COLORADO MOUNTAIN COLLEGE   SP
CB361.F72   Fraser, Russell A.
The Dark Ages & the Age of Gold,

I 03 0000008816   S0-ALN-255

CB   FRASER, RUSSELL
361   The Dark Ages & The Age
F72   of Gold

DISCARDED

COLORADO MOUNTAIN COLLEGE
LRC--WEST CAMPUS
Glenwood Springs, CO 81601

COLORADO MOUNTAIN COLLEGE
LRC--WEST CAMPUS
Glenwood Springs, Colo 81601

CB
361
F72

The Dark Ages and the Age of Gold

PRINCETON UNIVERSITY PRESS

PRINCETON, NEW JERSEY · 1973

The Dark Ages & the Age of Gold

BY RUSSELL FRASER

COLORADO MOUNTAIN COLLEGE
LRC---WEST CAMPUS
Glenwood Springs, Colo   81601

Copyright © 1973 by
PRINCETON UNIVERSITY PRESS

ALL RIGHTS RESERVED

LCC: 70-39786
ISBN: 0-691-06216-1

Publication of this book has been aided
by the Whitney Darrow Publication Reserve
Fund of Princeton University Press

Printed in the United States of America
by Princeton University Press

Pur remembrer des ancessurs
Les diz e les faiz e les murs.

WACE

The minde of man hath two Ports, the one alwaies
frequented by the entrance of manifold vanities;
the other desolate and over-growne with grasse,
by which enter our charitable thoughts and divine
contemplations.

SIR WALTER RALEGH

Somewhere in sands of the desert
A shape with lion body and the head of a man,
A gaze blank and pitiless as the sun,
Is moving its slow thighs, while all about it
Reel shadows of the indignant desert birds.

W. B. YEATS

Preface

UNDER THE ASPECT of the Dark Ages and the Age of Gold, metaphors which lie but like the truth, I have sought to describe and interpret the breaking away of the present from the medieval past. I locate this break in England in the sixteenth century, on the Continent two hundred years before. The emergence of the modern world—our world still—from the dying Middle Ages is surely among the signal "facts" of Western history. In my view, it is the decisive fact to the present time. The Catholic and Protestant, the humanist and new philosopher who is the father of classical science, even the atheist and pietist, as they postdate the Renaissance, are superficially different, brothers under the skin. Loyola, the Roman Catholic reformer, is far closer in spirit to Luther and Calvin than to a co-religionist like John of Salisbury, who lives on the other side of the great divide. Charles Kingsley, Cardinal Manning, Christian men of truculent assurance, are closer to T. H. Huxley, whatever the formal bias that sets them apart, than they are to Suger, the twelfth-century statesman and abbot of St.-Denis.

The great divide I am hypothesizing is coeval with the birth of rationalism. My subject is consequently the swallowing up of the old by the new, or the way we live now and how we got that way.

The Age of Reason Begins: that is the right title for a book on the Renaissance. The passion it signalizes for the unambiguous truth is associated customarily with a much later time. The source of the mistaken association is the gigantic and atavistic presence in the Age of Reason of Shakespeare. But Shakespeare is out of key with his time. Shakespeare is the last and greatest of medieval artists, and in him is summed up wondrously the capacity to entertain concurrent truths which may be contradictory. With the death of Shakespeare, this capacity by and large disappears; it begins to be recovered in the nineteenth century, is more powerfully emergent in the literature and psychology of our own time. So far, simple statement, which the argument of this book is intended to illustrate and support.

Though the rationalist figures here as a kind of villain, I see that I have emulated him in stipulating a coherent pattern in the events I record. This activity is sometimes reprehended by the modern historian. In the past, he thinks, are neither lessons nor laws but only *"l'infinie variété des mobiles"* (Pierre Renouvin). I think it is possible to see the past becoming the present, and to say how and when the transformation occurred, and for what reasons. On the assumption that the problems of the present are adumbrated in the past, I suppose it possible to awaken from history, as one begins to understand it. That is not to argue for a vulgar assurance. "No man can draw a stroke between the confines of day and night." Nevertheless, says Edmund Burke, "light and darkness are upon the whole tolerably distinguishable."

Value judgments arise as one attempts to distinguish. In my judgment, the dispossessing of the medieval past by a supposititiously more enlightened present is an event so important as to make of subsequent history little more than an epilogue or gloss. One reads that, in the middle years of the thirteenth century, the Mongol city of Karakorum was effectively the center of the world; or that, when put against the rise of physical science, the Renaissance in art and letters is only a provincial episode. My absorption in the Renaissance, as in the life of thirteenth-century Europe, makes it difficult for me to entertain these assertions with the seriousness they possibly deserve.

In the opinion of a contemporary American historian, to write a worthwhile book one has got to engage the interest of the commuter as he journeys to work on the train. That is perhaps a flippant opinion but I should like to accept it as stated. I hope to arouse interest in this man on whom business presses, for I believe that no story is more consequential in terms of his everyday concerns. The foreshortened interest in the present or the immediate past is founded, says Haskins in his history of the

Normans, on a sound principle, "namely, that it is an important function of history to explain the present in the light of the past from which it has come." It is explicitly this function I hope to fulfill. My interest in the annals of men who are not much remembered is, no doubt, partly personal, but not altogether. I see the long past as speaking to us still and as able, hypothetically, to instruct us.

Sir Walter Ralegh, under sentence of death in the Tower of London and writing concurrently a "history of the world," is apposite. The offences committed of old, he thinks, are still committed in the present. And therefore, inditing the afflictions of Israel, he is concerned to insure that the causes always be set down, "that they might be as precedents to succeeding ages." Karl Popper in our time decides to tell the story of the open society and its enemies on the day he gets the news that the Nazis have invaded Austria. "Only connect." The enemies of freedom in the Age of Pericles, as in the Renaissance, are not exclusively the province of the antiquarian. They are quick, or rather virulent, as their direct descendants are abroad. My effort is to relate the past and the present, to open a dialog between them, that the sins of the fathers may not be visited in perpetuity on the children.

Events of real magnitude, like those described in this account, are amenable to different interpretation. William Tyndale, who appears here as a dull-witted bigot, is also the author of the immortal riposte (in answer to a theologian who had rather be without God's law than the Pope's): "If God spare my life, ere many years I will cause the boy that driveth the plough to know more of Scripture than thou dost." I have given short shrift to this side of Tyndale's character. The same negligence or partiality describes my treatment of his fellow reformers, whether Protestant or Catholic. *Caveat lector.*

A more subtle kind of bias results as one limits his range of reference. The subject with which I am dealing is infinitely ductile. I plead guilty to constricting, partly deliberate, partly involuntary. Like the classical scientist, I have elected to speak only to a corner of things—to Ramus but not to Lefèvre d'Étaples, to Aquinas but not Albertus Magnus. Martianus Capella is here but not Aulus Gellius, Marx but not Bakunin. These omissions make the book less comprehensive and, to a degree, more orderly than true. I do not want to forfeit the good opinion of the erudite man in coming down on the side of form (exclusion) as against the endless marshalling of fact. And so I propose that he excuse me on the ground that, like the poet of the sort hypothesized in these pages, I know what little I know.

In reprinting passages from Renaissance books, I have normalized the spelling of *i* and *j*, *u* and *v*, and have expanded archaic contractions. In a few cases, superfluous or obsolete punctuation has been omitted or altered, and obvious misspellings silently corrected. Gratuitous italics have been dropped from quoted material.

The research which underlies the book was supported by the generosity of the American Council of Learned Societies and the National Science Foundation, and was carried on chiefly in the British Museum. Documenting this research has been a problem: footnotes in a work of this kind are not really dispensable, if one is to trust the argument; and yet they distract attention from the argument as one is forced to move constantly from the text to the bottom of the page. I have tried to resolve the problem by confining my argument to the text. One need not consult the notes, unless for corroboration or further reference.

Sections of the book have appeared in different form in the *South Atlantic Quarterly*, *College English*, and the *Sewanee Review*. I thank the editors and publishers of these journals for permission to reprint. I am grateful also to friends and colleagues for reading and commenting on my writing—to Austin Warren, Robert Hollander, S. F. Johnson, and Robert Stilwell. As before, I owe much to my editor at Princeton, Lalor Cadley.

I want in this preface to remember my former graduate assistant and friend, John Nadeau, now dead, who first instructed me in the Middle Ages. I suppose that everyone who writes addresses himself to a putative reader. Mine was R. P. Blackmur who, on his principle that the best thing about knowing writers was not having to read them, would perhaps have devoted little time to what follows. Still, I found it important that he was there.

RUSSELL FRASER
Ann Arbor, 1972

Contents

The Dark Ages and the Age of Gold

I   The Past As Prologue

THE LATE sixteenth century in England is defined by a seriousness that might have satisfied Matthew Arnold, and that makes the centuries before it appear irresponsible in contrast. The Middle Ages, conversely, are like a Georgian prologue to the earnest Victorian thing, or like Shrovetide before the austerities of Lent, when

> The people take their fill of recreation,
> And buy repentance, ere they grow devout.

Or they are the Dark Ages, and the Renaissance a purposive scattering of the dark.

This is the aspect under which sixteenth-century writers were most apt to see their own time in relation to the past. Here is a cursory but a representative sampling of what they say on the subject. The Elizabethan critic William Webbe knows of "no memorable worke written by any Poete in our English speeche until twenty yeeres past."[1] That eliminates Chaucer, whose talent is generally conceded but who is thought to have been unlucky in his birth. It is this unluckiness that Thomas Nashe has in mind, in commiserating the lot of "Chaucer, Lidgate, Gower, with such like, that lived under the tirranie of ignorance."[2] When Sir Philip Sidney, who is more catholic in taste than his contemporaries, is moved to praise the medieval song of Percy and Douglas, he is constrained to temper praise, "so evill apparrelled [is it] in the dust and cobwebbes of that uncivill age." Reading and admiring Chaucer's *Troilus and Criseyde*, he does not know "whether to mervaile more, either that he in that mis-

---

[1] *Discourse of English Poetrie*, 1586; in G. G. Smith, ed. *Elizabethan Critical Essays*, I, 239.

[2] Preface to *Menaphon*, 1589.

3

tie time could see so clearly, or that wee in this cleare age walke so stumblingly after him."[3] Mistiness describes the perception of the past and rationalizes the benighted authority of those medieval writers and thinkers whom Renaissance Englishmen are apt to revile as "the barbarous nation of scholemen."[4]

This reviling of the Middle Ages as a barbarous time is not peculiar to the English. In France, Guillaume Budé, the friend of Erasmus and an ardent panegyrist of the Greeks, declares himself thankful and a little surprised that anything of merit has been "saved from the deluge of more than a thousand years; for a deluge indeed, calamitous to life, had so drained and absorbed literature itself and the kindred arts worthy of the name, and kept them so dismantled and buried in barbarian mud that it was a wonder they could still exist."[5] Peter Ramus, perusing the medieval commentaries on Aristotle, discovers in them "nothing that points to nature: nothing, if you regard the truth of nature, that is not confused, muddied up, contaminated, and distorted."[6] Observation is distorted; so is the language in which it is couched. "The script was so ancient," says a German historian who is reading in the Lives of the Fathers, "that I had to become a boy again and go back to the elements."[7] The Italian humanist, for example Lorenzo Valla, displays the same contempt for the Latin of the Schoolmen, those "confused, bloodless, and dry dialecticians!" Pico della Mirandola is instructed by a friend that the medieval writer, in his ignorance of good latinity, can hardly be said to have lived at all.[8] Pico does not argue the point.

But now "after so many yeares of barbarisme," in the phrase of the poet Thomas Campion, the age of dross gives way to an

---

[3] *Apologie for Poetrie, c.*1583; Smith, I, 178, 196.

[4] Roger Ascham in the *Scholemaster,* 1570; Smith, I, 22.

[5] *De studio literarum,* 1527; C. S. Baldwin, *Renaissance Literary Theory and Practice,* p. 4.

[6] Quoted J. H. Randall, *Career of Philosophy,* I, 234.

[7] Aventinus, quoted H. Waddell, *Desert Fathers,* p. 149.

[8] Quoted Randall, I, 233, 232.

age of gold.⁹ By convention the golden age is supposed to precede our own, which is held to represent one more stage in the decay of nature. That is the medieval supposition. Already in the fourth century, the Christian apologist Lactantius is disinclined to wonder "that a kingdom established on a mighty foundation, increased by the long labor of mighty men, fortified with mighty resources, should one day fall." Whatever is built up by human strength, even the greatly durable edifice of the Roman state, is open to destruction "since the works of mortals are mortal."¹⁰ The ultimate authority for this melancholy view of things is the Book of Esdras: "So you too must consider that you are smaller in stature than those who were before you, and those who come after you will be smaller than you, for the creation is already growing old . . . and past the strength of youth" (ii, 5:54-56).

Medieval man, though not obsessed with decay like the Apocryphal writer, assumes that history moves in the direction of entropy. "Ripeness is all." The assumption is not a trouble to him nor is there implicit in it any genuine sense of historical time. Typically, and waiving the great and fanatic exceptions like Joachim of Flora, he is not an eschatologist. He does not look backward or forward but is satisfied to live in the present. Abbot Suger, the master of St.-Denis, is notable for piety among the prime movers of twelfth-century France. But his piety is neither lugubrious nor fearful. On January 13, 1151 the old man lies dying and is observed by a contemporary thus: "He did not tremble in the sight of the end, because he had consummated his life before his death; nor was he loath to die because he had enjoyed to live." He is not ridden—like most of us?—by the consciousness of "unlived lines," is no longer striving "for something still to be attained" (Rilke). This equable man does not go out "like one who is rejected, who is thrown out against his will." In his death as in life, he is *humanus satis et jocundus.*¹¹

⁹ *Observations in the Art of English Poesie*, 1602; Smith, ii, 332.
¹⁰ *Divine Institutes*, Bk. vii.
¹¹ E. Panofsky, *Abbot Suger*, pp. 37, 13.

To man in the Middle Ages, all time is present time. For this reason, the myth of the Golden Age does not excite him to speculation and has not much currency in his writings.[12] Renaissance man differs on this head as he is increasingly the victim of incertitude and dislocation. Equilibrium is already a kind of dying and a welcoming of death: "his first minute, after noone, is night" (John Donne). As every day is frustration, conceived in prelude to that more propitious day which must succeed in unknown fate, equilibrium gives place to despair. To the man at sixes and sevens, the wasting towards death is insupportable:

> Death, at whose name I oft have been afeard
> Because I wished this world's eternity.
>   (*2Henry VI*, II, iv, 89-90)

It is this man who engenders the consciousness of historical time. In the Renaissance the pastness of the past is first perceived; concurrently the future, unspoiled because unrealized, begins to beckon seductively. To look backward and forward is the hallmark of the modern age (in which the classical past is resumed) and betokens its sickness. "*Non omnis moriar*" is perverse.

Perverseness is figured in the heaping up of memorials: "These fragments I have shored against my ruins"; as also in the hypothesizing of a better time to come. (The present is an interlude, or vale of tears.) In the formulations of Renaissance poets, the better time is discovered initially in the past.

> The Golden Age was when the world was young,
> Nature so rich, as earth did need no sowing,
> Malice not known, the serpents had not stung,
> Wit was but sweet affection's overflowing.[13]

But how explain the sense of progress and even millennium which the Reformation communicates, exactly as it seeks to re-

---

[12] H. Levin, *Myth of the Golden Age*, p. xx. P. Burke, *Renaissance Sense of the Past*, treats the lack of historical awareness in the Middle Ages and its emergence in the Renaissance. See esp. Chs. I, II, VI.

[13] Fulke Greville, *Caelica*, XLIV. And see Tasso, *Aminta*, I, ii, Chorus; and Guarini, *Il Pastor Fido*, IV, Chorus.

turn to the primitive purity? The answer is that progress in the "modern" age is implicitly regressive, an attempt to repudiate the old-fashioned or medieval acquiescence in the darkness that awaits us all. In contemporary jargon, the master-motive is "genito-fugal" (Ferenczi), where the modifier denotes not only the beginning but the end.

> The earth that's Nature's mother is her tomb,
> What is her burying grave, that is her womb.
> (*Romeo and Juliet*, II, iii, 9-10)

The ending and beginning are the same. The proclaiming of a millennial future differs only lexically from the invoking of a vanished Saturnian Age. Each is despairing and fraught with good hope. Potentially, "What's past is prologue." In the Renaissance, as the implications of this hopeful saying begin to be grasped, the convention of decay begins to be inverted. The process of inversion is as follows.

First comes the backward glance that takes in despondently the breaking of nations and the colossal heap of detritus that is the past. Example: Edmund Spenser, after Du Bellay, reflecting on the *Ruines of Rome*.

> Behold what wreake, what ruine, and what wast,
> And how that she, which with her mightie powre
> Tam'd all the world, hath tam'd herselfe at last,
> The pray of Time, which all things doth devowre . . .
>   O worlds inconstancie!
> That which is firme doth flit and fall away
> And that is flitting doth abide and stay. (III)

When Roger Ascham muses on the corruption of the Latin tongue, which in its pure state endured scarcely a hundred years, he is reminiscent of Lactantius in the "good cause" he postulates. "No perfection is durable. Encrease hath a time, and decay likewise, but all perfit ripenesse remaineth but a moment."[14] All things fall and are built again; or, more poignantly, having fallen, continue to decline.

---

[14] *Scholemaster* in Smith, I, 26.

But Ascham is a reformer and optimistic with respect to the present. Having spoken to his morose point of view, he does not infer, as he might logically, that our old stock cannot be inoculated. Instead he looks about for a nostrum. He finds it in antiquity, which comprehended all knowledge to the degree that men can do so. That is in the beginning the orthodox view. Early in the sixteenth century, Erasmus bespeaks it. "I affirm that with slight qualification the whole of attainable knowledge lies enclosed within the literary monuments of ancient Greece. This great inheritance I will compare to a limpid spring of whose undefiled waters it behoves all who truly thirst to drink and be restored."[15]

There is in Erasmus's prescription no thought of transcending antiquity. The great excitement that attends on the rediscovery of classical learning derives initially from the more modest hope of retrieving the Golden Age. This hope inspires the fifteenth-century humanist and supports him in his task of rendering Greek poetry and history in Latin. To Lorenzo Valla it appears that if the Middle Ages were unhappy in producing no single scholar, "the more we may congratulate our own times, in which, if we but strive a little further, I am confident that not only the Roman city, but still more the Roman language, and with it all liberal studies, shall be restored."[16] Contemporary physicians see that restoration as imminent with the translating of the Greek physician Galen.[17] Like Andreas Vesalius of Brussels, the first man of modern science, they look forward to the time when "anatomy will . . . be cultivated in our Academies as it was of old in Alexandria." They are not yet imbued with the philosophy of progress. Their commitment to the past is, therefore, a kind of enslavement. Like Jacobus Sylvius, who taught Vesalius at the University of Paris, they are inclined to believe that any structure occurring in modern man and not in the writings of Galen can only be due to degeneration in modern man.[18] To

[15] Quoted G. K. Hunter, *John Lyly*, p. 21.
[16] *De Elegantia Latinae Linguae*, 1477; Baldwin, *Renaissance*, p. 8.
[17] Rendered in Latin by Nicolò Leoniceno, 1509.
[18] Discussion draws on J. Saunders and C. O'Malley, *Vesalius*.

arrest the process of degeneration and decay, they seek to emulate the antique past. "For what naturallie can go no hier must naturallie yeld and stoupe againe."[19] That is Ascham's law.

But now it is qualified, as art is enlisted in nature's redress. In the great house near St. Albans where Sir Francis Bacon passed his youth, a picture of Ceres, to whom man is indebted for the sowing of grain, is moralized with the words: *Moniti Meliora*. Instruction begets improvement. Years later the auspicious saying appears again—it is verified now—in preface to the *Great Instauration*.[20] Charles II, as confidence grows on the age, commits his subjects to "a further repairing [of] the Decayes of Nature, untill Art have done its last, or, which is most probable, Nature cease to be, or be Renewed."[21] Art enhances Nature (*Ars Naturam adiuvans*) and puts an end to yielding and stooping. That is how the Italian jurist Andrea Alciati interprets an emblem in which Fortune or instability is posed against Mercury, in whom art and application are personified and fused.[22] On that fusion the Renaissance relies to reverse the decay of things.

In attesting to its success the emblem writers, who render the common understanding in moralized pictures, are unanimous. Mercury tunes the broken lute in an illustration contrived by Joannes Sambucus, who offers the hopeful legend, Industry corrects Nature (*Industria naturam corrigit*).[23] Death, who is depicted by Gabriele Rollenhagio as toying with the sceptre and crown, is overmatched at last by erudition, depicted as the wise man with one hand on a book and—a nice and significant conjunction—the other grasping a globe.[24] It is the emblem that presents Francis Bacon, whose ambition is "to make the mind of man, by help of art, a match for the nature of things."[25] Rollenhagio's motto (*Vivitur ingenio, caetera mortis erunt*) ap-

---

[19] Smith, I, 26.

[20] C. D. Bowen, *Francis Bacon*, pp. 27-28.

[21] Prefatory letter to George Dalgarno's *Ars Signorum*, 1661.

[22] *Emblemes*, 1564, H8r, p. 127.

[23] *Emblemata*, 1564, D5r, p. 57.

[24] *Nucleus Emblematum*, 1611, emblem 1.

[25] Quoted L. Eiseley, *Francis Bacon*, p. 53.

pears also in Vesalius, on the tomb of the mourning skeletal figure of the *Fabrica* (1543). "Genius lives on, all else is mortal." The sense of the epitaph adorning that great recension and modernization of anatomical knowledge is not mournful but exuberant. Knowledge is power.

But Bacon and his age have got it wrong, and so much we are learning belatedly, after some cost. Baudelaire anticipates this learning more than a hundred years ago: "*la vraie civilization,*" what is it? "*Elle n'est pas dans le gaz, ni dans la vapeur, ni dans les tables tournantes. Elle est dans la diminution des traces du péché originel*" (*Mon Coeur Mis à Nu*, XXXII). The Age of Reason has little truck with the doctrine of original sin, does not estimate the problem Baudelaire is posing—or say, to qualify: the master spirits of the age, the great men in whom the *Weltanschauung* is realized, these men are impervious to the idea of "concupiscence." All problems, on the resolving of which progress attends, are—as we should say, "exogenous." (The argot of different times and "theologies" is amusing; the point of view which informs the exotic words is familiar enough, over the centuries.)

One entail of the hopeful psychology which I associate to the Age of Reason is the doctrine of Imitation. Ascham, who conceives it as a means of retrieving our fallen condition, provides a directory to the restorative virtues of classical writers. On his diagnosis, the study of Cicero nourishes and revivifies more than all others. That is because Cicero was an imitator himself, able and willing to enlarge his own capacity by going to school to the past. Just as "Tullie did not *obiter* [incidentally] and bichance, but purposelie and mindfullie, bend him selfe to a precise and curious Imitation of Plato," so we who come after are to imitate Tully, that the world's great age may begin anew and the golden years return.[26] To bring back the age of gold, the early sixteenth-century critic Marco Girolamo Vida advises aspiring writers "to follow the trusty footsteps of the ancients" and to "steal and

---

[26] Smith, I, 11. Ascham advises also imitation of Sallust, Varro, Caesar, Homer, Virgil.

drive the spoil from every source."[27] Joachim du Bellay, defending his native language, proffers the same advice. On his view, "Being natural does not suffice to make poetry a labor worthy of immortality."[28] Art, which is founded on the imitation of Greek and Latin authors, must collaborate in the work.

Horace, as he is the great spokesman for this position, becomes the great Cham to Renaissance critics. His admonition, never to lose touch with the Greek patterns by night or day, is taken as emphasizing the sovereign value of artifice in salving and recurring the fall.[29] Thomas Campion, interdicting rhyme as "vulgar and unarteficiall," equates what is merely natural with what is unlicked or unamended by art.[30] He proposes to compass the *siglo de oro* by imitating the more artful verse of the ancients.

There are of course skeptics, even in the Renaissance, who do not believe in artifice (or in anything else) as the *vade mecum*. Rabelais is one of them. "How comes it," he inquires, affecting stupefaction, "that in the abundant light of our century, in which by some special gift of the gods we see all the better disciplines recovered, there are still found everywhere men so constituted as to be either unwilling or unable to lift their eyes from the more than Cimmerian darkness of the gothic time to the evident torch of the sun."[31] John Donne almost a century later sees his hopeful contemporaries as still involved in that darkness. He is therefore bemused that "the world . . . should glorifie it selfe, or flatter, or abuse us with an opinion of eternity." On his less sanguine understanding, "there is a reproofe, a rebuke born in

---

[27] *Art of Poetry*, 1527, tr. G. Saintsbury, *Loci Critici*, p. 85.

[28] 1549; Ch. III. For a different and more primitivistic view, see E. Armstrong, *Ronsard and the Age of Gold*.

[29] *Epistle to the Pisos*, ll. 278-79.

[30] Smith, II, 327.

[31] Letter to Tiraqueau, June 3, 1532; Baldwin, p. 207. And see Ch. VIII of *Gargantua and Pantagruel*: Gargantua remembering his youth. George Hakewill (1578-1649), the follower of Bodin and proponent of a cyclical theory of history (*An Apologie or Declaration of the Power and Providence of God in the Government of the World*, 1627), belongs in this skeptical company: modern men are no better than their predecessors—who were themselves no giants.

. . . [nature], a sensible decay and mortality of the whole world."[32] The disconcerting conclusion of a skeptical observer like Donne is that modern man, so far from overgoing his forebears, is in comparison to them a diminished thing. And in fact to be modern, in the lexicon of an unprogressive poet like Shakespeare, is by definition to be trivial or slight. The "modern quill" of the Rival Poet, whom Shakespeare reprehends in the Sonnets, comes too short as it is modern. The "wise saws and modern instances" at which he glances in *As You Like It* are not so wise as pretentious.[33]

In this dyspeptic view Shakespeare is joined by Samuel Daniel, a fine poet and the author of a superb tragedy but written in the classical manner and at a time when the romantic or panoramic play was establishing itself as the dominant kind. And so no one today reads Daniel's *Cleopatra*. In the last year of Elizabeth's reign, Daniel also wrote a *Defence of Ryme* in answer to Campion's *Observations in the Art of English Poesie*. It is the most sophisticated of Elizabethan critical treatises and, except for Sidney's *Apologie*, the most agreeably written. And it is antithetical to the eupeptic spirit of its time. The latter-day notion that mechanical or artificial change is decisively enabling finds no support from Samuel Daniel. To him, "Nature . . . is above all Arte."[34]

---

[32] *LXXX Sermons*, 1640, p. 357. In the *First Anniversary*, Donne expatiates on the inherent reproof:

> Then, as mankinde, so is the worlds whole frame
> Quite out of joynt, almost created lame . . .
> The world did in her Cradle take a fall,
> And turn'd her braines, and tooke a generall maime.
>
> (ll. 191-7)

[33] Sonnet 83; *AYLI*, ii, vii, 156. The pejorative sense is conventional in Shakespeare's time. *OED* defines as "ordinary," "commonplace," 1591-1610.

[34] Smith, ii, 359. Daniel's position is eccentric but not unique. Puttenham, *Arte of English Poesie*, 1589, thinks the poet "is then most admired when he is most naturall and least artificiall" (Bk. iii, Ch. xxv). Rhyme is more natural and "more ancient than the artificiall of the Greeks and Latines . . . even as the naked by prioritie of time is before the clothed"

The modernist does not repudiate nature in his exalting of art. The imitation of nature is one of his great shibboleths. But he apprehends nature through art, which fortifies and revises it. Art is more powerful than Nature (*Natura potentior Ars*): that is the motto with which Titian glosses an emblem of the bear cub who is licked into shape by its mother, even as nature is redacted by art. Titian, as befitting a child of the Age of Reason, chooses the emblem as his device.[35] In the new art of Italy, Giotto is commended as against Cimabue. What makes Giotto the better painter is his emphasis on naturalness, understood to be recovered from antiquity, but conceived not as a copying, rather as a redacting of nature. This is imitation at a remove. The forms of nature are defined by the canon of proportions. To be a painter is therefore to be a student of proportion, to be a scientist who is versed in rules and laws.

This implicit definition is signalized in a couplet by the dramatist and poet William Cartwright. His intention is to eulogize the plays of an admired colleague; he describes them accordingly as

> like to Dürer's pencil, which first knew
> The laws of faces, and then faces drew.[36]

Leonardo, in a treatise on painting, compares those who affect this art, "without having previously applied to the diligent study of the scientific part of it . . . to mariners, who put to sea in a ship without rudder or compass." Neither is very likely to arrive at the wished for port.[37]

The commitment to anterior learning is bequeathed to the present by the classical past. With the advent of the Renaissance it is included in the requisite equipment of the painter who, if he wishes to delineate the truth, must familiarize himself with

---

(1, v). But Puttenham, who desires the reformation of poetry, is uncertain in assessing the respective merits of "artificial" and "natural" verse.

[35] M. Praz, *Studies*, I, 96-97.

[36] "Upon the dramatic poems of Mr. John Fletcher."

[37] *Treatise*, tr. J. F. Rigaud; quoted L. B. Campbell, *Scenes and Machines*, p. 30.

the rules of perspective and, like the Greeks, with mathematics and anatomy. The classicism of Dürer and Da Vinci is denoted in part by their concern with the principles of anatomical form. Literally, they go to school to the human body. It is in Titian's *atelier* that the meticulous and scholarly plates are created for the *De Humani Corporis Fabrica* of Vesalius. When King James VI of Scotland, who a little later becomes the first of the Stuart kings in England, composes a manual on prosody for his countrymen, he urges them not merely to copy but to redact, which is to bring into form according to the rules: for "if Nature be chief . . . rules will be ane help and staff to Nature."[38] On that assumption, Campion proposes that quantity and not rhyme furnish the help and staff to support the writing of a new English verse. Quantity means obeisance to classical rules. Like the new Italian painters, Campion is summoning the past to the aid of the present.

The massive assistance afforded by antiquity (and dramatized in school books to the present time by the hoary figure of the Greek scholar fleeing west on the fall of Constantinople and bringing his codices with him) is important in enabling the Renaissance to see itself as superior to the Middle Ages in learning and hence in understanding. This is the first step in inverting the convention of decay.

"We are reanimated Ancestours," Joseph Glanvill, the propagandist of new science, asserts proudly, "and antedate their Resurrection."[39] Medieval man continues to moulder. Dust blinds him to that "morning brightnesse before the Sunne rising," which is the breaking forth of "the light of all good knowledge."[40] Renaissance man is not so myopic. The task he has undertaken, to regularize the writing of poetry, is, so King James assures himself, relatively simple: now, "quhen the warld

---

[38] *Ane Schort Treatise Conteining some Reulis and Cautelis to be Observit and Eschewit in Scottis Poesie*, 1584; Smith, I, 210.

[39] *Vanity of Dogmatizing*, 1661, p. 138.

[40] John Brinsley, *A Consolation for Our Grammar Schooles*, 1622, pp. 47-48.

14

is waxit auld," we have in our scrip all previous opinion.[41] The past is not wise by virtue of its pastness, but puerile because it is earlier in time. Had we cleaved "to the eldest and not to the best," says Richard Mulcaster, the progressive headmaster of the famous Merchant Taylors' School when Edmund Spenser was a student there, we should still be eating acorns instead of grain and wearing old Adam's pelts.[42] It is the present that is mature and enlightened. Towering above the littleness of the past, it is able to see more and see further.

To the eupeptic temperament in whatever period it impinges on history, the idea of progress is an article of faith. When in the fourth century the pagan prefect Symmachus enters a moving protest against the banishing by the Christian party of the Altar of Victory, he invokes the authority of the past. St. Ambrose, who epitomizes the progressive point of view, replies abruptly: "Why cite me the examples of the ancients? It is no disgrace to pass on to better things." A generation later the Latin poet Prudentius makes of this story a Christian poem, in which the annals of Rome figure as no more than prolegomena to the triumph of Christ.[43] Like Mulcaster (or like Karl Marx), like the vulgar progressive in our own time, Prudentius scorns the past. History is still to begin. "Back to our caves" (*Redeamus ad antra*): that, he says satirically, is the motto of the traditionalist.

Classical science, the principal achievement of the Age of Reason, is optimistic and anti-traditionalist as it affirms "that idea of progress in animated nature which palaeontology in the main so plainly teaches."[44] A powerful and beneficent selecting agency scrutinizes man in his infinite variety, "favoring the good and rejecting the bad." The curve of things is ineluctably upward. There is no asymptote breaking this curve (no entropy). "As

---

[41] Smith, I, 209.

[42] *First Part of the Elementarie*, 1582, Hhiiiv.

[43] *Contra Symmachum.*

[44] Robert Chambers, *Vestiges of the Natural History of Creation*, 1844, "General Considerations Respecting the Origin of the Animated Tribes." The passage I quote is omitted in subsequent editions.

natural selection works solely by and for the good of each being, all corporeal and mental endowments will tend to progress toward perfection."[45] Each generation makes the immediate past obsolete. The corollary, as Herzen knows already, even before the advent of the Soviet state, is that men are caryatids whose function is not to live but to support the future—"a millennial future" (it is Hitler who descries it) "in the face of which the wishes and the selfishness of the individual must appear as nothing and submit."[46]

But life in the present is worth postponing indefinitely, for in the beckoning future is "the victory of socialism"—Socinianism, the Fifth Monarchy, whatever ideal system one chooses—which "lays the foundation of a new civilization, without class oppression or exploitation, one which opens up unlimited prospects for the progress of technology, science, and art, and hence for the development of all the physical and spiritual potentialities of man."[47] History is progress: the root wisdom of the great historians of the Age of Reason: David Hume, Blackstone, Macaulay, Motley, Treitschke, Parkman. "The majority of the 'groups' which win and conquer are better than the majority of those which fail and perish, and thus the first world grew better and was improved."[48] Culture also is progressive, moves forward in quantum jumps not less than material knowledge. Shakespeare in important particulars is outdated, Sophocles still more as he is farther back in time. "In bourgeois art man . . . is only a half-man. Communist poetry will be complete, because

[45] Charles Darwin, *Origin of Species*, 1859, Ch. xiv, "Recapitulation and Conclusion."

[46] *Mein Kampf*, pp. 402-4.

[47] *Handbook of Philosophy*, ed. H. Selsam from M. Rosenthal and P. Yudin, pp. 23-24, "Civilization."

[48] Walter Bagehot, *Physics and Politics*, 1872, Ch. vi, "Verifiable Progress Politically Considered." From the same ch.: "Conquest is the premium given by nature to those national characters which their national customs have made most fit to win in war, and in many most material respects those winning characters are really the best characters. The characters which do win in war are the characters which we should wish to win in war."

it will be man conscious of his own necessity as well as that of outer reality."[49]

The writer is Christopher Caudwell, who gave his life in the Spanish War only a few decades ago but whose ingenuous saying is as old as Methuselah. If that is so—if the good-natured or fatuous progressivism of the modern age is adumbrated in the distant past—it seems hardly admissible to speak of the Renaissance, in which the optimistic point of view is enshrined, as representing a splitting off or new departure from the antecedent age. But it is the enshrining or canonizing that makes the difference. Modern man, who enters history in the fourteenth century, in England two centuries later, is generically progressive. The psychology by which he is recognized is manifest occasionally throughout the Middle Ages. But the manifesting is less important in terms of this account than the adverb which describes it.

In the twelfth century John of Salisbury, the friend and counsellor of Thomas Becket and the greatest scholar of the age, dismisses the claim of the *moderni* in his time to superiority over the ancients by reciting what is almost a medieval commonplace. John is moved by the impudence of the new logicians, who reject the Trivium of Grammar (the study of literature), Dialectic, and Rhetoric, to compose a treatise on behalf of those studies. He reminds his enthusiastic contemporaries that "Bernard of Chartres used to compare us to dwarfs perched on the shoulders of giants." The so-called "Cornificians" whom John is reprehending take their name from a celebrated detractor of Virgil. That is perhaps gratuitous information. What we want to grasp about these twelfth-century men is their role as hair-splitters from whom all the answers come readily and who, as Henry Adams instructs us, "made a practice of inventing horns of dilemma on which to fix their opponents." It is interesting that John of Salisbury, who has no difficulty in getting free of the horns, should be put down by Adams as "a typical Englishman of the future

---

[49] *Illusion and Reality*, conclusion to Ch. xii, "The Future of Poetry."

17

is disinclined to see our modern understandings "built by the square of Greece and Italie. We are the children of nature as well as they; we are not so placed out of the way of judgement but that the same Sunne of Discretion shineth uppon us; we have our portion of the same virtues as well as of the same vices."[55]

What rubs worst in this assertion is its positing of a community of vices. Men do not and cannot get better and better, or not by their own effort. In consequence of the Fall, says Donne in his *Sermons*, we lost not only our freedom from pain and death but, what is more critical, "all possibility of recovering any of this by our selves."[56] If that is so, books are no remedy in making men judicious, "but onely," in Daniel's words, "that great booke of the world and the all-overspreading grace of heaven."[57] But to invoke the grace of Heaven as decisive is to spoil the game of the Renaissance, which is to build the kingdom on earth of itself. If vice is endemic and all men are prone to it and wisdom is apportioned equally and gratuitously to the present and the past, there is no reason to be especially optimistic about this present moment. Neither is there reason to exalt Greece and Rome above the Middle Ages. But on that exalting depends the faith of the Renaissance that it can transcend the past. Assertions of our common frailty are likely, therefore, to fall on deaf ears. We "are earthly Angels by the noblenesse of Creation," says the Puritan preacher. Frailty is caused by "voluntary degeneration," is not endemic.[58] "Man was made sound at first." His enfeeblement grows from free will![59]

In the Renaissance and later, psychology is moralized. It is

---

[55] Smith, II, 372, 370, 366-67.

[56] Quoted F. Manley, ed., *Anniversaries*, p. 17n.

[57] Smith, II, 367.

[58] Robert Bolton, *Directions*, 1625, p. 162.

[59] The poet and playwright John Day, in the *Parliament of Bees*, 1641:
>   If he grows ill,
> 'Tis not by course of nature, but free will.
> Distempers are not ours; there should be then,
> Were we ourselves, no physic: men to men
> Are both diseases' cause and the disease.

Day concludes: "Thank Fate, I'm sound and free from both of these."

true that Shakespeare in his reading of aberrant behavior is partly voluntaristic: passion collies or blackens judgment, assays to
lead the way; the guilty man collaborates and to his own destruction. But this oversetting passion or debility, which is fatal in its
issue, is understood also and critically as physiological, involuntary: the "mother" or *hysterica passio*, an organic displacement
from below, which suffocates and maddens King Lear; the case
of Leontes, who has *tremor cordis* "on" him. The older psychology supposes that when wisdom and blood combat in so tender
a body as ours, "we have ten proofs to one that blood hath the
victory."[60] There is no help for that, failing "gratuitous" inter-
cession:

> As true we are as flesh and blood can be,
> The sea will ebb and flow, Heaven show his face,
> Young blood doth not obey an old decree.
> We cannot cross the cause why we were born.
> (*Love's Labour's Lost*, IV, iii, 215-18)

Now it is proposed that the disobedience of the blood is meditated disobedience altogether. Madness (or criminality) is the
willful adhering to "false principles of moral philosophy." The
lunatic asylum, as the rationalist describes it, is the habitat of
"guilty creatures," a place of penance "where shame and turpi-
tude fetter crime." In the heyday of the Age of Reason, "indi-
gence, laziness, vice and madness mingled in an equal guilt with
unreason; madmen were caught in the great confinement of
poverty and unemployment, but all had been promoted, in the
proximity of transgression, to the essence of a Fall." Michel
Foucault in his *History of Insanity* locates this metamorphosis
in the second half of the eighteenth century.[61] In fact the horrid
"promotion" is occurring already, more than a hundred years
before. Ordericus Vitalis, the twelfth-century historian of the
Norman Church, is old fashioned as he disputes it. The lucky
man "who supplants vices ascribes all the good he possesses to
the grace of God." That is not what the Pharisees think (and

---

[60] *Much Ado About Nothing*, II, iii, 169-71.
[61] Foucault, pp. 130-32, 153, 161, 169, 208-9.

we may take them in this context as emblematic of the modern spirit), in rebuking the disciples of Jesus because they do not fast. But the rebuke is inapposite, says the Norman chronicler: a piece of new cloth is not to be joined so easily to an old garment: "the severe observances of the new law are not to be required of carnal men who have not yet been regenerated," made lucky by the conferring of grace.[62]

It is the quotation from *Twelfth Night*! "Anything that's mended is but patched. Virtue that transgresses is but patched with sin, and sin that amends is but patched with virtue" (I, v, 51-54). The latter-day Pharisee closes his ears to this equable and also melancholy proposition. There is no "imposition hereditary ours" (Shakespeare in the *Winter's Tale*), or else we can annul it as we "follow the immutable laws of morality!"[63]

This strident psychology, which argues implicitly for the withholding of compassion and which imposes an intolerable burden on the man who accepts it, every modern man takes in with his mother's milk. " 'Tis in ourselves that we are thus and thus": Iago, a self-congratulating prophet of the modern age. Here, to get at the difference between modern and medieval, is a tenth-century abbot reflecting on his native insufficiency. "Observe"— it is Odo of Cluny who exhorts us—"that I have never acted well of my own accord. Judge, then, my ill character as seems right, while you make known and praise the mercy which was always looking down on me."[64] Pelagianism, as this humble exhortation is taken to heart, is cast in a less pleasant light.

The logical and farthest extension of the new Pelagianism is to disvalue not only the immediate past but the whole of the past. Time, says Bishop Wilkins in a hopeful phrase which might so easily be uttered in despair, is "of the nature of a river or streame, which carrieth downe to us that which is light, or blowne up, but sinketh that which is weighty and solid." As the

---

[62] *Ecclesiastical History*, I, 16, 20-21 (Bk. I, Ch. vi).

[63] The eighteenth-century "reformer" Philippe Pinel, quoted Foucault, p. 161.

[64] *Life* by John of Salerno, trans. and ed. Sitwell, p. 11.

analogy holds, it is "a false conceit, for us to thinke, that amongst the ancient variety and search of opinions, the best hath still prevailed."[65] The reverse is true, and so the past can teach us little.

This declaration of independence is the second and the critical step in annulling the idea of decay. Spenser's friend Gabriel Harvey takes that step, in proclaiming his indifference to what was transacted "in ruinous Athens or decayid Roome a thousand or twoe thousande yeares ago."[66] It is a spectacular saying. This is its purport: the new men of the Renaissance are the first of their kind; all who preceded them were more or less unsuccessful improvisations.

To the whittling down of antiquity, the Italian critic Julius Caesar Scaliger brings to bear his considerable powers of misconstruction. Scaliger is indignant at the primacy conceded to the past, "As if we were servants of the Greeklings, and not correctors." Poetry, as an art responsive to principles, "has hardly been an art before us." So much, observes Scaliger laconically—he is introducing his *Poetices* (1561)—"is evident from our discussion." It follows with equal transparency that "The Greeks are mistaken if they think we have taken anything from them except to improve it."[67]

Aristotle, as he is improved, is transcended. And not only Aristotle. Now the claims of Galen are scrutinized and found wanting, as by Vesalius, whose observations on bloodletting and the venous system call the received anatomy in question.[68] Sidney a little later is unequivocally contemptuous of Galen's adopted sons, the old-fashioned doctors who remain unaware of the new scientism and "who by a beaten way/ Their judgements hackney on."[69] Sir Thomas Browne in the seventeenth century

---

[65] Wilkins is following "the learned Verulam," in preface to his *Discovery of a World . . . in the Moone*, 1638. Bacon says: "Antiquity, as we call it, is the young state of the world . . . the present time is the real antiquity" (*Advancement*, Bk. 1).

[66] Letter-Book, between 1573 and 1580.

[67] Quoted Baldwin, *Renaissance*, pp. 171-72.

[68] *Venesection Letter* of 1539.   [69] *Astrophil and Stella*, 102.

wonders at the "obstinate Adherence unto Antiquity."[70] A hundred years later, the poet James Thomson bundles together the mouldering stones and towering pyramid and proud triumphal arch which memorialize the past—and consigns them all to dust. "What grandeur can ye boast," he inquires rhetorically,

> While Newton lifts his column to the skies,
> Beyond the waste of time.[71]

Ancient poetry is also understood to have met its match in the poetry of the renascent age. Ben Jonson applauds Shakespeare as standing the comparison with "all, that insolent Greece, or haughtie Rome sent forth." To the Restoration poet Sir John Denham, it is apparent that "By Shakespeare's, Jonson's, Fletcher's lines/ Our Stage's luster Rome's outshines."[72] The literary clergyman Francis Meres, essaying "A comparative discourse of our English Poets, with the Greeke, Latine, and Italian Poets," makes equals of Ovid and the "mellifluous & hony-tongued Shakespeare" and, less happily, of Sophocles and Michael Drayton, and Dante and the obscure Matthew Roydon and, as writers of comedy, Aristophanes and "Doctor Gager of Oxforde."[73] The judgment is absurd, and just for that reason significant. Bacon, who sees the long past "but as the dawning or break of day," is not content to argue for the equality of the present. He "cannot but be raised to this persuasion, that this third period of time will far surpass that of the Grecian and Roman learning."[74]

The headiness explicit in this trumpeting of the present and the concurrent depreciating of the past denote the age that has been granted the Pisgah-sight. It is an intoxicating vision and it does not make for humility. The twelfth century partakes of it also and so prefigures and illuminates the modern age, which

---

[70] *Pseudodoxia Epidemica*, 1646, Bk. I, Ch. vi. See also Ch. viii, all of Bk. II (esp. Ch. iii, a comparison of ancient myth with modern induction), and VI, i. (Browne, like so many of his contemporaries, is inconsistent as an advocate of modernity.)

[71] "A Poem Sacred to the Memory of Sir Isaac Newton," 1727.

[72] "On Mr Abraham Cowley," 1668.

[73] *Palladis Tamia*, 1598.

[74] *Advancement of Learning*, 1605; quoted Eiseley, *Bacon*, p. 17.

the sixteenth century announces. In the twelfth century, the rise of a new logic or dialectic engenders the feeling that the present has the key to all things in its hand. Those who are most notably imbued with this feeling and whom John of Salisbury calls the Cornificians "are ignorant of grammar, physics, and ethics alike." Their ignorance is, however, unashamed; it is even meditated: and this because they are rationalists who went to school "when there was no 'letter' in liberal studies, and everyone sought 'the spirit,' which, so they tell us, lies hidden in the letter." Contempt for language follows, except as language is a tool for dialectical disputation. The marriage of Mercury and Philology is dissolved. As the spirit is immanent formal study of the letter becomes gratuitous, for example the study of the old-fashioned logic, which John defines in part as "the science of verbal expression." The *moderni*, although they are great "public criers of logic," attach little value to what they conceive as an affair of mere words. Professing to "despise everything save logic," in their own austere and more exclusive sense, they are really mounting an attack on literature as anciently practiced.[75] Compare the neo-romantics of our own time—for example Artaud, the propagandist of the theatre of cruelty: "The library at Alexandria can be burnt down. There are forces above and beyond papyrus."[76] That is certainly true. It is the fierce alacrity with which the truth is urged that defines the new departure.

The almost mystical reverence for the science of grammar—what we should call literature—is suggested in the history of the world itself: *glamour* is a later form of *gramarye*. Modern man is incurious of etymologies. It is a part of his winnowing temper that the past, incarnate in the curriculum of the schools, should be rejected by him as obsolete. "Old things are passed away; behold, all things are become new": the saying of Corinthians (II, 5:17) is the rallying cry of the Moderns in their war on the conventional course of study, which means essentially the literature of the past. To Cassiodorus (*c*.480-*c*.580) at the beginning of the Middle Ages, the antiquity of that literature is an earnest

[75] *Metalogicon*, Bk. II, Ch. vi; I, iii; I, x; II, vi.
[76] *The Theater and Its Double*, p. 10.

25

COLORADO MOUNTAIN COLLEGE
LRC---WEST CAMPUS
Glenwood Springs, Colo   81601

of its worth. Because he wishes his monks to profit from their reading, he assures them that "it will be more efficacious not to sip at the cup of audacious novelty, but to drink deeply from the fount of the ancients." Modern man inquires, however: "But who has drunk at the sources of life?"[77]

In the twelfth century as in the Renaissance, the venerating of the past becomes a target for satire. "History is bunk!" says Amadeus of Bourg-Dieu, the type of the eschatologist. Like Coriolanus, equating the long past with the dust of antique time, he endeavors to sweep away the "old and obsolete." (These two words he understands as synonymous.) In fulfillment of his impatient design, "all things were 'renovated.'" John of Salisbury explains what this means. Rhetoric is vilified. It is only what Galileo, four hundred years later, will call flowers or prettification. Grammar or literature is turned upside down: the scum rises to the top. In place of the Latin writers, the canonical *auctores* who for centuries have given nourishment to the mind and spirit, more topical writers are enshrined in the curriculum. The student is an autodidact; necessarily, as he acknowledges no provenance, a bigot, violently indignant with the past.[78]

This indignation describes the rationalist as also the barbarian who appeals from reason to blood prescience. Each is himself alone. The barbarian thinks that "masterpieces of the past are good for the past: they are not good for us." If *Oedipus Rex* does not please any more, "that is the fault of *Oedipus Rex* and not of the public." The style of Sophocles, to his ear, "is too refined for this age, it is as if he were speaking beside the point." The rationalist differs from the barbarian in that he is preoccupied not so much with relevance as with the imperial view. To the patient assaying of concrete particulars he prefers "abstract systems of renovation applied wholesale."

The first quotation, which might be adapted from the *Metalogicon*, comes from Antonin Artaud, whose manifesto is entitled

[77] *Divine and Human Readings*, p. 69; Artaud, *The Theater and Its Double*, p. 146.

[78] John, who cultivates the past as in his learned defense of the Trivium, is called a reprobate, a dullard, a blockhead. *Metalogicon*, ii, vi; i, iii.

"No More Masterpieces," the second from Matthew Arnold in the opening chapter of *Culture and Anarchy*. The young radicals of the twelfth century have become the Establishment, some centuries later. For an apposite quotation from the literature of the 1970s, see almost at random the memoirs of Nadezhda Mandelstam, the widow of the Soviet poet. The elevating of rationality by the true believers of the twentieth century, who are their "reanimated ancestors," inclines them to reject the merely personal consideration in favor of "an irrefutable scientific truth by means of which . . . people can foresee the future, change the course of history at will and make it rational." Men invested with god-like authority require no tutelage. (If, says John of Salisbury in the earlier time, "anyone applied himself to studying the ancients, he became a marked man and the laughingstock of all.") Provisional faith in the past and what it teaches, "the sacred succession of interlinked events," gives place to "absolute faith in the new, scientifically obtained truth." The end of doubt is assured, at the same time "the progressive loss of a sense of reality."[79] The rationalist or maker of systems, deifying the abstract truth, isolates it from flesh and blood. His dessication follows, as also the perverting of the system.

There is this important difference between the twelfth-century *modernus* and his contemporary exemplification. The latter is more imperious and not content with the renovation of the schools. Devoted to his fellowmen in the mass, not so devoted to Tom, Dick, and Harry, he sponsors "a new doctrine drawn up in black and white for elaborating down to the very smallest details a rational society for the future" (Arnold). This doctrine touches the million and in that sense is new. But the psychology which informs it is the same, yesterday and today. Once more, what's past is prologue.

Late in the twelfth century, the Arthurian romancer Chrétien de Troyes honors his teachers only so far as to grant that they possessed the first fame of chivalry and learning. But he asserts that it was lent to them only. Now it is domiciled in France: "for

[79] *Hope Against Hope*, pp. 162, 164, 247-48.

27

the Greeks and the Romans no one any longer says either much or little; their word has ceased, their bright flame is put out."[80] That is the judgment of the *modernus* and theoretician Matthew of Vendôme, in his treatise on the art of versification (*c.*1175): "The old authors are found wanting; the new press upon them."[81]

The quenching of the old flame and the supervening of a new have important consequences for the doctrine of imitation, whose currency begins to wane with the waxing of the idea that we have got hold of the key to the mysteries. Matthew of Vendôme, who casts a cold eye on classical poetry, is unwilling to countenance the imitation even of giants like Ovid and Virgil. It is not simply the presumptive ignorance of the past that offends him but the manner in which that ignorance is couched. On his reading, the manner determines the matter, in the same sense that manners maketh man. The heart of his objection—and here the parallel is very close to modes of thinking and feeling that receive their most notable development in the Renaissance—is that the style of the ancients darkens and obfuscates the content. But style is too little inclusive a word: say, the habit of mind that characterizes their writing. Critically, it is his impatience with the old-fashioned style or temper that impels modern man to turn away from the imitation of the past. The ancients, says Matthew, "ought to supply more matter with less art, and rid themselves of excess baggage altogether." That is what they ought to do. Instead they are prone to digression and to an overabundance of similes and rhetorical figures. "*Hoc autem modernis non licet*": this, however, the moderns will not permit.[82] What the moderns will permit, what in fact they insist on as the staple of the new curriculum, is the cultivating of dialectics.

This denigrating of the past as so much poetry, in our pejorative sense of the word, is exciting and portentous. Peter Abelard,

---

[80] Quoted E. Curtius, *European Literature*, p. 385. J. Seznec, *Survival of the Pagan Gods*, sees Chrétien not so much as repudiating as continuing or "claiming" the ancient heritage (pp. 18-19).

[81] IV, v; in E. Faral, *Les Arts Poétiques*.

[82] IV, ii, iv, v.

as he is committed to the exercise of the unrefracted reason, wants to know why "the bishops and the doctors of the Christian religion do not debar from the city of God those poets whom Plato restrained from the city of the world."[83] His contemporary Hugh of St. Victor confirms the opposition between the *civitate Dei* of the dialectical intelligence and the *civitate saeculi* of the empiric: between philosophy which is concerned more basically with the noumenal world, and poetry which dallies with particular fact. Philosophy, says Hugh in his treatise on the arts, "investigates comprehensively the ideas of all things, human and divine." Poetry is distracted by phenomena. As its pronouncements are "scattered and confused," it figures among "the appendages of the arts [which] . . . are only tangential to philosophy."[84]

Four centuries later, this criticism recurs powerfully. It is because poets "be so farre wyde from all studye of Philosophye," says the mathematician Cardano, that "they be shut out of Plato his common weale." In the opinion of Renaissance man, they are "banished worthilye."[85] The philosopher, whose business is with disclosing the truth, should stop his ears against "the songs of the poets . . . who are always taking some small matter and dragging it out through long verbal detours, obscuring a simple meaning in confused discourses."[86]

The injunction bears fruit. The study of the classics is abolished (as at the University of Paris in 1215); formal logic replaces it. The result is the blighting of the twelfth-century renaissance in literature but also the triumphant emergence of Scholastic philosophy in the century that follows. Albert the Great succeeds to John of Salisbury as, in the seventeenth century, Thomas Hobbes succeeds to John Donne. The judgment of literature in Hugh of St. Victor's *Didascalion* is the judgment of the new men in the later Renaissance. In consequence and in each period, the doctrine of imitation is either repudiated

---

[83] *Theologia Christiana, c.* 1122-25, Bk. II; *Opera,* p. 445.
[84] *Didascalion,* late 1120s, Bk. I, Ch. iv.
[85] *Cardanus Comforte,* 1573, Clv.
[86] *Didascalion,* III, iv.

29

(as by Sir Philip Sidney: "I am no Picke-purse of an others wit"), or considerably abridged (as by the Florentine Platonist Poliziano, who urges his fellow academicians to "swim . . . without corks, take sometimes your own advice . . . risk your whole strength").[87] Originality and inspiration begin to be esteemed. Shakespeare is detected, warbling his native woodnotes wild. Cicero is put away, whom Ascham requires his less venturesome compatriots to follow. "I am not Cicero," explains Poliziano, a little impatiently now. "I am expressing, I think, myself."

The new poetry of the Elizabethans, forswearing (at least ostensibly) corks and bladders and "Dictionarie's methode," seeks to indite what is written in the heart.[88] Originality is the proud possession of Thomas Nashe, who boasts "that the vein which I have . . . is of my own begetting, and calls no man father in England but myself."[89] Discerning it also in the work of the romancer Robert Greene, he commends that author especially in that he does not borrow but invents.[90] In contrast, Nashe is scornful of his costive and timorous contemporaries who "praise the mountaine that in seaven yeares brings foorth a mouse, or the Italianate pen that of a packet of pilfries affoordeth the presse a pamphlet or two in an age." As a free-born Englishman, he identifies imitation with servility. The kind of writer he admires is "the man . . . [of] extemporall vaine."

Partly, this paean to self-sufficiency is mere bravado. Neither the Renaissance nor the twelfth century ceases to drink from the fount of the past. Only, the draughts are not so deep as they were in the more leisurely days of Cassiodorus. A conviction that business presses describes the new or renascent age. In the earlier period *abbreviatio* is exalted as an ideal of style. Condensations of classical authors are produced in large numbers by contemporary poets. In the later period the ideal is equally congenial, as

---

[87] Sidney, *A&S*, 74; Poliziano, in letter to Paolo Cortese, who is reproved for attending only to the learned dead. Baldwin, *Renaissance*, pp. 48-49.

[88] See, for example, *Astrophil and Stella*, 15, on "Petrarch's long deceasèd woes."

[89] *Strange Newes*, 1592.   [90] Preface to *Menaphon*, 1589.

witness the enormous success of the great compendia of classical wisdom known as *florilegia* (the past boiled down); and the revival of the epigram, which is "fitted to the season/ Of such as best know how to make rhyme reason";[91] and the currency of the emblem book, available in literally hundreds of editions, whose appeal is to the dictum that a picture is worth a thousand words.

This lust for clarity and for the *brevitatis via* is an inseparable component of the rationalist mind. The French moderns of the early eighteenth century undertake to improve Homer by making him shorter; Dryden and Pope purge and illuminate Chaucer and Shakespeare and Donne.[92] A taste for mottos and devices and *impresas* characterizes the waning Middle Ages, in which the Renaissance is augured. From the beginning of the fifteenth century, Italian humanists like Marsilio Ficino sponsor the study of Egyptian hieroglyphics.[93] Erasmus, in the next century, is intrigued by that study. The great gain potential in it, to the new and more compendious psychology, is the discarding of language altogether and the supersession of language by picture.

Of all forms of poetry, the epigram is chariest of language and least inclined to divagate and meander, and hence its renewed popularity in the Renaissance. But what of the concurrent taste for *copia* and amplification?[94] I would explain it by asserting that this taste is "superficial." It characterizes an age which, be-

[91] Henry Parrot, *Laquei Ridiculosi*, 1613.

[92] Dryden on Chaucer: "the father of English poetry [but] his verses [were] lame, unequal, his sense is scarce to be understood. He is a rough diamond, and licentious; he mingles trivial things with those of greater moment, knows not when he has said enough. Having observed this redundancy in Chaucer . . . I have not tied myself to a literal translation" (conflated from Preface to *Fables*, 1700).

[93] E. Iversen, *The Myth of Egypt*; G. Boas, trans., *The Hieroglyphics of Horapollo*. And see the extensive discussion in J. Summers, *George Herbert*, Ch. VI, "The Poem as Hieroglyph."

[94] As described in M. J. Rauh, *Rhetoric in Shakespeare's Time*, pp. 33-40; W. G. Crane, *Wit and Rhetoric*, Chs. V, VI; J. Cousin, *Études sur Quintilien*, Vol. I, Bk. IV, Ch. III, "Théorie de la Digression." And see G. Williamson, *The Senecan Amble*, for extensive discussion of brevity and amplitude in Renaissance prose.

lieving in the simplicity of the truth that bides below the surface, is willing, when only the indifferent cover is in question,
to "expatiate and confer." Indulgence of the husk or cover is an
exercise or *jeu d'esprit*, appropriate to frivolous matter but not
to matter of truth. The truth-telling poet who has his ear to the
ground understands that divagation and meandering are out of
fashion. As he would attract a public, he proclaims that understanding in introducing his compendious verses:

> This is my subject, reader, I confesse,
> From which I thinke seldom I doe digresse.[95]

Divagation is equally abhorrent to the reductive spirit of the
twelfth century. To make against it, the practice is instituted of
setting epigrams as models for school children to emulate.[96]
Now in the Renaissance the cultivating of the genre is resumed,
and for the same reasons.[97] The penchant for economy and for
hewing to the line that had inspired the Latin poet of the earlier
period to write epigrams in imitation of Martial inspires the imi-
tations of the later sixteenth century (as by Sir John Harington
in the 1580s, and Sir John Davies in the 90s), and the great
spate of collections prompted by them in the next generation.[98]
The hallmark of these collections is an eagerness to come at once
to the point without resort to evasion or circumlocution. The
epigrammatist Thomas Bastard comes straight to the point and

[95] Thomas Bastard, *Chrestoleros*, 1598.

[96] See William Fitzstephen (d.1190?), *Description of London* (pub.
Stow's *Survey*, 1598), in preface to his biography of Becket.

[97] The vogue begins in England with Sir Thomas More, and the arch-
priest of prosodic reform, the Rev. Thomas Drant; and on the Continent
with Theodore Beza, whose Latin epigrams (*Juvenilia*, 1548) are tr. by
Nicholas Grimald (in Tottel, 1557) and later by Timothe Kendall (*Flowers of Epigrammes*, 1577). Jonson, as he includes "To Penshurst" and
other longish poems among his *Epigrams*, is transcending the convention,
aiming rather "at providing an English equivalent of Horace's *sermones*—
'conversational poems' or, literally, 'talks' " (J. Bamborough, *BJ*, p. 160).

[98] For the earlier period, see Godfrey of Winchester, d.1107. In the
years 1598-1620, more than 50 editions of epigrams were published. See
H. Hudson's (unfinished) study, *Epigram*.

thereby earns the suffrage of a fellow poet who is also a kindred spirit:

> Thy epigrams are of no bastard race,
> For they dare gaze the world's eye in the face.[99]

The style of antiquity is more reticent and circumstantial than this. *Hoc autem modernis non licet.* Modern man, in the twelfth century as in the Renaissance, is impatient of getting on with the job, and this because he is hopeful of concluding it once and for all. Erasmus, in rationalizing antiquity as a series of topics (*Adagia*, 1500), associates the twelfth century to his own. His *Similia* or *Parabolae* (1513) recall the reductions of Bernard of Chartres and Alan of Lille and the dictionaries of Christian symbols in vogue a little later. The impulse to concision which moves Hugh of St. Victor in twelfth-century France, and occasions his strictures on poetry, recurs in sixteenth-century France and this time not in the Schoolman but in the poet. Jean-Antoine de Baïf is, as a poet, devoted to the ancients. But he wears his classicism with a difference. Like Erasmus, he encapsulates the wisdom of the past as so many saws and sayings.[100]

There is a nice conjunction here of the new and the old, as if history for once were emulating art. For the father of the poet, Lazare de Baïf (d.1547), a Hellenist and neo-Platonist and avid like his kind of expressing the kernel in things, establishes his residence in Paris within a stone's throw of the Abbey of St. Victor, the institution which sheltered the compendious Hugh.

The deprecating of imitation and the abridging of the ancient past by the age that is mewing its youth make possible a reevaluating of the immediate past. This is the third and the ultimate step in the process of reversing the convention of decay. As the reigning Czar is executed and interred, his predecessors are taken into the pantheon. As the literati of the sixteenth century proclaim their independence of Greece and Rome (for example, through the mouth of Gabriel Harvey), they begin to look with

[99] John Heath, *Two Centuries of Epigrams*, 1610.

[100] In his most popular work, *Les Mimes, ensignemens et proverbes* (1576), which ran through 9 editions to 1619.

sympathy on the literature of their own past, which they had just now been stigmatizing as barbarous. Self-consciousness and uncertainty with regard to their position require the visiting of the stigma. Burgeoning assurance allows of its removal. The belittling of the Middle Ages as a means of aggrandizing the self-esteem of the Renaissance is conditional on the adoration of Greece and Rome. But now it is proposed that the Renaissance stands at the zenith. And so the medieval legacy is inquired into and used to acquit the present of its debt to the antique past.

By the middle of the sixteenth century, Chaucer is being celebrated as "our English Homer" (whatever the velleities of William Webbe).[101] Ascham proposes that "his sayings have as much authority as either Sophocles or Euripides in Greek."[102] The poet Thomas Freeman goes further than this in allowing authority not only to Chaucer but also to Lydgate and Gower, and in claiming for them equality with "all the sages . . . of former ages." Because these medieval poets "could see and shine" with any and "did their learned lights advance," even if in a time less favored than the present time, the darkness of the Middle Ages is made less dark than it was and—what is more to the purpose—the splendor of antiquity is made less daunting.

> Nor Greece nor Rome could reckon us
> As then among the barbarous,
> Since these three knew to turn, perdy,
> The screw-pin of philosophy
> As well as they; and left behind
> As rich memorials of the mind.[103]

[101] *Toxophilus*, 1545. Already in the Henrician period, the conventional view of the Middle Ages begins to be tempered. The literary patron Sir Brian Tuke, though he laments the past as a time when "all good letters were layd a slepe throughout the worlde," praises the style of Chaucer (V. Rubel, *Poetic Diction*, p. 17). In the next century Denham salutes Chaucer as a presage which, "like the morning star, To us discovers day from far," and as a dissolver of the mists "Which our dark nation long involved" ("On Mr Abraham Cowley," 1668).
[102] Smith, I, 355.
[103] *Rub and a Great Cast*, 1614.

But if the vernacular poet is conceded authority, vernacular speech must be granted it too. Boccaccio, in the beginnings of the Renaissance, admires Dante but this side idolatry, for "he wrote in his mother tongue."[104] Even so late as the seventeenth century, Galileo is odious to the Inquisition not only as he sponsors the Copernican theory but as "he does so in Italian, surely not the language best suited for the needs of . . . scholarship."[105] Galileo is, however, in key with his time. Compare Descartes, to whom the vulgar French of Lower Brittany seems, when choice is incumbent on him, as suitable an instrument as Latin. Newton, who cleaves to Latin in writing the *Principia* (1687), abandons it for English in the dissertation on *Opticks* (1704). Bishop Sprat is so moved by the staunch behavior of London in time of plague and fire as to declare "that not only the best Natural, but the best Moral Philosophy too, may be learn'd from the shops of Mechanicks."[106] Ascham, a hundred years earlier, had come to a similar conclusion. Though he asserts the primacy of Latin and Greek as "the two onelie learned tonges," he is of Sprat's opinion in believing that "the rudenes of common and mother tonges is no bar for wise speaking."[107]

There is in his position a certain equivocalness, as of the man who wants to have it both ways. In this he is like his contemporaries Sidney and Bacon, who are quite capable of speaking to either side of a question and often with equal eloquence and fervor. Sidney, who eschews imitation as in the famous dictum, "Look in thy heart and write," is also a great imitator and even in the sonnet whence that quotation comes. Bacon, who virtually personifies the passionate belief of the Renaissance in the possibility of ordering and rationalizing existence, owns nonetheless that "There is no Excellent Beauty that hath not some strangeness in the Proportion."

The abiding sense of proportion makes of the Renaissance an uncommonly hopeful time, already preparing to inhabit the

---

[104] *Genealogy of the Pagan Gods*, xiv, xxi; Osgood, ed., p. 99.
[105] 1633. G. de Santillana, *Crime of Galileo*, pp. 246-47.
[106] *History*, ed. Cope and Jones, p. 121.
[107] *Scholemaster*; Smith, 1, 5.

realms of gold. It is also a time given over to the blackest despair, bred of a conviction that the cosmos is running down. It rejoices in man as having climbed up from darkness to the summit of things. It sees him concurrently as the slime of the dungpit. In the phrase of John Marston, the sublunary orbs cast their excrements there. This capacity to equivocate does not much commend itself to the historian, who is by trade and temper one of the rationalizing kind. It is true, he insists that he is treating of history *wie es eigenlich gewesen*. But he is enamored of a certain consistency in history. It is his characteristic humor always to be looking for the figure in the carpet. This makes him in his myopic intensity faintly comic, for the figure is hardly ever so clear of line as to yield itself up to immediate perusal. But this is not to say that no figure is there.

It is perceptible, for instance, in the growing impatience of Renaissance man with the claims of antiquity, and this despite the fact that real homage is paid to the classical past even as the desire quickens to enfranchise the present. Bacon, though mostly he chafes at further servitude to the fruitless preoccupation of the past with verbal questions, is not absolutely consistent in that chafing. In his character of Mr. Facing-Both-Ways, he wants it to "be kept in mind that experiments of Light are more to be sought after than experiments of Fruit."[108] Girolamo Cardano, who is very much of the party of progress, is yet concerned to remind us, in looking back over his life, "that there is practically no new idea which one may bring forward."[109] The self-reliant Harvey, as he reflects on that less than hopeful observation, is often pedantically attentive to the goings-on in Athens and Rome. So, two centuries later, is Alexander Pope, the presiding poet of the Age of Reason. In *An Essay on Criticism*, Pope offers his respects to old authority and the rules, whose chief seat he locates in France. There, "Critic-learning flourished most." And then, in an astonishing and revealing *volte face*, Pope rounds on that hypothetically civilized country and derides it as "a na-

[108] Quoted Eiseley, *Bacon*, pp. 94, 54.
[109] *De Vita Propria Liber*, 1643, Ch. 44.

tion born to serve." By the time of John Keats, the tension be-tween homage and impatience is broken. Keats knows nothing more hateful or risible than adherence to the classical formula-tions: "musty laws lined out with wretched rule/And compass vile" and epitomized for him in "The name of one Boileau!"[110] The self-sufficiency of the Romantics is the end of the road on which Harvey in the 1570s sets out so jauntily.

It is a significant progress, however vexed with turnings again; and like Saul's on the road to Damascus, it is fraught with revelations. These are prone to ambiguity in the way of divina-tory things. Call them "visions and revisions." Their ultimate purport is, nonetheless, fairly clear. I should describe it as fol-lows. The golden age is not behind us; man has not suffered an irremediable fall; he may throw away his crutches; the golden age is now.

[110] *Sleep and Poetry.*

II   Poetry and the Illative Voice

GABRIEL HARVEY, in writing down the past as abortive, is the optimistic man. He sneers at Greece and Rome the better to laud his own time and to establish its uniqueness. Samuel Daniel, who is not inclined much to sneering, scrutinizes Greece and Rome more narrowly than most of his contemporaries because he sees no time as exemplary. He is the old-fashioned or pessimistic man. His root assumptions are two, and either, if received, would have nipped the modern world in its making. The first: "Perfection is not the portion of man." From Daniel's disbelief in perfectibility all his other positions derive: his tolerance, his indifference to the framing of rules and regulations (here, to govern poetry), his more judicious assessing of the classical past, I should say finally his rejoicing in the role and title of mere poet.

And the second assumption, which is really a codicil to the first: everything is provisional and nothing finally avails or endures. What is cried up today as the ultimate nostrum "is but a Character of that perpetuall revolution which wee see to be in all things that never remaine the same."[1] On "the condition of things in general," compare John of Salisbury, a man of Daniel's kind: "all things under the sun are but the sport of chance; for the flight of time, the mutability of things, the blindness of men's minds, the fickleness of their souls, all by their own vast nimbleness, spin round the axle of Fortune." Like Daniel, John of Salisbury predicates of the condition of man "perpetual revolution."[2] Those who address themselves to the building of

---

[1] Smith, II, 374, 384.

[2] Letter to Peter of Celle, 1-8 April 1157. The early correspondence is ed. by W. Millor and H. Butler (rev. C. Brooke). See also H. Arendt, *Human Condition*, esp. pp. 7-21.

the kingdom on earth (and the attempt to reconstitute prosody in Daniel's time is one part of that grand endeavor) are just as much in fee as the often-ridiculed Schoolmen to what Daniel describes as that corroding "law of time, which in a few yeeres will make al that for which we now contend Nothing." This is the nightmare that troubles the sleep of Francis Bacon.

When Daniel refuses to legislate the language of poetry, he expresses in a single phrase the old point of view: "there is no necessitie in Nature."[3] It is hard to conceive of a more reactionary proposal in the context of the early seventeenth century. The antithetical saying is Bacon's, who picks up the gage two years later in the *Advancement of Learning*. Interpreting the fable of Typhon, made captive by Pan, Bacon concludes that "whatever vast and unusual swells, which the word Typhon signifies, may sometimes be raised in nature, as in the sea, the clouds, the earth, or the like; yet nature catches, entangles, and holds all such outrages and insurrections in her inextricable net, wove as it were of adamant." To abandon "the necessity of fate" is to be more indulgent of fancy than patient of truth—"as if anything in the frame of nature could, like an island, stand apart from the rest." Nothing at last is unamenable to law, and therefore Bacon "would introduce into primary philosophy a real and solid inquiry . . . according to the laws of nature."[4]

Poetry affects to stand outside these laws. It is anarchic and therefore mendacious. That in brief is the criticism of poetry as urged by the rationalizing intelligence, which has dominated in our councils from the sixteenth century forward. Francis Crick, the molecular biologist and Nobel laureate in medicine, exemplifies this intelligence in announcing—with a zestful pugnacity that makes for entertainment as it seems a little quaint in this more tentative time—that "the old, or literary culture, is clearly dying, whereas the new culture, the scientific one . . . is growing with great rapidity." One is reminded irresistibly of that truculent contender for the truth, Thomas Henry Huxley, a hundred years ago.

[3] Smith, II, 378.   [4] Bk. II, Ch. xiii; III, i.

But not to play the petulant role of the latter-day "humanist": what the scientist announces is true. It is the facile optimism that galls and the jejune assumption that progress attends on the swapping of old and new dogma. As for "people with training in the arts"—the modern optimist in rounding on these people is conscious only of his modernity, not conscious at all of the old-fashioned character of the rationalism for which he is spokesman—"tomorrow's science is going to knock their culture right out from under them."[5]

The Bible epitomizes this moribund culture. Against the tissue of impossibilities it fashions is the adamantine net: the perception of necessary form. The Bible, which depends for its continued currency on the laconic assumption that it is not truth but poetry ("The Bible As Literature"), associates the creation of living matter with whimsy or caprice. The biblical Typhon is oblivious of law. Adam is formed as by fiat from the dust of the earth, Eve from Adam's rib. The rationalist knows better. On his more orderly understanding, human life is the product of a nicely reticulated evolutionary chain that links together in iron sequence every sentient thing on the planet. The impulsive and essentially personal artificer, the God who walks in Eden in the cool of the evening, is an outrage or insurrection. The rationalist pins Him down. In the same muscular way he deals with the arbitrary fictions of the poet, who wills us to believe that dead men rise and push us from our thrones, or that prayer is efficacious (Henry Plantagenet before Agincourt, Henry Tudor before Bosworth Field), or that the red right hand of God is lifted to punish our mistreadings.

Rationalism in this context does not denote the honoring of reason but the idolatrous worship of reason and an exclusive attending on it, as when Brutus seeks to disjoin flesh and spirit:

> We all stand up against the spirit of Caesar,
> And in the spirit of men there is no blood—

or Wallace Stevens bids us ironically to dismiss "the half colors of quarter-things . . . The single bird, the obscure moon," to

[5] *Of Molecules and Men*, pp. 93, 95.

cleave in place of them to "The ABC of being . . . The vital, arrogant, fatal, dominant X" (*The Motive for Metaphor*). The rationalist, who assigns scant importance to the body, prefers to it the paradigm or ABC of being, has little patience with indigenous (hence qualified) things, elusive to the hand and eye, our life as a mingled yarn. His forte is to "bottom" the yarn, in process to unravel the inextricable net it composes. Ernest Jones, the biographer of Freud, presents him fairly, in attempting to account for the supposed lack of harmony in Andrea del Sarto's *Virgin with the Harpies* (Uffizi Gallery). The Madonna in the painting is smiling but the pedestal on which she stands is adorned with grimacing monsters. How explain this incongruous juxtaposition? The rationalist has an answer. He points to the unhappy marriage of the artist, thence to his hatred of women, thence—as each effect must show forth its cause—to latent homosexuality in him. Iconographic tradition: the symbolizing of the triumph of Christianity over the unregenerate past (Mary bruising with her heel the head of the serpent) eludes the explicating man; but never mind. Really what is missing here is the sense, the possibility even, of the *discordia concors*: "wild laughter in the throat of death."[6]

The Age of Reason I define, then, as the age of factitious clarity, no chiaroscuro, a "humorous" age in which the master motive lies open to inspection. Gustave Mahler, conversing with Freud, hits suddenly on this motive. At last it is clear to him why, in his music, profound and banal melodies should tend to intermingle, why for instance the funeral march in the *First Symphony* should take its rise from the popular children's song, *Frère Jacques*. As a boy, the composer had been forced to participate in the incessant quarrelling of his parents. One day, fleeing the house which rings with altercation, he encounters in the street a barrel organ playing "Ach, Du lieber Augustin." There it is! the "etiology" of all that comes later, the connecting thread which must associate bathos and sombre feeling. But the chance conjunction of early panic and the barrel organ "carolling down

[6] Discussion draws on D. Fernandez, *Diacritics*, p. 10; quotation is from *Love's Labour's Lost*, v, ii, 865.

41

a golden street" is not solely, perhaps not chiefly, the engendering agent of the sentimentality to which the mature composer is prone. "My mother cried," says Beatrice in *Much Ado About Nothing*; "but then there was a star danced, and under that I was born."[7] Mahler, in his art, in his person, is like the rest of us, a huddle of contradictions in the face of which explication must quail.

The rationalizing man—let us call him Polonius—is recognizable, however, as he continues to pursue the connections on which his psychology is founded. "If circumstances lead"—circumstantial evidence, in which he trusts absolutely—he will find "Where truth is hid, though it were hid indeed/ Within the center." Alternative explanations, varieties of truth, these are renounced, certainly as they appear contradictory. *Tertium non datur*. The bundle of *fasces*—man the integer whose ambiguous existence is a mediating between body and spirit, "ontogeny and phylogeny," between the universal truth and its particular exemplification—is picked to pieces. "Mind obtains the monopoly of interpreting, manipulating, and altering reality—of governing remembrance and oblivion, even of defining what reality is and how it should be used and altered. . . . [Mind is made] the sole repository of judgment, truth, rationality . . . decides what is useful and useless, good and evil" (Marcuse).

The civilization that depends on the aggrandizing of mind is not a plenary civilization nor worth the "discontents" it imposes. Freud, who accepts the imposition, is more persuasive on his descriptive side. "Originally the ego includes everything." Later, as reason grows more imperious, it bates and dwindles. What is left is "only a shrunken vestige of a far more extensive feeling—a feeling which embraced the universe and expressed an inseparable connection of the ego with the external world."[8] The connection is renewed, the demise of the Age of Reason is predicted—now, in this second half of the twentieth century—

[7] Mahler and Freud are discussed in Fernandez, p. 12; Beatrice is quoted *Much Ado*, II, i, 348-50.

[8] Marcuse is quoted in *Eros and Civilization*, pp. 128-29; Freud in *Civilization and Its Discontents*, p. 6.

when the Cartesian impulse to bifurcation: here blood, there spirit, gives way to a laconic accepting of blood and spirit together, reason and will, id and ego, not as antinomies but one: "That subtle knot, which makes us man." Now, as the clarity is rejected which does not enlighten but casts in a false relief,

> We more than awaken, sit on the edge of sleep,
> As on an elevation, and behold
> The academies like structures in a mist.
> (Stevens, "Notes Toward a Supreme Fiction")

Implicit in this discussion is the hypothesizing of an antithetical kind of temperament, which I call medieval as it is, not everywhere supreme but only ascendant, in the long period which stretches from the early Christian era (when the millennial expectation of the Ante-Nicene Fathers is dashed) to the reviving of dogmatic assurance in fourteenth-century Italy and later, and which I see as conspicuous once again in the immediate present: this antithetical temperament is apt to sponsor a view of life and art that is marked by dubiety, tentativeness, accommodation, and not least of disparate things. Shakespeare's characters are endlessly bemused (though not palsied), and for that reason I associate their creator not to the modern or rationalizing age but rather to the medieval past. I see that the term "medieval" is likely to give trouble, especially when used of a very wide range of persons, ideas, and institutions, disposed in a great gap of time. Like "rationalism," it is amenable to different interpretations. In my role as expositor (or rationalist) I do not despair, however, of suggesting what it means.

Shakespearean man is medieval in temper as he forbears to instruct us in last things. His magniloquent language is "like a clamor in a vault" that cannot be "distinguished" or parsed, or not in preceptorial ways. (It is the fool in the grain from whom answers come readily.) Addressing himself to all the vexed situations, he is characteristically at a stand, is discovered exclaiming:

> My thoughts are whirlèd like a potter's wheel.
> I know not where I am, nor what I do.

43

The world as he perceives it strikes him with amazement—he is entoiled as in a maze—and apt to lose his way,

> Not knowing how to find the open air,
> But toiling desperately to find it out.[9]

The black night which environs Racine's Oreste—"*Mais quelle épaisse nuit, tout à coup, m'environne?*"—it is the business of the "modern" playwright or psychologist to dispel. Racine in his art prosecutes this business successfully; in Shakespeare, as in his medieval antecedents, it is burked. Prince Hamlet, in whose heart there is a kind of fighting that will not let him sleep, starts from his bed, starts up from his cabin: "in the dark/ Groped I to find out them." It is not easy to say just what he finds. The natural habitat is evidently the tickle point between light and dark. Man, evidently, is in a parlous case and there Shakespeare, who is not wanting in ruth but only in capacity, is constrained to leave him.

In the Age of Reason, the modern age of which Bacon is the prophet—the bucinator, he calls himself—and which has maintained its hegemony to the present, the environing darkness is banned. The effect follows ineluctably from its cause. There are no mysterious lacunae. "Duncan is in his grave." It is certain that he remains there. God does not hurl thunderbolts at guilty men and is in fact on the side of preponderant power. Everything resolves itself to a question of power—as the physicist would say, of force. This physicist—like I. I. Rabi, whose conversation I am paraphrasing here—is verified in the event: only he misses the sense of metaphorical representation. On his literalistic view, prayer is a muttering to no purpose. The wise man will save his breath to cool his porridge.

Whatever is, is in fee to necessity. That is the first premise on which the modern age is founded. It is the discovery, perhaps it is the invention of the immediate predecessors and contemporaries of Shakespeare: Copernicus in astronomy, Vesalius in anatomy, Peter Ramus in logic, in physics Galileo and Kepler,

---

[9] Conflating *3HVI*, v, iv, 43-45; *1HVI*, 1, v, 19-20; *King John*, iv, iii, 140-41; *3HVI*, iii, ii, 174-78.

in physiology William Harvey, in mathematics Vieta and Descartes. Shakespeare, who sums up the medieval or anarchic intelligence just as it reaches its term, casts a cold eye on this modern discovery. His apologists for order and necessary form are the sycophantic Rosencrantz in *Hamlet*, and the devious Canterbury in *Henry V*, and the dog fox Ulysses, and the bumbling Menenius Agrippa. Shakespeare's plays are themselves explicitly formal but also peculiar. Necessary recurrence is to seek. In each play the writer is at a new beginning. The pattern he discovers has no necessary reference to what has gone before.

Implicit in the paeon to order is a second premise, which also bequeathes its important legacy to subsequent times. This second premise is teleological: the orderly course of things is a "progressive" course. In the words of a modern activist and man of good hope: "The tide of evolution never flows backward."[10] (Here the eschatologists of the Renaissance, like John Foxe in the sixteenth century and, a hundred years later, the Fifth Monarchy men, confess their affiliation to classical science.) Evolution is purposive, signifies not simply flux but advance. So Lamarck and Samuel Butler but also Charles Darwin, who has incidentally little time for the fabulous content of poetry.[11] The victorious march of progress is like the ascendancy of truth which, crushed to earth, will rise again. J. S. Mill is reactionary in supposing it "a piece of idle sentimentality that the truth, merely as truth, has any inherent power denied to error."[12]

[10] Jack London in his utopian novel *The Iron Heel* (1907), Ch. IX.

[11] According to Lamarck the giraffe grows a long neck because it wants and needs it. According to Butler "effort, endeavor, purpose, have something to do with biological evolution . . . living forms evolve because they want to" (*Life and Habit*). According to Darwin all "corporeal and mental organs . . . have been formed so that their possessors may compete successfully with other beings, and thus increase in number" (*Autobiography*, pp. 88-89).

For Darwin on poetry and art in general, see p. 138: "But now for many years I cannot endure to read a line of poetry: I have tried lately to read Shakespeare, and found it so intolerably dull that it nauseated me. I have also almost lost any taste for pictures or music."

[12] "On Liberty."

Modern or progressive man is animated by a belief that is certainly mystical—inconsequently, given his insistent adherence to rationality—in the power of truth to prevail and to make for the establishing of the kingdom of God on earth.

The man who takes himself seriously in any generation—Plato and Yeats, Friedrich Engels, Francis Crick—is imbued with the sense of an ending. "America is up against the wall." Inevitably, says Eldridge Cleaver, a millenarian of the 1970s, we must assign "This whole apparatus, this capitalistic system and its institutions and police . . . to the garbage can of history."[13] The millenarian of the twelfth century, like Joachim of Flora, perceives the ending as imminent and is able to fix it precisely in time. In the seventeenth century, a conviction of the ending of all things recurs. Cromwell has seen the writing on the wall. Here we are, some centuries later. No doubt it is melodramatic to anticipate the last day. Every today is an ending and beginning. The new moon is always there, cradled in the arms of the old. Nonetheless it is tenable to speak of a climactic or critical change. "We are living in a very singular moment of history. It is a moment of crisis, in the literal sense of that word. In every branch of our spiritual and material civilization we seem to have arrived at a critical turning-point" (Max Planck).[14]

Tenably, in the second half of the twentieth century, the Age of Reason is drawing to its close. The world goes on. The psychology which directs it is dramatically different. Already in the nineteenth century, this different psychology begins to be bruited. Bacon, who makes no question but what two times two is four, is controverted—but in terms less beholden to reason than intuition or simple asseveration—by the Underground Man: "two times two makes four is, in my opinion, nothing but an impertinence . . . two times two makes four looks like a dandy, struts like a cock of the walk blocking your way." The predictable equation is fatiguing. "Two times two makes five is sometimes a most delightful little thing."[15]

[13] D. L. Brown, "Black Power," *Illinois Quarterly*, xxxiii, 32.
[14] *Where Is Science Going?* p. 64.
[15] Dostoevsky, *Notes from Underground*, pp. 32-33.

46

In the affront to rationality, the sense of an ending is clamant. The waning of the Middle Ages communicates this sense, for example in the prevalence of witches.[16] As the classical period verges on decay, preoccupation with the esoteric infiltrates the study of mechanics and natural law. Science, increasingly, gives ground to superstition and magic. Demonology flourishes and its obverse, the obsession with God. The appeal to the occult, as by the Neoplatonists of the third century, displaces the appeal to reason.[17] Compare the modern penchant for turning off the mind but, not to stupor, rather to attain another and hypothetically superior order of awareness: the cult of Esalen, the incantatory noises of Hare Krishna, art as vaticination, the credibility which goes to the astrologer as to the revelations of Annie Besant. The master of Kundalini Yoga seeks to enfranchise within his disciples of the Healthy, Happy, Holy Organization the all-enabling genie who is Satnam, the personification of Truth. It is not by intellection that this more puissant truth is known.

The repudiating of the conventional wisdom is immensely hopeful; and accompanied by vast unease. Human mentality, as conceived by Renaissance thinkers, is unchangeably established. So with the law of action deriving from it; so with its creation, the social world. Now this immutable order which takes its warrant from reason is subject to irreverent interrogation. The result, says the Steppenwolf in the novel by Hermann Hesse, is the reduction of life in our own time "to real suffering, to hell," as "two ages, two cultures and religions overlap." Modern or amphibious man, who has forfeited the power to understand

[16] Generally the witch-craze is read as a Protestant phenomenon, for example by Trevor-Roper who documents the relative disbelief in witches in the Middle Ages and the astonishing "recrudescence [of belief] . . . from about 1560" (*European Witch-craze*, p. 140). The conventional view is epitomized by W.E.H. Lecky, who sees the dying-down as coincident with the rise of rationalism; and by Andrew Dickson White, who interprets its flourishing as an aspect of "the warfare of science with theology" (quotes from Trevor-Roper, p. 98). They have got it backwards.

[17] Seznec illustrates in *Survival of the Pagan Gods*, p. 42.

47

himself and the situation in which he is involved, "has no stand-ard, no security, no simple acquiescence."

The complement of disequilibrium is violence.

> I was dreaming of a lot of fat faces . . . and how they'd look with that smashed, sticky expression that comes with catching the butt end of a .45 across their noses. I was dreaming of a slimy foreign secret army that held a parade of terror under the Mafia label and laughed at us with our laws and regula-tions and how fast their damned smug expressions would change when they saw the fresh corpses of their own kind day after day.

The dreamer is presented by Mickey Spillane, an obscene and enormously popular writer of detective thrillers in the 1950s. The fantasizing of this writer's sadistic hero is the consequence of frustration (inanition), the long commitment to rationality as a universal panacea. "Words are no deeds," says Shakespeare's heroine in *Measure for Measure*.

"The great human tomorrow" which the rationalist is always proclaiming and for which he is content to postpone indefinitely an equable life in the present, is discovered suddenly to consist in the abrogation of order. Now, "the proud *Homo erectus* is dropping to all fours, is growing fangs and fur; the beast takes ascendency in man. The brutal Middle Ages are returning." That is a gloomy point of view, as enunciated by the Soviet apostate, Yevgeny Zamyatin.[18] To sustain this point of view is not difficult. The record of the past fifty years offers sufficient corroboration. This, then, is where we are. My business in what follows is to suggest how we got there.

Bacon, the graceless or Pelagian man, only thinks he sees the future. In declaring for law, Bacon speaks for the new men. Their revolutionary and hypothetically more enlightened pro-posal is that the tables of the law, in which necessity is codified, are open to them and, when disclosed, will strike the shackles from the mind and body of man and make the earth bloom like

[18] Zamyatin, *Essays*, p. 52.

48

a garden. After the skepticism of the Age of Faith comes the dogmatism of the Age of Reason.

The opposition between the two is fundamental, as with two stars of contrary aspect. Nowhere is that opposition more sharply defined than in the art of either period, and the differing attitudes each evinces towards it. Here are two quotations in which the difference is encapsulated. The first is from Quintilian, who is writing in the Silver Age of Rome but whose point of view reflects the Middle Ages precisely: "The enjoyment of literature does not become wholly pure until it withdraws from action and can rejoice in the contemplation of itself."[19] The second quotation is Sir Philip Sidney's, and in it the Renaissance esthetic is affirmed: "It is not Gnosis but Praxis must be the fruit."[20] In the Renaissance the opposition between these two formulations is resolved, and with considerable consequence to poetry as a significant form of discourse.

The high seriousness of Renaissance literature and criticism derives from the notion that man can know the truth and that the truth will make him free. The Middle Ages have no notion that the whole truth is open; or, what is more important, that the truth is literally efficacious. Medieval art is therefore much humbler, only a functional thing, dedicated to uses that are intermediate and not final. Medieval music is ancillary entertainment, one part only of worship or ceremony or banqueting or mumming. The homophonic music of the eighteenth century—post-Renaissance music—as it is often written to accompany the religious service, is also functional in kind. From the exercise of this function come masses which astonish by their beauty and vigor—Mozart and Haydn are the great exemplars—but which partake of the character of sacred concerts. The business of the priest at the altar recedes. The music is the thing.

The same exalting or isolating is observable of post-Renaissance art. Donatello, turning his back on the Middle Ages, begins to create what had not been attempted since antiquity: isolated heroic statues in the round. The medieval preference is for

[19] *Institutio Oratoria*, Bk. II, Ch. xviii, 4.
[20] Smith, I, 171. Sidney is quoting Aristotle, *Ethics*, I, iii.

pilgrims that they marry teaching and delighting, entertainment and signification: "Tales of best sentence and moost solaas."[27]

The same requirement governs in the medieval drama. When the banner bearer or *vexillator* announces a performance of the *Ludus Coventriae* cycle, he declares that its purpose is to please the people "with plays full glad" and to demonstrate to them "How that this world first began,/ And how God made both earth and man." The matter in prospect is a "game well played in good array." There is also the undertaking that "Of Holy Writ this game shall be." The subject is serious; it is at the same time sport or diversion. The banner-bearer who announces "The Play of the Sacrament" calls on Jesus to save the audience from pain and to confer on it the joys of life everlasting. But he finishes: "Now minstrel, blow up with a merry stevin!"[28]

This conjunction of pleasure and profit, which is the basis of the medieval esthetic, is crystallized in a moving phrase by John of Salisbury, who "is certain that the pious and wise reader who spends time lovingly over his books . . . comes close to life in all things." It is explicitly "the pleasure of letters" that he wishes to celebrate in commencing the *Policraticus*, that encyclopedic treatise on the art of good government. Literature is delightful in that it offers "solace in sorrow, rest in labor, cheerfulness in poverty, self-restraint in pleasure and in wealth." But literature is also of practical use. "In books there is something profitable for everybody," on the principle that "all that has been written . . . [is] ordained for man's utility."[29] For that reason, John of Salisbury is a student of the poets. It is, however, unnecessary to hunt quotations in this medieval writer. One has only to read him a little to appreciate the value and the kind of value he attaches to verse. Though the *Policraticus* is essentially a political treatise, it is also a cento of classical poetry. Citations abound, to Horace and Ovid and Persius and Juvenal

---

[27] General Prologue, l. 798.

[28] J. Q. Adams, ed., *Chief Pre-Shakespearean Dramas*, pp. 81, 85.

[29] *Policraticus*, 1159, Bk. vii, Ch. 10; intro. to Bk. i. Even pagan literature is valuable so long as one remembers the snake in the grass (vii, 10). See Pike edn., pp. 255, 6-7, 253, 251.

and Lucan and Statius. The function of the poets is twofold. They are there to point a moral and to adorn the tale.

This notion of poetry's function is a long time in giving over. Mostly the sixteenth century is satisfied with it. Sidney, who is the first in England to modify the old esthetic decisively, also enunciates and honors it in his *Apologie*. "Poesie therefore is an arte of imitation," the end of which is "to teach and delight."[30] Sidney's master, the Italian humanist J. C. Scaliger, is satisfied to paraphrase Horace essentially as his medieval predecessors had done. The end of poetry is to instruct (*docere*) and also to give pleasure (*delectatione*; elsewhere *jucunditate*).[31] This is the whole business of art.

In the beginning, the yoking together of these two functions is understood to describe the Renaissance esthetic not less precisely than that of the Middle Ages. The Irish poet and translator Richard Stanyhurst locates "thee chiefe prayse of a wryter . . . in thee enterlacing of pleasure wyth profit." According to Webbe, "the right use of Poetry is . . . to mingle profite with pleasure, and so to delight the Reader with pleasantnes of hys Arte, as in the mean time his mind may be well instructed with knowledge and wisedome."[32]

All this is sufficiently familiar. But now a change begins to be perceptible. To teaching and delighting, the venerable functions of art, a third is added, which is acting or doing. The new formula reads: *et prodesse et delectare et movere*. Art impels to action. I take this revision to be of central importance, in the splitting away of the present from the past.

One ought not to speak of the "present" without comment or qualification. Purposive activity is canonized in the modern age which commences with the Renaissance. The "orchestra and noblest seats of Heaven" the modern hagiographer reserves for

[30] Smith, I, 158-59.

[31] *Poetices*; Smith, I, 398. Scaliger is, however, "anticipatory," like Sidney: "*Sed & docendi, & movendi, & delectandi*" (*Poetices*, III, xcvii).

[32] Stanyhurst dedicating his trans. of Virgil (1582); Webbe in his *Discourse of English Poetrie* (1586); Smith, I, 136, 234.

those "who have held up shaking hands in the fire and humanly contended" (Sir Thomas Browne). Now increasingly the applause which goes to action is withheld, or it is muted. The immediate present is detected, as belief in the efficiency of action begins to wane. Maybe the goal is not attainment but process and consists, says Dostoevsky, "in life itself and not actually in the goal proper." A fixed goal is a formula and already "the beginning of death."[33] Maybe the true believer is not the forthputting man who "dares trust his proposition, and drives it on to the utmost issue"—that is what the Renaissance preacher supposes[34] —but the indolent man, who is the hero and pariah of the 1970s, who mistrusts himself and all propositions, all reduction of thought to action, who abhors contention and is willing simply to observe.

Medieval man is a dreamer, whose dreams remain untranslated and inert. That is the hostile judgment of his successor. But perhaps "the one person who has more illusions than the dreamer" is this successor, who is "the man of action." Oscar Wilde, the most perceptive intelligence of the later nineteenth century, is very much of the immediate present in asserting that man is made perfect "by the rejection of energy," that the intentional life is the guarantee of damaged goods. "It is always with the best intentions that the worst work is done."

The deprecating of purposive and ostensibly useful behavior, in the 1890s and now in the second half of the twentieth century, signalizes a return to the "brutal Middle Ages" (Zamyatin)— which means, in this context, not the knout and the pogrom but the exalting of the inward or contemplative life. In the opinion of the Age of Reason, "Contemplation is the gravest sin of which any citizen can be guilty, in the opinion of the highest culture it is the proper occupation of man." Far more difficult, says Wilde, with his customary insouciance in which there is much more than a kernel of sense, "to talk about a thing than to do it." In fact, "to do nothing at all is the most difficult thing

---

[33] *Notes from Underground*, p. 31.

[34] Jeremy Taylor in a Univ. of Dublin sermon, quoted F. L. Huntley, *JT and the Great Rebellion*, pp. 6-7.

in the world, the most difficult and the most intellectual."[35] The connection between the dead past of the mystic and saint and our often enervated present is the deprecating of activity to a particular end. "Don't just do something, Buddha said. Stand there" (Daniel Berrigan).

In our own time as in the Middle Ages, it is often the activist, the man committed first of all to political or social engagement, who commends to us the "law of reversed effort" or the life of non-striving and surrender, and it is only from this man that such praise comes acceptably: Father Berrigan, in the older time Suger of St.-Denis, one of those greatly active personalities who, in his own phrase, "are men of action by virtue of their prelacies"—the station in the vineyard to which they have been called—not by private compulsion or predilection. To Suger's contemporary, St. Bernard of Clairvaux, commitment to the purposive life is fetishistic and absolute. "You perform all the difficult religious duties," says an acid-tongued contemporary to the self-denying man. "You fast; you watch; you suffer; but . . . you do not love."[36] Suger does not shirk the difficult duties but he undertakes them only *ultra possibilitatem humanam*. Recall the moving line Shakespeare gives the aged Bolingbroke and one has him to the life: "Are these things then necessities? Then let us meet them like necessities." Suger is in the world, necessarily. He is not of it.

The man who has discovered how little "laws or kings can cause or cure" is not, as he says so much, discommending action per se but frenetic action, the end of which is the assuaging of guilt, as also the ingenuous belief that action in the world is finally or entirely efficacious.[37] Joseph Conrad is morbid, in asserting that "Man is a worker, or he is nothing." Conrad works to detect but also to obliterate the void: "the true horror behind

---

[35] *Intentions*, 1891; quoted R. Ellman, *The Artist As Critic*, pp. 359, 384, 400, 381.

[36] E. Panofsky, *Abbot Suger*, p. 17. The contemporary is Peter the Venerable, quoted in Adams, *Mont-St.-Michel*, pp. 313-14.

[37] See Arendt, *Human Condition*, esp. Ch. vi, "The 'Vita Activa' and the Modern Age."

the appalling face of things" (*Lord Jim*). J. S. Bach is an indefatigable worker but for the glory of God and the innocent pleasure of man. The goal toward which his music directs us is passivity or stasis but it is won, like Tamino's guerdon in the *Magic Flute*, through unremitting attention: commitment.

"Out of the man of conscience is formed the child." That is Dietrich Bonhoeffer, who dies a martyr to his conscience but whose life is in no sense to be read as prolegomenary. Bonhoeffer the activist yields himself to the present, makes that surrender to it which is not slothful capitulation but fulfillment. "Willingness to be determined by the future is the eschatological possibility of the child. The child sees itself, in all fear and wonderment, gripped by the onrush of things to come, therefore it can live only for the present"—the committed life, precisely!— "but the grown man, willing to be determined by the present, lapses into the past, into himself, in death and guilt. It is only out of the future that the present can be lived."[38] The early Fathers, despairing of things as they are, reject the present in favor of the eschatine—but prematurely.[38a] Hysteric rejection denotes the cultist of the twentieth century—like Robert de Grimston, the founder and leader of the Process Church of the Final Judgment. "There is not much time. The distant rumblings that are heralds of the End have become a mighty roar closing in about us . . . the whole world . . . [is] stricken by the sound of its own approaching doom." But this sound is overpowering, not as the revolted man is preternaturally acute, rather as he stifles his senses. Suger, contemplating the precious stones on the main altar of St.-Denis, the work of his hands, is rapt, sees himself as dwelling, like the mystic, like the child, "in some strange region of the universe which neither exists entirely in the slime of the earth nor entirely in the purity of Heaven." How does one attain to this trance-like state, not torpor but perfect elation, in which purpose is suspended and "external cares" are qualified as they are merged in the whole of things? Suger answers obliquely, in a poem commemorating the bronze

[38] *Act and Being*, p. 182.
[38a] Paraphrasing Bultmann, in F. Kermode, *Sense of an Ending*, p. 25.

reliefs on the doors of his church: "The dull mind rises to truth through that which is material."[39] Existence is definable at last and at best as inturning, the love and exploiting of the self, but the road to this proper preoccupation or homecoming leads through concern with the world outside the self. "Socialism is a cry of pain" (Durkheim).

The pain is perhaps the engendering agent. The end is equability, the absence of pain. One approaches the end as one participates in the laboratory experiment which is being seeking to understand or verify itself: the search for authenticity.[40] God, for whom alone solipsism is possible, is honored, says Luther—one might say, is authenticated—as "he passes into the flesh, the bread, our hearts, mouths, entrails, and suffers also for our sake that he be dishonorably handled, on the altar as on the Cross."

But this sacrificial progress, if it signifies for the Creator, does not signify absolutely for His subjects. It is just this proposition that the modern or more hopeful age which commences with the Renaissance is concerned to deny. To affirm it (to discountenance the kingdom on earth) is not to suggest that action is nugatory but only—as one perceives the limits of action—to make clear that Yeats is greater than Lenin and Handel than Sir Robert Walpole, and that energetic behavior, whether febrile or truly humane, is to be valued more as process than in terms of the end for which it bids.

Bacon, as the seventeenth century opens, calls for "a more intimate and strict conjunction of contemplation and action." His enormously ambitious endeavor is to reconcile the two stars of contrary aspect which are the Middle Ages and the Renaissance and to effect a benign conjunction of the two, "a conjunction like that of Saturn, the planet of rest and contemplation; and Jupiter, the planet of civil society and action."[41] The result of the Baconian synthesis, as Bacon himself is an impure amalgam,

[39] Panofsky, *Suger*, pp. 21, 23.

[40] The title of an important book by J.F.T. Bugental, subtitled "An Existential-Analytic Approach to Psychotherapy."

[41] *Advancement*, Bk. 1. And see, for a "recension" in our time, Harvey Cox, *Feast of Fools*, p. 117.

is, however, the eclipsing of the old by the new. In terms of art, in terms of life, the result for the future is the ascendancy of the transitive element.

It is not an inevitable result. Bacon's dream of the saint and revolutionary together awaits its translation in the present time. Only now the bias is different and the sharp demarcations to which new philosophy is inclinable break down. Now we are summoned "to reconcile the corrosive nature of laughter to the habits of reason" (Artaud).[42] Baconian man is not much given to laughter. The true active-contemplative man is more nearly an integer as he does what he does not from dogged resolve or black bile but *con amore*—commitment for the joy of it. The freedom he seeks to realize is not defined in the ceaseless activity of domination, the ego as a hammer coercing the world, but as a "coming to rest in the transparent knowledge and gratification of being."[43] His "socialism" is at last a cry not of pain but exultation, as when God looks on what He has made and sees that it is good. His engagement is, however, conditioned by a "saturnine" awareness that "the foolishness of God is wiser than men, and the weakness of God is stronger than men."

Does this mean that only Heaven avails? That is the radical saying of the disaffected man: St. Bernard of Clairvaux. The vision to which modern physics compels our attention of the black holes in space into which all matter is inexorably sucked will induce in us a certain reserve—but not despair. "All things fall and are built again, And those that build them again are gay."

A rueful aristocrat in the reign of Henry VIII thinks that "It was merry in England before the new learning came up"[44]— before the claims of the active and intentional life were made overmastering. The honoring of these imperious claims is the lugubrious business of modern or post-medieval man who is always, however grudgingly, coming up to the mark. To him

[42] *The Theater and Its Double*, p. 91.

[43] H. Marcuse, *Eros and Civilization*, p. 104.

[44] The Duke of Norfolk speaking in his capacity as High Steward of Cambridge. C. D. Bowen, *The Lion and the Throne*, p. 54.

it does not signify merely to think; it is necessary to do. *Il pensare non importa, ma il fare.* That is Gabriel Harvey, in a phrase which bristles with implication for the future.[45] Already the future for poetry is augured in the analyzing and disposing of religion by Sir John Cheke, "who taught Cambridge and King Edward Greek." Religion is divided by Cheke in two parts. One he places "in the searching after *knowledge* and in the tracing out of those things which are grateful and well-pleasing unto God." In the searching and tracing, pleasure accrues to men as well as to their Creator. That is the old conception of the business of art. The new is prefigured in Cheke's description of the second part of religion, a transitive part which leads to praxis and which "we may name piety." The humanist makes it his touchstone of value. He is avid of knowing. But he insists that knowledge be "employed in *action*."[46]

What the early humanist requires of religion, his successors require of the arts and sciences in general. The fruit and goal of all studies, as Juan Vives defines it, is to turn the knowledge we have acquired "to usefulness, and employ it for the common good."[47] Descartes insists that it is "possible to arrive at a knowledge highly useful in life; and in room of the speculative philosophy usually taught in the schools, to discover a practical [philosophy] . . . and thus render ourselves the lords and possessors of nature."[48] To Bacon, it is apparent that some men "seek in knowledge a couch for a searching spirit . . . [or] a walk for a wandering mind . . . [or] a tower of state." *Hoc non licet modernis.* The old proneness and passivity, which makes contemplation an end in itself, is no longer allowable. In future, "all knowledge is to be . . . referred to use and action." In the theatre which is man's life, "it is reserved only for God and angels to be lookers on."[49]

[45] *Marginalia*, p. 141; Hunter, *Lyly*, p. 33.

[46] Hunter, *Lyly*, p. 6.

[47] *De Tradendis*, Ch. 1; Appendix, p. 283.

[48] *Principles of Philosophy*, sections lxxi, lxxii; B. Willey, *Seventeenth Century Background*, pp. 95-96.

[49] Bacon in *Adv. of Learning*, Bk. 1; *Valerius Terminus*; Bowen, *Bacon*, p. 112.

Effectively, the conjunction of Jupiter and Saturn is denied. Delight, which belongs to the latter, is admitted as a valued concomitant of poetry, only as it "stirreth up men to take that goodnesse in hand, which otherwise would bee loathsome & unpleasant."[50] The poets are admitted, only as they are militant poets who galvanize to action. Their forebears, "those lither [lazy] contemplators . . . which sit concluding of syllogisms in a corner," as Stephen Gosson describes them,[51] are henceforward to be denied even a corner to conclude in. Here in the womb of time, the bureaucrat as overseer of the artist is detected—for example, Stalin's henchman, the unlamented Andrei Zhdanov. But the Stalinist conception of art is implicit in the Renaissance. It is the rationalist who first elaborates and sponsors that conception. Communism is Rationalism at the end of the road. To the rationalist, then and now, poems are marching songs or they are nothing. Will not the strident tenor of these songs destroy the creative spirit? "Oh yes, it will," answers Mao Tse-tung. "It will destroy . . . the creative spirit that is rooted in liberalism, individualism, abstractionism; the creative spirit that stands for art-for-art's sake and is aristocratic, defeatist, and pessimistic. It will destroy any brand of creative spirit which is not of the masses and of the proletariat. And is it not right that these brands of creative spirit should be destroyed . . . ? I think so. They should be extirpated to make room for the new."[52]

If today is really the end of the road, the terminus of four centuries of proselyting activity, that is not obvious to the proselyting intelligence which continues to be nourished in the belief that the arts are kinetic, even programmatic. "Writers," says a Marxist critic, who might be quoting Stephen Gosson, "must march at the front, not at the rear."[53] How old-fashioned it

[50] Henry Crosse, *Vertues-Commonwealth*, 1603, O1. "The true use of Poetrie standeth in two parts: the one in teaching the way to Vertue; the other to move with delight thereunto."

[51] *Schoole of Abuse*, 1579, E2-v.

[52] *Problems of Art and Literature*, pp. 44-45.

[53] Howard Fast, *Literature and Reality*, p. 8.

sounds. A writer like Ehrenburg, in crude and obvious ways, exemplifies this musty intelligence—see his didactic exercises in fiction, for example the Stalin Prize-winning novel, *The Storm*. On a higher level are the formulations of a critic like Lukács, a more considerable figure but speaking from the same point of view, as in his (necessary) strictures on Pasternak's "very bad epigonistic novel."[54] The invidious word is misleading. What is reprehensible in *Dr. Zhivago* is the author's unwillingness to assume that art conducts to the making of a better society.

This assumption is simply endemic to the critical discourse of the Age of Reason. It remains widely current, it is even conventional. If we want an "accurate evaluation of societal problems," we should go to the academy, says a modern academic astronomer; we should initiate within the schools a dialog which, as it involves "the Humanities Department, cannot fail to develop and communicate to the public at large the relevant essence of the important issues."[55] The involvement of the "humanist" is understood to be crucial. His dealings are with literature and therefore he is efficient in prescribing for social change. This is to say: literature enables.

It is a hard saying to address to the poets. Its rigor and substance are, however, predictable, given the belief of the new men that the truth is ascertainable and also availing. Believing so, they are impatient with whatever distracts from their effort to unlock the mysteries and put them to use. They demand of the artist that he justify his existence by collaborating in the building of the kingdom on earth. One of their spokesmen is Henry Peacham, a mathematician, a writer of epigrams, and the author of a practical treatise on art. Since it is self evident, as Peacham announces, that "all virtue consisteth in action," it follows that "hardly they are to be admitted for noble who (though of never

---

[54] "The Importance and Influence of Ady," *NHQ*, x, 62. Why the strictures are necessary is made clear in the collection of essays entitled *Realism in Our Time*.

[55] H. Arp, "The Need for a New Kind of Academic Responsibility," *AAUP Bulletin*, LV, 367.

so excellent parts) consume their light, as in a dark lanthorn, in contemplation and a stoical retiredness."[56] The poet, if he is in key with his time, accepts the proposition and agrees, like Henry Vaughan, a poet himself but energetic and purposeful, to exclude as mere versifiers "those ingenious persons" who "cast away all their fair portion of time in no better employment than a deliberate search or excogitation of idle words."[57]

John of Salisbury, addressing his *Policraticus* to Becket, dismisses the years he has devoted to ecclesiastical administration as so much time trifled away (*nugatum esse*). It is a source of sorrow to him, as he acknowledges in preface to the *Metalogicon*, that "Administrative concerns and the [time-consuming] trifles of court life have precluded study." He believes that, at bottom, what counts is the passive life, given over to scholarship and religion, as against the active life of public and political business. Even Augustine, who distinguishes seven grades in the ascent of the soul to perfection, identifies the highest grade, in which the soul attains to a vision of the City of God, not with purposeful activity but contemplation.[58] The identification is no longer felt as respectable.

The answer of the new poet to the charge of inactivity is that he can and will take part in prosecuting the business in hand. In so answering, he is coming directly to grips with the Platonic objection to poetry, that after all it does not fructify. That objection, compelling in the febrile atmosphere of Periclean Athens, which believes in the possibility of building the kingdom here and now, is powerfully renascent, after a lapse of two thousand years, in the sixteenth century. "All the enormous gain of dream," which Saintsbury in a great phrase ascribes to the sleep of the Dark Ages, is scrutinized with a hostile eye and rejected.[59]

The ancients see literature as dynamic, essentially like rhetoric. The Renaissance resumes this view, after the medieval hiatus. When Ascham, for example, attacks medieval romances,

---

[56] *Compleat Gentleman*, 1622; Hunter, *Lyly*, p. 352.
[57] Preface to *Silex Scintillans*, 1655.
[58] *De Quantitate Animae.*
[59] *History of Criticism*, I, 444.

he does so because, as they were "made in monasteries by idle monks or wanton canons," they breathe the spirit of the indolent past.[60] Art as anciently practiced is a creature of the Dark (or quiescent) Ages, and hence alien to the questing present. In Thomas Nashe, the connection is very clear. It is the enervating character of the romance, forged by the "idle pens" of "exiled Abbie-Lubbers," that excites his indignation.[61] Art is idle dreaming. If the business in hand were not more hopeful or compelling than in the days of the abbey-lout, there would be no great cause for decrying the sloth it engenders. But in fact business presses. Whatever makes against it becomes, therefore, a matter of urgent concern. Study of the Bible inspirits us to do. The antithesis of learning in the service of doing is the perusal of romance. The moralist is dejected that we "spend our time in trifling toyes, to our perpetuall shame," for he sees that we might be creating the New Jerusalem.[62]

It is the vision that describes modern man. Participating in it, Macaulay, the rationalist in motley, derides Socrates and Plato as unfruitful philosophers exactly as they had derided the poets. Against the finely reticulated edifice of their thought, he directs the crucial question: "What has it enabled us to do . . . ?"[63] Only the practical arts, which flower in action, are to be countenanced.

The Middle Ages, though in many respects eminently practical and certainly dedicated to—or, what is perhaps more precise: greatly productive of—doing, are innocent of the demand

---

[60] *Scholemaster*; Hunter, *Lyly*, p. 140.

[61] *Anatomie of Absurditie*, 1589; Smith, I, 323. "What els I pray you doe these bable bookemungers endevor but to repaire the ruinous wals of Venus Court [*The Court of Venus*] to restore to the worlde . . . those worne out impressions of the feyned no where acts of Arthur of the rounde table."

[62] Nicholas Baxter (who claimed significantly to be a tutor to Sir Philip Sidney) in preface to his trans. of the *Sermons of Calvine . . . upon the Prophet Jonas*, B8v. Baxter enjoins his readers to close up "the booke of Arthurs knights. . . ./ And Guy of Warwicke, Scoggins gests, and Gargantua,/ The court of Venus, Howleglasse, Legenda Aurea."

[63] "Lord Bacon," July 1837 in *Edinburgh Review* (on Basil Montague's edn. of Bacon).

that art conduce to action. The medieval conception of the nature of music, as against that of the Renaissance, illustrates how very recent is the ascendancy of the transitive principle as the end of artistic endeavor. The public music of the Middle Ages is, like its poetry, functional rather than expressive. This is what is meant by describing it as ancillary music. The practice of medieval composers will support the description. There is in their work no thought of arousing and manipulating emotions suggested by the words they set. What they seek is an effect: to imitate sadness or exhilaration but not to incline to it. It is the emphasis on inclining, which is action, that separates yesterday and today. Even so late as the fifteenth and early sixteenth centuries, there is in esthetic theory no conception of art as an expressive agent whose end is an ethical result. The end of music, as of poetry, until the new men of the Renaissance give to either art a new or augmented purpose, is only to teach and delight.

Dante, in the famous letter to his patron Can Grande, appears to anticipate the view of poetry as an instrumental art. The *Commedia* is written "not for the sake of speculative philosophy, but for the sake of practical needs." The emphasis on use for living recalls John of Salisbury and the author of the *Philobiblon*, who think that the written word is appliable or else "ordained for man's utility." What this means is that poetry is (among other things) heuristic. But how is the poet, unless he is also kinetic in his function, to fulfill Dante's prescription: "to remove those living in this life from a state of misery and to guide them to a state of happiness"?[64] The answer is that the poet, like Orpheus or like Amphion, is powerful in action: but the change he works is a spiritual change and independent of reward or punishment, here or hereafter. The state of misery from which the reader of the poem is transported is that of an impoverished imagination.

But now the sixteenth century, in music and in poetry, joins effect to expression. It is a union of profound significance. One consequence is the extraordinary cultivation in the later sixteenth

[64] *Letters*, ed. G. Carpenter, p. 199. The authenticity of the letter has been questioned; I suppose Dante to have written it.

century of the affective resources of music, which will aim increasingly—I quote Richard Hooker—at representing "the very image and character" of the virtues, not simply that we may know them, but that "the mind delighted with their resemblances" may be "brought by having them often iterated into a love of the things themselves."[65] Sir Thomas More speaks obliquely to this revolutionary esthetic in contrasting the music of the early Tudors with that of his Utopia in which "the fassion of the melodye [music] dothe so represent the meaning of the thing, that it doth wonderfullye move, stirre, pearce, and enflame the hearers myndes."[66] From now on the end is not merely knowing but doing. The new music of the Elizabethans will inspirit the heart by representing to it, in Hooker's words, "the very standing, rising, and falling, the very steps and inflections every way, the turns and varieties of all passions whereunto the mind is subject."

Of course medieval man pays homage to a connection between music and morality. *Musica voluntatem malam revocat*: Music hath a charm to soothe and so forth. Alternatively, music incites to "likerous lusts." (This inspiriting or allaying power is imputed, as by Dante, to poetry also.) But modern or Renaissance man desires a more explicit and dynamic connection. He wants music actively to be a part of *boni mores*. And so, like Father Mersenne, the friend of Descartes, he seeks to discover the root and cause of those ethical effects Greek music had supposedly engendered.[67] He experiments with a new theory of

---

[65] *Ecclesiastical Polity*, 1597, v, xxxviii, 1.

[66] Robynson's trans., 1551.

[67] *Quaestiones . . . in Genesim*, 1623, cols. 1607-82. "*Quod optima instrumenta si quis illorum beneficio passiones movere velit, & voces eligi debeant, si ad scopum pervanire volveris*" (1607-12). For the theory of Glareanus, see 1625-26. "De Modis Harmonicis . . . Antiquorum" described 1627-32, 1665-82. John Hollander, *Untuning of the Sky*, and F. Yates, *French Academies of the Sixteenth Century*, Ch. III, trace the revival of Greek ethical theory in Renaissance music. D. T. Mace, *JWCI*, XXIX, 297, 299, 301, documents the disappointment of "moderns" like Wallis and St. Évremond in contemporary music as it fails to appeal in more than sensuous ways.

modes, like Glareanus, the friend of Erasmus, who "flattered himself with the hope of restoring that very practice of music to which such wonderful effects had been ascribed." Like Josquin des Prés and his contemporaries, he creates what the sixteenth century calls *musica reservata*, characterized by its power to produce an emotional commentary on the text. The emotional color assigned to the wind instrument is illustrated perhaps by the squealing of oboes or the braying of trumpets as Titus Andronicus serves up his gruesome feast, and Claudius and Antony keep wassail, and Duncan enters under the battlements of Macbeth. Pericles, as he hears a different kind of harmony, is nipped "unto listening, and thick slumber hangs upon . . . [his] eyes." Evidently, he has no choice but to sleep. It is this supposedly coercive or dynamic property to which Orsino adverts in the opening line of *Twelfth Night*; and the Duke of Vienna in claiming for music "a charm/ To make bad good, and good provoke to harm."

All things get a hearing in Shakespeare and even the old Platonic and Pythagorean view, now revived in the Renaissance, of music as an ethical agent. But Shakespeare, if he is willing to entertain this view, is mostly concerned to disallow it. Antony, as he listens to Dorian music, is impelled to his proper business. This Antony merits our suffrage. As he indulges soft Lydian airs, he grows slack and effeminate and so incurs our contempt. That is the customary formulation. In Shakespeare's play, it functions largely as a straw man. Mostly, the use of song in the plays is not to dispose but to characterize. It is true that Shakespeare resorts often to so-called magic songs, whose office, hypothetically, is to move. But the music of the elves and fairies in *A Midsummer Night's Dream* or in the *Merry Wives of Windsor* is essentially a blind. Titania and Falstaff are not enchanted; they make love to their employment. Brutus occasions his own demise, and even though the slumbrous song of young Lucius is in prelude to that event. Neither is Ariel's music in the *Tempest* really decisive in allaying the fury and passion of the wicked conspirators. The incantation of the witches in *Macbeth* ought, as one adheres to the ethical theory, to afford the supreme example of the power of music to conduce to good or ill. But music in *Macbeth*, at least of Shakespeare's designing, is omitted altogether. It is the protagonist himself who works the fatal imposition. Man at some time is master of his fate.

The determinist is paradoxically more hopeful, exactly as he urges his deterministic theory. His basic premise is that the music of the planets (*musica mundana*) is mirrored in that of human beings (*musica humana*). If, he argues, appropriate music is performed by men (*musica instrumentalis*), and whether vocal or instrumental or both, virtue and harmony will be engendered in their conduct. He cites as illustrative the public banquets of the Romans, whose idea is to implant wisdom in their magistrates by playing the dulcet music of strings.[68] The music of the spheres is also affective: a psychological or, better, a physiological reality that literally disposes behavior. But the music must be appropriate: not the pipes of Pan, the wind instruments associated with martial business or with the importunities of the flesh, but the lyre, the strings of Apollo. Gosson is alive to this distinction. That is why he describes his *School of Abuse* as containing "a pleasant invective against poets, pipers, players, jesters, and such like caterpillars of a commonwealth." Music, like poetry, is valued or feared as it manifests an ulterior power, which is the ability to incline.

There are men in the Renaissance who remain devoted to music or to poetry simply for its own sweet sake. But it never occurs to them to say so. From that day forward, the defenders of each art speak the same vocabulary as the detractors. Church music is good for ethical reasons: according to Hooker it edifies "the affection, because therein it worketh much." Exciting the congregation to "inflammations of all piety," it "stirreth up flagrant desires and affections correspondent unto that which the words contain, allayeth all kind of base and earthly cogitations, banisheth and driveth away those evil secret suggestions which

---

[68] Discussion follows Jean Bodin, *The Republic*, 1576.

our invisible enemy is always apt to minister, watereth the heart to the end it may fructify."[69] Fructification: that is the great thing.

Music and poetry, committed anciently to teach and delight, have become kindred to oratory, whose ultimate function is to persuade us to do. The imputing of that third function to the sister arts constitutes a major shift in sensibility.

No doubt the idea of impelling to action is nascent in earlier times.[70] But it must await the Renaissance which, given its dedi-

[69] *Ecclesiastical Polity*, v, xxxviii, 3; xxxix, 1, 4.

[70] Here from the classical period are important approximations. Pindar, as he is alert to the glozing power of poetry "which often causes the incredible to be credited," thinks it seemly that the poet "should tell noble tales of the gods—the guilt is less" (*Olympians* 1:30-35, 52-53). And see 9:100; and *Nemeans* 7:22. Plato's discussion of the "ethical" character of music and poetry rests on the assumption that each art is affective. *Laws*, II, 655: "One class of harmonies is akin to courage and all virtue, the other to cowardice and all vice." (Aristotle enforces the connection in *Politics*, VIII, 7: "just as the souls of . . . [men] are distorted from their natural state, so there are musical modes which are correspondingly perverted.") Since "vicious measures and strains do . . . harm . . . to the lovers of them," the poet is not to circulate his poems "until they have first received the *imprimatur* of the director of education" (*Laws*, II, 656; VII, 801). Art, Socrates thinks, aims not simply to delineate but to persuade (*Gorgias*, 453d, 502). The rhetorician Gorgias of Leontini, with whom Socrates is disputing, entertains the same view. "The power of song . . . persuades and moves as if by magic . . . through words the soul comes to feel a sorrow of its own at the good or ill fortune of others" (*Encomium of Helen*). See as illustrative the antics of Ion the rhapsode (*Ion*, 535); or the Homeric minstrel whose singing of old disasters moves Odysseus to tears (*Odyssey*, VIII, 83ff). As poetry possesses this energizing power, Socrates insists that it inculcate only the principles of justice and truth (*Phaedrus*, 278). Euripides is attacked as his instrumental art is put to other and inferior ends: "Your lessons have brought our youngsters, and taught our sailors to challenge, discuss, and refute" (Aristophanes, *The Frogs*). Horace, who as preceptor reads sometimes like Dante (*Art of Poetry*, ll. 95-100, 335ff), reads also like Boccaccio in proposing that ancient poets were able to build towns and prescribe marriage laws and abate our lusts or else inflame our spirits to war (ll. 389-90). Strabo, at the end of the classical period, sees the fables of the poet as provoking to emulation or deterring from vice (citing the stories of Lamia and the Gorgon, *Geography*, Bk. I,

68

cation to the earth and its usufructs, is the right or propitious time to come to birth. Boccaccio, abruptly, is new as he pounds on the table. The Italian critics who resume his fevered discussion—Pico, Francesco Patrizzi—are new, not in what they say, for every phrase is reminiscent, but in their insistent bias.[71] The emphatic statement of it belongs to the sixteenth century. Doors open on the future and close on the past in this passage from Antonio Minturno: "It will be the business of the poet so to

---

sect. 2, subhead 8). Plutarch, supposing poetry to be dangerously dynamic, measures out the proper dosage by analogy to eating and drinking (*De Audiendis . . . Poetis*).

The classical reading of poetry dies, however, with the Middle Ages. It is true that Augustine asserts the triple function: one is "not only to teach that he may instruct and to please that he may hold attention, but also to persuade that he may be victorious" (*On Christian Doctrine*, end of Ch. xiii). But Augustine is legislating, like Cicero, for the orator (*De Oratore*, i, viii, xvi; *Pro Archia*, i, ii, vi, xiv), in this case the preacher. Perhaps the Renaissance conception of art is hinted at by "Longinus." The harmony which is literature is said to ravish the soul as it "bewitches and disposes us to elevation, and dignity, and sublimity, and all that itself contains, exercising universal royalty over our minds" (*Peri Hupsous*, Ch. xxxix). S. Monk, *The Sublime*, p. 233, quotes Joseph Wharton on Longinus: "it is impossible not to catch fire and rapture from his glorious style." Monk, p. 11, traces the ancient association of rhetoric and "emotional transport," in which the idea of praxis is bruited—but far off. So with Dante, who makes the reading of an adulterous romance the occasion for the sin of Paolo and Francesca (*Inferno*, v); and earlier St. Jerome: "After frequent night vigils, after shedding tears which the remembrance of past sins brought forth from my inmost heart, I would take in my hands a volume of Plautus" (*Epistula ad Eustochium*, no. 22, p. 165 in *Letters*, trans. Mierow).

But this attesting to the charm of poetry or music, which may be insidious, is as old as the hills and not at issue here. In sum: the idea that art impels to action is first of all a classical idea, is revived and aggrandized even crudely in the Renaissance, and by and large is aloof from the medieval understanding. The fully fledged appropriating to poetics of the traditional view of rhetoric is the business of the fourteenth century and later.

[71] Boccaccio, *Genealogy of the Gods*, xiv, vii. For Pico and Patrizzi, who differ from Boccaccio in stressing the maleficent power of poetry, see quotations in Weinberg, *History of Literary Criticism in the Italian Renaissance*, i, 256, 253.

speak in his verses that he may teach, that he may delight, that he may move."[72] The poet is made to assume the galvanic function reserved from the time of Cicero to the orator.

Anciently, "Three thinges are required of an Orator." (The preceptor is the rhetorician Thomas Wilson.) These are "To teach. To delight. And to persuade."[73] Poetry cannot participate, or not easily and naturally, in that third requirement. The orator, in commencing his address, will direct the attention of the auditor to the business he wants to see transacted. As he would persuade, he will fashion at once a clear statement of his purpose. But poetry, by convention, is indifferent to persuading. And so it commences without preamble and often without direction. Even the need for a title does not always occur to the medieval poet. Titles are not customary in the days before poetry is assimilated to rhetoric. Neither is the formal or studied conclusion. The orator depends on it absolutely. When he comes to the close of his exordium, it is his job to pull together all the points he has adumbrated, and then to speak explicitly to the emotions of the auditor, that he may be roused to some particular action. But this procedure is alien to poetry, as it is to non-polemical prose. The conclusion of a poem, in the sense of an appeal to sympathy or to militant behavior (Workers of the world, unite!), is apt therefore to be aggressively laconic, as in the closing line of the *Song of Roland*: "*Ci faut la geste. . . .*" or even lacking altogether, as in the *Aeneid*. Prudentius, as he sees that his "book is growing long," observes that "It is time now to halt its march, lest my song be drawn out endlessly, and bring disgust."[74] Chaucer, or his copyist, concluding the *Canterbury Tales*, says simply: "Here is ended the book." Ovid's conclusion to the *Remedia Amoris* is as abrupt and unstudied: *Hoc opus exegi*: I have finished my work.

It is a reasonable conclusion. There is nothing more to be said and certainly there is nothing to be done. But the Renaissance is committed to doing. And so increasingly what is requisite for

[72] *De Poeta*, 1559.
[73] *Arte of Rhetorique*, 1560, Bk. i.
[74] *Contra Symmachum.*

oratory or rhetoric becomes requisite for poetry also, as the third or persuasive function is imputed to it by those critics and not least by those poets who are anxious to cultivate purposiveness, too. In all the "endless stream of idiotic drivel" which is the achievement of Rudyard Kipling, the purposive critic can recall only one line worth retrieving—when Kipling says of the Sudanese:

> We sloshed you with Martinis,
> An' it wasn't 'ardly fair.

This single reference—which refers, we are told, "to the latest repeating rifle of the time, not the cocktail"—is memorable as it communicates "ethical consciousness." It is itself, what good poetry must be, a weapon. "The 'manner' of our times is two-fold—in its simplest statement, *for fascism and imperialism or against it.* No one remains aloof; there are no neutrals; the writer must share the manner in one way or another."[75]

No one ever demanded so much of poetry before. It used to suffice that it presented a picture of the City of God. This is how the critic George Puttenham conceives its business, in dilating on the *Arte of English Poesie.* "The learned clerks who have written methodically of this Arte"—Puttenham's point is to figurative language—"have sorted all their figures into three rankes, and the first they bestowed upon the Poet onely." This first is the auricular figure which has to do, I suppose, with sheer or mere delight and which "forces the mynde little or nothing." In the second rank are the figures which Puttenham calls sensible. These are conceits which appeal to the fancy and which engage not only the ear but the mind. They are bestowed on the poet and orator impartially. The sententious figures of the third rank, whose end is an ethical result, belong, however, to the orator alone.[76]

But now the poet is asked to employ them, and not only to depict the kingdom but like the preacher to conduct us thither.

[75] Howard Fast, *Literature and Reality*, pp. 82, 105.

[76] Bk. iii, Ch. x. The auricular figure "extendeth but to the outward tuning of the speach, reaching no higher than th'eare."

It is his justification that he does so. The translator and traveler George Sandys, considering the affective power of classical stories, sees some myths as not merely teaching but "inflaming by noble examples, with an honest emulation and leading, as it were, by the hand to the temple of Honour and Virtue." Sandys is introducing his commentary on Ovid, who remains to the Renaissance as to the Middle Ages a treasure trove of morality but allegorically rendered.[77] Early in the fourteenth century, the *Ovide Moralisé* interprets the *Metamorphoses* as supplying a complete lexicon of the passions. So does Arthur Golding (1565-67) in the sixteenth century and George Sandys in the seventeenth. But there is this important difference, as between the redactions of the earlier period and the later. The Middle Ages are satisfied to spy out the truth concealed in the fable. The Renaissance, detecting it, wants to put it to work and this on the supposition that what the allegory conceals is not only, in Sandys's phrase, "agreeable to the high affections of the soul" but actively "conducing to magnanimity."[78]

Conduction, the orator's province, is usurped by the poet. At the heart of poetry is a moral but also a goad: in the words of Sir John Harington, "the Morall sence profitable for the active life of man."[79] The English humanists, in adding play acting and declamation to the curriculum of the schools, are moved to do so not because they see the drama as virtuous in itself but as a rhetorical instrument for moving the audience to virtue. "The principal end of making Themes," the Elizabethan school-

---

[77] *Metamorphoses*, trans. 1626. For *Ovidius ethicus* or *theologus*, see Seznec, *Survival of the Pagan Gods*, pp. 91-95; E. K. Rand, *Ovid and His Influence*, pp. 112-49 (medieval), 150-65 (Renaissance).

[78] The medieval writer finds his truth in "annexing"—the divining of complementarities—as when in telling the story of Saturn and his children, he intercalates a passage on Abraham, whose union with Sarah is understood to parallel that of Juno and Jupiter (*Ovide Moralisé en Prose*, ed. C. de Boer, Bk. I, sect. xiv). In a discussion of the Sibyls, Isaiah comes to mind (II, xxxii); the Rape of the Sabines is analogous to the Massacre of the Innocents (XIV, xxiv). The Renaissance writer has in mind more than the adducing of parallels. His end is kinetic.

[79] Preface to trans. of *Orlando Furioso*, 1591; Smith, II, 201.

master supposes, is not to create professional actors—though the practice in declamation in fact helps to create them and so gives a powerful impetus to the drama—but to work in the declaimer "a greater love of the virtue and hatred of the vice" and to enable him "with soundness of reason to draw others" to his opinion.[80] Harington honors Virgil because of this proselyting power. In the *Georgics* there are "many . . . lessons of homly husbandrie but"—and this is what really makes them valuable—"delivered in so good Verse that me thinkes all that while I could find in my hart to drive the plough."

The model equating of goodness with persuasion is in Sidney's *Apologie*.[81] The true poets, writes Sidney, "make to imitate, and imitate both to delight and teach, and delight to move men to take that goodnes in hand . . . that goodnes whereunto they are mooved."[82] Sidney is the chief of the academy in which the new esthetic is fashioned. "His end was not writing, even while he wrote; nor his knowledge moulded for tables, or schooles; but both his wit, and understanding bent upon his heart, to make himself and others, not in words or opinion, but in life, and action, good and great." That is the judgment of his friend and biographer, the poet Fulke Greville.[83]

But Sidney remains also in significant ways a medieval man. New and old are at war in him as in so many of his contemporaries, for example in Greville (and his preceptor Calvin), in Spenser and in Donne. The old-fashioned psychology is dominant in this mournful observation: "our erected wit maketh us know what perfection is, and yet our infected will keepeth us from reaching unto it." Sidney's career, in art as in life, exemplifies a reaching toward perfection. He believes that the end of art is more than educative. But the medieval man still speaks in the qualifying phrase, instinct as it is more with wistfulness

[80] John Brinsley the Elder, quoted Hunter, p. 14.

[81] Later in publication (1595) than Harington and others who make the same equation, but written early in the 1580s and very obviously familiar in ms.

[82] Smith, I, 159.

[83] *Life of Sidney*, 1652, Ch. 1; edn. of 1907, p. 18.

than with assurance: "the final end is to lead and draw us to as high a perfection as our degenerate soules, made worse by theyr clayey lodgings, can be capable of." He pays homage to the past in assigning to the sciences only this limited scope, "to knowe, and by knowledge to lift up the mind from the dungeon of the body to the enjoying his owne divine essence." This is the conventional statement, that "the highest end of the mistres Knowledge . . . [is] the knowledge of a mans selfe."

But then Sidney proceeds, and as he does so the new trenches in fascinating ways on the old: self knowledge is the goal but "with the end of well doing and not of well knowing onely . . . the ending end of all earthly learning being vertuous action."[84] What is at issue here is not the conventional union of faith and good works but a newly optimistic reading of the latter, and in consequence a receding of the City of God before the City of Man. Medieval man commits himself to good works to expiate his sins, to glorify God, and also to lay up treasures in Heaven. The commitment, or what follows from it, is understood to have its limits: "For every man with his affects is born, Not by might mastered, but by special grace."[85] Sidney is adumbrating the revolutionary proposal that works are instrumental—decisively so—in the making over of man.

Why should the Calvinist, who ties salvation to faith, be preeminently, even in hysterical ways, the active personality? The answer—a piece of it—is that progress in the modern age turns on the diminishing of the individual, whose every instinct, not least the instinct for pleasure, is harnessed in the pursuit of what is useful. Poetry is pushpin. Modern man may be, like the Marxist, theoretically secure in the working out of the Dialectic. But he sees or feels himself rather as psychologically attenuated by the passive role his deterministic theology prescribes. He is an instrument or cipher. Frenetic action, on this reading, is a desperate attesting to one's role as more than cipher in the preordained unfolding of things. The ego is disvalued: and inclined *pari passu* to assert its substantial importance. That is what

[84] Smith, I, 157, 160-61.   [85] *Love's Labour's Lost*, I, i, 152-53.

is happening in the murky world within the self. In the public world, however, repression in the service of utility goes unchallenged. As the stress on purposive behavior is accepted, the modern or Enlightened Age is announced. Poetry must either be modernized or jettisoned altogether.

The opponents of poetry, as Sidney very acutely represents them, allege "that before Poets beganne to be in price our Nation hath set their harts delight upon action, and not upon imagination: rather doing things worthy to bee written, then writing things fitte to be done." This is the cutting edge of one half of Plato's criticism, now current once more in the Renaissance, that poetry is inimical to action. Sidney sympathizes with the ground of the criticism: "that a man might better spend his time is a reason indeed." He is therefore uneasy at breaking a lance with Plato: "but now indeede my burthen is great; now Plato his name is layde upon mee, whom, I must confesse, of all Philosophers I have ever esteemed most worthy of reverence." Because he himself "doth intende the winning of the mind from wickednesse to vertue," he must agree that if poetry does not take part in that contention it ought to be banished from the commonwealth.[86]

But Sidney is enamored of poetry. He resolves the conflict between his philosophical proclivities and his love for poetry— by making poetry manifest those proclivities. Already in the 1560s, his friend Thomas Wilson had given a hint by suggesting that "The Poets were wise men and wished in heart the redress of things."[87] Now Sidney takes the deed for the wish. "What that before tyme was," when the poets were supposed to have diverted the nation from action to imagination, "I thinke scarcely Sphinx can tell." From the beginning they have studied redress. And so the poet is ushered into the modern age and by the prince of poets in his time, "For he dooth not only show the way, but giveth so sweete a prospect into the way, as will intice any man to enter into it."[88]

After Sidney, the threefold conjunction of teaching and de-

[86] Smith, I, 187, 183, 190, 172.   [87] Smith, I, xxiv.
[88] Smith, I, 187-88, 172.

lighting and doing becomes the accepted convention. Ben Jonson endorses the definition of "the wisest and best learned" who find "Poesy a dulcet and gentle Philosophy, which leades on and guides us by the hand to Action with a ravishing delight and incredible Sweetnes."[89] Hobbes, in the middle of the seventeenth century, speaks for all serious partisans of poetry in describing the poet's task as "to avert men from vice and incline them to vertue and honorable actions."[90]

The task is onerous, perhaps impossible. The new poet accepts it and even courts it. Partly, that is because of the optimistic spirit he shares with the critics of poetry. He stands with them in repudiating the deferential attitude of a medieval writer like Peter of Blois, five centuries before: "Knowledge is with the ancients."[91] He sees himself as bestriding the summit of creation and possessed of a fund of knowledge not conceded to the ancients. He believes that his endowment is all in all sufficient, and so he is indifferent to the melancholy question uttered by John of Salisbury in that same twelfth century: "who can believe that from reading alone, without the presence of grace which illumines, creates, and gives life to the virtues, man can attain wisdom?"[92] Modern or Renaissance man is a Pelagian, optimistic of attaining to wisdom by his own unaided efforts. He is willing to dispense with the idea of grace, which reminds him of his own insufficiency. As against the dyspeptic past, he asserts that the wisdom belonging to him is not static but kinetic. His poetry is, therefore, more than sagacious and pleasing. It is programmatic. It seizes the reader by his lapels. "Hot blood begets hot thoughts, and hot thoughts beget hot deeds." This, to paraphrase Shakespeare's Pandarus, is the right generation of verse. That, at least, is the Renaissance construction. In the seventeenth century it hardens into law. The day of the contemplator, self-delighting, self-appeasing, is over.

[89] *Timber, or Discoveries,* 1620-25.
[90] *Answer to Davenant's Preface to "Gondibert,"* 1650.
[91] Atkins, *Literary Criticism,* p. 70.
[92] *Policraticus,* VII, 9; Pike edn., p. 250.

III The Father of Lies

THE TASK of the votary is threefold: "to pray, beare, and doe."[1] On the maker of poetry in the renascent age, a similar function is enjoined. But that poetry inclines to action does not answer perfectly to the criticism of the detractors of poetry. The ancient functions of teaching and delighting, though made preliminary now, continue to be equally weighted and approved. The pragmatic spirit is jealous of their equality. And so, in its avidity for profit, it disturbs the old and nice equivalence of profit and pleasure. Teaching gains inexorably on delighting. Utility is exalted. Erasmus makes a hero of Prometheus, who tutored mankind in the practical arts. To a poet like Nicholas Grimald, the tutorial function displaces every other. Grimald is dedicating his didactic tragedy on John the Baptist. It is his promise that "Here the reader or the spectator will learn . . . He will also see how . . . Nor will he be without an opportunity for noting."[2]

But to learn or see how does not suffice, and not even if one is promised an opportunity for noting. "Mere power and mere knowledge exalt human nature but do not bless it." That is Francis Bacon, who concludes that "We must gather from the whole store of things such as make most for the uses of life."[3] Poetry, as it turns its back on use, is rejected as yielding "to no Commonwealth commoditie": Nashe on medieval romances. Or poetry, if it is accepted and praised, is depicted as yielding us "infinite commodities": Webbe on the *Iliad*. The reiterated word is portentous, smacking as it does of palpable gain as the goal or mark of all endeavor. And in fact Webbe affirms that the "best kinde of Poetry [does] . . . direct ones endeavor al-

---

[1] John Donne, *A Litany*, XIV.   [2] *Archipropheta*, 1548.
[3] *Advancement of Learning*; quoted Eiseley, *Bacon*, p. 23.

wayes to that marke, that with delight they may evermore ad-
joyne commoditie to theyr Readers."[4]

At first pleasure is harnessed in tandem with profit. Then it
is seen as subordinate to profit. At last it becomes an embarrassment. Poetry is redeemed only as it is didactic. "It profiteth a
man nothing that he should delight himself with God."

In the Renaissance, the old debate between the Owl and the
Nightingale is resolved in favor of the former. Antique poets
are censured as missing the mark, who "had speciall regarde to
the pleasantnesse of theyr fine conceytes, whereby they might
drawe mens mindes into admiration of theyre inventions, more
then they had to the profitte or commoditye that the Readers
shoulde reape by their works." Theocritus, for example, is de-
preciated as "tending most to delight and pretty inventions."
Hesiod is better "for his Argument" and because he "dealt very
learnedly and profitably . . . in precepts of Husbandry."[5]

There is something to this opposition of the delightful poet
and the profitable. Theocritus had written of the waving of the
poplar and the elm and the welling forth of murmurous waters.
In the opulent summer of his imagining, "the burnt cicalas keep
their chattering toil, the owl cries in the thorn brake, the yel-
low bees are remembered as they flit about the springs." That
is very well in its way; but now here is Hesiod who is concerned, in the *Works and Days*, not only to delight with the
pretty inventions of mythology but also to communicate profitable instruction: "Never make water in the mouths of rivers
which flow to the sea, nor yet in springs; but be careful to avoid
this." Hesiod is privy to use and Theocritus only to pleasure.
Still it is too bad to let Theocritus go. That is, however, the
price of compounding with the new men, to whom the acid test
of value is use.

Both the poet (Sir Philip Sidney) and the poet-hater (Stephen
Gosson) refer their critical positions to this test. The gentleman
duellist at whom Gosson sneers is no doubt a knave. But the
crucial objection is that the trade he plies, though certainly it

[4] Smith, I, 323, 235.   [5] Webbe, quoted Smith, I, 236-37.

tends to action, is—like the trade of the gentleman poet—not useful but simply ornamental. It is therefore understood as having no credentials that the man who labors fruitfully and to a positive end must honor. The pragmatic text, narrowly interpreted and always in the direction of what one can press in his hand, is urged against poetry, more insistently now than ever before, by the new realist or practical man who holds his warrant from Plato, the quintessential idealist. The modern age and the ancient past discover their identity when Bacon locates "the ultimate end of knowledge . . . [in] the use and benefit of mankind."[6]

In the spirit of that momentous equation Plato, addressing "Friend Homer"—the appellation is of course ironic—asks him to tell us what state was ever governed the better for his help. Bishop Sprat, raising the same question so many centuries later, turns the argument against metaphysics. "What help did it ever bring to the vulgar? What visible benefit to any City, or Country in the World?"[7] But the question, in Sprat as in Plato, is rhetorical. The lack of visible benefit, in poetry or in a merely speculative philosophy, is felt as self-evident. When Isaac Casaubon, the humanist and classical scholar, visits the Sorbonne, he is greeted with the words, "In these halls, for four hundred years, men have disputed." Casaubon responds: "Qu'a-t-on décidé?"[8]

The old-fashioned poet (like the duellist) makes a trade of disputation. Opposed to him is the active or practical man—Themistocles, for instance, as the moral preceptor Richard Braithwait reports him. "His aimes [were] not to delight himselfe or others with the effeminate sound of the Lute" but to labor "for the publike state." Asked to play, he says pointedly, "I cannot fiddle, but I can make a small Towne a great City."[9] In this distinction the poet is reproved. What war did his counsels ever direct? He has sponsored no invention applicable to

[6] *Advancement*, Bk. 1.   [7] *History*, p. 117.

[8] F. Farrar, *History of Interpretation*, p. 291n.

[9] *The English Gentleman and the English Gentlewoman*, 1641, p. 98.

the arts or human life. He has given to the world no ethical system or course of conduct.

The record is depressing, and the followers of Plato from the Renaissance to the present have not wearied of reciting it whenever the poet enters a claim to serious attention. "This is not playhouse poetry; it is sober fact": Thomas Carlyle, in token of important business at hand.[10] Though the Victorian philanthropist Sir Josiah Mason would have bristled at the linking of his name with Socrates and Plato, those Greekish professors of long beards and long words (the phrase is Macaulay's), he also is a Platonist in his commitment to the truth that pays. That is why, on founding a College of Science at Birmingham (1880), he forbids the new institution to make any provision for "mere literary instruction and education." (Francis Crick is adumbrated.) On his reading, beauty is assimilated to use. Macaulay, as befitting a literary gent, is not so purblind as this. He admits that "if the tree which Socrates planted and Plato watered is to be judged of by its flowers and leaves, it is the noblest of trees." But he adds that "if we judge of the tree by its fruits, our opinion of it may perhaps be less favourable." His own opinion is determined by a resort to the scales. "When we sum up all the useful truths which we owe to that philosophy, to what do they amount?"[11]

Here a vision of the Crystal Palace ought to supervene to give point to the question that follows: "What profitable truth has it taught us?" The answer to the question is patent if, emulating Plato, assaying the heuristic value of poetry (or Macaulay on Plato), one weighs his gross product against that of the applied or Baconian philosophy. Jeremy Bentham emulates Plato. For that reason, in fashioning his *chrestomathia* or program of a Utilitarian education, he suppresses classical teaching but justifies the teaching of science by invoking the criterion of use.

It is the criterion Thomas Nashe had invoked almost three centuries earlier—but not to disparage poetry. On the contrary. Poetry, says Nashe, "is the hunny of all flowers, the quintessence

---

[10] *Past and Present*, IV, 4.   [11] "Lord Bacon."

of all Sciences, the Marrowe of Witte, and the very Phrase of Angels."[12] The least important attribute of poetry is the last. In his truculent anatomizing of contemporary abuses, Nashe includes licentious romances but not because they are licentious. The want of utility galls. Gosson, like Nashe, is hostile to the romance, which has to do with "the adventures of an amorous knight, passing from countrie to countrie for the love of his lady, encountering many a terrible monster made of broune paper." Hypothetically, pleasure accrues as this progress is dramatized, but not profit. "What learne you by that?" the utilitarian inquires.[13] Partly, an anxious sense of the imbalance between profit and pleasure begets Gosson's attack on the theatre and his attempt to prove that it ought "not to be suffred in a Christian common weale." The indictment of poets as "the fathers of lies" is not exclusively a moral indictment.[14]

Sidney's *Arcadia*, like Plato's *Republic*, is more inclusive and hence more discouraging:

> Poor Painters oft with silly Poets join,
> To fill the world with strange but vain conceits:
> One brings the stuff, the other stamps the coin,
> Which breeds nought else but glosses of deceit.

Against the counterfeit makers who traffic in deceit, Nashe adduces the fifteenth-century humanist and cleric Giovannantonio Campano, who is represented as stigmatizing "our English Poets" because "lying is their lyving, and fables are their mooveables." You cannot feed capons so. Take away the trifles on which the poets subsist and "sillie soules, they will famish for hunger." The whole business of art "is but to yeeld pleasure by lying."[15]

[12] *Pierce Penilesse*; Smith, I, 194.

[13] *Playes Confuted* [? 1590]; D. Bevington, *From "Mankind" to Marlowe*, p. 190.

[14] *Playes Confuted*, D5v; *Apologie of the Schoole of Abuse*, 1579, L2v-3.

[15] Campano in Smith, I, 327; Matthieu Coignet's manual of instruction for princes (trans. Edward Hoby as *Politique Discourses*, 1586), in Smith, I, 342.

Hamlet, in a famous passage, seeks to rebut this charge. The end of playing—inferentially, of art in general—is "to hold, as 'twere, the mirror up to nature; to show virtue her own feature, scorn her own image, and the very age and body of the time his form and pressure." Poets, as they prosecute that end, are not the fathers of lies but the champions of truth. But the rebuttal, so far from exonerating the poet, only adds another count to the indictment. What is at issue is not so much a distinction between truth and fancy as between profit and loss. The romancer who deals in fantastical shapes makes nothing for the uses of life. But neither does the realist who, holding up the mirror, delineates indifferently and hence irresponsibly the form and pressure of what is. Congreve, in his defense of the stage, pleads as the chief imperative fidelity to fact. Collier, rejoining, is not so conscientious. "If there must be Strumpets, let Bridewell be the Scene."[16] The poet or playwright, in his mindless preoccupation with superficies, fails to distinguish between the truth that dispirits and the more cordial truth that gladdens and pays. As he is unconcerned to sift or assay, useful enterprise is impossible to him. He is an amoralist who trades in the unbolted fact. Better if "the name of the vice is omitted," says the Puritan theologian William Perkins. Vicious matter presented to the ear or the eye is infectious, and even if the triumph of virtue is in train. "This being true, then by proportion the visible representation of the vices of men in the world, which is the substance and matter whereof playes and interludes are made, is much more to be avoided."[17] To this position Plato adheres. That is why the Master of the Revels and the contrivers of the Licensing Act and Dr. Thomas Bowdler find in him a common father.

Plato, in his role as the pontiff of utility, thinks it natural to draw a line of demarcation between the two kinds of truth. The poets, as their bent is to promiscuity, do not winnow what is fruitless or vicious but seek to encompass experience as a whole. The benevolent dictator, on the other hand, restricts his "support to those creative searchings which serve best the ideas of social-

[16] *Defence of the Short View*, 1699, pp. 10-11.
[17] *Direction for the Government of the Tongue*, 1615, pp. 18-19.

ism and the needs of the widest social circles." Comprehensiveness, the métier of the poet as chameleon, is under ban: "we will
oppose," says the party boss, who is resolutely avuncular, "any
effort leading towards the exploitation of artistic creativity as a
stepping stone to antisocialistic activity."[18] (How unexpectedly
cruel it is, to say that the style is the man.) Art, as it holds the
mirror up to nature, confounds fruit and chaff. The best men,
who are the rulers or guardians, must therefore be innocent of
art. They are not to "depict or be skilfull at imitating any kind
of illiberality or baseness, lest from imitation they should come
to be what they imitate." The artist, who concerns himself "with
an inferior part of the soul"—as Shakespeare is concerned in
depicting Iago or Christopher Sly—"awakens and nourishes and
strengthens the feelings and impairs the reason." Representing,
now inordinate grief: Lear's cry to Cordelia, "Never, never,
never, never, never"; and now an unseemly jest: Hamlet's retort on Ophelia, "Do you think I meant country matters?" he
leads his auditor to give a loose to sorrow or to be ribald himself, he betrays him unconsciously into playing the vulgarian or
the melancholic or the spleenful man at home.[19]

"What is to bee thought of stage Playes?" asks the clergyman
William Ames; and answers: "Such stage playes as are now in
use, are utterly to be condemned." That is because they "consist
in the lively representation of vices and wickednesses." But
mimesis is not neutral. "In the representation of such wickednesses, the actours doe not onely put on the resemblance of them
. . . they as well conceive them internally, as expresse such matters externally." In this way it happens that "by exercising themselves to it, they dispose themselves to the same vices, whence
they become ready and prone to execute them without shame."[20]

On the evening of May 10, 1933, on the Unter den Linden
across from the University of Berlin, the works of Thomas

---

[18] Wladyslaw Gomulka at the Fifth Party Congress, 1968; T. Z. Gasinski, "Signs of Dissent and Detachment in Recent Polish Poetry," *MQR*,
x, 29.

[19] Discussion draws on *Republic*, Bks. II, III, and x.

[20] *Conscience*, 1639, p. 216.

Mann, Stefan Zweig, Arthur Schnitzler, Gide, Zola, Proust—pretenders to impartial representation—are committed to the fire. The mob that exults in the burning of the books must be seen for what it is: not merely crazed but austerely moral. This mob is Plato walking. In the words of a student proclamation, which reads like a redacting of the Tenth Book of the *Laws* or like the typical polemicist of the English Renaissance, any book, any author lies open to destruction "which acts subversively on our future or strikes at the root of German thought, the German home and the driving forces of our people." Painting is also scrutinized and rejected as its content is felt as acting subversively: art is kinetic. Picasso, Gauguin, Matisse, Van Gogh, Cézanne are taken down from the museums. The National Socialist in his role as *fidei defensor* has determined "to purge the German Reich and our people of all those influences threatening its existence and character."[21]

The Platonist, who is as often to be met with in the Renaissance as in fifth-century Athens and whom we have with us still, is paradoxically the humanitarian. As he thinks himself devoted to the use and benefit of mankind and to the extirpating "of all those influences threatening its existence and character," he endeavors to drive a wedge between mankind and the maleficent distracting he associates with poetry. Like William Alley, the Bishop of Exeter, he fears the virulent power of an unholy truth encapsulated in poems or enacted in plays. Alley is only a conventional preacher in framing his attack on "Wanton Bookes."[22] He is, however, a Platonist in attacking the theatre for giving scope to the dram of eale within us all, as we watch it flourish in the doomed protagonist. He, and the unappeasable or Platonic critics who hold with him, are hostile to poetry and the drama not as they are mendacious but as they engender "unchasteness, uncleanness, whoredom, craft, subtlety, and wickedness." The writer is Peter de la Primaudaye, a homiletic tutor to the late sixteenth century, who counsels his readers to withdraw from

[21] Quotations from Shirer, *Third Reich*, pp. 241, 244.
[22] *Poore Mans Librarie*, 1571.

"the theater of players" because, as they attend there, "they soon receive into their souls a lively impression of that dissoluteness and villainy which they see and hear."[23]

Plato's counsel is notoriously the same. Poetry "feeds and waters the passions instead of drying them up . . . [and] lets them rule, although they ought to be controlled." If mankind is ever to increase in happiness and virtue, poetry and her sister arts or fellow malefactors must be rooted from the commonwealth. The sense of this general proscription of poetry is not lost on the poets themselves. Thomas Hardy conveys it succinctly.

> Let him in whose ears the low-voiced Best is
> killed by the clash of the First,
> Who holds that if way to the Better there be,
> it exacts a full look at the Worst,
> Who feels that delight is a delicate growth
> cramped by crookedness, custom, and fear,
> Get him up and be gone as one shaped awry;
> he disturbs the order here.

Order is more than inclusiveness and therefore the poet, as he seeks to be inclusive, has got to be put to silence. A full look at the worst comes too dear if the price we pay to apprehend it is the blunting of our purpose. It is the conclusion of the utilitarians, who are not bigoted but only pragmatic, that too much risk attends on the indulgence of art. "No muse is good muse" (Peter De Vries).

Here is the modern utilitarian or Platonist, as Solzhenitsyn (ironically) reports him: "to tell the people the truth doesn't mean to tell the bad, to poke into shortcomings. You can speak fearlessly about the good, so that it will become even better. Where do these false demands come from for the so-called 'harsh truth'? And why should truth be harsh, all of a sudden? Why shouldn't it be the shining truth, attractive and optimistic? Our whole literature ought to be festive!"[24] The writer who,

[23] *French Academy*, trans. 1586, p. 216.
[24] *The Cancer Ward*, Ch. XXI.

85

declining to be festive, evokes "horror and nausea," is proscribed. Kafka for instance in *Metamorphosis* performs the equation "man and roach are the same; they are each as worthy as the other; they are each as glorious as the other; they cancel out—and thereby we have the whole miserable philosophy of the 'new critics,' " who preach that our "sole cultural recourse lies in a literature . . . based on helplessness, disgust, self-loathing, mysticism, and contempt for social action."[25]

This last—social action—is the great desideratum. Literature and art, says Chairman Mao (after Lenin), are but "a screw in the machine." As they are "subordinate to politics," it is idle to speak of art for art's sake. Art is "a powerful weapon." The artist is acceptable as he shoulders this weapon to "contribute to the democratic struggle."[26]

But even though the artist engages to contribute, he has not satisfied his detractors. For the judgment of art, as formulated by the Mysomousoi or poet-haters (Sidney's phrase), is not merely negative. The negative judgment, that art is lacking in utility, is answered by those poets who exaggerate the element of profit in poems and plays. The dramatist Thomas Heywood tells of a secret landing of the Spaniards in Cornwall. Catastrophe impends. But now the players arrive, "presenting a battle on the stage." In the course of this mock battle, "their drum and trumpets strooke up a lowd alarme: which the enemy hearing, and fearing they were discovered, amazedly retired . . . and so in a hurly-burly fled disorderly to their boats."[27] After all, plays are useful.

But the apologist is still at a beginning. At bottom, his art is excoriated not simply as it is valueless but as it is actively vicious. This is the positive and more formidable objection to art, that the profit it affords is inseparable from loss. A lasting concordat with the poets is impossible, but not because of their ancient

[25] Milton Howard, quoted Howard Fast (with whom the passage begins), in *Literature and Reality*, pp. 10-11.

[26] Mao Tse-tung, *Problems of Art and Literature*, pp. 7-8, 32-35; Fast, *Literature and Reality*, p. 22.

[27] *Apology for Actors*, 1612, G2.

commitment to what Gosson calls the "Pipes of vanitie." *Autre temps, autre moeurs*. At issue is the nature of poetry itself which, as it feigns, engenders feigning. The poet may fetter his torment in verse and thereby assuage it. That is a happiness to the poet.

> But when I have done so,
> Some man, his art and voice to show,
> Doth Set and sing my paine,
> And, by delighting many, frees againe
> Griefe, which verse did restraine.
>
> (Donne, "The Triple Foole")

It does not matter that criminality is reprehended. Comedy and tragedy are evil in the grain as they lead us to imitate the evil depicted in them. That is what Gosson means in asserting (with Plato) that poetry is effeminate.[28] Its point of view is assimilated in the representation of fact and therefore the condoning even of a didactic theatre, as by Gosson himself, is inappropriate. Comedy and tragedy, simply as kinds, must water the passions and not least when their design is coercive or remedial or explicitly pious. Religious and irreligious plays are generically the same.

Gosson, who equivocates on this head, has his own ax to grind. He is a reformed playwright. William Perkins, who has nothing to extenuate, is more consistent. Perkins sees only a specious distinction between good and bad plays. Even the Biblical drama, which one would suppose the preacher to endorse enthusiastically, is proscribed. Though plays "may have an honest end, a laudable subject, as a history of the Bible," they "cannot bee made honest by the intention of the doer."[29] For the ultimate end, says William Ames, is dishonest: the raising of turbulent emotions.[30] Philip Stubbes, in his encyclopedia of the vices of Ailgna (Anglia), employs against the drama the technique of dramatic debate. In the posing of questions whose an-

---

[28] *Ephemerides of Phialo*, 1579; Second Action of *Playes Confuted*; *Schoole of Abuse*, A3.

[29] *A Case of Conscience*, 1595.

[30] *Conscience*, p. 219.

swers are foreordained, he imitates Plato in the *Republic*.[31] He is like Plato also in his discovery of the peril attendant on mimesis or feigning. Plays in general, and sacred plays among them, are "sucked out of the Devilles teates, to nourishe us in Idolatrie, Heathenrie, and Sinne."[32]

There is in the Platonic indictment no intimation of catharsis. Aristotle, asserting that despair, enacted, drives out despair is a better esthetician and psychologist than Plato. "Form, which is the birth of passion, is also the death of pain."[33] Milton is of the party of Aristotle in defending tragedy because of the power it possesses "by raising pity and fear, or terror, to purge the mind of those and suchlike passions; that is, to temper and reduce them to just measure with a kind of delight, stirred up by reading or seeing those passions well imitated." The truth is not entoiling. Paradoxically it is the truth that makes one free: and makes one happy. If the hero is destroyed, the "true experience [acquired] from this great event" engenders, not despair

---

[31] Plato's device of the dialectic is intended to force men to awake from the spell of poetry and to think in general terms. It makes them, by asking questions, think about Odysseus rather than identify with him. Philo, predictably, copies Plato in boiling down Scripture to a series of questions and answers. In the sixteenth and seventeenth centuries, the device becomes a staple of the detractors of poetry and plays. It is employed, for example, by J. Northbrooke, *Treatise*, 1579; R. Rogers, *Practice of Christianitie*, 1618; J. Rainolds in his dialog with John Hart (*Summe of the Conference*, 1584); R. Hill, *Pathway to Prayer*, 1613; G. Babington, *Exposition of the Commaundements by way of Questions and Answeres for greater plainnesse*, 1583; E. Dering, *Catechisme*, 1572. William Crashaw in his sermons uses a syllogistic method of presentation. R. Junius (pseud.), *Compleat Armour*, 1638, states a position, sometimes called "Objection," and follows it with a statement explicitly labelled "Answer." The method is not peculiar to the haters of poetry (the mathematician R. Recorde casts his *Whetstone of Witte*, 1557, in the form of a dialog between Master and Scholar), but is reflective of and suited to the temper of a rationalizing age. It is, in contemporary jargon, the right "tagmemic" structure.

[32] *Anatomie of Abuses*, 1583, N2v.

[33] Wilde, *Intentions*; Ellmann, *Critic*, p. 399. G. Else, *Aristotle's "Poetics,"* challenges the conventional notion of catharsis as producing an emotional end-effect on the spectator, describes it rather as a feature of the structure of tragedy. See esp. pp. 224-32, 423-50.

but "peace and consolation . . . And calm of mind, all passion spent."[34] This, I think, is what Dante means, in undertaking to remove his reader "from a state of misery . . . to a state of happiness."

The journey itself is not necessarily agreeable. Stendhal (after Hamlet) likens art to a mirror passing down the road. Stendhal is more consistent than Hamlet, in that the mirror he imagines has, properly, no "point of view." Should it find evil on the way, it is not to omit the representation, however appalling or seductive. The business of the mirror, in which the artist is figured, is neither affirmation nor denial. Knowing nothing before the fact, it seeks only to discover and to body forth what is. Entertaining no assumption, oblivious of the event, in a sense indifferent to it, it is content to pay homage to the visible universe. That indiscriminate celebration is, according to Aristotle, not only the hallmark of art but also the characteristic habit of *homo sapiens*, who finds his highest gratification in apprehending the truth. In defending that proposal, Aristotle appeals to experience which shows that "though the objects themselves may be painful to see, we delight to view the most realistic representation of them in art." The explanation of this paradox Aristotle locates "in a further fact: to be learning something is the greatest of pleasures not only to the philosopher but also to the rest of mankind." One rejoices in the witnessing of art and even when it witnesses to evil, because he is "gathering the meaning of things."[35] It is not that the truth is availing, but rather that the attaining to truth—if man is to be defined as a rational creature—fulfills in highest measure the ends and purposes of our being. All men, says Descartes, "yearn . . . after . . . some good of a sovereign nature much higher than the goods they possess. Now this sovereign good . . . is nothing but the knowledge of truth."[36]

[34] Preface and conclusion to *Samson Agonistes*; Marcuse, *Eros and Civilization*, p. 94: "Happiness involves knowledge: it is the prerogative of the *animal rationale*."

[35] *Poetics*, III, 4.

[36] *Letter-Preface to "Principles of Philosophy,"* 1647. Freud is like Descartes and Aristotle in asserting that the reality principle "also seeks

That is why the scabrous and smutty discourse of Thersites, or the unremitting horrors of a novel like *The Cancer Ward*, or the monstrous death of Cordelia or Julien Sorel, are entertaining. In listening to the one, in bearing witness to the other, we make contact with the sources of reality. To pierce directly to those sources and so to communicate—I quote Eliot in the *Dialogue on Dramatic Poetry*—"the full quality of a moment as it is actually felt to consist" is the whole duty of the artist.

The Platonist acknowledges a higher duty. His more pragmatic commitment is to the building of the kingdom. Given that commitment, he is as indifferent to the easy pleasure afforded by lying romances as to that more exquisite pleasure of savoring the full quality of a moment as it is actually felt to consist. The allegiance of the poets is to pleasure, and therefore he seeks to compass their destruction. It is better that poetry die than the whole people. The gravamen of his charge is that the poets, whether they are involved with fantastical dreams or with holding the mirror up to nature, are not sufficiently consequential. Because more is incumbent on man than delectation and dreaming, or even than gathering the meaning of things, the "idle" monks and canons had been exiled a half century ago. Today it is the turn of the poets. Warfare is open and manifest now, as between profit and pleasure.

Among the poets a dejected minority see no choice but to capitulate. The new day is already triumphant. It is dazzling and even inspiriting in its triumph, and so to contend against it is apparently irrational. More and less than pragmatic conviction is involved. The poet who throws in with his detractors is not simply a time server, or not always. He is mesmerized, as by looking on the basilisk. He desires from the highest motives to participate in the great work of transformation, "to come to terms with reality and make excuses for it." There is pathos in this desire and instruction for the present time. The Renaissance

---

pleasure—although a delayed and diminished pleasure, one which is assured by its realization of fact, its relation to reality" (*Collected Papers*, IV, 14).

poet, divided in himself, is like our contemporary, the poet Osip Mandelstam who "wanted to be with everybody else," who "feared the Revolution might pass him by." One thinks of the aged playwright Gerhart Hauptmann, in earlier days the pane-gyrist of the downtrodden, leaving the theatre after a perform-ance of his last play—arm in arm with Dr. Goebbels.[37] Not the least but the most worthy feel the pull to come to terms: Pasternak, Ben Jonson, Andrew Marvell, Stevens in the mid-1930s (the poems of *Owl's Clover*). The capitulation of the artist does not depend finally on cajolery or violence but on the talismanic power of a noble idea. The artist collaborates in his own destruction. Like Richard II, he gives his soul's consent. That is as he wishes to save his soul. "One wonders," writes Mandelstam's widow, mindful of the force of this talismanic power, "why our rulers still needed prisons and capital punish-ment."[38]

The poet George Gascoigne is one of those who capitulates. His nosegay of *An Hundred Sundrie Floures* (1572) begins to stink in the nostrils. Lilies that fester smell far worse than weeds. Addressing the Queen on her progress to Kenilworth (1575), he fans the air as he can. "Behold here," he adjures her, "nott Gascoigne the ydle poett, wryting tryfles . . . but Gascoigne the Satyricall wryter, medytating eche Muse that may expresse his reformacion." In token of that reformation, and "to make amendes for the lost time . . . misbestowed in wryting so wan-tonlie," Gascoigne turns tractarian.[39] Now, all his travail is ex-pended "in matters both serious and Morall," for example in elaborating a *Delicate Diet, for daintiemouthde Droonkardes* (1576).

Sir John Harington, in acknowledging the limitations of poetry, is not so euphonious as this. His abasement before what is serious and moral is, however, as thoroughgoing. It is true, he

---

[37] Shirer reports the scene, p. 243.   [38] *Hope Against Hope*, p. 126.

[39] As in the homily entitled *The Droome of Doomes day*, prefaced by a trans. of the *De Contemptu Mundi* of Pope Innocent III (1576). The end is to persuade the Queen to forget "the poesies which I have scattered in the world" (C. Prouty, *Gascoigne*, pp. 90-91, 85).

has much to say of the "many good uses to be had of [poetry]."
But in the last resort he has got to concede that "to us that are
Christians, in respect of the high end of all, which is the health
of our soules, not only Poetrie but al other studies of Philosophy
are in a manner vaine and superfluous."[40] Aquinas finally says
the same thing, of reason relative to faith. In his (normative)
case the admission is positive; it is even laconic: he is acknowledging the supremacy of God. The Renaissance apologist differs
as he has seen the flaw at the heart of his pleading. Essentially
he is throwing up his hands. That is what Boccaccio is doing.
After much vociferous defense of poetry, he is compelled to
grant "that it would be far better to study the sacred books than
even the best of . . . poetical writers."[41] Fulke Greville is a poet
and also a dramatist in the Senecan kind. He has, however, too
much conscience to enter a plea for the stage or, by implication,
for vain and superfluous poetry.[42] Greville's genius, as he acknowledges in the biography of Sidney, is "more fixed upon the
Images of Life, than the Images of Wit." It is an interesting
antithesis and in it is implicit the repudiating of art as, at bottom,
an elegant diversion. In a splendid phrase, Greville announces
his decision not to write to the connoisseurs of pleasure "on
whose foote the black Oxe had not already trod . . . but to those
only, that are weather-beaten in the Sea of this World, such as
having lost the sight of their Gardens, and groves, study to saile
on a right course among Rocks, and quicksands." In ordering
his sententious reflections "together for the use of life," he elects
to write tragedies, but "no Plaies for the Stage . . . against whom
so many good, and great spirits have already written."[43]

[40] Smith, II, 197.

[41] *Genealogy*, XIV, xviii; Osgood, p. 82.

[42] His doubtful view of either is set forth in *A Treatie of Humane
Learning*:

> Then if our Arts want power to make us better,
> What foole will thinke they can us wiser make,
> Life is the Wisdome, Art is but the letter,
> Or shell, which oft men for the kernell take. (st. 35)

[43] Ch. XVIII; Oxford edn., p. 224.

But though Greville allies himself with the detractors of stage plays, he remains a considerable poet. His kind of poetry is, however, not much given to poeticness. It is efficient, it is Augustan, and notable for its use of educative figures like *antitheton* and *paroemia* or the gnomic proverb.

> Oh, wearisome condition of humanity,
> Born under one law, to another bound;
> Vainly begot, and yet forbidden vanity,
> Created sick, commanded to be sound.
> What meaneth nature by these diverse laws?
> Passion and reason self-division cause.[44]

And yet even for this powerful and emphatically serious poetry its maker cannot honestly claim, what is indispensable if poetry is to be admitted, that it enables us to navigate among the rocks and sands.[45] The signal fact in Greville's long life is his early friendship with Sir Philip Sidney, the most highly honored of Elizabethan poets. It is, in Sidney's work, his moral fervor and his commitment to the idea of use that chiefly compel the admiration of contemporaries and of those who, like Greville, live on to regret and to embellish in legend his untimely death. Nevertheless, and for all his undoubted devotion, Greville's praise is given not so much to the beauty of the work as to the beautiful man who was its creator. In the *Life of Sidney*, he arrives in his dour integrity at the conclusion that even the great soul whom he cherished as his brother failed in the *Arcadia*, that

---

[44] "Chorus Sacerdotum" from *Mustapha*, 1609.

[45] Compare *Treatie of Human Learning*, sts. 111-12:

> Poesie and Musicke, Arts of Recreation,
> Succeed, esteem'd as idle mens profession;
> Because their scope, being meerely contentation,
> Can move, but not remove, or make impression
>> Really, either to enrich the Wit,
>> Or, which is lesse, to mend our states by it.
> This makes the solid Judgements give them place,
>> Onely as pleasing sauce to dainty food;
>> Fine foyles for jewels, or enammels grace.

most purposive of all romances, to transcend the vanity endemic in art.

Sidney is before him in this consciousness of failure and more severe in reprehending it. The *Arcadia*, "being but a trifle, and that triflingly handled," is an "idle work ... which ... like the spider's web, will be thought fitter to be swept away, than worn to any other purpose." That is too harsh a view, and Sidney does not adhere to it consistently. It is, however, a part of his nagging sense of guilt at having trafficked at all in "glosses of deceit" that he should feel the compulsion "to cast out, in some desert of forgetfulness, this child, which I am loth to father." On his deathbed, he consigns it to the fire. After all it is no "better stuff than as in a haberdasher's shop, glasses, or feathers."[46]

That is the conclusion at which the new men have also arrived, and it leads them to impose conditions on the makers of verse. Like Plato, they are willing to concede the attractiveness of poetry. But like him they insist that poetry, to be suffered, must "show not only that she is pleasant but also useful to States and human life."[47] To a man like Fulke Greville, whose honesty and intensity are bound up with his narrowness of vision, it is an impossible condition. He does not protest against it as essentially impertinent. Agreeing that resistance is irrational, he declines to make resistance and gives his allegiance, in Sidney's phrase, to the regiment of virtue on whose banner *Utilitas* is blazoned.[48] Imaginative literature, as its scope is merely "contentation" or satisfaction, cannot bring us a jot nearer our ultimate goal. There is accordingly no profit in it. True profit consists in looking to the high end of all.

[46] Dedication to the Countess of Pembroke.

[47] *Republic*, Bk. x.

[48] *Old Arcadia* 33:

> Reason, tell me thy mind, if here be reason
> In this strange violence, to make resistance,
> Where sweet graces erect the stately banner
> Of vertue's regiment, shining in harnesse
> Of fortune's Diademes, by beauty mustred.

94

> What then are all these human Arts, and lights,
>> But Seas of errors? In whose depths who sound,
>> Of truth finde onely shadowes, and no ground.[49]

In this melancholy verdict, John Lyly concurs. At the fag end of a glittering career, out of favor and out of pocket, Lyly addresses a begging petition to the Queen. That is a poignant fact but not otherwise remarkable. What gives it special point is the kind of support the broken playwright is after, not the wherewithal to make a fresh start but only a plank "to wafte me into the country where in my sad and settled devotion, I may in every corner of a thatched cottage write prayers instead of plays—prayers for your long and prosperous life and a repentance that I have played the fool so long, and yet live."[50] The note of bathos in Lyly, which lets one know that he is speaking from the heart, is muted in George Whetstone, who finds little profit in writing for the stage and hence informs against it in a disingenuous exposure of London low life.[51] Whetstone forswears his craft as an unsuccessful gambler leaves off play. Joseph Hall, in the next generation, abandons the writing of satire to enter on a less parlous career in the church. Robert Greene, as he is a more considerable figure than either, makes a more convincing apostate. His forswearing is, however, belated, and as such avails him nothing.[52] Interment in the Poets' Corner is denied to Robert Greene. He is buried in the heart of industrial London, underneath the trains, on the site of the Liverpool Street Station. It is too gross an irony and hence it is inaccessible to art: the Poet insulted over by the Machine. As a melodramatist in the grain who went off at thirty-two from a surfeit of Rhenish wine and pickled herrings, Greene himself

---

[49] *Treatie of Humane Learning*, st. 34.

[50] Hunter, *Lyly*, p. 86.

[51] *Promos and Cassandra*, 1578; *A Mirror for Magistrates of Cities*, 1584, to which the attack on the stage (*A Touchstone for the Time*) is appended.

[52] *A Groatsworth of Wit bought with a million of Repentance*, 1592—supposedly a deathbed tract.

would have sanctioned it. That is partly his trouble. He is an old-fashioned poet who composes in the aureate style and who is not so much preoccupied with ends as with means. His despairing response to the invidious question of use is not engendered, like Greville's, by an instinctive repudiating of the credentials of poetry. It derives from and is envenomed by the perception, borne in upon him by penury and unsuccess, that his kind of art no longer passes muster and that the old and sustaining context inhabited by the poet has begun to decay. Greene in his embittered isolation is closer to Richard Savage (the artist in his garret), two centuries later, and even to Dr. Johnson, than to a poet like Stephen Hawes, groom of the chamber to Henry VII, who almost overlaps him in time. In him is prefigured the separation of the poet and his patron or public, as sensibility or superstitious regard are tempered increasingly by the desire to achieve a negotiable return.

With the waxing of that desire, the poet is asked to give value. What he gives, in the case of Robert Greene, is an hysterical indictment and not only of himself but of his art. He needs no Bishop Burnet to put him to his responses. On his own involuntary confession Greene is a failure, and by virtue of the indifferent profession he has chosen to follow, "That fruitless and unprofitable art,/ Good unto none, but least to the professors."[53] That Shakespeare just then is coming into his force does not signify, unless to exacerbate the hatred and self-loathing evinced by the dying poet. Shakespeare is only another idle (and larcenous) singer: "an upstart Crow, beautified with our feathers." But so are his fellows, Greene's "Quondam acquaintance, that spend their wits in making plaies." To these gentlemen the repentant sinner proffers as his legacy "a better exercise, and wisedome to prevent his extremities," in which a bootless dedication to the vanity of art has involved him. Among those he admonishes are George Peele, the finest of Shakespeare's pre-

---

[53] *Every Man in His Humour*, I, i. For a fuller discussion of the changing relation between poet and patron and, more generally, the progressive disvaluing of the former, see my *War Against Poetry*.

cursors in the drama, excepting only Christopher Marlowe; and Marlowe himself, at the apogee of his wonderful powers.

The renunciation of art, whether sad or splenetic, is one response to the intensifying of the attack on poetry. It is not the only response. If Plato and his followers assail the poet as useless, it is open to the poet not to surrender but to cry in Plato's teeth: to plead guilty to the indictment not wanly but cheerfully, and then to resume what he agrees is his indolent business. This audacious and revolutionary tactic, which gives away at one stroke the centuries-old insistence on the usefulness of poetry, is adopted by the epigrammatist John Heath. More arrogant or frivolous than Fulke Greville and Robert Greene, he cuts the ground from his adversary Zoilus by affecting to agree with him:

> I might be better busied; I grant so.
> Could I be better idle? Surely, no.
> Then hold your idle chat, for I profess
> These are the fruits but of my idleness.[54]

It is a startling profession and not much heard before the Renaissance. Ancient Alexandria is notorious in professing it; and in a way that is what it means to be Alexandrine or meretricious, to declaim to no purpose like the polymath Eratosthenes (275-195 B.C.), the librarian of Alexandria, who holds that poets are not teachers but only entertainers. Eratosthenes, grown tired of entertainment, starves himself to death. "Beware of the merely learned man," says Bernard Shaw. "He is an idler who kills time with study."

Quintilian, as his interest is absorbed in oratory, to which as a practical matter the triple function of teaching and moving and delighting is annexed (*docere, movere, delectare*), is not much preoccupied with poetry, whose function he sees as exhausted in pleasure alone (*solam voluptatem*). That is Lyly's fulsome idea of his own art. The ladies who constitute his audience are to handle the cloying stuff he has confected "as you do your junkets,

---

[54] *Two Centuries of Epigrams*, 1610.

that when you can eat no more you tie some in your napkin for children . . . [or] for your waiting maids. Euphues had rather lie shut in a lady's casket than open in a scholar's study."[55] Puttenham, in his role as cicerone to aristocratic persons who have more and less to do than cudgel their brains, is chiefly concerned to tutor "Ladies and young Gentlewomen, or idle Courtiers . . . for their private recreation to make now & then ditties of pleasure." Serious instruction is no part of his purpose. The governing principle is that expressed by the fop in Congreve's play: " 'tis well enough for a servant to be bred at a university, but the education is a little too pedantic for a gentleman."[56] As Puttenham is aware that "to such manner of mindes nothing is more combersome then tedious doctrines and schollarly methodes of discipline," he undertakes to devise "a new and strange modell of this arte, fitter to please the Court then the schoole."[57]

But this is eccentricity. That it ceases to be so in the seventeenth century is owing to the more vehement insistence on use of an age to which all good things have suddenly become attainable. The England of the later Tudors and Stuarts, as it has much, is covetous of more. And therefore it scrutinizes questions of profit with an intensity quite unknown to the Middle Ages. The result of this scrutiny is a repudiating of poetry's claim to be useful, in any case to be useful enough. The poet himself, as he is disinclined either to capitulate or to argue, has got to choose a new line. The line he chooses is sufficiently flamboyant. Poetry, he agrees, is a toy or drossy trifle (Philip Massinger).[58] It is therefore irrelevant to ask of the poet that he demonstrate an import in which he affects to disbelieve and from which, in his studied elegance, he recoils. "Rhymes are guards on wanton

[55] *Euphues and His England*, 1580.

[56] *Love for Love*, v.

[57] *Arte of English Poesie*, iii, x.

[58] Massinger, dedicating *The Bondman*, 1623, to Philip Earl of Montgomery, prays him "to shroud this trifle under the wings of your noble protection" and give it "a gracious pardon." In dedicating his elegiac poem, "Sero, sed Serio," 1636, to the same patron, he depreciates "my Toyes" and "my foule drosse."

Cupid's hose,"[59] fashioned without effort and only to afford a grace to the moment as it passes.

Between poetry and utility a gulf is opened, deliberately, and by the poets themselves. Donne declares: "I will have no such Readers as I can teach."[60] In his obscurity and metrical harshness, Donne is hanging out his sign. It reads: "Wits and Amateurs only."[61] The playwright John Marston varies this impudent message a little. That his *Dutch Courtizan* (1604) is no better than she should be is not an embarrassment to Marston. On the contrary, he is at pains to let his auditors know that "if our pen in this seem over slight,/ We strive not to instruct, but to delight" (Prologue). Look not for profit but only for sport in "these puntillos of dreames and shewes": that is Samuel Daniel, introducing a masque to the King and Queen at Hampton Court.[62] Partly, the advice is gratuitous. King James knows better than to anticipate profit in poetry. His own verses are entitled *Poetical Exercises at vacant hours* (1591). That is on the way to becoming the conventional description and as such it is utilized by George Chapman, in dedicating his sequel to Marlowe's *Hero and Leander* (1598). He has condescended, says Chapman with the requisite negligence, "to employ some of my serious time in so trifeling a subject." Even a poetaster like Henry Petowe, attempting an enfeebled version of the same erotic story, is concerned to remark that these "my forward indeavours ... [were] done at certaine vacant howers."[63]

I do not suppose that either Chapman, a powerful poet and not least in the poem he dismisses as ephemeral, or the scribbler who echoes him, were altogether in earnest. The depreciating of

[59] Berowne in *Love's Labour's Lost*, IV, iii, 58.

[60] Preface to the *Progresse of the Soule*.

[61] A. Alvarez, *School of Donne*, p. 32. E. Miner, *The Metaphysical Mode from Donne to Cowley*, locates the "chief literary radical" of Metaphysical poetry in its private mode (pp. 3-47).

[62] "*Ludit istiis animus, non preficit*": *Vision of the Twelve Goddesses*, 1603/4.

[63] "To the quicke-sighted Reader," *The second part of Hero and Leander*, 1598.

poetry as *pueriles pupae*[64] is, on one side, in the nature of a meditated *topos*. Montaigne, who deprecates his *Essays* as *"cette fricassé que je barbouille,"* does not wish, presumably, to be taken at face value. Sincerity is, however, not so important or so consequential as formal adherence to the brazen new fashion, which holds that poetry is only an "exercise, or rather divertisement." This scornful and slighting opinion is voiced by the poet Abraham Cowley,[65] whose judgment is approved in the heartlessness of most of his verse. Poets like Cowley, who sponsor the new and enduring conception of poetry as an amiable diversion, continue to assume that most women and some men do really find pleasure in poetry. Only they assert that the element of profit is to seek. On their more modern understanding, the poet is a tunesmith or sciolist who does not offer knowledge but only entertainment. Thomas Kyd, in the most popular play of the age, defines what is essentially the anti-esthetic of the new Alexandrians:

> When I was young I gave my mind
> And plied myself to fruitless poetry;
> Which though it profit the professor naught,
> Yet is it passing pleasing to the world.[66]

The kind of poet whose allegiance is given only to entertainment concurs with as much spirit as his languid disposition can muster. He does not acquiesce in the banishing of poetry which, if it is nugatory, is nonetheless charming. But he insists on the profitless character of what he is doing. The new poet or sciolist composes simply "for his own exercise and his friends' pleasure," and always "at ydle times . . . to avoyde greater ydlenesse or worse businesse."[67] This cultivating of poetry as the lesser evil does not occur inevitably to Saint-Évremond, who devotes his

---

[64] William Vaughan, *The Spirit of Detraction*, 1611, p. 112.

[65] Preface to *Works*, 1668.

[66] *The Spanish Tragedy*, v, i, 69-72.

[67] Thomas Howell, dedicating his *Devises*, 1581, to the Countess of Pembroke.

exile at the court of Charles II partly to making love and mali-
cious conversation. Still, as he has "much leisure" and is looking
constantly "to pass away the time," he "writes sometimes on one
subject, sometimes on another," but only, as his eighteenth-
century editor asserts, "for his own amusement" or that of the
gentlemen "with whom he converses." In his own lifetime,
Saint-Évremond publishes nothing. His contemning of a useful
role in society, if it baffles and inflames his detractors, serves to
confirm their bias and to make their arguments against him more
plausible and convincing. When the Devil quotes Scripture, they
are willing to listen.

The Devil, in his folly and to his ultimate confusion, continues
to edify his opponents. Poets and romancers vie with one another in self-depreciation. Even the sage and serious Spenser is
willing, in an uncharacteristic mood, to describe the *Faerie
Queene* as "these ydle rimes . . . The labor of lost time."[68] The
storyteller disdains the tale. Barnabe Rich, "seeing trifles of no
accompt to be now best in season, and such vanities more desired
than matters of better purpose," puts forth his own book because
he "would follow the fashion."[69] George Pettie's "idle opportunity" begets "those tragical trifles" which compose his *Palace
of Pleasure* (1576). Not a serious novel but a "silly present" is
the best that Emmanuel Ford can proffer. The romantic fiction
he is dedicating, "being but a fancy . . . [is] to be read for
recreation."[70]

In the next century the negligent manner becomes more practiced and the disavowing of serious pretension more insistent, as
poetry is relegated to the periphery of things. Wycherley wrote
"not for Benefit, or ever made it his Livelihood." He would
not have written anything, says Lord Lansdowne, "if it had
been a trouble to him to write." But there needs no ghost from

[68] Prefatory poem to Lord Burghley, who concurs in Spenser's opinion.
"All this for a song": Burghley's response to the pension of 50£ granted
the poet by Queen Elizabeth (P. Magnus, *Raleigh*, p. 48).

[69] To the readers of his *Farewell to Military Profession*, 1581.

[70] *Ornatus and Artesia*, c.1598.

the grave to tell us this. Wycherley is really, what Congreve wished to be, a "Gentleman-Writer" (the description is Rochester's) and not a painful "Trader in Wit." His greater contemporary, who notoriously would meet with Voltaire "on no other footing than as a gentleman," affects to write his first comedy in the spirit of that invidious distinction, not to make a good thing but merely "to amuse myself in a slow recovery from a fit of sickness." Dr. Johnson is perplexed: "There seems to be a strange affectation in authors of appearing to have done everything by chance. The *Old Bachelor* was written for amusement in the languor of convalescence. Yet it is apparently composed with great elaborateness of dialogue and incessant ambition of wit."[71]

But the hint of ambition is anathema to the artist, in his new character of the useless but delightful macaroni. With respect to "this Trifle," his novel *Incognita* (1691), "begun and finished in the idler hours of a fortnight's time," Congreve is hopeful only that as "It has been some Diversion to me to Write it . . . [so] it may prove such to you when you have an hour to throw away in Reading of it."[72] Alexander Pope is not willing to evince even so bashful a hopefulness. Though Pope is ostensibly the most exacting of poets, he does not want it supposed, any more than Congreve, that toil has entered into the framing of his verses or that profit attaches to them. And hence he disvalues poetry as "this idle trade," and his own consummate labors as the tuning of "many an idle song." His more nerveless ambition is to make it appear that poetry and criticism are "only the affair of idle men who write in their closets, and of idle men who read there."[73] The artist is hateful as he pretends to be a serious craftsman. Amateur status redeems him. "I crave the gentleman's pardon," says Britannus in the play by Bernard Shaw. "I

---

[71] Johnson's perplexity is recorded in his *Lives of the Poets* ("Congreve"); Congreve's affectation in his reply to Collier's *Short View*. Of the nature of his sickness Collier declined to inquire, but felt it "must be a very ill one to be worse than the remedy."

[72] Dedication and Preface of 1713.

[73] *Epistle to Dr. Arbuthnot*; Preface to *Works*, 1717.

understood him to say that he was a professional."[74] After all, the repudiating of the usefulness of poetry is not a Romantic affectation, though Lord Byron is faithful to it when, harking back unconsciously to the mock-humble style of James I, he entitles his initial collection of verses *Hours of Idleness* (1807).

Most memorable, in the laconic mode, is the offhanded remark addressed by the players Heminge and Condell in dedicating the First Folio of 1623 to William Herbert and his brother Philip. Their Lordships, observe the compilers of Shakespeare's *oeuvre*, "have beene pleas'd to thinke these trifles some-thing heeretofore." One cannot be certain: the best in that kind are but shadows.

It is, however, not enough to pretend to indifference or to a lack of purposiveness in the matter of plays and poems and romances. The true Alexandrian has got to manifest an aversion to the printing of that matter, as if black letter were the ultimate soilure. Castiglione gives him his cue: "Onely hee may shew . . . [his writings] to a friende whom he may trust." Any wider dissemination than this is forbidden: "least he make other men to laugh at him."[75] Shakespeare is circumspect in allowing his "sugred Sonnets" to circulate only "among his private friends." The lyrics and satires of John Donne, written in the same years, are withheld from publication until their author is dead. The sciolist makes poetry "only to please his own fancy upon emergent occasions." He is unwilling even "to accept the name of a poet, having neither published in print nor kept copies of anything he writ."[76]

As a working poet, Michael Drayton is indignant at such elaborate affectation, by which "Verses are wholly deduced to chambers, and nothing esteemed in this lunatic age but what is kept in cabinets, and must only pass by transcription."[77] Inditing

---

[74] *Caesar and Cleopatra*, III.

[75] *The Courtier*, 1528, Bk. I.

[76] The description is of the Scotch poet and courtier Sir Robert Aytoun, whose Latin verses (*Delitiae Scotorum*, 1638) are introduced by his nephew Sir John Aytoun, addressing the "Courteous Reader."

[77] Preface to *Poly-Olbion*, 1612.

an epistle *Of Poets and Poetry* (1627), he consigns to oblivion those who pretend to court it:

> For such whose poems, be they nere so rare,
> In private chambers, that incloistered are,
> And by transcription daintyly must goe,
> As though the world unworthy were to know
> Their rich composures, let those men that keepe
> These wonderous reliques in their judgement deepe,
> And cry them up so, let such Peeces bee
> Spoke of by those that shall come after me,
> I passe not for them.

The recondite Donne takes the point, and stoops to print his elegiac *Anniversaries* (1611–12). That unwonted lapsing becomes, however, a source of festering regret, compounded of wonder "how I declined to do it" and of a morbid resolve "not [to] pardon myself" for having "descended to print anything in verse," even "though it have excuse, even in our times, by example of men, which one would think should as little have done it, as I."

Among those who should as little have done it is Ben Jonson, who is so pretentious as not only to publish but to accord to his plays the grandiose title of *Works* (1616). His more sophisticated contemporaries know better than Jonson what to make of such puntillos of dreams and shows. And hence the jesting question addressed to their author:

> Pray tell me, Ben, where doth the mystery lurk,
> What others call a play you call a work.[78]

The question is implicit in the angry and embarrassed reaction of John Marston, Jonson's early antagonist in the War of the Theatres, to the unsanctioned appearance of his own collected plays (1633). Marston, as a young man, is not greatly perturbed at being known as a writer for the stage. That is a young man's amiable failing. But to make so great a thing of his idle and

[78] *Wit's Recreations*, 1640.

immature effusions is, he feels, not only in poor taste but disabling of his reputation as the more thoughtful and more provident incumbent, in later years, of an ecclesiastical living in Hampshire.

There are playwrights and poets who, though as sensitive to social stigma as Marston and Donne, still nourish in secret an illicit passion for print. Puttenham is acquainted with "very many notable Gentlemen in the Court that have written commendably, and suppressed it agayne, or els suffred it to be publisht without their owne names to it: as if it were a discredit to a Gentleman to seeme learned and to shew him selfe amorous of any good Art."[79] In fact it is a discredit, and so the gentleman who wishes to indulge his shameful passion has got to resort to a vulgar sleight of hand to insure publication while seeming to deplore it. George Gascoigne, for example, although he is desirous of publishing his *Hundred Sundrie Floures*, must contrive in a series of introductory letters to clear himself of responsibility for the printed book. It is no fault of his: he had been absent from England, soldiering in Holland, when the volume was printing.

That his story is untrue, as his biographer has demonstrated, ought not to be held against him.[80] Untruth is incumbent on an author in these matters. When the poet and translator Robert Tofte wishes to publish a collection of sonnets, he is put to the inventing of an unveracious friend who, "having promised to keepe private the originall," violates that promise and "Without the Authors knowledge." The friend, as he knows his business, takes the blame on himself, acquitting the poet or rather "the Gentleman . . . [who] suspecting what is now prooved too true . . . earnestly intreated me to prevent" publication. Tofte's entreaties come too late. They are still unavailing when, some years later, another work of his, written by the author, "Cursorily, and in hast . . . [without] so much leisure, as to over-

---

[79] *Arte of English Poesie*, I, viii.

[80] In an introductory letter to the revised edn. (*Posies*, 1575), Gascoigne denies receiving money for the book. His soldiering story is controverted by Prouty, pp. 59-60.

looke one leafe, after he had scribbled out the same," falls from his own hands into those of the omnipresent printer who, like the poet's untrustworthy friend, is also deaf to entreaties.[81] Thomas Nashe confesses to the same disillusioning experience. A work he had wished to suppress is "wrested" from him by "the urgent importunitie of a kinde friend."[82] The progress of the work from the friend to the printer, whose maw is always gaping, follows on the author's indulgence.[83]

The reforming zealot, who is elsewhere so insistent on telling the truth, is not above this disingenuous posturing. Though he does not wish "to affront a little structure with too large a Portall," he feels it necessary to apologize for the publication of his "hasty, and artlesse home-spun web (the rapted Corrolarie of my more busie howers)." This web, "warpt and woven in some few sad minuts, softly stolne from the humide bosome of the silent Night," is now to endure "the pittiful payne of Pressing" but—the author is adamant on this point—"without my knowledge or perusall."[84] Even the clergyman is put to the same formulaic recital. Richard Rogers, who makes his handbook on godly behavior "for the use of my selfe and some private friends," had not "any the least cogitation of permitting it to come into Print."[85] The Christian Reader, whom this declaration is intended to reassure, is very much like Britannus in the play.

If importunate friends are not at hand to compel publication, pirate printers are. It is at least ostensibly to anticipate the pirates that Daniel's sonnet sequence is given to the press, and Sidney's *Arcadia* (1593), and the tragedy of *Gorboduc* (1565) which, though "never intended by the authors therof to be published," is purloined by an avaricious printer while the noble collabora-

---

[81] *Laura*, 1597, A3v-4 ("Printer to the Reader"), E7 ("R.B's just excuse"); *Honours Academie*, 1610, "The Printer to the Readers."

[82] Dedication to the *Terrors of the Night*, 1594.

[83] For the discomfiture occasioned by false or overzealous friends, see the lament of George Pettie, preface to *Palace of Pleasure*; and Barnabe Rich, "To the Readers in General" and "The Conclusion," *Farewell to Military Profession*.

[84] "To the Reader," J. H., *This Worlds Folly*, 1615.

[85] *Practice of Christianitie*, 1618, a4.

tors are absent from town and "put . . . forth exceedingly cor-
rupted." Thomas Norton, who expresses himself as "very much
displeased that . . . [the play] so ranne abroad without leave,"
does not ask the Privy Council to suppress it. He gets out another edition.[86] Bacon also declines to take proceedings to block
the publication of an unauthorized edition of his *Essays*. As he
explains with the right *hauteur*, "To labour the staie of them had
bin troublesome." Bacon's alternative is to authorize an edition
himself, "like some that have an Orcharde ill neighbored, that
gather their fruite before it is ripe, to prevent stealing." That
is a plausible argument. Still it must be urged in a negligent
manner, proper to "These fragments of my conceites."[87]

There is a certain *cachet* in professing an art which blenches
at the name of utility. The artist who aspires to genuine elegance is enabled to maintain without spot the lustrous image he
conceives of himself. One may say of him that his work is merely conceitful. That is to concur in his own estimation. One must
not say that it is toilsome or useful or purposive. Castiglione,
who provides a breviary of behavior for this negligent writer-
in-spite-of-himself, exalts to a point of honor the facile nature of
poetic composition. There is no thought in him, as in the coarse-
fibred Ben Jonson, of striking a second heat upon the Muses'
anvil. Jonson, whose high seriousness with respect to his art is
signalized in the literally unprecedented decision to publish his
collected works, is a poet and playwright who desires to get in
step with the utilitarians. Unlike Fulke Greville, he continues to
believe that poems and plays avail. Unlike the new sciolists (who
mock him for his pains), he strives to confer respectability on
poems and plays, which he sees as hammered out with as much
craft and sweat as any other commodity. His vision is, however,
uncongenial to those who believe that a good poet is not made
but born. Castiglione commends, as characteristic of the right
sort of maker, the ability to contrive verses without contrivance.

[86] From motives of "common honestie & shamefastnesse," according to
John Day (to the Reader), who represents this edn. as "new apparelled,
trimmed, and attired," 1570-71. P. Simpson, *Elizabethan Drama*, p. 187.
[87] Dedication to his brother, 1597. Simpson, p. 188.

It is a business (or sport) as little arduous as pulling a daisy and it is about as consequential.

But that is what the detractors have been affirming all along. The poet had been in the habit of imputing at least a modicum of consequence to his poems, in accordance with the old principle that poetry teaches as well as delights. But as he would keep free from dust and soil, he does not deign to say so. It is a part of his splendid affectation that he should be, by nature, too proud to fight. And so he talks of *sprezzatura* and of poetry as a game or *jeu*, and is in the process estranged from his own time and vilified by it. Precipitated out of society, no longer a political creature, he becomes, necessarily and painfully, a kind of revenant who haunts the fringes. His premises are not those of his fellows, nor is their business any business of his. Like the old gentleman in Jonson's comedy, he concedes that poetry is a "vain course of study" and that a reasonable man will wish "to distinguish/The vain from the useful learnings." Only he finds brute reason fatiguing and does not really desire to be weaned from what he agrees is a "Dreaming on nought but idle poetry."[88] His cheap resort is to the pretense that usefulness is vulgar. He does not wince or not visibly at the saying of Marlowe's Tamburlaine but affects to applaud and endorse it: "And 'tis a pretty toy to be a poet."

In professing to agree with the detractors, he intends to aggravate their distemper. Unluckily, his descendants accept that profession of agreement at face value. And so a real identity is forged between those who stigmatize poetry as worthless and those who, assenting, continue to write it. That is what Wilde means, in observing that "Cavaliers and Puritans are interesting for their costumes and not for their convictions." It is one consequence of the attack on poetry that the thoroughgoing Puritan and the absolute or essential Cavalier should come together at last on the subject of art. Prynne, who writes against the theatre, and Davenant, who unhappily writes for it, are not so much antinomies as brothers under the skin.

[88] *Everyman in His Humour*, I, i.

In the seventeenth century, the extremes suppress the middle. The old-fashioned man, who claims utility for verse, is attacked from both sides. At last he is discredited altogether. The average man three centuries later may suppose—a little vaguely and without caring very much one way or another—that poetry is useful. But those who read and write poetry know better. The maker of art, in his capacity as maker, is like the lilies of the field. "No work of art ever puts forward views; views belong to the Philistines and not to artists": Oscar Wilde on trial. Art and ethics are discrete. "Colour-sense is more important . . . than a sense of right and wrong." The ultimate in gaucherie is to ask for the moral of a piece. "There is no such thing as morality or immorality in thought": Wilde digging his grave.[89] To this position, most of the hard-headed sort would adhere. They realize instinctively that art speaks a different discourse from their own.

As they grow more clamorous and forthputting in their endeavor to seize the world by the scruff of the neck and move it forward, the poet grows more studied in his insolence. He is no longer a man of business, like Chaucer, or like Shakespeare a great buyer of land. Business is beneath him. He is understood to be an irresponsible man. He does not baffle understanding. He ceases to reply at all to the arguments advanced against him. Like Milton, he betakes himself to the country for seven years and this to write poetry. Like Donne, he dismisses with undisguised contempt the real world of merchandise and litigation.

> And if unfit for tombes and hearse
> Our legend bee, it will be fit for verse;
> And if no peece of Chronicle wee prove,
> We'll build in sonnets pretty roomes;
> As well a well wrought urne becomes
> The greatest ashes, as halfe-acre tombes.

Proclaiming his indifference to the petty travails of "schoole boyes and sowre prentices . . . Court-huntsmen . . . countrey

[89] Quotations from Frank Harris, *Oscar Wilde*, pp. 67, 144-45; and *Intentions* in Ellmann, *Critic*, p. 406.

ants," the poet, with increasing bravado, flaunts a code and carriage that mirror his own only remotely. But he acknowledges the caricature to be a faithful resemblance just to the degree that it scandalizes the critics, who are instructed that what he does is devoid of point or substance and is nonetheless to be admired.

In time his pose hardens to a formal position. The Romantic poet, obsessed with the memory of "mighty Poets in their misery dead," laments but accepts as a matter of course the lot of the dedicated writer, whose portion is "Solitude, pain of heart, distress, and poverty." That is a condition of the gulf that has opened between him and the rest of society.

> We Poets in our youth begin in gladness;
> But thereof come in the end despondency and madness.[90]

The poet of the Mauve Decade, out of key with his time, unaffected by "the march of events," glories in his isolation.

> Beneath the sagging roof
> The stylist has taken shelter,
> Unpaid, uncelebrated,
> At last from the world's welter
>
> Nature receives him;
> With a placid and uneducated mistress
> He exercises his talents
> And the soil meets his distress.
>
> The haven from sophistications and contentions
> Leaks through its thatch;
> He offers succulent cooking;
> The door has a creaking latch.[91]

From this dubious haven come curious proposals, in which the element of truth is not so important as the impulse to exasperate the early bird who gets the worm. Gwendolen Fairfax announces that "In matters of grave importance, style, not sincerity, is the

[90] Wordsworth, "Resolution and Independence."
[91] *Hugh Selwyn Mauberly*, x.

vital thing"; and Lord Illingworth, with superb effrontery, that "A well-tied tie is the first serious step in life." Whistler retorts pleasantly on a presumptuous critic, "My dear fellow, you must never say that this painting's good or that bad, never!"[92]

But the public, as it is denied the right to make a value judgment, responds not so much with the looked-for exasperation as, less dramatically, with a shrug of the shoulders. Finally there is no public. That is not a matter for regret but satisfaction. "There is nothing worse for our trade than to be in style," says the poet Archibald MacLeish. To Ford Madox Ford it is apparent that Henry James could not "by any possibility be the great writer that he is if he had any public aims."[93] One thinks of Keats, on the writer as chameleon. But sympathy and dispassion are not what Ford has in mind. Writers like Shaw and Dickens, as they enter into the political life of the time, are felt to be diminished. Commitment is the *trahison des clercs*. "In England," Wilde declares, "the arts that have escaped best are the arts in which the public take no interest. Poetry is an instance of what I mean. We have been able to have fine poetry in England because the public do not read it, and consequently do not influence it."[94] What the public reads is bad, by definition. "The imaginative writer today can be widely popular only by writing falsely," says the poet Edwin Muir. Robert Frost, who is intimate in his beginnings with solitude and pain of heart, who writes for years unattended by a public, finds his public at last only as a homilist. And hence he is the butt and the despair of the *cognoscenti*, who recognize the dull-witted man in that he requires utility of verse.

His is no doubt a narrow view, although it is shared by the

[92] Harris, p. 44.

[93] S. G. Putt, *Henry James*, p. 244. This is not to ignore James's own deeply moral view of his craft. One might assemble without difficulty a beadroll of quotations from the Renaissance to the present in which writers —like Milton, Dryden on the epic, even Wycherley—attest to the high seriousness of what they are doing. This is in part the business of Ch. IV. My focus in this chapter is, however, on the "new" or countervailing psychology: the poet as sciolist and private man.

[94] *The Soul of Man Under Socialism.*

greatest number of those who once constituted a public. Characteristically, the modern poet dismisses it. He does not invoke the Social Muse. "Is it just," he asks rhetorically, "to demand of us also to bear arms?" He wants it understood that poetry does not apply. He advises his reader, "if the sages ask thee why . . ./ This charm is wasted," to reply to the sages in rhyme:

> Tell them, dear, that if eyes were made for seeing,
> Then Beauty is its own excuse for being.[95]

In so fatuous a manner is the ancient bond between teaching and delighting torn and canceled, and by the poets themselves. "And give up verse, my boy," says Mr. Nixon in *Mauberly*. "There's nothing in it."

Professor X, the typical exponent of literary study in our own time, inclines without conscious acknowledgement to this slighting view. Delight in good books is a "delicate growth," and so he conserves it. He presents literature to his students under glass. False alternatives are of the essence of his critical discourse. The poem is not a message or vector but an artifact which confesses its own excuse for being. Poetry should not mean but be. In its remoteness from sociology or politics, it resembles an airborne spore, or it is like a machine that runs to no purpose.

Budé, the early French humanist, comes to mind. Assuming, perhaps too easily, that all learning is for use, he ventures an analogy: "a machine that no one can operate is no longer a machine but a heap of scrap-metal."[96] That is a half truth and faithful to the activist bias of sixteenth-century humanism. The latterday humanist errs on the other side. Literature, he supposes, has no *parti pris*, is antithetic in its origins and in its working out to the didactic impulse of the preacher. Activism and literary study are immiscible: the gravamen of remarks by a recent president of the Modern Language Association.[97]

In dealing with ticklish business, the declarative statement is

[95] Emerson, "The Rhodora."

[96] Paolo Rossi, *Francis Bacon*, trans. S. Rabinovitch, p. 63.

[97] Henry Nash Smith in his Presidential Address to the MLA, 1969 (reprinted *PMLA*, LXXXV, 417-22).

rarely very helpful. Best, then, not to supersede it with another but to hedge it round with qualifiers and modification. For example: "in all my plays," says Bernard Shaw, "my economic studies have played as important a part as a knowledge of anatomy does in the works of Michael Angelo."[98] But Shaw, emphasizing the context from which art arises and the uses to which (the artist thinks) it is put, is a musty polemicist whose art we depreciate as it smells of drains and blue books? On the contrary: all art is involvement (James not less than Shaw), whence its enduring appeal. *Universalia post rem.* "The writer is neither Vestal nor Ariel: he is in it up to his neck . . . marked, compromised," says Sartre, "right into his most distant retreat." The compromise or stigma is the quickening agent, precisely.

Say this too emphatically and one is down on the floor with the Marxist utilitarians. What the poet sees, his final reservation in first and last things, is outside their ken and is therefore discounted: "New skies the exile finds, but the same heart."[99] Applause goes by fiat to the more hopeful writer who traces every problem to "its roots and its concrete origins in society."[100] This writer, as he answers "the call of the age," will give militant support to the society which is understood to have formed him. He will play an honored role, not as he exists "in splendid isolation from [the] contending classes," but as he makes "common cause with that class and its allies, which in a given age represent the forward thrust of history. In our age, in the assault against monopoly power, this means common cause with the working class and its allies."[101]

The poet Osip Mandelstam, though venturing now and then in the tepid waters of Socialist Realism, mostly holds himself aloof. In consequence he is destroyed, made a sacrifice, says his widow in a deeply suggestive phrase, to "the inverted 'human-

[98] Letter to Archibald Henderson, 30 June 1904; quoted in Henderson's biography, p. xvii.

[99] Horace, *Epistles,* Bk. I, no. xi, I. 27: "*Coelum, non animum mutant.*"

[100] Lukács, "Franz Kafka or Thomas Mann?" in *Realism in Our Time,* p. 79.

[101] *New Program of the Communist Party U.S.A.,* p. 72.

ism' of the times."[102] What is the sanction for the thoroughgoing materialism of Lukács or a behavioral calculist like B. F. Skinner or the All-Russian Writers' Union? It is Platonic, and descends to the present from the humanism of the Renaissance.

Skinner is no fool and not an easy mark to shoot at. But he is, in this context, exactly the right mark. His eye is exclusively on "defective social environments," his root position assumes that "it is the contingencies which must be changed if . . . [man's] behavior is to be changed." With this position, contrast the line from Shakespeare: "There is no time so miserable but a man may be true." The intelligent and skeptical behaviorist will answer: "What man?" and "how 'true'?" or, if Auguste Comte: "*Comment!*" But the refinement is niggling. The position Shakespeare's character expresses is also a root position and not invalidated yet by the attempt at formulating a "technology of behavior."[103]

Formalist criticism, the far more considerable achievement of the earlier Ivor Richards and his numerous disciples, also comes down to us by way of Plato and the Renaissance. It is first of all a retort on the fathers of humanism as it is or seems to be "free-standing" criticism, like the sentences of R. P. Blackmur or stanzas in a late poem by Yeats. The social or heuristic function of art does not much preoccupy the critic of this persuasion nor the social matrix in which art is nourished. But the negation or lack of interest is also an affirmative act, and only less consciously ideological than the tiresome affirmations of the ideologue, who enjoins on the writer the perception that all "tensions increase . . . with the evolution of capitalism" and the task of seeking the nodal points—materialistic, by definition —of these tensions.[104]

Art is assayed in a vacuum: the "scientific" error; or anatomized as a repertory of semiotic signs—"pseudo statements"— which designate without denoting. Words are endowed with an

[102] *Hope Against Hope*, p. 134.

[103] Skinner is quoted in *Beyond Freedom and Dignity*, pp. 15, 147; Shakespeare in *Timon of Athens*, IV, iii, 161-62.

[104] Lukács, p. 75.

independent existence: the "Hegelian" error, which confuses real power with its verbal precipitates. The verbal icon or configuration of morphemes is felt as sufficient to itself. The artificer who fashions this icon first appears in history three centuries ago. In his modern incarnation, he is paying off an old score. Like the Alexandrian poet of the Renaissance, he is taking his revenge on his moral and ethical tormentors. Now to look in detail at these tormentors: to resume the Renaissance past, to possess it, that we may lay it to rest once and for all.

IV   The Regiment of Virtue

THE Renaissance poet who justifies art for its own sake is not essaying a defense of pure poetry. He is incapable even of the concept. Really he is retorting on his critics, *Je m'en fiche*, as to men of another order and so beneath his notice. The argument advanced in the *Republic* that pure poetry is worthless bites deep, and especially in an age which, like the Renaissance, makes a fetish of worth. That is why, though there are ironists who bid goodbye to use, the more conventional response of the Elizabethan poet is to insist on what is useful and commit himself to it with as much assiduity as his critics. Should the critics interrogate him on matters of profit and loss, he does not reply that they have failed to put the proper questions. In deference to the master spirit commodity, he endeavors to satisfy the audit required of him, item by impertinent item.

He is supported in his endeavor by recollecting that the putting down of the monasteries did not entail the putting down of religion but only of the old feckless religion, now reformed and reconstituted. By analogy, and to forestall the interdicting of poetry, he undertakes its reformation: he proclaims for the future a strict adhesion of poetry to use. He recalls that even Plato was willing at least to hypothesize a scruple of use in the arts. Plato denies to the poet the more useful ability to contrive, like Philip of Macedon, a new order of battle or, like Archimedes, a new reading of natural phenomena, or to write, like Plutarch, a treatise of morals, or, like Themistocles, to make a great city. But the Platonic critique is not absolutely demeaning. If it insists that the poet is not so useful as these others, it grants that he may be useful in less spectacular ways. For example, it is open to him to fashion pious hymns and sing in praise of famous men. The concession is of course an injunction.

116

The totalitarians of the twentieth century, in their estimation of art, are the legatees of Plato and his Renaissance disciples. Sometimes the connection is obscured, as when the modern preceptor commits the artist to "realistic" representation. "Truthful writing," he is apt to argue, is "the highest criterion" and "is always dependent upon the relationship of the writer to reality, but"—now the mask is slipped a little—"the truth itself must be seen in the dialectical sense."[1] Not until artists have grasped this dialectic or higher truth—according to Mao Tse-tung, who might be commending the Platonic doctrine of Forms—"can they give our literature and art a rich content and a correct orientation."[2] The orientation is insistently positive. "Only that which contributes to the abolition of human exploitation, poverty, and degradation, and to the building and strengthening of a system of social life from which such inhuman phenomena will be absent is moral and ethical."[3] The quotation is from a Soviet "catechism" on philosophy. I do not see that it differs in essentials from Plato, pronouncing on art, or from the more thoroughgoing Platonizers of the seventeenth century: Richard Baxter, Henry Burton, Collier on Congreve, a little later his satellite Arthur Bedford, Thomas Rymer, who introduces to our language the phrase "poetical justice."

The prescription comes down to this: applied or didactic poetry is "the only poetry which ought to be admitted" (*The Republic*). Its function is to falsify but in the direction of good hope, to present a world "where life is not 'an ague of nature,' but a proud and glorious and heart-breaking and splendid achievement."[4] The denizens of this better world, which resembles the "brazen" world only linguistically,

> walk home remembering the straining red flags,
> And with the pennons of song still fluttering through their blood
> They speak of the World State
> With its towns like brain centres and its pulsing arteries.
> (Stephen Spender, "The Funeral")

[1] Fast, *Literature and Reality*, p. 8. [2] *Art and Literature*, p. 14.
[3] *Handbook of Philosophy*, p. 42 ("Ethics").
[4] Fast, p. 16.

Like the universe of discourse asserted by the symbolic logician, this wished-for place is defined as the "world of reality." If the poet is going to present it, he must submit to a drastic correction.[5]

The kind of correction envisaged is as new as the *Family Shakespeare* or the strictures of Mao Tse-tung and as old as Plato's *Laws*. The impulse behind it is benevolent. To make our citizens pious and heroic, to nourish in the young "ideas . . . which we should wish them to have when they are grown up" —sound ideas: our ideas—we must institute, says Plato, a censorship of fiction. We must require the poet—Socrates, with his wonted courtesy, would have us beg him—"not simply to revile, but rather to commend the world below," and to obliterate those obnoxious passages in which death appears fearsome. "These things we shall forbid . . . [the poets] to utter, and command them to sing and say the opposite." What does not inspirit to temperance or continence or magnanimity or submission to authority must be cut away. Let no poet say complacently, like the player in *Hamlet*, "I hope we have reformed that indifferently with us, sir," lest he be bruised by the law. "O, reform it altogether": that is the Socratic injunction. Heroes in future are to be, wholecloth, heroes. "Another and nobler strain must be composed and sung by us." For example:

> Comrade, are you cold enough,
> Lean enough, bold enough—
> Hush!—to march with us tonight
> Through the mist and through the blight?
> Dare you breathe the afterdamp?
> Can your cunning foot the swamp
> Where you tread on the dead?—
>   Red! Red!
>   (Sylvia Townsend Warner, "Red Front")

The burden of this new song is the empery of poetic justice: "Swear"—whatever the distressful fact—"that our dead fought

[5] *Republic*, x, 607.

118

not in vain."[6] The countervailing of the fact attests to the currency of Plato's roseate esthetic. St. Jerome in the Christian era defines and enjoins it: *Quod malum est, muta. Quod bonum est, prode.* Here is a contemporary definition and enjoining. "Should we praise our enemies . . . ?" Mao Tse-tung inquires, and answers: "Certainly not," even though they may manifest "some strong points" and their creative work a "measure of artistic quality." Nice discrimination is not the business of "our cultural army," which is to undertake without reservation "the task of exposing the atrocities and treacheries of our enemies, of making it clear that their defeat is inevitable, and of encouraging . . . [our friends] to rally with one heart and spirit." *Quod malum est, muta.* But what of our friends? "We must praise their accomplishments," understanding that "it is certainly reprehensible" to dwell on the dark side. Then follows the rhetorical question: "Why should we not extol the people, the creators of history and civilization?" *Quod bonum est, prode.* "Political standards come first and artistic standards come second."[7]

To the new Platonists of the Renaissance this insight, or precept rather, is the first commandment in legislating the business of art. Their suffrage is given to art only as it sponsors beneficent fictions. "The good end happily, and the bad unhappily," says Miss Prism. "That is what Fiction means." Thomas Drant, the translator of Horace and a great promoter of poetry, quotes Jerome with approval. "Suppress what is evil; advance what is good."[8] Treating of plays and dancing, the Oxford physician John Case is "sure that neither of them . . . not overreaching their honest and lawfull circumstances, can want either good groundes to authorize them, or sufficient patronage to maintaine them," provided that they are resolute in "keeping themselves under saile."[9]

[6] For poetic justice, see *Republic*, III, 386-87, 390-92. The quotation is from John Cornford, the poet of the International Brigade, "Full Moon at Tierz: Before the Storming of Huesca."

[7] *Art and Literature*, pp. 9, 38, 42-43.

[8] *Medicinable Morall*, 1566.

[9] *The Praise of Musicke*, 1586, pp. 80-81.

The proviso is crucial. Plato, as he is unwilling to hear that "wicked men are often happy, and the good miserable," is adamant on this question of keeping under sail. He identifies overreaching with the imitation of vicious and hence inutile truths, which "engender laxity of morals among the young." He proposes accordingly to grant a hearing only to "the pure imitator of virtue," and to him only as he undertakes to "follow those models which we prescribed at first." If he is a poet, this amenable man will strive as he is wise to "express the image of the good" and nothing but the good, "on pain . . . of expulsion from our State." If he is a musician—inferentially another idler who daffs the world aside and bids it pass—he will be deaf to all strains and intimations but those which reflect a courageous and harmonious life.[10]

The proviso is accepted by those poets who covet something more than the dilapidated haven from sophistications and contentions that is reserved to the unregenerate among them. The unregenerate "make . . . Poetry an occupation," says Campano.[11] It is a withering sentence, and is meant in reproof of men who should be laboring to a useful purpose but who instead are penning "quires fraught with amorous discourses." But Campano himself is a poet, and also the editor of the fables of Aesop; and Nashe (who quotes him with approval) is a poet and playwright, and elsewhere a partisan of poetry. He does not want it supposed that all poetry is under ban. What is under ban is that sterile kind of poetry which renders "youth effeminate, and men more given to wantonnesse, pleasures, passion, & vayne opinions, then to virtue."[12] Aesop is not bad absolutely, but only

---

[10] *Republic*, III, 392, 397-98, 400-1.

[11] *Smith*, I, 327.

[12] Cf. E. Hoby's trans. of Matthieu Coignet's *Politique Discourses* (*Instruction aux Princes*, 1584): "This which I have spoken of must not be understood of Poesies wherein much trueth and instruction is contained, nor of pictures which represent the actes of holye and vertuous personnages, nor of fables taken out of hystories, whereof, there may growe some edifying." Smith, I, 343.

Aesop the fabulist. Properly construed, he also is a fruitful preceptor.

On the poetry of Campano, I am mute; but the poetry of Nashe is not serious stuff in the energetic or Renaissance sense of the word. It is not meant to be. Here, Nashe is not toiling *ad astra*. The zeal of the Renaissance for purposiveness and the naked truth is complemented, whenever the pragmatic spirit is off duty, by an abandonment to whatever savors least of ulteriority and use.

Most of the time the pragmatic spirit is formidably alert, and not least in the poets themselves. When, therefore, Plato or some sixteenth-century epigone demands of Homer or Shakespeare what state was ever governed the better for his help, those poets and critics who are really *au courant* do not reply that the question is irrelevant. They attempt to adduce states that were better governed, in consequence of poems that point to the right course of conduct and galvanize men to essay it. They argue from utility, to snare the enemy with his own springe. Their argument is shrewdly conceived. But the enemy is permitted, with a courtesy that is ultimately decisive, to choose the ground on which the issue is joined. There is no help for that. The Renaissance poet, to the degree that he responds to the new and governing imperatives, will speak to them more than shrewdly: he will speak to them as a matter of course. He will endeavor, from conviction as well as for tactical reasons, to justify himself in terms of use.

> Who sayes that fictions onely and false hair
> Become a verse? Is there in truth no beautie?

The question is George Herbert's.[13] He does not ask if there is no truth in beauty. His commitment as a poet is to bring men to God. That is a useful enterprise, and beside it the sterile cultivation of the beautiful pales to insignificance. But qualification is in order. Herbert's greatness depends substantially on

---

[13] *The Temple*, 1633: "Jordan."

121

a powerful countercurrent one feels in his religious poems, the
pull of the world he is abjuring.

> I know the wayes of Pleasure, the sweet strains,
> The lullings and the relishes of it;
> The propositions of hot bloud and brains;
> What mirth and musick mean; what love and wit
> Have done these twentie hundred yeares. ("The Pearl")

This complicating tendency, to regret the old man as one is putting him off, to confess in one's heart that if everything is gained
as one embraces the new dispensation, something is lost, makes
the story I am telling here more than the conventional account
of mistaken purpose and unwholesome zeal.

> But when I view abroad both Regiments;
> The worlds, and thine:
> Thine clad with simplenesse, and sad events;
> The other fine,
> Full of glorie and gay weeds,
> Brave language, braver deeds:
> That which was dust before, doth quickly rise,
> And prick mine eyes.
>
> ("Frailtie")

Herbert, as he does not cleave easily to the regiment of virtue,
is a poignant figure. So is John Donne, whose agitated career is
more a seamless whole than most criticism is willing to acknowledge. Though Donne's poetry is notable for "many curious
and daintie conceits," he ought, says a disapproving contemporary, as "a man of . . . years and place to give over versifie-
ing."[14] He does not give over: evidently he cannot. "Dost thou
love Beauty?" he inquires in the *Anniversaries*; and adds with
a truculence that belies his asserted contempt: "Poore cousened
cousenor." Donne's progress "from the mistress of my youth,
Poetry, to the wife of mine age, Divinity,"[15] is a serried progress
and always throwing back to his concupiscent past. In age, as

[14] John Chamberlain, *Letters*, ed. N. McClure, ii, 613.
[15] He is describing his books, in a letter to Buckingham.

Jonson tells us, he "repenteth highlie, and seeketh to destroy all his poems,"[16] but that is not as discrimination quickens. Hysteria bears a part in this abortive and melodramatic attempt to repudiate what is of the essence of the man, and an agonized consciousness—as in St. Jerome—that one loves too much "Brave language, braver deeds." The praise bestowed on the collected poems by Donne's friend and biographer Walton is moving and no doubt genuine, but in respect of the progress it delineates it is more artistic than true.

> This was for youth, Strength, Mirth, and wit that Time
> Most count their golden Age; but 'twas not thine.
> Thine was thy later yeares, so much refind
> From youths Drosse, Mirthe, & wit; as thy pure mind
> Thought (like the Angels) nothing but the Praise
> Of thy Creator, in those last, best Dayes.
> > Witnes this Booke, (Thy Embleme) which begins
> > With Love; but endes, with Sighes, & Teares for sins.[17]

Who can say to what extent the histrionic refusal of Abraham Cowley to work his former vein (drossy poems of love) any longer is dictated by fashion, an opportunistic coming to terms, to what extent by exacerbated guilt? The Old Testament epic to which the poet turns reads like a manifesto and a summoning to battle.[18] I suppose Cowley, announcing that divinity is the poet's proper subject, to be seeking absolution. Of the nature of this "occulted guilt" one does not presume to speak, except to note that he is hardly singular in his conviction of it.[19] "It is

[16] Jonson's conversations with Drummond.

[17] Charles Cotton, "To . . . Walton, on his Life of Dr. Donne, etc.," offers the same reading: Donne, "Led on by vanities, error, and youth,/ Was long e're he did find the way of truth."

[18] *Davideis*, 1656. Cowley, rejecting amorous poems like *The Mistress*, 1647, will "unbind the charms that in slight Fables lie,/And teach that Truth is truest Poesie." For the prevalence of Biblical themes in Renaissance writers, including Cowley, see D. C. Allen, *Legend of Noah*, Ch. VIII, esp. pp. 176-81.

[19] Cf. the Latin poet George Buchanan, to whom there is no use any longer in singing "how the golden hair of Phyllis is dearer to me than

time," he writes urgently, to recover poetry "out of the Tyrants hands, and to restore it to the Kingdom of God. . . . It is time to Baptize it in Jordan, for it will never become clean by bathing in the Water of Damascus." Commodity is to seek in "the obsolete thread-bare tales of Thebes and Troy." Noah's story is more than Deucalion's because it is more fruitful. "The actions of Sampson" afford "plentiful matter" in contrast to the labors of Hercules. The progress of the Chosen People toward the promised Land, whitened on their way by the manna from Heaven, yields "incomparably more Poetical variety, then the voyages of Ulysses and Aeneas." Point, counterpoint:

> From the debris of hollow celestial kingdoms . . .
> We must emerge . . .
> to work for the worldstate, to feel its flags as
> personal pulses in the blood—

Randall Swingler, another hag-ridden poet but of the 1930s.

Only the idiom varies. The Christian poet who misses in the fabulous content of poetry "such copious hints to flourish and expatiate on, as the true Miracles of Christ, or of his Prophets and Apostles" is adumbrating faithfully his militant successor three centuries later.[20] The fables which tell of the transformations of the gods are weighed and found wanting. Increasingly (now and then), more gravid and useful stuff fills up their room.

> Doth poetry
> Wear Venus' livery, only serve her turn?
> Why are not sonnets made of thee, and lays
> Upon thine altar burnt?[21]

---

the locks of Bacchus." Buchanan, the author of love lyrics in his youth, does not "know whether to be chagrined or ashamed at the trifling character of the greater part of . . . [those] poems." H. Hudson, *Epigram*, p. 114.

[20] Cowley, Preface to *Works*, 1688, C3v; Preface of 1656; D. Bush, *Mythology*, p. 247. Swingler's poem is called "Toward the City."

[21] Herbert, "To his mother," pub. 1670.

Henry Vaughan, who had worn the livery of Venus as a writer of "idle books" and "vicious verse," suppresses his "greatest follies" and urges "a wise exchange of vain and vicious subjects for divine themes and celestial praise."[22] Suppression, conversion are notable in English poetry from the early sixteenth century forward. So far, perhaps, mere "literary history": inert information. But the information, as we are able to construe it, preserves for us the record of an epidemic disease coeval with the birth of modern times. What it signifies is a burgeoning hatred of *terra damnata*, in the beginning a hatred of the self.

The secularism of the Renaissance, its glorification of the body are complemented by a fierce abjuring of the world and the body and an appeal from phenomena to "forms more real than living man." Concurrent with the rise of a secular drama, Biblical drama enjoys a renascence. As wild music burdens every bough, more edifying music swells with it. Surrey versifies Ecclesiastes, and Spenser the Book of Revelations, and Donne the Lamentations of Jeremiah. Drummond of Hawthornden repudiates profane poetry, vows allegiance to a new kind of writing:

> Thy nail my pen shall be, thy blood mine ink,
> Thy winding sheet my paper, study grave.[23]

Thomas Carew, "that excellent wit, the King's carver," and famous as the author of the lovely lyric, "Ask me no more where Jove bestows," finds that loveliness no longer answers. Carew

[22] Preface to *Silex Scintillans*, 1655. Compare "Mount of Olives" (Vaughan applying to God): "Yet if poets mind thee well,/ They shall find thou art their hill/ And fountain too." Joseph Beaumont, in preface to his epic poem *Psyche* (1648), undertakes to demonstrate "that a Divine Theam is as capable and happy a Subject of Poetical Ornament, as any Pagan or Humane Device whatsoever."

[23] *Poems*, 1616. For Surrey as pious versifier and redactor, see C. Huttar, "Poems by Surrey," *English Miscellany*, pp. 9-18. Spenser contemns secular verse ("lewd layes") in "An Hymne of Heavenly Love." The sonneteer Thomas Rogers prefers religious to profane poetry (*Celestial Elegies*, 1597). The moralist and epigrammatist John Davies of Hereford writes in both kinds (*Wit's Pilgrimage*, ?1605).

resolves to leave off, as to no purpose, the frivolous question of his youth:

> no more
> In molds of clay will I my God adore;
> But tear those idols from my heart, and write
> What his blest sp'rit, not fond Love, shall indite.
> Then I no more shall court the verdant bay,
> But the dry leafless trunk on Golgotha;
> And rather strive to gain from thence one thorn,
> Then all the flourishing wreaths by laureates worn.[24]

The clichés of the militant poet are indifferent to time. Carew is better than his modern avatar who, supposing that angry declamation will do the business ("let the wrong cry out as raw as wounds"), determines to "weave no tracery of pen-ornament," to "paint ... no draped despairs, no saddening clouds."[25] But the self-loathing that underlies the rejection of one's craft is constant. So is the governing idea.

This idea is that mere poetry, in the context of the breaking of nations, is not so persuasive as "tools, dynamos, bridges, towers,/ Your tractors and your travelling-cranes."[26] In the Renaissance, the poet who is alive to his context puts away the laurel wreath and aspires to a more substantial crown. Wyatt and Surrey abandon "this foolish rhyme"—the belittling phrase is Wyatt's—to indite the psalms in English meter.[27] Theodore Beza, who writes love poems as a young man, tears those idols from his heart and turns a psalmist in age. Baïf's renderings constitute the important business of the last years of his life. Sir John Davies ruminates in quatrains on the immortality of

---

[24] "To my worthy friend, Master George Sandys On his translation of the Psalms." Carew's resolution is prompted by Sandys' *Paraphrase upon the Psalms of David*, 1636. Against the lines quoted here, see Carew's most famous and influential poem, "A Rapture," probably written "In wisdoms nonage, and unriper yeares" (Dunlap edn., p. 236).

[25] Stephen Spender, "The Pylons."

[26] C. D. Lewis, *The Magnetic Mountain*.

[27] H. A. Mason, "Wyatt and the Psalms," *TLS*, Feb. 27, 1953, p. 144; March 6, 1953, p. 160.

the soul.[28] Bacon, in illness and fallen from power, translates the psalms into verse (1625). For Sidney, they are the ultimate refuge. To the great poem which concludes his *Certain Sonnets*, "Leave me, O Love, which reachest but to dust," he appends the somber line, in token of his rejection of secular verse for religious, *Splendidis longum valedico nugis*:

> Foul vanities, to you
> Forever more, adieu.[29]

It is not a new thing, this expropriating to godly use by a sprinkling of holy water on the works of the ungodly. St. Jerome in the fourth century, allegorizing a celebrated passage in Scripture, instructs his co-religionists who, like himself, are unable to resist the charm of profane learning, to purge it of error and make it their own. "I have in mind particularly," he says, "the figure of the captive woman described as naked, shaven, and with closely pared nails; the Israelitish bride with hair close-cropped."[30] To marry this woman (to make poetry acceptable), it is necessary to "cut her hair and her nails" (Deuteronomy

---

[28] *Nosce Teipsum*, 1599. Davies also versifies psalms. Michael Drayton, like Davies, turns from secular poetry to Biblical paraphrases, and renders in 14ers the last chapter of the *Lamentations of Jeremiah* (*Harmonie of the Church*, 1591). Henry Lok is more consistent: even his sonnets delineate the Christian passions (1593). Joshua Sylvester leaves off amorous sonnets to translate the pieties of Du Bartas (1592). Henry Constable's sonnet cycle *Diana* (1592) is complemented by his (unpublished) *Spirituall Sonnettes to the Honour of God and Hys Sayntes*. Barnabe Barnes as sonneteer imitates *Astrophil and Stella* (in *Parthenophil and Parthenophe*, 1593), but writes his *Divine Century of Spiritual Sonnets* (1595) "in honor of the greatest Disposer of all great honors."

[29] Trans. John Lilliat. Other renderings: the ecclesiastic Edmund Prys turns the Psalms into Welsh poetry (1621). His fellow-countryman William Myddleton undertakes a metrical version (1603), as does the musician and poet William Hunnis (1578), and the composer Thomas Tallis, who sets Archbishop Parker's versifications of 8 psalms (printed John Day, *c.*1567). Bp. Bale's *Index* attributes to Nicholas Grimald "Metrical Songs ... [from] the Old Testament," "Commentaries on the Psalms," "A Restoration of the [penitential] Psalms of Thomas Wyatt."

[30] In Boccaccio, *Genealogy*, xiv, xviii; Osgood edn., p. 85.

21:12). In the tenth century, Hroswith, the nun of Ganders-heim, is charmed by the comedies of Terence. Admiring the style and yet finding the matter repellent, she reconstitutes the plays she imitates, to the end that the inconsequential and bawdy Roman playwright is made to write consequentially of the martyrdom of virgins.[31] Terence, put to his purgation, becomes, like the Biblical favorites of the Venerable Bede, *apud nos.*

But it is in the Renaissance that the compulsion to put everything to use achieves its most notable victories in penetrating the modes and forms of secular literature. Whining poetry is invested, as by Donne in the Holy Sonnets. Popular lyrics are redacted and made to serve a higher good, as by the Catholic priest and poet Robert Southwell; and the Protestant priest and martyrologist Thomas Brice, who is able to express profit even from a notorious poetical miscellany.[32] Epic poetry is metamorphosed: matter of divinity, as it is more solid stuff, displaces the Matter of Britain: Milton sings not of Arthur but of "one greater Man."

The burden of the new music is the same and for the same reasons: music, like poetry, is intent on establishing its claim to be useful. And so it is felt as no longer sufficient to set, as to versify, the matter of a lover and his lass. From now on, the composer will exercise uncommon vigilance in scrutinizing the nature of the Word. Protestant and Catholic are, in this respect, equally vigilant. The dedication to consequence of the men of the Counter-Reformation and their close kinship to the men of Reform are manifest in the deliberations of the Council of Trent (1545-63), which adjures Catholic bishops to "exclude music in which anything impious or lascivious finds a part."[33]

[31] "I have used those plays of his . . . in which the foul lewdness of lascivious women was pictured, to make known to the world the noble chastity of holy virgins." Hroswith, quoted in E. Duckett, *Death and Life in the Tenth Century*, p. 259.

[32] *The Court of Venus Moralized*, which survives only as an entry in S.R. 1566-67.

[33] 1563. The result is the supersession of most Church music—most of it being "tainted" by derivation from popular and often ribald melodies.

Palestrina reacts by burning his madrigals. Victoria is more circumspect. He writes no madrigals nor, through a long life, any secular music whatsoever, and this in homage to the new principle that "The art of song should be entirely devoted to the end and aim for which it was originally intended, namely, to the praise and honor of God." The unconscious equations this composer performs are interesting. Music means, ideally, "divine things," what is whitened or purged. Music that excites us to "earthly delights" brings to mind words like "evil" and "depraved." The music of Victoria is delightful but only incidentally. The intention is to drive out *terra damnata*, to assist men in "raising themselves" to God.[34] Comeliness is not in question, or not first of all, but use.

When, a little later, William Byrd desires to promote the popularity of his songs, it is their utility that he insists on and not their indubitable beauty, in offering "Reasons . . . to persuade everyone to learn to sing." Singing is most to be commended in that it is an "exercise . . . good to preserve the health of man." It "doth strengthen all the parts of the breast, and doth open the pipes . . . [and] is a singular good remedy for a stuttering and stammering in the speech."[35] Byrd is a recusant; but his Protestant contemporaries are at one with him here in this justifying of music on utilitarian grounds. The strategy of Reform in assimilating beauty to use is enunciated, for example, by the Protestant composer John Hall, in redacting secular

Exceptions are notable: Crashaw, for instance, who professes "dumb eloquence" and yet in his "music" ignores almost completely the austere prescriptions of the Council of Trent. See M. Praz, *Flaming Heart*, esp. pp. 204-63. I see the prescriptions as the rule.

[34] The masses, motets, and hymns of the ecclesiastical year, composed during Victoria's residence in Rome, represent the first collection to be issued in compliance with the decree of the Council of Trent forbidding secular song tunes in the religious service. Quotations are from Victoria's dedication of his hymns to Pope Gregory XIII.

[35] *Psalms, Sonnets, and Songs of Sadness and Piety*, 1588. What Byrd is ostensibly looking for is "the best means to procure a perfect pronunciation, and to make a good orator."

verse,[36] and by the madrigalist Thomas Whythorne, in moralizing his own compositions. Hitherto he had rejoiced in embracing his lady's grace. Now it is the grace of Heaven he embraces. Whythorne, as he is concerned to vindicate the credentials of music, tells of the eminent persons who have loved it. He begins with Nero.[37] The Puritan, who cannot be too much maligned, insists that what he sings makes for "the encrease of vertue: and abolishing of other vaine and trifling Ballades."[38] That is the point of a woodcut adorning the Book of Job in Cranmer's Bible and depicting a reproachful saint before whom musicians are playing.[39] The saint wears a long face as his ears are assailed by immoment or secular music: it gives pleasure. He is, however, not yet so draconian as, like the Clown in *Othello*, to bid the musicians put up their pipes and go vanish in air. Instead, he commands them to sing a new song.[40] Action, an ethical result, is the end he enjoins.

The enjoining is successful. Scripture is melodized.[41] Sternhold and Hopkins, rendering the psalms, see them as "meete to be used of all sortes of people, laying apart al ungodly songes and Ballades which tend only to the nourishing of vice and corrupting of youth." The extent to which they are used is sig-

[36] *The Court of Virtue*, 1565: "As prayer in sadness is mete: In myrthe so godly songes to synge, For Christen men lo this is fytte," B6v.

[37] *Autobiography*, c.1576, ed. J. Osborne. Whythorne's book is "made in the commendation of vertue and the reprehending of vices." Though Whythorne is a pioneer in the new secular music and publishes the first set of English madrigals (1571), he is increasingly preoccupied, as Master of Music to Archbishop Parker, with versifying and setting the Psalms.

[38] John Day, *Medius of the whole psalms in four parts, which may be sung to all musical instruments*, 1563.

[39] 1539; Ch. xv.

[40] So *Court of Virtue*, p. 16: "make a boke of songes holy,/ Godly and wyse, blamyng foly . . ./ Compyled of gods holy lawes:/ Of vertue and wyse olde sayd sawes." The end is kinetic: these "Ryght sober songes" will "to goodnes men procure,/ Whyle here their lyfe dayes doe indure."

[41] The Ten Commandments are set to music, and the Song of Simeon and Lord's Prayer, as by William Whittington, dean of Durham, and Thomas Sternhold.

nalized by their enormous popularity.[42] In England as in France, what is sacred or useful is employed to drive out what is idle or profane. The *Goostly Psalmes and Spirituall Songes* of Miles Coverdale, the translator of the Bible, are not composed to gratify the author's taste for music, but "to give our youth of England some occasion to change their foul and corrupt ballettes into swete songs and spiritual hymns of God's honour."[43] The better to drive out idle matter, the tunes to which it is sung are appropriated by the saints (who in this are less finicking than their Catholic contemporaries), and made to bear a more sobering burden. When, says John Donne, paganism went down before Christianity, "Temples were not demolish'd, though prophane:/ Here Peter Joves, there Paul hath Dian's Fane." The monastery established by St. Jerome at Monte Cassino, as it replaces a temple of Apollo, converts a "stronghold of Hell and Death" to a "stronghold of life."[44]

This same process of redintegrating occurs in the Renaissance. The reformers of poetry and music, like their prototypes in an

[42] Ninety metrical versions of the Psalms, set to music, were printed 1500-1600; before the middle of the seventeenth century, editions of Sternhold and Hopkins, as listed *STC*, exceed three times that number. See H. E. Rollins, *Old English Ballads*, p. xxv. The popularity of these renderings is general. An early edition of Sternhold claims the approval of the King, whose "tender and godly zeal doth more delight in the holy songs of verity than in any feigned rimes of vanity" (1551). At the Court of François I, the royal family sings psalms versified by Marot.

[43] Printed before 1539. Coverdale in a preface to the Christian reader proclaims his distaste for "the corrupt ballads of this vain world." The Scotch poet John Wedderburn, whose renderings perhaps furnish the basis for Coverdale's, changes his ballads "out of prophaine sangis in godly sangis for avoyding of sin and harlatry," that the young may "put away baudry and uncleine sangs." So Archbishop Parker in setting to music the *Whole Psalter* (1567): "Depart ye songes: lascivious,/ from lute, from harpe depart:/ Geve place to Psalmes: most vertuous,/ and solace there your harte." Sternhold's Psalms are valued by William Baldwin (dedicating his *Canticles or Ballads of Solomon*, 1549, to King Edward) as they will "drive out of office the baudy ballades of lecherous love that commonly are indited and song of idle courtyers in princes and noblemen's houses."

[44] E. K. Rand, *Founders of the Middle Ages*, p. 239.

131

earlier time, do not level what is potentially a useful habitation. It is their subtler and more economical achievement to "have hallowed a Pagan Muse,/ And denizend a stranger."[45] As early as the fourteenth century, zealous ecclesiastics had composed Latin songs and set them to the tune of popular lyrics, that the minor clergy "should not pollute their throats and mouths, sanctified to God, with disgraceful and secular minstrel songs."[46] In the sixteenth century, the purposive instinct is sturdier. Its invasion of the province of secular melody is therefore more sustained and less prey to a distracting sense of humor. It sees nothing incongruous in the redacting of profane songs like "O Sweete Olyver altered to the scriptures,"[47] or in the fitting of psalms to popular tunes, as at the court of François I. The polemical poet in the twentieth century makes capital of nursery rhymes:

> The banker turns his gold about
> But that won't sell the rye.
> Starve and grow cold without,
> And ask the reason why
> The guns are in the garden
> And battle's in the sky. (Julian Bell, "Nonsense")

Four hundred years earlier, this same poet is detected bidding the Lord stand up to revenge his quarrel, to the air of a dance of Poitou.[48] He does not doubt that the Elizabethan ballad, "Fain would I have a pretty thing to give unto my lady," is made more comely because more useful by the transmuting of the pretty thing to a godly.[49]

[45] Donne, "Letter to the Countess of Bedford."

[46] Bishop Richard de Cedrede: "*ne guttura eorum et ora deo sanctificate polluantur cantilenis teatralibus turpibus et secularibus.*"

[47] 1586; Bush, *Mythology*, p. 60. Cf. the fortunes of the popular ballad of 1564-65: "I myghte have leved meryly morralysed."

[48] J. Holland, *Psalmists of Britain*. For the prevalence of moralizing secular verse, see "Six Ballads, with Burdens, from MS. No. CLXVIII in C.C.C.C.," ed. J. Goodwin, Percy Soc., XIII; "The Bannatyne MS. Written in Tyme of Pest 1568," ed. W. T. Ritchie; Chambers and Sidgwick, *Early English Lyrics*; Dyce MS. 45 in Victoria and Albert Museum.

[49] *Stationers' Register*, 1566.

The pretty thing has its own specious charm. There is, however, nothing to prevent the accommodating of it to a loftier
purpose, as in this enfeebled redacting of a famous song by the
courtly maker Sir Thomas Wyatt:

> Blame not my lute, nor blame not me,
> Although it sound against your sinne:
> But rather seeke for to be free,
> From suche abuse as ye are in.
> Although we warne you to repent:
> Whiche grant you God omnipotent.
> Blame not my lute.[50]

To the men of Reform, there is a certain piquancy in the hoist-
ing of their antagonist with his own petar.

There is also benevolence in their correcting of him. The
homilist who plagiarizes secular lyrics is endeavoring to make
the profit more.[51] His practical objection is to the high proportion of incidental chaff as against the scantling of preceptorial
matter. "My fruits are only flowers," says the poet Andrew
Marvell; and that is the trouble. It is a foolish man "that
wouldst debase with them/ And mortal glory, heaven's dia-
dem!"[52] That man is, however, not foolish but sagacious and
truly pious who writes poetry that stiffens the sinews and inspirits its auditors to a useful end. The case of the medieval
troubadour is instructive, in that it suggests and helps to define
the pragmatic impulse that contributes to the interdicting of
poetry. The troubadour, as he celebrates ephemeral things, is
attacked as a limb of the Devil. Toleration is inconceivable for
"the songs of poets and the sentences and verses of comedians,

---

[50] *Court of Virtue*, M2v.

[51] Like the sixteenth century Scot who teases the stuff of secular poetry
until it approximates to his *Gude and Godlie Ballatis*, the homilist—in this
case John Hall—is not prodigal of beauty but thrifty of truth. Under color
of an amorous song he "toucheth, replieth, and rebuketh, the wycked state
and enormities of most people, in these present miserable dayes" (*Virtue*, L8).

[52] "The Coronet."

133

which render the mind effeminate."[53] But toleration is forth-
coming as he sings of saints and Christian heroes, or edifies his
hearers with the *chansons de geste*, or—*mutatis mutandis*—as
he records of his Stakhonovite hero "How this one excelled all
others in making driving belts."[54] The matter is everything.

The first formal treatise in defense of poetry is written early
in the 1570s by the Oxford don John Rainolds.[55] But this is the
same Rainolds who is a tutor to Stephen Gosson at Corpus
Christi and who, late in the 1590s, calls for the overthrow of
stage plays. There is in this apparent disjunction no basic
change of heart, as with the man who is a socialist at twenty
and who . . . etcetera. It is only that the utility Rainolds finds
and praises in his poets is not obvious to him on stage. And
hence he condemns the stage. The same criterion is appealed to,
in the defense as in the attack. One of the questions that agitates the poet and colonist William Vaughan is "Whether Stage
Playes ought to be suffred in a Commonwealth?"[56] Vaughan is
a practical man, and subsequently a pioneer in the wilderness
of Newfoundland. His treatise on contemporary manners mirrors his practical temper. It is "a work very necessary for all
such as would know how to governe themselves, their houses,
or their country." The theatre, in his view, does not offer much
instruction on how to govern, and not even on how to govern
houses. He also denounces the theatre. But a subsequent chapter of his book is entitled "Of Poetry, and of the excellency
thereof," and in this chapter he proposes that poets, of whom
Moses and Deborah are the most ancient, brought civility to the
heathen and were the first to "observe the secrete operations of
nature."[57] The definition of excellence and hence of toleration
is use.

The definition is seductive in that one is tempted not to dismiss it as false but to mollify those who frame it by discovering
use and exaggerating its extent in all that they stigmatize as use-

---

[53] M. Valency, *In Praise of Love*, p. 94.
[54] Stephen Spender, "The Funeral."
[55] *Oratio in Laudem Artis Poeticae.*
[56] *Golden Grove*, 1600, Bk. i, Ch. 51.   [57] III, 42.

134

less. John Northbrooke defines the terms in which the controversy will be conducted. Though in general an opponent of the drama, Northbrooke is willing to tolerate academic plays. He does not want to "be thought too Stoical and precise."[58] But he appends this proviso, that plays be mounted solely for instruction. The burden of proof is on the friends of the drama. Dr. John Case, in the following decade, is equally magnanimous and canny. Popular plays are scurrilous. But academic plays may possibly constitute good "training."[59] Owen Feltham sniffs out that scurrile taint in the drama; and yet discerns also a scattering, not of mighty lines but "weighty."[60] Gosson, in his benighted youth a playwright, establishes the right measure of avoirdupois. Some players and some plays, he concedes, are tolerable in that they aim at beneficial instruction.

Increasingly, it is the aim to which the partisans of the theatre refer and defer. In his treatise on perspective scenery, the German designer Joseph Furtenbach, as he believes that "The putting on of plays is a most delightful and useful training for growing youth," concludes that "there is a special need for the private citizens of cities to build such beneficial theatres to save the growing youth from sins, shames, and vices."[61] Burghley, the Lord Treasurer, provides an amusing gloss. Sitting in a Star Chamber dispute, in which students of the Inns of Court are shown to have been fleeced by the Elizabethan version of the confidence man, Burghley lays the blame to parental neglect and proposes as a remedy that playwrights make a comedy on the case, in which actual names are to figure. His reasoning is that fathers will thereby be prompted "to look over their sons and certify their manner of living."[62]

[58] *Treatise wherein . . . Vaine plaies . . . are reprooved*, p. 28.

[59] *Speculum Moralium*, 1585, Lib. IV, p. 307.

[60] *Resolves*, c.1628, no. xx.

[61] *The Noble Mirror of Art*, 1663.

[62] E. K. Chambers, *Elizabethan Stage*, I, 267-68. On the usefulness of art, see Gosson, *Schoole of Abuse*, C6v-7v, adducing his early play of "Catilins conspiracies." Because Gosson is embarrassed by his youthful affiliation to the stage, he has got to deprecate the play ("a Pig of myne owne Sowe") even as he commends it.

The new principle of preponderant utility, as gross as may be, is established. It is the legacy to poetry and the theatre of the pragmatic spirit of the age. Those who dislike it can hardly say so explicitly, and not even to themselves. If they wish to save what it condemns, they must couch their bill for reprieve in the same language as the bill of indictment. If poetry is to be defended against the poet-haters who reject it as useless, poetry will have to validate, which means to heighten, its claim to use. And so the poets, in an evil hour, scant delight in favor of doctrine. With the exaggerated zeal of the convert, who is always an ultramontanist, they abase themselves before utility as if they had never known another god.

To regret the sour and uneasy aspersing of delight, as by the militants of the Renaissance and now again in our time, is not to depreciate a total view of art (*prodesse et delectare*) in favor of entertainment alone (*solam voluptatem*) but to find out a mean between these endless jars. Characteristically, the "modern" writer is radical, flees the mean. Already William Caxton, late in the fifteenth century, announces his discovery of Sir Thomas Malory the homilist. Caxton is more than a printer; he is a cultural go-between who introduces and interprets the Middle Ages to the Renaissance. As he is earnest in this function, he is necessarily selective. His selections are determined by the quotient of use. Malory is applauded only incidentally as a writer of romance. In his melancholy tale of Lancelot and Guinevere, "all is written for our doctrine, and for to beware that we fall not to vice ne sin, but to exercise and follow virtue."[63] A hundred years later, Sir John Harington, commending Ariosto, makes clear how the morbid insistence on utility has grown on the age. Harington, who translates a bawdy canto of his author to amuse the bawdy ladies at court, is required by Queen Elizabeth to translate the whole of the *Orlando Furioso* as a penance (1591). That is the old story, and whether it is true or false does not signify. It establishes the popular and very accurate opinion of at least one aspect of the poem. Whatever may be said of Mal-

---

[63] Caxton's preface to *Morte D'Arthur*, 1484.

ory, it may not be said of Ariosto that everything is written for our doctrine. And so Harington has got to equivocate. He concedes that in certain places Ariosto "is too lascivious." But then observing "that sweet meate will have sowre sawce" (there speaks the Italianate Englishman), he counsels a reading of those places "as my author meant them, to breed detestation and not delectation." This is sufficiently barefaced. Worse is to come. Having got hold of the cathartic principle that lust exhibited drives out lust, he can now take his oath that "in all Ariosto . . . there is not a word of ribaldry or obscenousness."[64]

What is true of poetry is true also of Tudor fiction. No matter how scandalous or lubricious the work, it seeks almost invariably to defend itself on moral grounds. Robert Greene, commencing his melodramatic novel *Pandosto* (1588), which Shakespeare in the *Winter's Tale* tugs into shape, sees it as a history which proves and so instructs. As it happens, *Pandosto*, which is only vulgar reportage, does neither. That does not lessen but rather enhances the need to establish its value. Thomas Lodge, concluding the story of *Rosalynde* (1590), in which Shakespeare finds the plot of *As You Like It*, is alert to that need, and so he admonishes his readers to "see in *Euphues' Golden Legacy*"—the subtitle of his book and an index of the way he wants it to be taken—"that such as neglect their fathers' precepts incur much prejudice; that division in nature, as it is a blemish in nurture, so 'tis a breach in good fortunes; that virtue is not measured by birth but by action," and so it goes on. The conclusion is cheap because inapposite, and also incumbent on both the author and reader, each of whom knows better than to plead entertainment as a reason for spending the time.

George Gascoigne knows better. Introducing a lascivious novel, he likens himself to Chaucer, not the ribald but the moral Chaucer, whose earnest intention was to put us on "the right pathway to perfect felicitie."[65] Even the ephemeral jest books are compelled to defend themselves by laying claim to utility.

[64] Smith, II, 214-15.
[65] *The Adventures of Master F. J.*, 1573; Prouty, *Gascoigne*, p. 83.

137

In the first of the *Merie Tales* (1567) foisted on the poet John Skelton, the hero, who is thirsting for liquor, summons the tapster and gets no response. At last he calls out "Fire!" and rouses the house, and in that manner his thirst is quenched: "Where is the fire?" the innkeeper asks him, and Skelton answers, "Here," pointing with his finger to his mouth. That, one would suppose, is a (moderately) funny story. But no, or not entirely. The conclusion follows: "Wherefore it is good for every man to help his own self in time of need."

What does one say of this perverted commitment to ulteriority? It is ludicrous, certainly unattractive: and it is distressingly familiar. The Renaissance on this side is like a concave mirror in which we perceive a comic version of ourselves: we, who find out meaning in everything, in boils and obesity and slips of the tongue, and delight especially in explicating what looks to be plain. Freud our father, who makes ubiquity of motive an article of faith, is for our time the archetypal "Protestant" or purposive man. It will not do to take dreams at face value, devoid of purpose, fulfilling no need. "All this is obviously not innocent." There are "no guileless dreams."[66] But just suppose the possibility of "pure, noncoping expression"! *Hoc autem non licet modernis.* "All action is motivated and expresses some purpose. All learning involves reward. Often behavior may seem unmotivated but only because we have failed to identify concretely the need or goal involved. Laziness, like all other human activities, serves an end beyond itself."[67]

Reading an exotic novella looks like self-indulgence: simple sloth. But the appearance belies the fact. We have failed, says William Painter, an entertaining storyteller of the 1560s, to identify concretely the need or goal involved. What Painter is offering in his *Palace of Pleasure* is pretty clearly titillation: "pleasant discourses, merry talk, sporting practices, deceitful de-

[66] *The Interpretation of Dreams*, pp. 90, 86.

[67] Conflating, partly adapting, the American psychologists W. McDougall, O. H. Mowrer, D. Krech and R. Crutchfield, R. L. Munroe—as summoned in Abraham Maslow, *Motivation and Personality*, pp. 294, 293n.

vises, and nipping taunts to exhilarate your Honor's mind." But this Renaissance author is sufficiently "modern" to see that he has got to have it both ways. And so he insists that what looks to be unalloyed pleasure is really a tractate "which may render good examples, the best to be followed and the worst to be avoided."[68] False morality is fullblown in the precious and sensational stories Sir Geoffrey Fenton derives from the French and Italian.[69] That the ladies who comprise his public may not confound his homiletic purpose with mere salacity, the author adjures them to "Behold here . . . a familiar profe." I suppose that the ladies detected the proof, or thought to detect it. It is their excuse for reading fiction, that—as Fenton explains in dedicating his book to the young bluestocking, Lady Mary Sidney— it "yields us freely presidents for all cases that may happen, both for imitation of the good, detesting the wicked, avoiding a present mischief, and preventing any evil afore it fall." The justification of these stories and their reason for being is that they "swarm with examples of all kinds of virtues . . . [and] teach by way of precepts" and confer inestimable "benefit . . . [by] presenting afore our eyes a true calendar of things." What *calendar* means in this crooked protestation is what it means to the farmer who looks into his almanac (or *Kalendar and Compost of Shepherds*) to ascertain the best time for planting.

To the humanist, poetry is such a calendar except that its business is not with husbandry but moral precepts. It is conventional to identify humanism with a cultivating of the classics. Partly, the identification is sponsored by those who seek to discriminate between the scientific and the literary man. Historically, however, there is on this head no particular reason for dissociating literature and science, or for identifying humanism with a love of books. The fathers of humanism, like Cheke and Vives and Erasmus, are students of the classics as also of patristic writings and the Scriptures. That is, however, not primarily because they love literature but because they are devoted to whatever makes

---

[68] Quotations from dedication to enlarged edn. of 1575.
[69] *Certain Tragical Discourses*, 1567.

times.''[75] Shakespeare's purpose, like Hilliard's or like Sidney's, is to limn exact pictures but by and large for the limning of them. In what he is doing, not much heed is paid to ulteriority or use: "that any man . . . might . . . see how to" accomplish this or that.

Utility is, however, Sidney's main card, and especially in his competition with the utilitarians. "Poetry," he assures them, "hath been the first light-giver to ignorance." To substantiate this claim, he cites "the Oracles of Delphos and Sibillas prophecies [as being] . . . wholy delivered in verses.''[76] The cloudy symbol is not more memorable or decorous but more educative than bald statement: in Sidney's words, "the fayned image of Poesie . . . hath the more force in teaching." For that reason, Sidney writes his *Arcadia* rather than an *Instruction aux Princes*. Of course he is animated, and not least as a romancer, by the same didactic impulse as an Elyot or a Matthieu Coignet: "in all these creatures of his making," says Greville very fairly, "his interest and scope was to turn the barren philosophic precepts into pregnant images of life,"[77] not because he honors life for itself but because he wishes to make the precepts breed. That is why Ascham prefers "gathering fit examples" to "declarying scholepoynt rules.''[78] Sidney is only more eloquent than Ascham. An estimate of efficiency governs in the preference of either, as it does in Sidney's celebrated dictum that "the Poet is indeed the right Popular Philosopher." And so Plato's fleering and rhetorical question, addressed to "Friend Homer," is answered rhetorically: "What Philosophers counsell can so redily direct a Prince . . . ?''[79]

Sidney takes the answer as given. George Chapman, writing a decade later, is not so reticent and perhaps not so sure, and so he rejoins circumstantially to Plato.[80] Chapman eulogizes Homer as being "so full of government and direction to all

---

[75] *Arte of Limning*, 1624, p. 17 in 1912 edn.

[76] Smith, I, 154.   [77] *Life*, p. 15.   [78] Smith, I, 21.

[79] Smith, I, 166-67.

[80] In a note "To the Understander" in preface to a second installment of his trans. of the *Iliad*, 1598.

estates . . . [that] soldiers shall never spende their idle howres more profitablie then with his studious and industrous perusall." And not only soldiers: "Counsellors have never better oracles then his lines: fathers have no morales so profitable for their children as his counsailes . . . Husbands, wives, lovers, friends, and allies . . . [have] in him mirrors for all their duties."[81] But if Chapman protests too much, Ben Jonson, writing still later, overgoes him. It is a kind of litotes or understatement to say that the poet is useful. He is that man who "can faine a Common-wealth . . . can governe it with Counsels, strengthen it with Lawes, correct it with Judgements, informe it with Religion, and Morals. . . . We doe not require in him meere Elocution; or an excellent faculty in verse; but the exact knowledge of all virtues, and their Contraries; with ability to render the one lov'd, the other hated, by his proper embatteling them."[82]

What dictates the extravagance of the claim is the necessity, in the context of the 1580s and after, to exalt the element of *prodesse* or profit. This exalting makes Sidney's *Apologie* a real *riposte* and not merely a polite epistle to the Goths outside the walls. It speaks the language of its time in that it owes allegiance to the master spirit of the time,

> he that wins of all,
> Of kings, of beggars, old men, young men, maids . . .
> That smooth-faced gentleman, tickling commodity.

The speaker is Philip the Bastard, an ebullient character in Shakespeare's *King John*, who concludes that "Commodity [is] the bias of the world." Our Philip, as Queen Elizabeth called him to distinguish him from Philip of Spain, is not so ebullient. But his allegiance is given to commodity, too:

> for if it be, as I affirme, that no learning is so good as that which teacheth and mooveth to vertue, and that none can both teach and move thereto so much as Poetry, then is the conclusion manifest that Incke and Paper cannot be to a more profitable purpose employed.

[81] Smith, II, 306.   [82] *Timber, or Discoveries.*

Sidney honors poetry, at least formally, because poetry "is used," for example "with the fruite of comfort by some, when, in sorrowfull pangs of their death-bringing sinnes, they find the consolation of the never-leaving goodnesse."[83] Significantly this is the fruit of psalm-singing also, whose vogue is concurrent with the rise of a utilitarian poetics. William Webbe, emphasizing "the great and profitable fruits contained in Poetry, for the instruction of manners and precepts of good life," is only echoing the pragmatism of Sidney. Webbe, as he is less civilized than Sidney, is less wary in applying his examples of instruction. He is therefore unself-consciously amusing, as when he alleges as fruitful the story of Orpheus, "who by the sweete gyft of his heavenly Poetry withdrew men from raungyng uncertainly and wandring brutishly about" (here is the germ of the *topos*: "keeping them off the street corners"); or the exemplary case of Ulysses, from whose "manifold and daungerous adventures" a man may "learne many noble vertues; and also learne to escape and avoyde the subtyll practises and perilous entrappinges of naughty persons." At the heart of Webbe's *Discourse*, more coarsely and hence more clearly urged than in Sidney, is the question of practical value: as Webbe puts it, to inquire into and to resolve "what hath been the use of Poetry."[84]

Increasingly it is the indicated question, and as pertinent to the considering of stage plays as of verse. The playwright concedes the tenuity of his plays. And yet in the past, grave men "from these trifles wonne morallytye, as the Bee suckes honny from weedes." The simile does not inspire much confidence in the theatre. It is apposite, however, as it makes the didactic element supreme. Plays show "the confusion of Vice and the cherishing of Virtue."[85] This is idealism with a vengeance. It tallies exactly with Plato's prescription to hand down the royal lie. "Properly express that which the people appreciate." In this case

---

[83] Smith, I, 184, 158.   [84] Smith, I, 232-35.

[85] George Whetstone, dedicating (i.e., defending) his comedy of *Promos and Cassandra*, 1578. "For by the rewarde of the good the good are encouraged in wel doinge: and with the scowrge of the lewde the lewde are feared from evill attempts." Smith, I, 59.

the Platonic prescriber is Stalin, who is recalling Lenin's "golden words."[86] Proper expression need not be truthful. Paper will put up with whatever is written on it. Only take the point that art is social engineering, and "writers and artists can correctly solve the problem of balance between praise and exposé. Every dark force which endangers the masses must be exposed. This is the fundamental task of . . . writers and artists."[87] The heuristic writer in the Renaissance is mostly not so strident; otherwise, where is the difference? The ghost of the comic actor Dick Tarlton vindicates the stage against its opponents as the stage has solved the problem of balance between praise and censure. If the playwright discovers vice, that is only to expose it: "neither is . . . [vice] in any play discovered, but there followes in the same an example of the punishment."[88] The objective is to eliminate "all that is evil and ugly. . . . Cannot our writers and artists understand it?"[89]

The chief business of Renaissance criticism is to promote this understanding. Tarlton's assurance, that he who "reads in a booke the description of sinne" has only "to looke over the leafe for the reward," informs the defense of the theatre in the next generation. John Owen typifies the defenders. "Owen is a pure Pedantique Schoolmaster sweeping his living from the Posteriors of little children, and hath no thinge good in him." That is Ben Jonson's opinion. As befitting the pure pedant, Owen countenances plays, not as they are pleasing but as they "check our crimes . . . with Jeers."[90] Late in the seventeenth century, the playwright Thomas Shadwell, than whom none is more licentious, is still burning incense to use. That Shadwell amuses is not so important as that he instructs.

[86] *Problems of Leninism*, p. 59.

[87] Mao Tse-tung, *Art and Literature*, p. 40.

[88] Henry Chettle is recapitulating Tarlton's arguments in *Kind-Harts Dreame* [1592], E4. The figure he employs recalls Whetstone: "from one selfe flower the Bee and Spider sucke honny and poyson."

[89] *Art and Literature*, p. 40.

[90] *Epigrams*, trans. from Latin by Thomas Harvey, 1624, no. 207. The same justification is proposed by Ralph Knevet in the Epistle to his pastoral drama, *Rhodon and Iris*, 1631.

> He to correct and to inform did write:
> If Poets aim at nought but to delight,
> Fidlers have to the Bays an equal right.[91]

The poet, averting his eyes from the blind crowder who begot him, has become as jealous of his position as the bourgeois. Like the bourgeois, he is not notably imaginative in his effort to maintain that position. The strategy of either is to mumble scraps and tags from Poor Richard. Shadwell announces, what might otherwise have gone unsuspected, that his design was to reprehend "the Vices and Follies of the Age." This design is equated with "the most proper and most useful way of writing Comedy." The writer understands that the equation is mandatory if he is not to forfeit respectability altogether. That is why he "must take leave to dissent from those who seem to insinuate that the ultimate end of a Poet is to delight, without correction or instruction."[92]

The dissent is made more poignant by Shadwell's uneasiness with regard to his place on the ladder of things. Title to gentility no longer turns on blood or birth; it turns on service. Gentility is earned.

> Worth makes the man, and want of it, the fellow;
> The rest is all but leather or prunella.

More than mere esthetics is at stake in acknowledging that the goal of poetry is pleasure. "Methinks a Poet should never acknowledge this, for it makes him of as little use to Mankind as a Fiddler, or Dancing Master, who delights the fancy onely, without improving the Judgement."[93]

Aroused gentility in Shadwell the dramatist, who is not to be confused with an entertainer in a music hall, sponsors a view of art that tallies in every important respect with that of Jeremy Collier, the chief opponent of the drama in Shadwell's time. When Collier attacks the plays of John Dryden as too little didactic, he announces in Shadwell's vein that "The Exposure of

[91] Shadwell on his comic drama, *The Squire of Alsatia*, 1688.
[92] Preface to *The Humorists*, 1671.　　　　[93] *Ibid.*

Knavery, and making Lewdness ridiculous, is a much better occasion for Laughter" than the cracking of jests for their own sake. It is not open to the dramatist to protest. Neither has he grounds to quarrel with Collier's conclusion, which makes the didactic impulse "the end of Comedy."[94]

The comic dramatist has got to bear arms. Next, tears are compelled to do duty. In the following century, George Lillo, dedicating his famous and lugubrious tragedy, the *London Merchant* (1731), affirms that "the more extensively useful the moral of any tragedy is, the more excellent that piece must be of its kind." On Lillo's reading, which squares with Collier's except that the genre is different, but not with Aristotle's which it apes, "the end of tragedy [is] the exciting of the passions in order to the correcting such of them as are criminal." An imperial tragedy, as by Nicholas Rowe, "may have its weight with an unsteady people." A domestic tragedy like Lillo's is even better: more useful, "by being accommodated to the circumstances of the generality of mankind." Hamlet only catches the conscience of the king. George Barnwell, Lillo's petty protagonist, warns and shames the entire age. The *London Merchant* is "more truly august in proportion to the extent of its influence, and the numbers that are properly affected by it." Samuel Goldwyn appears at the window.

This adducing of useful plays as "the best answers to them who deny the lawfulness of the stage" is not a countering of the utilitarians but an amalgamating with them, and similar in its issue to the amalgamating of the fox and the gingerbread man. Lillo, and the poets and playwrights who stand with him, are basically in fee to the same dubious esthetic as Jeremy Collier. It is only that the one sees pith and the other vapidity. Each, in his choice of criteria, announces himself the practical man. Put money in thy purse. Each is sealed of the tribe of Plato.

But the appeal of the poet and playwright to utility had driven out every other, long before. It is dominant, on Gosson's testimony, in the allegorical *Play of Playes* (1581), an early

---

[94] *Short View of the Immorality, and Profaneness of the English Stage,* 1698, p. 156.

attempt, and characteristically malapropos, to allay the storm rising against the theatre. The playwright, in seeking to establish his case, dwells on the bag of honey (not a sweet but a vendible thing). The flower itself, stamen, pistil, and petal (or plot or structure or style), is only of instrumental importance. The play, to alter the metaphor, is only a stalking horse. One sees where the modern heresy comes from. Style means, to the modern heretic: "Many phrases, abstractions, much book knowledge and show of learning." In his view—he might be paraphrasing John Rainolds or, what is more dispiriting, a defender of the theatre like Thomas Lodge—"It does not matter if . . . [our writers] be unable to write good theses . . . as long as they know how to organize and lead."[95] Since the purpose of writing is didactic and kinetic, writers and artists will speak "the language of the masses," not "the language of the intellectuals."[96] T. S. Eliot and his erudite company are odious as they cling to the latter: their poetry is "titivated with plumes of voodo jargon to overawe the young."[97] Good sense suggests its own delivery: Faust in a bad moment to Wagner. The artist who lets one have it straight from the shoulder "will create excellent works of art which will be enthusiastically welcomed by workers, peasants, soldiers, and the masses of the people."[98] Lenin, as a young man, is criticized by Plekhanov for a slovenly piece of prose. "This is not 'written,' as the French say. This is not a literary work. This does not look like anything."[99] But Lenin has no idea what his editor is telling him.

The Renaissance polemicists, attacking and defending the theatre, prefigure the modern heretic in his myopic fixating on

[95] Georgi Dimitroff, *United Front Against Fascism*, p. 128.

[96] Mao Tse-tung, *Art and Literature*, p. 12.

[97] Robert Hillyer, "Poetry's New Priesthood," *SRL*, xxxii, 7.

[98] *Art and Literature*, p. 48. The primary law in writing or speaking is to "have in mind the rank-and-file worker" (Dimitroff, p. 118). In obedience to this law, says Antonio Gramsci, Marxism "often has recourse to metaphors which are terribly vulgarized" (*Open Marxism*, p. 64). Gramsci, who as a man and writer stands far above the company he keeps, at least deplores the vulgarization.

[99] Quoted in B. D. Wolfe, *Three Who Made a Revolution*, p. 150.

content. Lodge, for instance, in his rejoinder to Gosson, proclaims that he also abhors "those poets that savor of ribaldry." Gosson is right to reprehend "the foolish fantasies of our Poets . . . which they bring forth on stage." He himself wishes "as zealously as the best that all abuse of playinge weare abolished." Having repudiated the savor, Lodge proffers the unadulterate or savorless salt. He discovers that "all the beginning of Poetrye proceeded from the Scripture," and hence is able to absorb art in homiletics and technology. "Ask Josephus, and he wil tel you that Esay, Job, and Salomon voutsafed poetical practises."[100] Even Milton, laboring to exonerate his craft, is not above this tactic of dropping names as an earnest of value. It is the lofty provenance of tragedy to which he refers the reader, who is to be impressed and persuaded because "men in the highest dignity," an emperor, a philosopher, a Father of the Church, have condescended to write in that kind.[101] By their practice, they confirm that

> Poetes were the first raysors of cities, prescribers of good lawes, mayntayners of religion, disturbors of the wicked, advancers of the wel disposed . . . and lastly the very fot-paths to knowledge.[102]

This looks like the medieval reading of poetry. It differs in this, that the element of *delectare* or delighting has by and large been dropped or rationalized as an emollient, and that of *prodesse* inflated to fill up all its room. As the attack on poetry and the stage is pressed harder, the apologist reacts to it by protesting with greater vehemence himself, and so with greater extravagance, the utility of what is despised. Puttenham is at pains to explain "How Poets Were The First Priests, The First Prophets, The First Legislators And Politicians In the World," and what is more "The First Philosophers, The First Astronomers And Historiographers And Oratours And Musitiens."[103] If they were also the first delighters, that is only a comment on the unexpected serendipity of things. Erasmus, translating Euripides into Latin, had little thought of engrossing our pleas-

---

[100] Smith, I, 76, 84, 71.　　[101] Preface to *Samson Agonistes*.
[102] Lodge, quoted in Smith, I, 75.　　[103] I, iii, iv.

ure. His real intent, as Lodge describes it, was "to manifest sinne unto us . . . [and] to confirme us in goodness." That is how one is to understand Chaucer, whose reputation for levity is exploded. If he wrote "in pleasant vein," his covert purpose was the better to "rebuke sin uncontrold; and, though he be lavish in the letter, his sence is serious."[104]

The complementary saying belongs to William Webbe who applauds Chaucer's poetry, as opposed to his sense, because the poetry is efficient in duping his readers. The poet's knack in delighting is honored by the critic and attended to officially only as it permits him to beguile those readers, who "respected nothing but the telling of a merry tale." Delight is a means. The forte of poetry is that it can manage "sweete allurements to vertues and commodious caveates from vices." Poets are tricksters who "will intice any man to enter into" the virtuous way, and who deign to delight, only "to move men to take that goodness in hande, which without delight they would flye as from a stranger": Sidney, demeaning his art. Poets, like good Phisitions," are cunning in framing "their potions that they might be appliable to the quesie stomaks of their werish [sick] patients."[105] Poetry is a spiritual bolus. Plays are "sour pills of reprehension, wrapt up in sweet words."[106] It is Harington's opinion that "in verse is both goodnesse and sweetnesse, Rubarb and Sugercandie, the pleasaunt and the profitable." But the function of the sugar candy is only to palliate the medicine it covers.[107] The classic statement of the view of art as medicine is Sidney's. In the *Apologie*, he affirms that poetry

> doth intende the winning of the mind from wickednesse to vertue: even as the childe is often brought to take most wholsom things by hiding them in such other as have a pleasant tast: which, if one should beginne to tell them the nature of Aloes or Rubarb they shoulde receive, woulde sooner take their Phisicke at their eares then at their mouth.

---

[104] Smith, I, 68-69.   [105] Smith, I, 251-52, 172, 159, 66.
[106] *Pierce Penilesse*, 1592; McKerrow's edn., I, 213.
[107] Smith, II, 207-8, 199.

But the poet forbears to tell them and so beguiles his patients, "ere themselves be aware, as if they tooke a medicine of Cherries."[108]

The effect of this metaphorical hovering about the sick bed is to transform the poet as well as the patient. He is not a poet any longer but a leech. The transformation is his own doing. To demonstrate utility is, he feels, the only way in which he can silence his detractors. And perhaps he is right, given the total context in which he and they reside. But the result of his insistent demonstrations is only and necessarily to play into the hands of the detractors. That is what Nashe is doing, in his defense of the theatre on pedagogical grounds.[109] Like an illustrated primer, it makes vivid the glories of English history or it dramatizes the evil consequence of vicious behavior or assists in reforming the drunk, the gambler, and lecher as it busies and narcotizes the brain. Plays are worth praise in that they keep the waterman sober: Sir Thomas Overbury's great point. The playwright Thomas Heywood lifts his eyes a little higher: plays constitute employment for the gallants who attend them.[110] An idle mind is the Devil's workshop. The question, what to do about that interesting and perennial problem, is still as vexatious to the diplomatist and friend of poets, Sir Thomas Roe, in the reign of King Charles, as it was to Robert Laneham, the chronicler of the Kenilworth entertainment, in the reign of Queen Elizabeth. Each is sufficiently exercised by it to give his approval to plays as impediments to popular mischief.[111] It is "a Principle in Policie, that the deteining of the multitude by publicke spectacles, is a great obstacle to many base and clandestine Actions." The drama is justified as a tub for Leviathan. If all were for the best in this worst of possible worlds, one would wish to see the drama put down: "notwithstanding, if we marke how young

<hr/>

[108] Smith, I, 72-73. [109] *Pierce Penilesse.*

[110] Commendatory verses in preface to Heywood's *Apology for Actors,* 1612.

[111] Roe, Letter to Sir Robert Anstruther, *State Papers,* 1630, p. 370; Laneham, *A Letter* [1575], ed. Alston.

men spend the latter end of the day in gaming, drinking, whoring, it were better to tollerate Playes."[112]

And so with a weary negligence, the new man approves the claim of art to a place in the sun. It is a qualified approval, and essentially it derives from the weighing and balancing of disagreeable alternatives. Art is admitted *faute de mieux*, and on the understanding that it is only a halfway house to be gained and left behind as one progresses to the City of God. Art is an expedient, the temporary resort of "men that are sickly and have weake stomakes or daintie tastes."[113] If their stomachs were not weak or werish, men might accept the real or salubrious thing, undiluted. As it is, and for a while longer, one agrees of necessity to settle for a watered-down version.

The agreement thus concluded, between the utilitarians and their quondam opponents, recognizes the former as rulers of the roast. But it concedes to the latter at least an inferior place at the board. The price exacted for that place is the redefining of art. There are eccentrics who, declining to pay it, cultivate defiantly, in isolation, and to the scandal of their more progressive and energetic contemporaries, "the obscure reveries of the inward gaze." The result of their defiance is also a new esthetic which, in the course of time, repudiates utility altogether.

But the day of the Alexandrian poet is not yet. The immediate and more dramatic result is the attenuating of the appeal to pleasure. In the seventeenth century, the favored appeal is to profit. The Social Muse is regnant, at whose "bidding darkness fled,/ Light shone, and order from disorder sprung." In the emergent light of the new day, plays and poems are discovered to be enabling. Commodity in her pale dominion checks the night. At last the darkness is routed absolutely, and the justifying of art in terms of use is confirmed.

How does one know that art is useful? The visible manifestation of use is material well-being. But if this is the standard

---

[112] Quotation from Joseph Wybarne, *New Age of Old Names*, 1609, p. 53. Wybarne's career is treated briefly by R. Dent, *RQ*, xxii, 360-62.

[113] Harington's *Apologie of Poetrie*; Smith, ii, 198.

against which all of man's work is to be measured, then a practical philosophy, as elaborated perhaps by Samuel Smiles, will conduct to it more effectively than art. The defense of poetry as inspiriting or homeopathic is, in its premises, patently unsound. These premises inform the thinking (the reflexive responding) of most persons in the twentieth century who do not read much themselves or look at pictures or listen to music, but who are persuaded nonetheless of the value of music and painting and poetry. Why are they persuaded? I think because, like the vulgar partisans of art in the sixteenth and seventeenth centuries, they cannot comprehend or come to terms with simple existence without ulteriority, what the medieval mystic calls *Istigkeit*: Is-ness, things sufficient in themselves. There is always God's work to be done, as anguished prophets like Carlyle do not weary of telling us: but that is not why the "machine that no one can operate" (Budé), that runs to no particular purpose is hateful. This machine, like the perfect and self-sufficient artifact, calls in question the ardors of the purposive man. It strikes at the heart of his being, and so he denies it.

In the Renaissance as again in the present, the cult of beauty begets derision, sometimes violent rejection. Love is a burnt match skating in a urinal (Hart Crane), or the subject of a rude contre-blason by John Donne. Romantic pretension is discovered to be threadbare: one hoots at the old pretension. Nothing mysterious here: the present is always fighting free of the immediate past: Sidney against Petrarch, Ezra Pound against the Georgians, Blake bidding us cast off the rotten rags and filthy garments of memory: "all that is not Inspiration" (*Milton*).

But take it further. In times of upheaval like the Renaissance, when old accounts are scrutinized and cast anew, beauty is repudiated, not in preface to the reinvesting of what is outworn, but for itself. Amenities are suspect as they are amenities. That is what the poet-haters are telling us. Devotion to the real world is evidently the intolerable sin to the man whose "calcined life is dissolving at its base." This man is Botticelli, who gives his paintings to the fire, or Antonin Artaud, who sees wherever he

153

turns iniquity, demanding destruction: no doubt a matter "for the theater to be preoccupied with," but "even more a matter for machine guns."[114]

This hysterical anathematizing is catholic, dowers with impartial hatred all the visible universe, "an unweeded garden" possessed by things rank and gross in nature. It is, first and crucially, the hatred of *"carrion man."* To the modern Misanthropos, harking back to his forbears in fifteenth-century Florence, in England a hundred years later, what is human stinks "of decadence and pus."[115] The exalting of work, like the savage denouncing of the abbey-lout—indolent man—takes its rise from this generalized hatred. It is not enough for plays and poems to exist: they must be felt as kinetic, winning to a positive goal. In the Middle Ages, art is frequently attacked, more often reconstituted, as it fails to make for the goal which is salvation. The allegory of the two covenants or cities (Galatians 4:21-31) tells powerfully on the minds of medieval persons, directs them from this earthly bondage to the heavenly Jerusalem which is free. But in the meantime and to the despair of the eschatologist, the earth is still exerting its claims. Pope John XXII prohibits in the polyphonic settings of the Mass the interplay of secular melodies. They smell of mortality. There the sour spirit is working. But the prohibition does not avail.

In the Renaissance it avails. The man who is satisfied to loaf and invite his soul is felt abruptly to be less than a man, and even by himself. The physical matrix—*terra damnata*—is execrated. Nothing is important for its own sake. This, the root proposition of rationalist thought, as of the venomous criticism of the *mysomousoi*, finds unconscious expression in the abstracting and causalist tendencies of classical science. The series x, y, z is preferable to a cluster of lower-case substantives, is in any event and implacably an on-going series. One never pauses, unless by design. Being, becoming, living on the razor's edge of contingency are not so good as striving and coping, addressing oneself to

[114] *The Theater and Its Double*, pp. 115, 42.
[115] Artaud, p. 42.

particular ends. To this energetic mode of behaving, art is made to adhere. The adhering of course is a fraud, and debilitating to the artist as also to the man who justifies art in terms of his own puddled spirit. Better to abandon the defense of art altogether than to pretend, with the Renaissance homilist and his successors in the modern period, that art is instrumental.

Here, from the eighteenth century, is an acute exploding of the old-fashioned defense. The "secondary kind of beauty" which Jonathan Edwards, in his character of Platonist or Cartesian, identifies with art, has no essential tie to true virtue. The "harmony of good music, or the beauty of a square or equilateral triangle"—or the cunning representations of the playwright and poet—are approved by the mind, not as they relish of salvation but as they "relish of uniformity and proportion." The Renaissance panegyrist who justifies plays and poems as their function is tutorial, or who equates the love of art with love of goodness is answered by reason and experience. Were approbation of this sort of beauty to spring from a virtuous temper, "delight in the beauty of squares, and cubes, and regular polygons," in the perfection of architecture, in the gorgeous traceries of art, "would increase in proportion to men's virtue; and would be raised to a great height in some eminently virtuous or holy men; but would be almost wholly lost in some others that are very vicious and lewd." That is how it would be; but that is not how it is, says Edwards, and he is right.[116]

This is not to deny value to art but to exorcise the old confusion, in which the seventeenth century has involved us, of art and homiletics. The ghost of the Renaissance past will be laid only as one agrees to transfer the argument to another plane, to accept that art is knowledge but not kinetic knowledge, rather that "unique and formed intelligence of the world of which man alone is capable" (Allen Tate),[117] to incline to Newman's view—as expressed, for instance, in his *Idea of a University*—that art

[116] *The Nature of True Virtue*, 1755, end of Ch. III; pp. 40-41 in 1960 edn.
[117] "The Present Function of Criticism," in *Collected Essays*, p. 15.

155

does not conduct to salvation, that it is not to be valued as the means to an end, and that its justification must therefore lie elsewhere, in a realm not tangential to use. Back, then, to the dark age before the new learning came up and with it the exalting of utility: for it is in that occluded time, so much reviled and misconstrued by modern man, that one gathers, interstitially, the right function and definition of art.

 **V** The Woman of Jericho

To the Middle Ages all things are grist, and poetry not less than philosophy. The definition of use implicit in this period is, however, eccentric and perhaps a contradiction in terms. Amplitude is of its essence, as in the advice the philosopher proffers to the voyagers whose ship has moored offshore. "If," says Epictetus, "you go on land to get fresh water, you may pick up as an extra on your way a small mussel or a little fish." Medieval man is engrossed and so detained by the prospect of this peripheral yield. Renaissance man, who rivets his attention to the important business in hand, is not so easily distracted. Erasmus, on the Gospels, epitomizes his singlemindedness: "Those who like" are bid sardonically to "follow the disputations of the schools" in which, no doubt, all manner of trivial yield is potential. The affinity of Erasmus to the new and more self-regarding age is detected, as he weighs the greater profit with the less. And hence the injunction: "let him who desires rather to be instructed in piety than in the art of disputation first and above all apply himself to the fountainhead."[1]

Application to the fountainhead requires the intermitting of little business. In the opinion of the preacher William Ames, "no word or sentence of men, ought to be mingled with the word of God . . . least by these meanes we does in some sort worship men instead of God."[2] The scientist or humanist who finds this prescription congenial substitutes for God the concept of Truth as a capital-letter abstraction. In his impatience with other and minor repositories of the Truth, he skips the "flowers of rhetoric"—like an aristocratic character in Sidney's *Arcadia*—

[1] In preface to his edn. of the New Testament; quoted Hunter, *Lyly*, p. 350.
[2] *Marrow of Sacred Divinity*, 1642, p. 274.

and hearkens instead to more substantial "reasons." He opposes to poetry the fountainhead or marrow of things, which is philosophy.

The contention of poetry and philosophy, and the partial capitulating of the one to the other, is as old as the beginnings of poetry and philosophy. Already Plato, exalting the philosopher above the poet as the chief authority in the state, is aware that there exists "an ancient quarrel between philosophy and poetry."[3] Perhaps the quarrel is inevitable. The philosopher, as Plato presents him, is the lover of wisdom, identified with the achieving of eternal truths. His commitment is to conceptual thought. It is not a commitment much honored by the poet. On this difference between them depends the old canard, which identifies poetry and falsehood. The philosopher Heraclitus dramatizes this identification in the strenuous saying that Homer "should be turned out of the lists and whipped."[4] Of course: for as he plays with the eidolons of mythology, he prevents us from ascertaining what is.

Homer is the first great poet; and Hesiod, the founder of didactic poetry and the regulator of the bodily functions, is the first to attack him. In criticizing the Homeric epic, Hesiod appeals, like the philosophers, to truth, but not to the ephemeral truth which the shifting particulars of the poet affirm and which is lost as they merge and dissolve. In Hesiod, the Platonic objection to poetry of the conventional or sensuous kind is anticipated. "But why all this," he inquires, "about oak or stone?"[5] The trouble with the imagery which the poet elaborates is that "the reality, after which it is modelled, does not belong to it, and it exists ever as the fleeting shadow of some other."[6]

But Hesiod is a poet himself. Apparently he believes that lying is not endemic to poetry. As the Muses advise him: "we know how to speak many false things as though they were true; but we know, when we will, to utter true things."[7] In this dis-

---

[3] *Republic*, Bk. x, 607b.

[4] Quoted G. de Santillana, *Origins of Scientific Thought*, p. 51.

[5] *Theogony*, 1. 35.

[6] *Timaeus*, 52c.   [7] *Theogony*, 11. 26-27.

closure, didacticism is sanctioned and Polonius, the dispenser of precepts, receives his charter.

The didactic point of view prefers to the evanescent and partial truth that diverts the more plenary truth that fructifies and pays. It is by no means to be despised. Whatever triumphs are achieved by the nascent natural philosophy of the Greeks are owing to it, as also the more spectacular triumphs engineered by the scientism of the seventeenth century and later. In the person of Francis Bacon, the scientist and humanist come together. "I was born for the service of mankind," says Bacon, in preface to a work on the *Interpretation of Nature*. "Among all the benefits that could be conferred upon mankind," there is none, he argues, "so great as the discovery of new arts, endowments, and commodities for the bettering of man's life."[8] It agrees with this devotion to the commonweal that the humanist, when he impinges on history, as in the Age of Pericles and in the Renaissance, should be denoted by an unquenchable ardor for truth. To this ardor is associated a singlemindedness that sometimes inclines him to error.

The attack on poetry as mendacious expresses the optimistic spirit of humanism. The Middle Ages, as they are not especially sanguine, are able to patch a truce between poetry and philosophy. The medieval compromise is not above reproach on logical grounds. That is the nature of compromise. But on the whole it is both successful and enduring. It is often assailed, as by Scholastic philosophy or millenarian zeal or, in the twelfth century, by the proponents of the new dialectics. But it does not break down finally until the Renaissance.

The Greek passion for truth, which impels Plato to banish the poets, derives from the same economic sources—one may call them humanitarian—as the passion of the Renaissance, which matches and perhaps overgoes it in intensity. The attempt to save poetry from being consumed in that holy fire is essentially the same in both periods. The didactic strain in poetry is emphasized, to the end that poetic truth may also be recognized as

[8] H. O. Taylor, *Philosophy and Science in the Sixteenth Century*, p. 124.

making for the uses of life. The allegorizing of Homer the polymath commences. In the mythology of the poet, a deeper meaning (whose sense is, generally, a more shallow meaning) is discovered: "hyponoia." The Homeric gods are represented as denoting aspects of man or nature. Juno is air, and Jupiter the heavens, Neptune is the sea, Vulcan is fire. Providence and also the wisdom of God are figured in Pallas Athene. The River of Lethe betokens the body which, as it is born, lapses in forgetfulness. Epimetheus, who rejects the blandishments of Pandora, suggests the wisdom of remaining in an ideal or intelligible world. Anaxagoras, early in the fifth century, finds the rules of dialectic embodied in Penelope's web. Cleanthes of Assos at the end of the third century invents the term "allegory" to describe what he takes and wishes to be happening in Homer. This wishing, which leads to divining, characterizes the critical writing of the Neo-Platonists. Because they are reluctant to extirpate poetry as their master advises, they get round him by hypothesizing purport and use.

The Greek and Jewish scholars of Alexandria, as they employ the same techniques in their reduction of Scripture, attest to the general currency of this impulse to reduction in the centuries just before and after the birth of Christ. Philo, in rationalizing the Bible, emulates the method of the Homeric allegories.[9] Origen (c.185-c.254), who is known as the "worker with brazen bowels" for his refusal to honor the demands of the flesh, commits the mind to abstention not less than the body.[10] Its proper office is to put "away all qualities from its conception, and . . . [to gaze] upon the underlying element alone . . . without any reference to the softness or hardness, or heat or cold, or humidity or aridity of the substance."[11] (The same exalting of abstraction describes the Renaissance. If, Bacon thinks, "a man be acquainted with . . . whiteness or heat in certain subjects only, his knowledge

[9] Attributed to Heraclitus of Pontus; Farrar, *History*, p. 138. For the beginnings of the allegorical method at the end of the pagan era, see Seznec, pp. 85ff.; and R. Hinks, *Myth and Allegory*, pp. 126-28.

[10] H. von Campenhausen, *Fathers of the Greek Church*, p. 50.

[11] *De Principiis*, Bk. IV, Ch. i.

is imperfect. . . . But whoever is acquainted with Forms, embraces the unity of nature.")[12]

Origen is the contemporary of Plotinus, and in more than chronological ways. The reductive process, to which both men are partial, is continued and extended by Porphyry (233-301), the pupil of Plotinus and the chief of the Neo-Platonic redactors. The cave of the nymphs in Odyssey XIII is presented by Porphyry as an emblem of the universe and the soul within. The flight of Odysseus from Circe and Calypso enacts the flight of the soul to its heavenly home. That is what Odysseus means in counselling a departure to our beloved fatherland. He is compelled to take leave, "even though he enjoys the pleasures of the eye and great sensual beauty."[13] Homer, as he is subjected to the hopeful labors of the didactic or allegorical critic, is seen as taking part in the endeavor to achieve the higher truth.

This possibly crooked expedient, which rescues the Greek epic poet from his detractors, serves in the next age to earn approval for the Roman. To the early fifth-century grammarian Macrobius, Virgil is not less an orator than a poet, and in fact is excellent and pregnant in all genres, for example in philosophy and theology, in augury and in law.[14] This putative excellence, for which Homer and Ennius are also remarkable, is documented by numerous quotations, as from the *Aeneid* and the *Georgics* and *Bucolics*.

It is in the *Saturnalia* (Book v), an account of a disputatious and incorporeal banquet, in which the dinner guests do not so much discuss the food before them as questions of etymology and myth, that these impressive claims are put forward. Their occasion is the skepticism of a certain Evangelus, who is moved to criticize what seems to him an eccentric celebrating of Virgil

[12] *De Augmentis Scientiarum*, II, 3.

[13] G. Boas, *Rationalism in Greek Philosophy*, pp. 396, 270, 457.

[14] *"Vergilium non minus oratorem quam poetam."* For fuller discussion of Macrobius and, more generally, the medieval "spoiling of the Egyptians," see P. Courcelle, *Late Latin Writers and Their Greek Sources*; and R. R. Bolgar, *Classical Heritage*, esp. pp. 26-45. Bolgar chronicles the labors of men like Servius, "the djinns of the unpretentious, somewhat battered, grammar-school lamp" (p. 41).

in the guise of a philosopher.[15] But Evangelus is beaten down by his friends. Virgil, as they construe him, is a diviner of the mysteries of heaven and earth: *"noster pontifex maximus,"* and *"tantam scientiam juris auguralis,"* and even *"admiratio de astrologia totaque philosophia."*[16] But I am abridging his titles.

In the next century, another grammarian, who is also a mythologist and a writer of allegory, extends the poet's competence into more recondite studies. This is the North African Fulgentius who, in an exposition of the real (the arcane) contents of the Master, asserts that the *Bucolics* and *Georgics* are literally dangerous for the *"secreta physica"* and *"mysticae . . . rationes"* they enclose. The Virgil of the *Eclogues*, as Fulgentius represents him, is adept not only as prophet and priest and musician but also as physiologist and botanist[17] and mage. In the *Georgics* he manifests, among other skills, those of the medical doctor, the astrologer, and the aruspex.

The poetry itself is not much attended to by these early contrivers of allegory. As they are of the Platonic persuasion, they do not say or relish the words on their tongue but seek to denude or invest them. The poem is a parable. In the opening books of the *Aeneid*, according to Fulgentius, the poet is offering stories for children (*fabulis*). Now childhood is put away: in Book IV, Man, a generic creature, falls in the flames of love. Subsequently, he exercises himself in sport (V) or sets himself to serious study (VI) and to learning the secrets of things. And so on. There is this to be said for Fulgentius that, in him, the medieval propensity for worrying the text is adumbrated but not yet fulfilled. The *Expositio Virgilianae Continentiae* is comprised, in the edition from which I am quoting, in less than thirty folio pages. To such a writer as Remigius of Auxerre, a few centuries later, that would hardly suffice to introduce his subject. But though Fulgentius is not long, he is not without longueurs.

---

[15] *Saturnalia*, I, xxiiii, 4.

[16] 10-18. The talents imputed by the Middle Ages to Virgil the magus and natural philosopher are considered by J. W. Spargo, *Virgil the Necromancer*; and D. Comparetti, *Vergil in the Middle Ages*.

[17] Text reads "notakinen"—presumably a misprint for "botanicen."

The medieval scholiast is concerned with the latencies of things. Ulteriority is central to his achievement. The contempt he sometimes evinces for what is taken to be of the surface anticipates the Renaissance. Fulgentius anticipates Boccaccio. He reads the *Aeneid* as a lexicon or thesaurus. What does it mean really, Fulgentius inquires, to write, "*Arma virumque cano*"; and answers: "*in armis virtutem, in viro sapientiam demonstrantes*"; or, more explicitly: "*Arma, id est virtus . . . Virum, id est sapientia.*" That is a fair illustration of his method.

But this ravishing of the surface in the commentaries of early writers like Macrobius and Fulgentius does not hold for medieval allegory as a kind. Comparison is relevant with the allegories of later writers, like Chaucer or Jean de Meun. In the former case, the surface is referential only. The interest is exclusively in penetrating the veil. By and large, that is true of the first sponsors of Biblical allegoresis. In the devious judgment of Origen, the greatest of the early Greek Fathers, "the Scriptures . . . have a meaning, not such only as is apparent at first sight, but also another, which escapes the notice of most."[18] This is an instance in which farsighted is sandblind. A preoccupation with the other meaning, which entails a severing of cause and effect and a disinclination to study the latter, is the hallmark of the eschatologist. He is a conspicuous figure throughout the whole of the medieval period. I do not think, despite the conventional view of this period, that he is the dominant or characteristic figure. (Against Origen's taste for latency one might pose the denial, by the twelfth-century Scholastic Robert of Melun, "that a person expounding the sense of an author and changing his words is the spokesman of authority.")[19]

The eschatologist achieves domination or aspires to it only, it seems to me, when the millenarian fever reaches a crest: Hitler, appealing to "the last great divine judgment." This fever is virulent in the Ante-Nicene Church, again in the twelfth century (Joachim of Flora, Bernardus Silvestris), and now again in our own time. Compare Christopher Caudwell, predictably a hero

[18] Origen, *The Writings*, trans. F. Crombie, p. 5.
[19] Quoted B. Smalley, *Study of the Bible in the Middle Ages*, p. 229.

and prophet to the New Left of the 1970s: "To-day all bour-geois culture struggles in the throes of its final crisis . . . a new system of social relations is already emerging from the womb of the old. The whole structure of society is shattered. This is a revolution."[20] I associate the millenarian impulse most of all to the greater renascence of the seventeenth century, in the sense that, in that period, the imminent coming of the kingdom, in this case a temporal kingdom, is predicted.[21]

Origen, the self-mutilated ascetic, is the perfect type of the eschatologist. Believing that the Apostles left "the grounds of their statements to be examined into by those who should de-serve the excellent gifts of the Spirit, and who . . . should ob-tain the gifts of language, of wisdom, and of knowledge," he sets himself the task of scrutinizing these ultimate grounds, to come to an understanding of first and last things. Intermediate business does not attract him. He is the allegorist in the simplis-tic or pejorative sense, I should say in the Renaissance sense, and in this he differs absolutely from an allegorist like Dante, who (in Auden's phrase) depicts in concrete detail

> the savage fauna he
> In Malebolge's fissure found,
> And fringe of blessed flora round
> A juster nucleus than Rome.

Origen is indifferent to flora and fauna. What excites him is the supposition that the writers he is expounding "merely stated the fact that things were so, keeping silence as to the manner or origin of their existence; clearly"—and here the Platonic lie is affirmed, that none merit salvation except the Elect—"clearly in

[20] Hitler is quoted in Shirer, p. 78. Quotations from Caudwell conflate *Illusion and Reality*, p. 271, and *Studies in a Dying Culture*, p. 157. Bernardus Silvestris, in his commentary on the *Aeneid*, c.1150, throws back to the simplistic Neo-Platonists of the early centuries. Allegory is merely a "wrapping up [of] the sense beneath a fabulous telling of the truth, whence it is called an envelope." R. Hollander discusses in *Allegory in Dante's "Commedia*," p. 102.

[21] E. Tuveson, *Millennium and Utopia*, documents the rise of millenari-anism in the seventeenth century and the way in which it informs the hopeful "progressivism" of the modern age.

order that the more zealous of their successors, who should be lovers of wisdom, might have a subject of exercise on which to display the fruit of their talents,—those persons, I mean, who should prepare themselves to be fit and worthy receivers of wisdom."[22]

The pernicious suggestion that the literal meaning is notorious and as such without particular interest is already implicit in the commentaries on Scripture of Philo Judaeus, writing early in the first century. To Philo it is apparent that when Moses describes the creating of heaven and earth, he is "speaking symbolically." Things are not what they seem: "he calls the mind heaven. . . . And sensation he calls earth." If he asserts that God completed his labors on the sixth day, "we must understand that he is speaking not of a number of days, but that he takes six as a perfect number." It is a dilating on the number that engrosses the Platonist. He does not find it of sufficient moment to read that on the seventh day God rested from all his works. "Now," he says, "the meaning of this sentence is something of this kind." His impulse is not so much "to describe accurately the character of those laws" he pretends to be explicating as to uncover "any allegorical meaning which may perchance be concealed beneath the plain language."[23]

Rachel, as he conceives her, is not a beautiful woman. Rachel is "beauty of body," and for that reason "is represented as younger than Leah, who is beauty of soul." The exegete thinks it important that Abraham was seventy-five years old when he departed out of Charran. Concerning the number, he promises to "enter into an accurate examination hereafter." He honors this promise at some length. But in the meantime fresh hares distract him: "first of all we will examine what Charran is, and what is meant by the departure from this country to go and live in another." Characteristically, he resolves the surface of Scripture to a volume of Questions and Solutions. "What," he asks, "is the rib which God took from the man?" and answers, "The

[22] Preface to *De Principiis.*

[23] *On the Allegories of the Sacred Laws*; *Works*, trans. Yonge, I, 52-53, 55; *Treatise Concerning the Ten Commandments*; *Works*, III, 136.

letter of this statement is plain enough. . . . But with respect to the mind, man is understood in a symbolical manner, and his one rib is virtue."[24]

In the soul of the Middle Ages, this fascination with the symbol as against the brute fact enters deeply. It does not achieve total mastery there, and its issue is not wholly contemptible. The exegetical method, which discovers a deeper truth in every commonplace phrase, frequently sponsors an interpretation peculiar to the exegete. That is why it evokes, in this quotation from Hugh of St. Victor, an ironical attack on those who hasten over the surface: "When they ought to disclose what is hidden, they obscure even that which is plain."[25] But the method gives warrant for the reading of poetry. At first poetry is allowable as it refers and so instructs. At last it instructs and delights. The ninth-century philosopher and theologian, Remigius of Auxerre, as he holds this warrant, finds it natural and fruitful to write commentaries on Virgil and Horace, and the comedies of Terence, and to quote often from the Roman poets, apparently from memory, as in his treatise on Martianus Capella. It is true that Remigius is constrained to interpret and employ. "*Poetae enim dicunt,*" he observes, in the *Commentary* on Martianus; and adds, divining what the poets had not perhaps understood: "*Re vera autem. . . .*"[26] Nonetheless, he reads the poets.

By the twelfth century the allegorical mode, on which the justification of poetry depends, has attained to full development. But curiously, and just as it makes of poetry a vehicle for anything under the sun, it allows of an abatement in the justifying of poetry. Vociferation dwindles in the high Middle Ages. The early panegyrists exalt the poet to the skies, and especially the Neo-Platonists among them like Macrobius. Partly, that is because they are reacting against the philosophic depreciators of poetry. The apology they formulate is, consequently, excessive and sometimes ridiculous—like the conventional apology of the

[24] *On Sobriety*; *On the Migration of Abraham*; *Works*, II, 82; IV, 296.
[25] Hugh in the *Notulae* is treating of the literal sense of the Octateuch. Smalley, p. 100.
[26] *Glossae in Martianum*, ed. C. Lutz, pp. 11-12, 23, 42.i.

Renaissance. There is in this particular not so much difference between Fulgentius and Thomas Lodge. There is, however, a world of difference between these two, on the one hand, as they belie with false comparisons; and, on the other, the more laconic and more equable reader of poetry in the period of a thousand years that supervenes. John of Salisbury attests often and sometimes in noble language to the medieval love of books. To the author of the *Metalogicon*, poetry is patently useful and delightful. But it is not to be equated with God's grace. It resembles philosophy and even merges with philosophy. But this merging does not turn on a desire to heighten or aggrandize its claims. It arises from the conviction (in which the eupeptic spirit of humanism receives its quietus) that all knowledge, whether poetic or philosophic, is provisional; and that this knowledge hints, but only obliquely, at the ultimate knowledge, which is of God. On this more modest understanding of the utility inherent in poetry, a utility which is real but not final, the medieval approval of poetry depends.

St. Augustine, the contemporary of Macrobius, although he is a great contemner of painted poetry, confers this qualified approval. The criterion Augustine invokes is enlightened self-interest. "We should not avoid music," he asserts, "because of the superstition of the profane if we can find anything in it useful for understanding the Holy Scriptures." On this same principle, "we should not think that we ought not to learn literature because Mercury is said to be its inventor."[27] The appeal to utility makes possible the scrutinizing of Virgil, "this great and most renowned poet," who makes his first appearance in the first chapter of the *City of God* and thereafter is never absent for long.[28] The admitting of the poet to the heavenly city is attributed customarily to the special character he bears. He is not only "famous" but "worthy." That is taken to mean: he is a poet only in the second place. This Virgil is primarily the prophet or seer,

---

[27] *On Christian Doctrine*, II, xvii, 28. For a less favorable opinion of literature, see the condemnation of the *Aeneid* in *Confessions*, Bk. I, xiii.

[28] I, iii. For Augustine's love of Virgil, see Hollander, *Allegory*, p. 11, n.8.

as when he foretells in his *Eclogues* the coming of the Messiah. It is "Christ, of whom the verse speaks," and "with a true reference." The versifier is approved because he is detected as speaking to the present as well as the past. Augustine makes this discovery when, holding out to the Christians the prospect of "an empire, universal, perfect, and eternal," he remembers and adapts to his own more inspiriting purpose the prophecy which Virgil gives to Jupiter, respecting the greatness of Rome (*Aeneid*, I, 278-79). In other words, utility governs in the recollection of the poem.[29]

That is the critical commonplace, and it is partly true. I do not think it reflects a plenary truth. Augustine, who honors the austere God of the Wisdom of Solomon (viii, I) in that he has ordered "all in a delicate decorum," also pays his respects to that more catholic deity whose greater achievement is to make "the world's cause, like a fair poem, more gracious by antithetic figures." Antitheton allows, in this less exclusive world, what a stricter decorum forbids: the raising of one's voice in "a new song sung unto the Lord"; and, at the same time, a continuing response to the older music of Virgil and Persius and Lucan. Augustine, who is ravished by the Christian ardors of St. Paul, is not moved for that reason to put away the poem of Homer (as translated by Tully), or to forego his pleasure in the lucubrations of Seneca. Stage plays are anathema to him, but Terence is not anathema. Though he deprecates what is of the senses, believing that God "speaks not corporally but spiritually," and that "His blessed and immortal messengers and ministers heard not with ears, but more purely with intellects," he rejoices that the poet "Claudian (though no Christian) sings . . . well."[30] Both points of view are true of him, although they are contradictory. That is his peculiar greatness. He is attracted to Christianity by the allegorizing sermons of St. Ambrose. "To Milan I came," he writes in the *Confessions*, "to Ambrose the Bishop" who, attending to the surface of Scripture only as a parable, re-

---

[29] *City of God*, VIII, xix; IV, 13-14; X, xxvii; II, xxix.
[30] XII, xxv; XI, xviii; VIII, xxiv; X, xv; V, xxvi.

solves it "ofttimes in a figure."[31] To Augustine, who is willing to set "the spirit that quickeneth" against "the flesh [that] profiteth nothing," it is a congenial resolution.[32] Augustine is like Ambrose, if not so consistent, in attending in his own sermons to the corporal cause. Christianity, he is quick to see, is often anticipated in the writings of Plato. "But that this word was made flesh and dwelt among us, that read I not there."[33]

The fact of the Incarnation is central. Augustine fulfills the symbolic sense of the two ribbons which depend from the bishop's mitre, in affirmation of the rule that one must interpret Scripture according to both the letter and the spirit.[34] "I warn you in the name of God," he says to his parishioners, "to believe before all things when you hear the Scriptures read that the events really took place as is said in the book. Do not destroy the historic foundation of Scripture; without it you will build in the air."[35] The history of ideas is better written in terms of second-rate men.

Like the medieval Janus, who is sometimes represented as bearing an old head and a young, Augustine bears in one person more than one man. His countryman Tertullian is more uniform and hence finally not so interesting a figure. Tertullian, in his exclusiveness, is like that terrible Christ who says to the son burying his father, "Follow me, and let the dead bury their dead." Augustine, who quotes the passage with approval,[36] is the more considerable man in having it both ways. He carries his baggage with him towards eternity.

---

[31] *Confessions*, v.   [32] *City of God*, x, xxiv.

[33] *Confessions*, VII, ix. For Augustine's appreciation of the surface— "irrelevant" detail—see the following passage from *City of God*, XVI: "The strings only do cause the sound in harps and other such instruments, yet must the harp have pins, and the other frets, to make up the music, and the organs have other devices linked to the keys, which the organist touches not, but only their keys, to make the sound proportionate and harmonious. Even so in those prophetic stories, some things are merely relations, yet are they adherent unto those that are significant, and in a manner linked to them."

[34] Emile Mâle, *Gothic Image*, p. 20.

[35] Sermo ii; Mâle, pp. 135-36.   [36] *City of God*, x, xxiv.

It is not a wholly gratuitous or unmeditated labor. Poetry gladdens the heart, and exercises the speculative and proselyting intelligence of the special pleader. But if the penchant for locating a more fruitful meaning associates Augustine with most medieval writers, the appeal to use which he voices is not so clamant or so narrow as the Platonic or Baconian appeal, and that is also characteristic of the Middle Ages. The difference is qualitative, and formally less of kind than of degree: but this is one case in which degree is so important as to entail a decisive modifying of kind. This modification is apparent when Augustine, approving music and literature as useful for understanding, goes beyond a bare sanctioning to enjoin on his readers an intelligent and even moving ecumenicism that is sharply at odds with the winnowing and exclusivist spirit of the opponents of poetry, and the heuristic redactors of poetry, and that is often conspicuous in Augustine himself. Art, he has observed, is not to be eschewed because it is myopic or of uncertain provenance. And then he adds this sentence: "Rather, every good and true Christian should understand that wherever he may find truth, it is his Lord's."

In this more liberal and yet more diffident construing of use, the distinctive medieval attitude toward poetry begins to be discernible. Since "the one true God is the sole author of all beauty," it does not matter to Clement of Alexandria whether this beauty "is Hellenic or whether it is ours." (That is a useful set-off to the denunciation of Origen, "because he did not think as a Christian but followed the chatter of the Hellenes.") Gregory of Nazianzus, whose prowess as an orator derives from impartial study of the Hellenes and the Church, is honored as the Christian Demosthenes. Gregory's avocation is to write poetical essays in as many classical metres as he can compass.[37] (He is like Sir Philip Sidney, a prime opportunist in poetry.) Even Tertullian, in his account of the celestial paradise, unconsciously echoes Virgil, in his description of Elysium. (The context is, amusingly, a disavowing of any debt to classical literature.)[38]

[37] Campenhausen, *Greek Fathers*, pp. 30, 160, 112.
[38] Tertullian, describing Paradise as *"locum divinae amoenitatis"* in

There are medieval writers who continue to make poetry respectable, only as it is a referrent. In this, their practice tallies with that of the early Neo-Platonists and the Florentine academicians of the Renaissance. I am thinking, for example, of scholiastic writers like Servius and Fulgentius. But even these simplistic persons are of the Middle Ages in their willingness to prey at large. The Renaissance, which is the age of dichotomizing, values only what it thinks it can use. That is why the Renaissance apologists seek insistently to demonstrate the usefulness of poetry. The Middle Ages, on the assumption that all things are of God, use indifferently whatever lies to hand.

This accommodating instinct is remarkable in the early fourth-century rhetorician Lactantius, who begins the Christianizing of Virgil. In the seven books which comprise the *Divine Institutes*, Lactantius attempts, for the first time in the West, to construct a synthetic treatise on theology. The argument is lofty, and yet poetry participates in it. Like the Bishop of Hippo, Lactantius, saluting Virgil as "that most excellent poet,"[39] enlists him in support of the unity of God. Elsewhere he levies (among many others) on Horace and Lucan and Cicero and Seneca. Despite the Christian hatred of the theatre, he discovers much that is cogent in Plautus, and employs him to bulwark or to illustrate his thesis. Homer is cited with approbation; so are Juvenal and Persius. Even Lucretius, whose philosophy is not notably Christian, finds a place.

But the *Divine Institutes* is literally solid with easy quotation of the classical poets. This intimacy with them which Lactantius evinces is manifest in an apology for Christianity, in the reign of the Emperor Constantine, who is officially the protector and promoter of the faith, and to whom the work is addressed. That is, however, only surprising on its face. The Lord's truth is effi-

---

Ch. xxxxvii of his *Apology*, is echoing *Aeneid*, vi, 638-39. See A. B. Giamatti, *Earthly Paradise and the Renaissance Epic*, pp. 68-69; and, for a more comprehensive discussion of medieval levying on classical poetry: Rand, *Founders of the Middle Ages*; and F.J.E. Raby, *Secular Latin Poetry in the Middle Ages*, and *History of Christian Latin Poetry*.

[39] iii, viii.

cacious wherever one finds it, in Jerusalem but also in Athens. Those who hunt it are defined by a provident ecumenicism. Lactantius is ecumenical, which is to say medieval, in his willingness to use and denizen the Pagan Muse, as he can. This enlightened willingness informs his observation that "The accounts of the poets . . . are true, but veiled with an outward covering and show." According to Lactantius, "the poets are not accustomed to speak that which is altogether untrue, but to wrap up in figures and thus to obscure their accounts." That they should "transfer many things after this manner [is] not for the sake of speaking falsely against the objects of their worship, but that they may by variously colored figures add beauty and grace to their poems." What they worship, however obliquely, is the one and indivisible God.[40]

The point of view is tendentious but it throws a vast umbrella over the poets, affording shelter to "our own Maro" and "even Ovid," whose lapses into salacity are tactfully ignored.[41] This shelter, like the Ark, does not discriminate much among kinds. A little later it is serving as protection for romancers like Apuleius, a favorite butt of the Renaissance detractors of poetry, who do not see how it is possible to hypothesize use or meaning of a fable like the *Golden Ass*. But the medieval writer is indifferent to the mode, and hence he is not so easily repelled. It is the account in Apuleius of the marriage of Cupid and Psyche (VI, 23ff) that furnishes a starting point for Martianus Capella, in his unromantic and wholly serious account of the *Marriage of Mercury and Philology*. Martianus, who observes with his customary inconsequence that "No one enters into Heaven except through philosophy,"[42] is certainly not a fabulist, or not by design. The function of Martianus is to conduct his readers to the City of God. He is not especially concerned how they get there.

The annulling of the Platonic categories, and the elevating of poetic fiction to the status of philosophy—or, what is much the

---

[40] I, xi; II, xi; I, xi; I, iv.

[41] Quotation is from *Epitome* (III), an abridging by Lactantius in his old age of the *Institutes*.

[42] 57, xv.

same thing, the depressing of philosophy—allows subsequently for the utilizing of Terence, a writer not often preoccupied with sacred themes. At the beginning of the eleventh century, Pope Sylvester II, declining to be put off by the robust surface of the plays, commends the Roman dramatist as a fruitful preceptor for virtuous conduct. In the century before, Hroswith, the nun of Gandersheim, makes him the model for her own dramatic writings on the struggle between the flesh and the spirit. On this reading, literature becomes an epitome of learning, and hence beyond question a valuable study. Like the conceptual thought which is philosophy, literature also, and in the same tentative ways, engages the higher truth. "Plato" is thereby answered and refuted. The refutation holds for something like a thousand years.

It does not suffice to the Renaissance, any more than to Plato himself, because the question of use has become at once more poignant and more narrow than it is to the Middle Ages. The new intensity belonging to it is what accounts for the shrillness of Renaissance polemics on poetry. The medieval reading of poetry is not shrill but laconic. This means it is accepted by and large without cavil. The defense of poetry is not conventional in the Middle Ages. There is no impulse to it. Poetry, like music, is functional, only one member of the grand consortium which includes grammar and rhetoric, ethics and theology. Those who practice it esteem their craft, and frequently they say so; but it does not occur to them to praise it from the rooftops. It is not until the Renaissance, which means until the fourteenth century in Italy, that formal treatises in honor of poetry are written. That they should be written at all argues a want of assurance in the poets, as if the merit of their profession had suddenly been called into question. The point is that it had been.

This is not to assert that only with the Renaissance do attacks on poetry commence, but that medieval hostility to poetry, which is never placated altogether, is mostly different in kind. Nor is the fruit of that hostility so exotic. There are of course Christians to whom all poetry is anathema, as a legacy of the pagan past. Among these uncompromising zealots, the most in-

173

teresting is Tertullian, the first of the Latin Fathers and the greatest spokesman of North African Christianity before Augustine. Tertullian is the type of the ultramontanist. As he is a convert, who makes the decision for Christ in middle age, he looks on the world he has forsaken with the new and hostile awareness of the radical puritan. He is far more puritanic than the ecclesiastical hierarchy, as represented in the person of his local bishop, whom he censures as too compassionate in absolving his frail communicants of mortal sin. His total abjuring inclines him to distinguish absolutely between the Academy and the Church. He is himself, as a scholar brought up to the law, the quintessential academician. With the rigor of his kind, he allows of no community as between Jerusalem and Athens, "between a philosopher and a Christian, between a disciple of Hellas and a disciple of Heaven." A Christian, he asserts, should build "not on a foreign foundation, but on his own."[43]

There is a certain logic and attractiveness in this rigorist view of things. I think of Georges Sorel, who insists that the only successful revolution is the total revolution, which does not reject but annihilates the past. "Reforms are not the solution," says the Maoist or Black Panther, returning in spirit to the Christian revolutionary. "Our problems derive from the system itself. We have to completely eliminate the capitalist system and replace it with socialism."[44]

The replacing of the "system," given the violence which attends it, is always a redacting of what has gone before, however different the formal sayings of "Robespierre" and "Louis XVI." Baudelaire is suggestive: "*La Révolution, par le sacrifice, confirme la superstition*" (*Mon Coeur Mis à Nu*, vi). But it is not the replacing of one system with another that warms the heart of the draconian or revolutionary man. It is the destructive act. "Bombs, for God's sake, bombs!" cries an embittered failure in Malraux's novel, *Man's Fate*. The "final explosive moment" is the end to which he looks. The past, about which his hatred col-

[43] Campenhausen, *Fathers of the Latin Church*, pp. 17-18.

[44] Eldridge Cleaver, quoted S. de Gramont in *NYT Magazine*, Nov. 1, 1970, p. 112.

lects and which stands as a surrogate for that part of himself he wishes to exorcise, has got to be rejected *in toto*, "like a whirling piece of metal thrown off by an exploding flywheel."[45] The man beset with devils is an elated "witness to the crushing of a world out of date." What he sings—it is Louis Aragon, the French Communist poet, who presents him—is "total annihilation." Hitler cries, in the final toils, "We shall yet master fate!" where fate is the ineluctable portion which the sick man, replete with unlived lines, must deny.[46]

As no man is self-engendered, no present moment stands without reference to the past which precedes it. Tertullian is right. Christianity, as it fails to conclude a Carthaginian peace in which the past is reduced to nothing, is henceforward and forever an amalgam of past and present. The pagan heritage lives on, to modify and, on the draconian view, to pervert the new dispensation.

> The liquor a new vessel first contains
> Leaves behind a taste that long remains.

That is Augustine, a little ruefully, on Virgil, the admired poet of his youth.[47]

This belief in the necessity of a total revolution is, however, the minority view. Medieval man is not given ordinarily to root-and-branch formulations. Unlike modern man, he is exempt from self-hatred, which is the price of hating others. Accepting himself, he accepts by and large the world in which he lives. See the bastard nature of medieval art, half pagan, half Christian. In his unwillingness really to deracinate, he is like that merciful or provident Joshua, who destroys the city of Jericho, but not absolutely. Rahab the harlot woman and all her kindred are spared. The children of Israel remember the service she has done them, in earlier days (Joshua 6:23). This is not to blink the iniquity of Rahab. Though the twelfth-century poet Alan

---

[45] Caudwell on "the last final movement" of the "bourgeois illusion," in *Illusion and Reality*, p. 88.

[46] Quoted Shirer, *Third Reich*, p. 1095.

[47] *City of God*, I, iii.

of Lille asserts that "The muse of Virgil tinges many falsehoods, and braids with the facing of truth his cloaks of fraud," he does not intermit his dependence on Virgil who is, with Cicero, Ovid, and Horace, one of the major sources informing his work. In a more generous mood, he understands and acknowledges that the literature of antiquity is indispensable to him. Seneca, as he confesses, "coins rational ethics. . . . Tully redeems the poverty of the word."[48]

This enduring attachment to the literary mode, and especially to Cicero, is conspicuous and amusing in St. Jerome. Describing the famous dream in which he is accused of preferring literature before religion ("*Ciceronianus es, non Christianus*"), Jerome engages for the future to cleave only to Holy Writ.[49] But Jerome is a notorious backslider, as his enemies do not fail to remind him. He will never "hold or read a secular codex again." That is the pious intention. But the vivid presence of "our Tully" (or Flaccus or Maro) is independent of reading or even of holding. "I must drink of the waters of Lethe," says Jerome in despair, "if I am to be blamed for remembering the poems that once I knew." Like Augustine, he has got to acknowledge that, though a man "may fill a jar with water . . . it still will smell of the wine that steeped it first."[50] Literary allusions do not dwindle but increase in his letters, as those who have analyzed the letters have shown. I think it is their frequency that accounts for the praise bestowed on this mundane writer in spite of himself by a greatly pious scholar of the twelfth-century Renaissance. To John of Salisbury, St. Jerome is *doctor doctorum* and even *doctorum doctissimus*. As for the anathematizing of literature which is the burden of the dream, that, John implies, was perhaps the work of a malignant spirit.[51] Whatever its provenance, this spirit is not notably efficient. So impregnated

[48] *Anticlaudianus*, I, iv.

[49] *De Custodia Virginitatis*. Rand, *Founders*, p. 106; L. B. Campbell, *Divine Poetry and Divine Drama*, p. 15.

[50] Waddell, *Desert Fathers*, pp. 41-42, 28.

[51] *Policraticus*, II, 22; VII, 10; II, 17.

is the century of Jerome with the style and thought of the invidious Tully as to merit the designation, *Aetas Ciceroniana*.[52]

Two centuries later, Bishop Isidore of Seville, who is with Cassiodorus perhaps the dominant intellectual figure of the Dark Ages, still adheres on one side to the draconian party. From the three books of *Sententiae* which he compiles on Christian doctrine and morals, the poets are explicitly excluded. "The Christian," announces Isidore, "is forbidden to read their lies."[53] (He is redacting the *Moralia* of Gregory the Great, who had rather hear a kitten cry mew.) But Isidore is not always unwilling to resort to the literary heritage, when that heritage seems useful to him. In the *De Rerum Natura*, his eccentric anatomizing of various aspects of the creation, he is described by a contemporary as resolving "certain obscurities about the elements by studying the works of the Church Fathers as well as those of the philosophers." But Cicero is counted among the philosophers. The more catholic intention of St. Isidore is to "expound [on] those . . . matters as to which we know that certain men of the heathen and of the church have opinions."[54] In fulfillment of this all-encompassing design, Isidore, like Fulgentius, addresses himself to the interpretation of classical myth.

This ability to find the Lord's truth even in the domicile of error characterizes the writings of Prudentius, who must bear the onus of having created the allegorical Christian epic. When Prudentius attacks the pagan gods (as in the Oration against Symmachus, which calls for their removal from the Roman Senate), he is attacking inferentially the classical poets, for example Ovid, Virgil, and Horace, in whose verse the infamous exploits of the gods are perpetuated. The legend that Saturn, fleeing from Jupiter, changed himself into a horse, provokes from the Christian poet the indignant observation that "The homeless stranger with his horse-lust . . . was the first fornicator that pretended divinity when he whinnied after the maids of Tuscany." Virgil, who recounts this legend in the *Georgics* (III,

---

[52] Rand, *Founders*, p. 255.   [53] III, xiii, 1.
[54] Isidore in a preface to his royal patron, the king of the Visigoths.

92-94), is no doubt to be censured and possibly eschewed. So are those poets who tell of the bestial transformations of Jupiter, as to a swan or bull or eagle. On the principle of guilt by association, the interdicting of poetry would seem to be required.

But Prudentius the hostile reporter is deeply conversant with the poets whose lubricious stories he reprehends. Often he quotes the classics verbatim, and not only from the wonted triumvirate of Virgil, Horace, and Ovid. Evidently the Lord's truth inheres also in Lucretius and Statius, Juvenal and Lucan. The verse in which the *Contra Symmachum* is written is sufficiently full of poetical reminiscence to earn for its author the title (in Bentley's phrase) of the Horace and the Virgil of the Christians. In the poem on the "Divinity of Christ," this reminiscence is even more striking. Though Prudentius clears himself of any taint of the older philosophy (a muddy composition of "the bearded Plato's ravings . . . the close-drawn reasonings which the stinking Cynic produces in his illusion, or Aristotle contrives in a dizzy whirl"), he is unable to get clear of the poets. In this he resembles St. Jerome who, like a sybarite renouncing self-mortification, finds it possible to repudiate the arid fare of philosophy. "What," he inquires, with a show of facile indignation, "has Aristotle to do with Paul? or Plato with Peter?" That is a fine rhetorical flourish and apparently it suffices: Jerome is not much of a philosopher himself. The repudiating of literature is not, however, to be managed by rhetorical formulations, as Jerome attests with some relish (he is writing long after the event): "I lay awake many nights, I wept with all my heart thinking about my former sins—and then I took Plautus in my hands."[55]

Prudentius, as his temper is not so melodramatic, is spared this wrestling with the angel or demon. One might suppose that as he wishes the Muse to put off her ivy crown for the mystical crown of the new dispensation, he would reject out of hand those heathenish writers who "devote smoking altars to a Saturn, a Juno, a Lady of Cythera and other monstrosities." But he does not reject them. They stand at his shoulder; he is forever within

---

[55] Campenhausen, *Latin Fathers*, pp. 180, 136.

their shadow. In Prudentius, the waters of Jordan are confluent with the waters of Helicon. "That unexplored stream" of which Lazarus is asked to tell is still the river of Phlegethon. From that river God returns, on the day of His Resurrection. At His death, "He enters Tartarus." Virgil personifies Morbus; so does Prudentius. Remembering Julian the Apostate, he describes him as waxing the knees of Diana,[56] a reminiscence of Juvenal; and as smoking the horse of Pollux with the burning of entrails, a reminiscence of the *Iliad* (III, 237), except that in Homer it is Castor who is the horseman. The error signifies. Prudentius, misquoting, is rather like Dickens, who knows Shakespeare so well as sometimes to get him wrong through not bothering to look up and to verify the line.

The nature of this medieval assimilating of poetry is illuminated by Boccaccio, with much charm but also with a certain defensiveness, in which the renascent age is augured. Boccaccio, like most of his predecessors, is sure that he has "little . . . to fear from the weapons of paganism." If he, a Christian, has "handled the foolishness of the Gentiles," he has only done "what many saintly men have done with highest approval, such as Augustine, or Jerome, or among others the neophyte Lactantius." Boccaccio is aware "that all pagans gods were devils," and certainly he disapproves "of their absurd misdeeds." But he has got to admit—and here the unwillingness of medieval man to play the draconian role to the hilt is caught and conveyed in a phrase—that, "their manner of worship aside, the character and words of certain ancient poets have delighted me."[57]

In Boccaccio, who stands on the utmost verge of the Middle Ages, this delight is not entirely unalloyed. Like Solomon, who is ensnared by the honeyed kisses of his Egyptian wife, Boccaccio in his contention with poetry is understood to be vanquished or unmanned. As he observes with some complacency, "Ah, how

---

[56] Quotations from "A Hymn Before Meat"; "A Hymn for the 25th of December"; "Hymn on the Burial of the Dead" (recalling *Aeneid*, VI, 275); "Divinity of Christ." For the debt to Virgil, see Hollander, *Allegory*, pp. 98-99.

[57] *Genealogy of the Gentile Gods*, xv, ix.

strong and irresistible are the love assaults of women, especially at night."

It is a cheerful analogy, but perhaps it is misleading and more definitive of the future than the past. Cassiodorus (*c.*480-*c.*580), who establishes the monkish tradition of scholarship and so assists in preserving the learning of antiquity, sees nothing un-Christian in attempting to relate divine letters "and the compendious knowledge of secular letters." He justifies his undertaking in that "the very holy Fathers have not decreed that the study of secular letters should be scorned." His cousin Boethius promulgates just such a decree. Cassiodorus undertakes to revoke it. He observes that "many of our Fathers, trained in letters of this sort and living by the law of the Lord, have attained true wisdom."[58] Like Augustine a little earlier,[59] Cassiodorus adduces Scripture in support of this eclectic position. The Jews are honored, he discovers, as they carried objects of gold and silver from Egypt. To the allegorical temperament, the passage from Exodus (ii, 3:22) gives sanction to the Christians, in their levying on classical verse.

This ingenious reading does not put down opposition altogether. The scholarly Aldhelm, England's earliest man of letters, remains suspicious of the classics. It is not Apollo but Christ from whom he draws his inspiration. But the rejection of Apollo, as by the Abbot of Malmesbury, is, it seems to me, mostly formal, and does not in any case preclude the writing and reading of poetry. I am tempted to describe it, always with the great and fanatic exceptions, as little more than an arbitrary genuflection. The recollection or savor of classical verse, despite the conventional deprecating of the old by the new, is never forgotten, and not even in the high Middle Ages when art and life become thoroughly and unmistakably Christianized. Tyndale is not absolutely out of the way, in protesting that poetry "is as good divinitie as the scripture to our scole men."[60]

---

[58] *Institutiones Divinarum et Secularium Litterarum*, trans. L. W. Jones, pp. 67, 129.

[59] Curtius, *European Literature*, p. 594.

[60] *Obedyence of a Chrysten man* [? 1536], O7v-P6v.

The case of Prudentius enforces and also qualifies the point. Prudentius, who levies on Virgil and Horace, is not so good a poet as Virgil and Horace, and that fact is more decisive than his manifold borrowings. Neither is he in spirit a man of the classical period. But though vastly inferior and alien in kind, he manifests in his poetry a tenuous but genuine affiliation to the past. This affiliation is perceptible in Romanesque architecture, which receives its crucial impetus and also its peculiar character from northern peoples—for example, from the Norman conquerors of Sicily—and yet is first of all Roman. So in the same qualified ways is Prudentius, and all those Christian poets he engenders, in whom the polluting or saving presence of Virgil remains of fundamental importance.

To Dante, at the close of the Middle Ages, there is no longer any thought of pollution. Virgil is the sapient guide and good instructor who is proof against the terrors of Hell. He is also the "Parent beloved!"[61] Dante, the supreme Christian poet, is proud to take rank after Virgil and Homer, Horace and Ovid and Lucan. Chaucer evinces this same humble pride. "Go, litel bok, go, litel myn tragedye," he writes in the envoy to *Troilus*; and adds the admonition:

> But subgit be to alle poesye;
> And kis the steppes, where as thow seest pace
> Virgile, Ovide, Omer, Lucan, and Stace.[62]

Dante, in acknowledging the preeminence of the older poets, does not palter or equivocate, as Boccaccio is to do. Neither is he fulsome, which is the other side of the coin. To him it is self-evident that "The renown of their great names That echoes through . . . [the] world above, acquires Favor in heaven."[63] On this favor is predicated the medieval acceptance of poetry. The amiable eleventh-century bishop, a certain Gunther of Bamberg, who versifies on profane subjects and prefers to the works of St. Augustine and St. Gregory romantic stories of Attila and

---

[61] Purgatory, iv. For Dante's debt to Virgil, "*lo mio maestro e'l mio autore,*" see Comparetti, Chs. xiv, xv; Hollander, *Allegory*, pp. 81-97.

[62] v, 1786, 1790-92.   [63] Inferno, iv.

the Ostrogoth kings, is perhaps to be censured for his trivial taste.[64] The heavenly favor which Dante hypothesizes acquits him of censure on the question of propriety or use. The question is not much belabored, until the Renaissance. Mostly, the Middle Ages take it as given.

In the fourteenth century, the climate begins to change. There is a vast uneasiness implicit in Boccaccio's justification of poetry, which did not require to be justified before. Boccaccio inaugurates the new habit of strident and exaggerated praise. His radical design is to conclude the *Genealogy* "with two books, in the first of which I shall reply to certain objections that have been raised against poetry and poets." He wants to inculcate "the right opinion about poets," that they not be taken "for mere storytellers, but rather for men of great learning, endowed with a sort of divine intelligence and skill."[65]

But this is meiosis. "It is absolutely certain," says the author peremptorily, "that poetry . . . is derived from God." As it "dwells in heaven, and mingles with the divine counsels," it presents "all that is clear and holy in the bosom of moral philosophy." (Here Boccaccio alleges as proof the compositions of his contemporary Petrarch, who, as a panegyrist, runs on in pretty much the same vein; and even, with some show of deprecation, "my own eclogues.") Affirming that John the Evangelist is essentially a poet, he turns the argument around and, on the authority of Aristotle, affirms also that "the pagan poets are theologians."[66]

But God is a poet, too, "the sublime Artificer of the Universe!" He speaks often in parables—appropriate, says Boccaccio in a startling aside, to the style of a comic poet—and even employs a verse of Terence against the stricken Paul: "It is hard for thee to kick against the pricks." (Boccaccio does not "suppose that our Lord took these words from Terence, though Terence lived long before they were uttered.")

Partly, the poetry of God is exemplified in Holy Writ, which

[64] Marc Bloch, *Feudal Society*, p. 100.
[65] Preface; Bk. xiv.
[66] Bk. xv.

represents Him "as sun, fire, lion, serpent, lamb, worm, or even a stone." As this figurative language springs "from God's bosom," it must offer us "many inducements to virtue." For example, it is "full of the sap of natural vigor for those who would through fiction subdue the senses with the mind." It suffices "to lift the oppressive weight of adversity and furnish consolation," and has also "been the means . . . of quelling minds aroused to a mad rage," and of recalling "the mind that is slipping into inactivity . . . to a state of better and more vigorous fruition." To labor the point that "the reading of poets conduces to righteousness" is, I think, to undercut it. Does Boccaccio really believe that Virgil and Horace, Persius and Juvenal are great "stimulators to virtue"? He says so. And more: poetry is "a practical art" which, as it "sharpens and illumines the powers of the mind," can "arm kings, marshal them for war, launch whole fleets from their docks."

Boccaccio, protesting that from poetry "the sap of philosophy runs pure," is a notable worrier. In this he enforces the principle that, as the attack on poetry waxes, the defense of poetry grows more self-conscious and shrill. The Italian poets respond initially to the new hostility; then, as the spirit of the Renaissance freshens elsewhere, the poets of other nations are obliged to confront it. The first full-dress eulogies of poetry in England date from the later sixteenth century. A kind of hysteria describes them. Poetry, they are apt to assert, can move stones and compel the attention of beasts. It is the treasure house of science, and also of morality, martial business, and statecraft. Philosophy and history enter into the gates of popular judgment, only by taking a passport of poetry. The poet is the ancient among learned men, and also the monarch of learning. His sovereignty encompasses astronomy, geometry, and arithmetic, music and rhetoric, logic and law. The Schoolman cannot touch him for insight. The physician, who only heals the body, is inferior to him; so is the metaphysician who, although he is counted supernatural, is constrained to build on natural foundations. In the poet's work, however, nature is surpassed.

Apparently the poet is a kind of alchemic. But that is not all.

He is the companion of camps, who teaches men their first motion of courage. In his verse is located the fount of true doctrine and the strengthener of wit. As poetry is mnemonic, it is the only handle of knowledge. But the best is still behind. Immortality on earth is in the giving of poetry, and more than this, the keys of the kingdom. In the "heavenly poesie" which is Holy Scripture, God is discovered, coming in His majesty.

But the uses of poetry are intermediate also. Poetry instructs a man how to behave "in stormes, howe in sports, howe in warre, howe in peace, how a fugitive, how victorious, how besieged, how besieging, how to straungers, how to Allies, how to enemies, how to his owne . . . how in his inwarde selfe, and howe in his outward government."

The writer is Sir Philip Sidney, in his *Apologie for Poetrie*, a work which represents fairly the eulogizing tradition in the English Renaissance. Hyperbole is meat and drink to the tradition, and that is instructive. The medieval reading of the merits of poetry is nothing like so insistent. It does not need to be. To the proposition that poetry offers much, most men would assent; as also to the corollary, that poetry is not absolutely efficacious. But medieval man does not pretend that it is.

VI The Language of Earth

THE MIDDLE AGES are the period of cultural assimilation. Medieval man does not select and exclude, like man in the Renaissance. He is more accommodating and opportunistic. The opportunism that defines him is commended, not surprisingly, by Shakespeare, who is the supreme opportunist:

> There is some soul of goodness in things evil,
> Would men observingly distill it out.

Another way of describing this accommodating instinct is to say that the Middle Ages do not canonize only what is or appears to be useful. That is why this period is able to come to terms with poetry. But as it declines to make a fetish of use, it sees no necessity to separate the wheat from the chaff. Discrimination is not conspicuous among its virtues. This means that the art it creates is largely indifferent to form. It is an impure art, not so clear and therefore not so enabling as the taste of the later age will require.

In the matter of poetry, perhaps the cardinal difference that distinguishes the Middle Ages from the Renaissance is the absence in almost all medieval writers, even those of indisputable genius, of an exclusively literary interest. Among the protagonists in the literary symposium described by Macrobius in his *Saturnalia*, the most learned is the grammarian Servius, the greatest Virgilian scholiast of the early Christian era. Boccaccio, and even on this side, is a much more considerable figure. But when Servius writes of Virgil, a thousand years before Boccaccio, there is for all the quixotry a largeness or amplitude about his description of the substance of the poem that narrows down in the descriptions of Renaissance poets and critics, as they comment on the work of their own time. William Ames is speaking

185

for the later time in deciding that "a contracted light, although it may seem small," offers more illumination than a light "dispersed by too much enlargement."[1] Enlargement or amplitude entails confusion. Medieval art is lacking in clarity, when compared with the art of the Renaissance. It does not manifest so strong a sense of explicit purpose or design. But it is the more ambitious art. Nothing is alien to it. The generalization applies to a medieval poet like Alan of Lille, for example in his discussion of the *Anticlaudianus*. It is exemplified best of all in Dante.

Superficially, this looks like a contradiction. The Renaissance poet is not much given to self-depreciation. Neither is the poet of antiquity. The convention to which both adhere affirms that the poet's work is more lasting even than the gilded monuments of princes. "Kings are known to posterity with the help of authors," says Boccaccio, who is addressing a king. He adds, with no consciousness of his own audacity, "Besides, if the work is really praiseworthy, what increase of authority can a king's name give it . . .?"[2] The same complacence describes the antique Roman as the new man of the Renaissance. It is illustrated in the proud boast with which Horace begins what seems to me his greatest ode: "*Exegi monumentum aere perennius*"; and fifteen centuries later in Michael Drayton's superb restatement: "My name shall mount upon eternity." In the intervening age, no one is quite so thrasonical as this.

But this largeness I am positing does not have to do with artistic pretension, or the aggrandizing of one's claims, or the imputing of supreme dignity to the burden of the poem. I see it rather as deriving from and attesting to the received and unargued conviction that a work of art, by its nature, is a kind of reticule in which all manner of business may be dropped and transacted. Shakespeare exemplifies that conviction. His plays are full of matter which, if not excrescent, is certainly tangential to the matter in hand. *Hamlet* is not exclusively the tragedy of the

---

[1] *Marrow of Sacred Divinity*, A6. Contraction is form and depends on a sense of causation. Medieval innocence of the latter is discussed by P. Burke, *Renaissance Sense of the Past*, pp. 13-20, 104-41.

[2] *Genealogy*, xv, xiii.

Prince of Denmark. It is also a text on the art of the theatre. In *A Midsummer Night's Dream*, this text is anticipated. But the rude mechanicals, insofar as they garble and misread it, have to do only in peripheral ways with lighting up the disjunction between love and reason which is the primary concern of the comedy but not the single concern. Shakespeare is not notably singleminded. It is an index of his affinity to the medieval temperament. Like Cassiodorus, he is prone to extramural enthusiasms and interests. The question, how to cope with the breeding of fleas out of urine, is as engrossing to him, in *1 Henry IV*, as the robbery at Gadshill which follows that poignant discussion. Sometimes his hospitality is distracting. Unaffiliated characters whose function is to seek are occasionally to be detected on the edges of his art, like the perfect spy of the time in *Macbeth*, or that enigmatical Varrius to whom the Duke of dark corners is indebted, or like Juliet's sister Susan, who is with God. "Where is my cousin, your son?" Leonato inquires, in *Much Ado About Nothing*. That is a good question. Shakespeare, who ought to know the answer, does not divulge it. Neither does he locate, except by report, the mother of Hero and the uncle of Claudio, who are named and left to their business. (The mother, I think, is lamenting in private her daughter's disgrace, the uncle is shedding grateful tears in his closet for the valor of his nephew in the wars.) "Marcus Lucchese, is not he in town?" asks the Duke, in *Othello*. "Write from us: wish him post-post-haste dispatch." For the balance of the action, nothing more is heard of this gratuitous person who, presumably in Florence, outside the stated bounds of the play, carries on an independent existence, indifferent to the tragedy that is preparing in Venice and Cypress and in fact oblivious of it.

The miraculous birth and the dreadful martyrdom, as Shakespeare presents them, do not hold the stage alone. The inconsequent clown who diverts and annoys the musicians is not of less moment than old Capulet, who grieves for the death of his daughter, or Michael Cassio, for the loss of his lieutenancy. I do not see that it is possible to rationalize the appearance in the play of that tedious poet who intrudes on the conference of

187

Brutus and Cassius; nonetheless, he displaces air, even as they do. Shakespeare, like the Old Masters in Auden's poem, is known for his inclusiveness. The heroes of modern art are known, conversely, for their abstention, and their unwavering determination to hew to a single line.

Bernard Shaw is an anti-hero. His habit of stuffing into his prefaces and plays whatever engages his interest at the moment does not commend itself to the modern temper. Shaw, as he is interested in almost everything, resembles Shakespeare (the qualifier denotes his inferiority to Shakespeare) and, like him, is infinitely seducible. As he writes of himself, early in his career, "I am a crow who has followed many plows."[3] The form of his art is not so much comely as accommodating, and this in deference to his impulse to get everything in. But the impulse is characteristically medieval. The Renaissance mathematician Cardano still exemplifies this impulse. "Avoid pond carp," he adjures the reader of his autobiography, "but not brook carp. A good dish is broth of beets with garlic, of cockles or crab or snails made with green bay leaves."[4]

It is not post-Renaissance man who takes all knowledge for his province but the man of the Middle Ages. He is the true *universale uomo*. His dedication, not simply to theology but to the greater corpus of the seven liberal arts, is summarized in a mnemonic couplet by the French Franciscan, Nicholas de Orbelis:

> *Gram* loquitur, *Dia* verba docet, *Rhet* verba colorat,
> *Mus* canit, *Ars* numerat, *Ge* ponderat, *Ast* colit astra.

This kind of intelligence battens where it can. It is luminous in Isidore of Seville, who undertakes to bring together within a single treatise "about all that ought to be known." The quotation is from Isidore's friend and correspondent, Braulio, the bishop of Saragossa, who is describing the encyclopedia known as the *Etymologies*. By virtue of this compendium of grammar

---

[3] A. Henderson, *George Bernard Shaw*, p. 71.
[4] *The Book of My Life*, trans. Jean Stoner, Ch. LII.

and rhetoric, mathematics, medicine, history, and theology, Braulio, very fairly, applies to its compiler "the famous words of the philosopher [Cicero]: 'While we were strangers in our own city, and . . . sojourners who had lost our way, your books brought us home . . . so that we could at last recognize who and where we were. You have discussed the antiquity of our fatherland, the orderly arrangement of chronology, the laws of sacrifices and of priests, the discipline of the home and the state, the situation of regions and places, the names, kinds, functions and causes of all things human and divine.' "[5]

This endeavor to assimilate "all that ought to be known" is equally remarkable in Cassiodorus, another miner in the dark galleries of the Dark Ages. Cassiodorus, as he concerns himself with the whole of mundane learning, encapsulated in the *Artes liberales*, makes nonsense of the casual identifying of monasticism and intellectual deprivation. It is his belief that "We can understand much through the art of grammar [literature], much through the art of rhetoric, much through dialectics, much through the science of arithmetic, much through music, much through the science of geometry, much through astronomy."[6] He attends to all these subjects in his writing.

Six centuries later, Alan of Lille, who combines in one person the triple character of poet, theologian, and philosopher, commends his Christian epic, the *Anticlaudianus*, in that it is "objectionable to no aspect of philosophy." In his work, as in the *Institutiones* of Cassiodorus, "there echoes a model of grammatical synthesis, of dialectic principle, rules for oratory, law of common arithmetic, paradoxes of learning, science of music, axioms of geometry, theorems of mensuration, the excellence of hebdomadal astronomy and signs of celestial revelation."[7] It is important to distinguish this characteristic encyclopedist of the high Middle Ages, who is honored as *doctor universalis*, from the omnicompetent poet hypothesized by Macrobius at the end of the classical period, or by Boccaccio in the beginnings of the

[5] *Isidore of Seville*, trans. E. Brehaut, pp. 23-24.
[6] *Institutiones*, p. 127.   [7] Argument and Prologue, pp. 51, 48.

189

Renaissance. The one is absolutely puissant; the other is absolutely engaged.[8]

The Middle Ages are not abstemious (not, at any rate, in their art), and not much preoccupied with unity or focus. Medieval drama will make the point. Its tendency is centrifugal. Its development is linear. Most of all it is characterized by inclusiveness. That is a fair description of medieval writing in general. When St. Isidore is asked by a king of the Visigoths "to explain . . . something of the nature and causes of things," he elects to begin with the day of Creation.[9] This mode of proceeding requires a certain fortitude of the writer and his audience. For a performance of the great mystery cycles, every waking hour is too little. To encompass the entire story, each actor who participates in the cycle at York (in which at least forty-eight plays are included) must "be ready in his pageant at convenient time, that is to say, at the mid hour betwixt 4 and 5 of the clock in the morning."[10] Niceness of articulation, in this kind of drama, yields to the rapacious or panoramic instinct. The York cycle, like Isidore's *De Rerum Natura*, begins with the story of Creation. It ends with the Day of Judgment. In struc-

[8] The encyclopedic character of the Middle Ages is illustrated in the addiction to *Summae, trésors, miroirs, mers des histoires*. See the discussion in Seznec, p. 123. Degory Whear, the first Camden professor of History at Oxford, suggests the more narrow or compendious psychology of the Renaissance. Treating the *Method and Order of Reading Both Civil and Ecclesiastical Histories*, Whear defines his subject as "nothing but Moral Philosophy, cloathed in Examples" (edn. of 1685, p. 298). Comparison with a less exclusive compilation like the *Historia Pontificalis* of John of Salisbury is indicated. See H. Baker, *The Race of Time*, p. 46. Though Bacon wrote much, he is still a compendious writer. Other Renaissance writers are more nearly helter skelter: Fludd, Browne, Nathaniel Wanley. I read them as atavistic.

[9] Preface, *De Rerum Natura*. So, one might interpose, Ralegh, Milton, Dryden. But to estimate the difference, compare the writings of Ordericus Vitalis, whose stated intention is, not to write a history of the world, but to chronicle the ecclesiastical history of England and Normandy—and yet who decides to "treat first of the Source of all things" (Preface), and who requires hundreds of pages before, as we should say, he has got started.

[10] H. Craig, *English Religious Drama*, p. 204.

ture, the analogy is to those clapboard houses of New England which add room to room or layer to layer, not in accordance with any master plan but as whimsy suggests or convenience requires.[11]

This indifference to a meditated and coercive design is illustrated vividly in the Easter trope or Sepulchrum, out of which the modern drama emerges. Initially, the Sepulchrum is only an efficient colloquy between the three Marys, lamenting the death of Christ, and the angel who watches over the tomb. In an English trope of the tenth century, the monks who represent the Marys are instructed to come forward, "slowly, in the manner of seeking something" or, alternatively, "as if straying about and seeking something." In front of the sepulchre, the angel accosts and resolves them. "These things," reads the MS, "are done in imitation of the angel seated in the monument, and of the women coming with spices to anoint the body of Jesus." That is the extent of the action. Given the revelation with which the play is concerned, it is enough. What the women discover, and the auditors who are watching and listening, is that "Jesus of Nazareth, who was crucified . . . has arisen as He foretold." With the imparting of this critical fact, the essential business of the play, and hence the play itself, is concluded. But the medieval instinct is not so much for efficiency as for proliferation of detail. To gratify this instinct ancillary business is added, like the Race to the Tomb of the Apostles Peter and John, and the Harrowing of Hell, and the *Peregrini* or Journey to Emmaus (which brings with it an impressive elaboration of stage properties: a "structure in the middle of the nave of the church, prepared in the likeness of the village of Emmaus"), and the incredulity of Thomas called Didymus, who has got to thrust his fingers in the wounds, and the appearance of the risen Christ to Mary Magdalene. Will Kemp is anticipated, doing his turn: a comic scene features an oil merchant or *unguentarius*, of whom ointment for the dead body is purchased.

But if it is legitimate and attractive to follow the Easter story

---

[11] G. Wickham, *Shakespeare's Dramatic Heritage*, p. 51, argues on the contrary for careful construction, not simply accretion, in the building of the medieval cycle dramas.

forward in time, there is as much reason to anticipate that story by dramatizing earlier episodes, in preamble to the day itself. And so not merely the Resurrection but the Passion of Christ is presented. Since Mary Magdalene figures in the Passion, her story engenders a dramatic cycle of its own, including and enacting her lurid life as fallen woman, and her subsequent conversion, and the conversion at her hands of the King of Marseille, and the winding up of her career as an anchorite in the desert. It is the whole of the story.

This same tendency to flatulence is observable in the Christmas play, which originates as a modest adaptation of the Easter Sepulchrum. Shepherds replace the three Marys, and midwives or *obstetrices* the angels. Apparently, the canonical gospels are too lean. To eke out the story they tell and so to satisfy the lust for completeness, the dramatist resorts to apocryphal writings, like the Gospel of Pseudo-Matthew in which the role of the midwives is hypothesized. The function of these persons is simply to announce the miraculous birth. But the medieval audience demands a representation that is more inclusive and more varied. And hence to the trunk, or *Officium Pastorum*, antecedent material is grafted. The shepherds attend on the cradle of Jesus. The Wise Men are presented, as they follow the star. But as it is niggarding to dramatize only that aspect of their story, so the Wise Men must be shown in their meeting with Herod; they must be warned by the angel to take a different way home. Herod himself must tear a passion to tatters. As one thing leads to another, he must resolve on the Massacre of the Innocents. In compliance with this sanguinary resolution, the Christmas play incorporates the *Ordo Rachelis*, in which Rachel, as an emblem of the mothers of Israel, bewails their slaughtered children. Still the impulse to completeness is not exhausted. Prophecies are dramatized of the coming of the Judge, as by Isaiah and Jeremiah, Daniel and Moses; and, for the sake of catholicity, by profane witnesses like Virgil and the Sybil.

But the interpolating of this *Ordo Prophetarum* only quickens curiosity. That means, necessarily, it aggravates the dropsical condition of the play. In the medieval drama, images beget fresh images. The introduction of Pontius Pilate (as in the Passion Play) begets the son of Pontius Pilate, a personage unknown to Scripture. The story of Balaam, the unwilling prophet of the Book of Numbers (22-24), suggests the braying of Balaam's ass. Daniel suggests Nebuchadnezzar. But this further accretion entails an account of the fiery furnace, and so leads to the igniting of flax and linen in the nave of the church. In an Anglo-Norman play of the twelfth century called *Adam*, the commitment to comprehensiveness requires the dramatizing of the Fall of the Angels, and the Casting Out from Paradise, and Cain's Murder of Abel, and a Prophet's Play like that of Balaam, and last, and as the culminating story, the Birth of Christ. For *Adam* is a Christmas play. That at least is the generic description.

In terms of the medieval mystery, it is, however, not really true that the end crowns the whole. The makers of the mystery, if they were given to rationalization, might argue for the circumstantial nature of their art in that it renders the climax more explicable. But it is not the need to prepare a climax that governs. Circumstantiality is an end in itself. "Sir, your honor cannot come to that yet," says Pompey the bawd, in *Measure for Measure*. He is replying to the justice who wants to know what was done to a respectable woman in the bawdy house where Pompey is employed. But the answer to the question must wait on the furnishing of the house itself, as with a lower chair in the inn room called the Bunch of Grapes, and a pair of stewed prunes in a fruit dish of threepence. As Pompey asserts, these also are truths. While they are attended to, the question, which is their occasion and the ostensible point on which the dialog turns, goes unanswered. The question, as it happens, is only ostensible. What is really at issue is totality of representation.

This unwillingness to admit of lacunae is equally conspicuous in the panoramic drama of the sixteenth century, before it is schooled and abraded by the focus drama of the Age of Reason. The schooling is artistically all to the good: Jonson as playwright is so immensely superior to his medieval predecessors as to make the observation merely banal. But the point is not to quality, rather to accommodation. In this particular, the Middle Ages

193

It is a source of unfailing interest to the playwright to observe

> how chances mock,
> And changes fill the cup of alteration
> With divers liquors![12]

Dr. Faustus, in which the action spans twenty-four years, testifies to this enthusiastic interest. "We must perform," says the Chorus, "the form of Faustus' fortunes, good or bad." George Chapman, in his most celebrated play, satisfies this requirement. The play begins with the stage direction: "Enter Bussy D'Ambois, poor." Not only the tragic climax engrosses John Ford, in his chronicle history of *Perkin Warbeck*, but the whole course of Perkin's fortunes and misfortunes, from the beginnings of his pretension to his death. Diastole and systole: not the final contracting as in the focus drama, but first the dilating and then the contracting: that is the rhythm which animates the *De Casibus* play:

> Stately and proud, in riches and in train,
> Whilom I was powerful, and full of pomp:
> But what is he whom rule and empery
> Have not in life or death made miserable?[13]

To traverse the whole course, as life yields to death, is to fail of that more strict subordination, in which the rationalist delights and which in fact he requires, of the component parts to a single effect. The business of the moment, in the episodic drama of the Middle Ages and the early Renaissance, as it is conceded attention and even devotion, aspires to autonomy. The aspiration is subversive of the principal achievement of the modern age, which is to generalize or bring to heel. What then? If modern man in his perception of things is approved, the indicated course is to leave the medieval maker in the dark backward and move on, as the satirical Rabelais adjures us, to the "evident torch of the sun." Medieval man is a curiosity, not important in himself, important only to antiquarians as the dead exponent of a discredited psychology. Description, as we have understood the

[12] *2HenryIV*, III, i, 51-53.   [13] *Edward II*, IV, vi.

process now for some hundreds of years, is a casualty of his myopic fixating on particulars without necessary reference to the whole. The annulling of random activity, to which we pin our hope, supposes the type or permanent configuration. What if the type does not inhere in reality, or—more precisely—represents an alternative mode of looking at reality?

In dealing with magnitudes—heights and weights, velocities of change—we are building on but not delineating individual cases. We are dealing rather with an affirmation or "universe of discourse." But this delimited universe—the *ensemble* of atomic physics—wins our suffrage only, says D'Arcy Thompson, as we employ the "equalising power of averages" or invoke the "law of large numbers."[14] To what degree is the generalizing law verified in nature? Evidently a decisive change in physical properties occurs when a thin film of oil "becomes attenuated to one, or something less than one, close-packed layer of molecules, and when, in short, it no longer has the properties of matter *in mass.*"[15] Critical mass alters what we perceive. That is not simply another way of saying that beauty (or proportion) is in the eye of the beholder. I take it to mean that generalization: coercive form is not a lie but a preference, expressing the relation between the man and the world he inhabits. It is the characteristic preference of the Age of Reason. Maybe the present time, which has learned to estimate discontinuity and to look with approbation on the indigenous thing, will not find the Middle Ages so remote as the immediate past.

Because the medieval temper is, in matters of art, essentially egalitarian, it does not discountenance but encourages and honors the pressing of individual claims. What it requires is not the depending of thing on thing but a multiplicity of things. "Infinite and perfect Beauty," asserts Hugh of St. Victor, "can only manifest itself properly when reflected by an infinite number of dif-

[14] Following the mathematician Poisson: *"Les choses de toute nature sont soumises à une loi universelle qu'on peut appeler la loi des grands nombres"* (*Recherches*, 1837; Thompson, *On Growth and Form*, I, 118 and n.).

[15] Thompson, I, 70, after the physicist Lord Rayleigh.

ferent forms.["16] Hugh is known as *Alter Augustinus* as he seeks
to honor the conflicting claims of mysticism and Scholastic philosophy. Augustine, in his fragmentary work on Christian learning, endeavors to rationalize the education of a Christian man
—and breaks off, having written four books. This education is
so various, superficially it is so disordered, as to frustrate description in terms of a meditated scheme. Medieval music is possibly
analogous. I think, for example, of the motets of Guillaume de
Machaut. By and large, they are episodic in nature. Partly, that
is a consequence of their polyphonic structure. Each line is invested with equal importance. The total composition is not de-
veloped retrospectively, in fulfillment of a single design. It is
built up word by word or phrase by phrase, and without regard
to the unity of the whole. Medieval architecture is like that. In
the abbey church of Mont-Saint-Michel, the Norman nave introduces the flamboyant Gothic choir. The cathedral of St. Vitus
in Prague, oblivious of the dictates of form, joins the style of
the Renaissance to French Gothic and ancient Romanesque.[17]
The twin towers of Chartres, as they differ radically in form, do
not reflect a master plan but the differing tastes and psychologies
of the generations which brought them into being. Their beauty,
taken together, is in their diversity.

The parallel is striking to the composition of the *Roman de
la Rose*, which is to the Middle Ages not only the incomparable
breviary of love but also a lexicon of the differing attitudes
towards love potential in different human beings. Like the
Gothic cathedral, the poem is a vast work-in-progress. Guillaume
de Lorris lays the cornerstone, in the first half of the thirteenth
century. At his death he bequeaths to those who come after him
a fragment of 4,000 lines. An anonymous poet undertakes to

[16] Quoted Hunter, *Lyly*, pp. 137-38.

[17] Spain offers predictably more violent illustrations of the yoking of
opposites. Santiago de Compostella adds Baroque to Romanesque. In Seville
the one remaining Moorish minaret is tied in completely, with no sense of
disjunction, to the fifteenth-century Gothic cathedral. Had the perpetra-
tors of this "oxymoron" thought about what they were doing, they would
no doubt have rejected the Moors. But their psychology is not "intellectual."

provide a brief conclusion or coping. Jean de Meun, perhaps forty years later, is dissatisfied with that conclusion. Jean adds more than 17,000 lines to the whole. The tastes of his predecessors are not to his own taste and he does not feel obliged to consult them. In what he adds, not much thought is given to coherence. Guillaume is the celebrant of courtly love. Jean de Meun is its satirist.[18] There is a degree of violence in the yoking together of these opposing points of view. The poem, nonetheless, is able to sustain it, and this because it is infinitely flexible in form. In a more familiar world, the vessel bursts asunder as the heated particles within drum with increasing velocity against the walls. In this recondite world of the high Middle Ages, the vessel expands. After all, it is a world for which the living man himself in his perplexing variety provides the model, and not a ghostly paradigm from which all vagaries and contradictions have been excluded.

It is just these contradictions that the Latin poet Alan of Lille sees as sticking the heart of human behavior and, by inference, of the world which man inhabits and seeks to recreate in his art. Man is "unequal in nature, unequal in substance, discordant in form, a dual being . . . [who] comes together in creation; one side of him knows the earth, the other smacks of heaven . . . this poor part is forced to yield tribute to death, the law of death exempts that other. This remains, that dissolves, this endures, that perishes; this wears the name of being, that manifests the godhead."[19] To subordinate these independent clauses to a single declarative sentence requires, perhaps, uncommon strength of will. One might compare the homogeneous and unified design of St. Paul's, which proclaims in every feature the strong and single hand of Christopher Wren, with an earlier and less self-conscious cathedral like that of St. Alban's, in which a discrete array of Norman and Gothic elements, intermixed with vestiges of late Anglo-Saxon, exist more or less amicably to-

---

[18] J. V. Fleming in his comprehensive study of the *Roman* disputes the notion that Jean is "Anti-Guillaume," and posits for the poem "a single and unified action" (pp. 69, 104).

[19] *Anticlaudianus,* c.1184, I, viii.

gether. This is the unity of what comes next. It is the art of catena. Its great quality is that it is able to assimilate the vagrant impulse, without fear of occluding or contradicting the ultimate point. For in a real sense, there is no such point.

That is why, in the art of the Middle Ages, divagation is not a blemish but a virtue, and *egressio* and *excessus* are words of praise. "He that treats of sacred writ should follow the way of a river." The injunction is uttered by Gregory the Great. He proceeds to develop and to justify his analogy:

> for if a river, as it flows along its channel, meets with open valleys on its side, into these it immediately turns the course of its current, and when these are copiously supplied, presently it pours itself back into its bed.

That is the pattern for the writer whose business is an elucidating of the Divine Word. If, says Gregory,

> in discussing any subject, he chance to find at hand any occasion of seasonable edification, he should . . . force the streams of discourse towards the adjacent valley, and when he has poured forth enough upon its level of instruction, fall back into the channel of discourse which he had prepared for himself.[20]

Lactantius is faithful to this pattern, though not precisely in Gregory's sense of lighting on seasonable edification. In the midst of a book devoted to the origin of error, he finds nothing amiss in turning aside to discuss the invention of wine.[21] Hugh of St. Victor is a little more circumspect. As Hugh is treating of history, and in particular of books that are useful for study, a different matter absorbs his attention. He pauses to consider it. "Possibly," he says, "if it did not seem childish, I should interject in this place a few instructions on the manner of construing sentences."[22] He does not want to be taken as laboring the obvious and so he puts his interjections away. But it is not a feeling of impropriety that restrains him.

John of Salisbury, writing what purports to be a history of

[20] *Moralia*, i, 6-7.   [21] *Divine Institutes*, ii, xiv.
[22] *Didascalion*, vi, 3.

the Papacy, is sufficiently willing to entertain whatever comes
to mind that he devotes almost a third of his narrative to an
account of the theology of Gilbert de la Porrée, the Bishop of
Poitiers, and his controversy with Bernard of Clairvaux. Concluding this swollen parenthesis, he confesses with superb understatement to his closest friend, Peter of Celle: "I have dwelt on
these matters . . . longer perhaps than the nature of the subject
required." What the subject requires is not without importance.
There are, however, other and equally weighty considerations.
"I was anxious," says John, "to give you a fuller picture of
the man whom you have had the good fortune to know." He
adds: "Now I must return to papal history."[23] It is worth re-
marking that the entire history encompasses only four years
(1148-52). Of course it is not a history at all. It is a series of
speaking oeillades, whose total range of seeing approximates to
360 degrees.

Cassiodorus is another who is prone to looking around. In his
case, the digressive habit is not confined to what he writes. First
a servant of the Ostrogothic rulers of Rome, he is subsequently
a Calabrian monk. That is a pretty fair disjunction. The work
overgoes it. In the introduction to divine and human readings
written for the edification of his monastic pupils, he subsumes
under the heading of divinity not only those reflections that are
augured by his topic, as on the Octateuch, or first eight books of
the Old Testament, and on the four accepted synods of the
Church, and the situation of the double monastery he had
founded at Vivarium and Mount Castellum; but also and with
no sense of a new departure, reflections on the adding of critical
marks, and on figures of speech, and on the remembering of
correct spelling. Having cited authorities "on first, middle and
last syllables, and on the letter B in three positions in the noun
and adjective," he observes, what is evident and characteristic:
"I have collected as many of these works as possible with eager
curiosity." If contemporary abuses engage his attention, he interrupts his train to offer admonition and advice, as to a greedy

---

[23] *Historia Pontificalis,* c.1164, xv (trans. M. Chibnall, p. 41).

abbot: "do not burden . . . [the peasants] with the weight of increased taxes"; or to the reformer of the language of Holy Writ: "let a laudable neglect hide a triple trochee." If it appears that among his readers there are persons of inferior capacity who cannot enter on philosophic writings, he attends to their plight by the intermitting of philosophy. It is not beneath his dignity nor outside his ken to expatiate on the humbler matter of husbandry. He considers that it is good to look to the high end of all: he is "modern," he is "artistic." But he is, unlike the modern régisseur, neither steadfast nor singleminded. He keeps turning the mirror, and what it reflects is endlessly engrossing. Form goes out the window as he remembers that "Gargilius Martial has written most excellently on gardens and has carefully explained the raising of vegetables . . . [and that] Columella and Emilianus among others are commendable authors on the tilling of the fields and on the keeping of bees, doves, and also fish." This, the business of Book 1 only, is in preface to an account of the seven liberal arts.[24]

The idea of form, as a modern writer conceives it, is unfamiliar to the Middle Ages and uncongenial. A writer of the ninth century, in his innocence of form, discourses concurrently on the love of God and one's neighbor and the nature of irregular verbs. The fourth-century monastic John Cassian lumps together in a single work remarks on synecdoche and the eight deadly sins. (He is not content with the conventional seven.) In the *Institutes of the Coenobia* there is not merely God's plenty: there is an inundation of words and heterogeneous things which overthrows the mind and staggers the senses. One complains of Saul Bellow?

Early in the fifth century Martianus Capella, in his account of the *Marriage of Mercury and Philology*, ekes out the romance which his title announces with a census of contemporary culture. Martianus is primarily an allegorical writer. But though he is concerned with what lies beneath the surface, he is not

---

[24] *Institutiones divinarum et humanarum lectionum*, after 551. Jones edn., pp. 134, 136, 107, 130.

hostile to the surface nor impervious to its charms. He does not indulge it only as a stalking horse. Neither is he noticeably sparing of words in his description of the union of the god and the learned maiden.[25] But his interests are too manifold to be exhausted in the recounting of a fable, and even though it is fraught with implication. Concluding Book II, at which point the more modern writer would be drawing to an end of the whole, he gives notice of a new departure. *"Nunc ergo mythos termina- tur,"* he says. Now the mythological narrative is finished. But the book is not finished. As Martianus makes clear, it has hardly begun:

> *infiunt*
> *artes libelli qui sequentes asserent.*
> *nam fruge vera omne fictum dimovent.*

In the more condescending words of Francis Bacon, who has also been intent on the meanings of mythology: "But perhaps we remain too long in the theatre—it is time we should advance to the palace of the mind."[26]

What occasions the advance, and hence the writing of another seven books, is the presentation to Philology on her assumption into Heaven of the seven liberal arts. Such a wedding gift as this is not especially conducive to the telling of an amorous story. The medieval author, as he has an eye for the fitness of things, perceives the problem, though with a minimum of per- turbation. His resolution is simple and characteristic. He puts aside the story (*omne fictum dimovent*) and attends hencefor- ward to the claims of fruitful truth (*fruge vera*).

This naïve resolution is not open to the modern maker. His anxious sense of the fitness of things commits him, as he grows adept in his craft, to the ruthless exclusion of peripheral matter, like Shakespeare's dish of stewed prunes or Cardano's reflections on brook carp and pond carp or the edifying meanders Pope Gregory is willing to accommodate. Modern art moves forward in a straight line. This line is also decorous: distinguished by

---

[25] Bks. I-II.
[26] *Advancement of Learning,* end of Bk. II.

propriety. "You cannot serve cod and salmon": an imperious hostess of the Victorian (high rational) period, instructing and admonishing her cook. To interpolate in one's novel the tangential account of an Old Man of the Hill (Fielding) or the Memoirs of an Unfortunate Lady (Smollett) is understood as self-indulgent and is accordingly reprehended. If, in a novel well carried, straight-line progression appears to be obscured (Caroline Gordon in *None Shall Look Back*; Stark Young, *So Red the Rose*; *War and Peace*, the great exemplar in this kind), that is a measure of artistic cunning: the ancillary stories of which the artist is treating are rationalizable after the fact. They bear; as James would say, they are reflectors. The impulse is insistently centripetal.

Very obviously in medieval art the impulse is to fly the center. It is a "natural" impulse: the medieval maker enacting in his work the Second Law of Thermodynamics. "Things fall apart." The ordered systems he begins to construct tend, like systems in nature, to evolve in such a way as to increase their degree of disorder or randomness. The implicit contradiction is startling: order governs in the abrogation of order. To entertain the possibility that time might run backwards and the twelfth century succeed again to the present is to annihilate sequence and form. But the concept of Time Reversal is the child of Newton's Second Law. To employ another and more familiar "metaphor": Dike, the Orphic principle of nonrational and even demonic becoming, is the child of Themis, the personification of the Olympian life view: pattern, stasis, predictability. One is led to say: in nature, as in the art of our predecessors before the new learning came up, the direction of things is centrifugal. "It is as if," writes Loren Eiseley, "everything alive had in it a tug of anti-gravity, a revulsion from the central fire or the mother sea. If stars and galaxies hurtle outward in headlong flight, the urge for dispersal seems equally and unexplainably written into the living substance itself."[27] So Eden, and the Tower of Babel.

If there is order in us, it is the order of change. The living organism, as opposed to the artifact elaborated by the modern

[27] *The Unexpected Universe*, p. 149.

régisseur, is—no doubt a configuration—but so constructed as to evade the coercive tendency of the laws of nature. Divagation, contradiction are of its essence. "We begin in infancy with a universe that our minds constantly strive to subdue to the rational. But just as we seem to have achieved that triumph, some part of observed nature persists in breaking out once more into the unexpected."[28] This persistent breaking out or turning aside is definitive of the medieval "esthetic." But the word is excessively portentous. Medieval man is too much in love with the mutable present, too little enamored of "God": unchanging form, and that is why his art, from a modern point of view, is imperfect.

Alan of Lille is illustrative: in his arbitrariness he is typical. Having got halfway through the *Anticlaudianus*, he changes course abruptly to pursue things unattempted yet in prose and rhyme. To this point his Muse has sung in faint murmuring; his page has sported in fragile verse. Now he resigns the petty and tunes a greater lyre. As Alan puts it (in hexameter verse),

> laying aside the poet entirely, I usurp to myself the rare sayings of the prophet; the terrestrial Apollo yields to the celestial muse, the muse of Jove; the manifest language of earth surrenders to the speech of heaven, earth gives place to Olympus.[29]

Of course no such surrendering or displacing occurs. In any case, it is not total. Neither is it in Martianus Capella. Though he advises his readers that from now on and for the most part he will devote himself to more serious learning—*"et disciplinas annotabunt sobrias pro parte multa"*—Martianus knows better than to promise more than he can pay. As befitting the author who declines to distinguish between a romance and a handbook, who moves impartially in his writing from poetry to prose, who, in the midst of a treatise on arithmetic can break without warning into song (Book VII), he adds—what is possibly a gratuitous observation—that fabulous matter will not be altogether forbid-

---

[28] After Eiseley, pp. 203, 218, 166-67.
[29] Bk. v, Ch. v (Cornog edn., p. 109).

den (*nec vetabunt ludicra*).[30] Formal cause, things happening *propter hoc*: where are these? *Omne fictum dimovent.* The crocus, as a modern physiologist instructs us, grows by fits and starts, each followed by a partial recoil. Growth and form are incremental. The medieval maker, as he confesses the language of earth, speaks also to the present moment. "We have come down" in the present "from a principle of continuity to a principle of discontinuity."[31]

William Carlos Williams on Marianne Moore is to the purpose here. "The only help I ever got from Miss Moore toward the understanding of her verse was that she despised connectives."[32] What follows is a favoring of the disjunctive mode. John of Salisbury, in what he despises and favors, is like the modern poet. Introducing the *Metalogicon* (1159), John defines his purpose as an essay in defense of logic. That is, however, only his stated purpose. Almost at once, he begins to dilute it. He announces that he has included various things, "according to the custom of writers." *Res varias*: it is the apposite title for the medieval book. What the book incorporates, as in a kind of emulsion, "each reader is at liberty to accept or reject as he sees fit." I think of Chaucer in the Prologue to the *Miller's Tale*:

> whoso list it nat yheere,
> Turne over the leef and chese another tale.

There is no coercive driving toward a single point but a setting forth by the author, and with an equanimity that is in curious contrast to the polemical matter in hand, of his highly diversified wares. "It is hoped," as John says (he is addressing Thomas Becket and also the anonymous reader who stands behind him) "that, at your convenience, you will examine all the points that I have made in detail, since . . . I have constituted you the judge

---

[30] Remigius (ed. C. Lutz, p. 209) glosses: "LUDICRA *id est fabulosa.*" The commentary of Remigius incorporates those of the ninth-century Irish bishop Dunchad, and John the Scot (Erigena).

[31] D. W. Thompson, pp. 170-71.

[32] Quoted Hall, *Marianne Moore*, p. 49.

of my little works." But the reader is more than judge; he is partly the contriver. To him and not the author the job of picking and choosing is assigned. In support of this rather casual view of the writer's business, John adduces a Latin quotation:

> Some things you will read herein are excellent,
>> some mediocre, and several defective;
> But this is inevitable—as otherwise, dear
>> Avitus, there would be no book.

That is Martial's opinion (*Epigrams*, i, 16). "I echo him," says John of Salisbury, and sets about the making of his emulsion.

This same predilection for randomness and ecumenicism is enunciated by Alan of Lille, in the prose prologue to the *Anticlaudianus*. The poem is a house of many mansions. In one, the literal, even a boy may dwell. There, pleasure is unalloyed. In another, the moral, his father may profit from instruction. Still another mansion, the allegorical, is reserved to the choice and master spirits of the age. In the words of Alan "the literal meaning's sweetness will allure the puerile ear; moral instruction will imbue the proficient mind; and the keener subtilty of the allegory will sharpen the perfected intellect." The medieval poet who builds so diversified a habitation, or hodgepodge, resembles only generically the more fastidious spirit who succeeds him. This successor is figured in Milton's *Il Penseroso*. It is not plenitude that delights him but "Spare Fast, that oft with gods doth diet." His watchword is exclusiveness. His dedication is to rigorous form. In this he dramatizes the characteristic preoccupation of modern man. Medieval man is, more humbly, a jack-of-all-trades. His intention, as a poet, is to offer something for everybody.

Milton is everybody's possession; not everybody, I think, is reading Alan of Lille. Still, the comprehensive mode in the earlier writer and the psychology that informs it speak to us suggestively as we contemplate our own psychology. Alan's business, in the *Anticlaudianus*, is to tell of Nature's appeal to God for the creation of a perfect man in whom all moral and physical virtues are united. That is to describe the poem, simply as narration. It is, however, much more than narration, and its total business is far from simple. From among the many matters it is concerned to explore, and with the aid of art, reason, and doctrine,[33] I select the following, pretty much at random:

> Why the consonants, with voice lowered in a thin sound, grow mute, but the vowel clearly cries aloud and gives breathing-holes to the remaining sounds. . . . In what manner the conclusion, summing up separate points, encloses all with a logical end, drawing up the reins of the discourse. . . . What number is called a point, what a line, or what a plane figure. . . . What tone may be double to a tone, or what song may echo in diapason. . . . Why the center sits in the middle, and why every angle either lies inactive and obtuse or stretches upward and acute. . . . What the movement of the moon is, what the sphere of the sun.[34]

But this perusal by the author of the *artes liberales* does not argue loss of interest in the narrative itself. In the medieval reticule, celestial language is conjunctive with the language of earth. Neither enjoys absolute priority. If Prudence is rendered vividly as she ascends to Heaven in her chariot to prosecute Nature's request, that is not because Alan is primarily concerned with description. It is rather in fulfillment of his express design to allure the puerile ear with the telling of an interesting story. The heart of that story is the journey to Heaven, which derives, I suppose, from Martianus Capella. In neither case, however, is the story felt as sufficient. It is understood that the author, as he is magnanimous, will seek to gratify not only the ear but the perfected intellect as well. And therefore, in the earlier narrative, Mercury personifies fluency of speech (*symbolum sermonis*), and Philology the love and pursuit of reason (*typus est rationis*).[35] In the later narrative, Prudence, as she requires a complement also, is conducted by Reason, who functions as the

---

[33] Bk. ii, Ch. vii, p. 75.

[34] Conflating the discussions of Grammar (ii, 7; p. 75), Logic (iii, 1, pp. 78-79), Rhetoric (iii, 2; p. 82), Arithmetic (iii, 4; p. 85), Music (iii, 5; p. 88), Geometry (iii, 6; p. 89), Astronomy (iv, 1; p. 91).

[35] The authority is Remigius of Auxerre. Lutz edn., p. 28.

charioteer. The chariot itself is drawn by five horses, and in these the five senses are figured.[36]

This running in tandem of the literal meaning's sweetness and the subtler allegory that pervades it is the mode of proceeding that Alan employs throughout the poem. "In this book," he asserts, "the substance is twofold: one a narrative, the other of mystic significance." If, in the course of the journey he is describing, "various natural phenomena are met," he does not huddle them up in a cursory phrase. That would be to leave unsatisfied the more proficient minds. Their temper is speculative. They are avid of knowing "Who binds up the rain in the cloud, why the air roars, who begets the winds, who engenders their rages, why the substance of a cloud comes out in so many formations." To avoid their discomfiture, the poet interrupts his narrative while "The cause of clouds is considered, and the cause of snow, the origin of hail and the source of lightnings . . . the divers orbits of the planets . . . [and] the various natures of the stars." It is not an unreasonable interruption. The claims of the puerile ear are neither more nor less urgent than those of the learned intelligence. For that reason, though the poem as a narrative is essentially completed, the poem as thesaurus is not completed at all when Prudence returns to earth with the soul that God has granted, and Nature begins to mould the body. "At this point," says the author, who has only been biding his time, "the opportunity is seized to describe the habit, residence, and wheel of Fortune."[37]

Jean de Meun avails himself of this same opportunity when, in the *Roman*, he also embarks on a long description of Fortune's wheel. To recite the story of the Lover and the Rose is only one aspect of his poetic intention. He is absorbed in that story; and in the contrast between the Golden Age and the present, and the more important contrast between ennobled blood and the higher nobility which belongs to the gentle heart. If the hypocrisy of the Mendicant Orders inflames him, he is bound to give it room. It is a part of the totality of things, like the matter

[36] Argument, p. 50.

[37] Argument, p. 51; II, iv (p. 68); IV, iv-viii; V, i; VII, viii-ix; VIII, i-ii.

of astrology, and the properties of mirrors and glasses, and the nature of frenzies and dreams. Historical persons populate his narrative, like King Manfred of Sicily, and Nero and Seneca, and Héloïse and Abelard. But so do abstractions. So do persons from mythology, like Dido and Phyllis, Oenone and Medea. What Venus did with Mars finds a place in the story. As it is exemplary, it whets the perfected intellect. The literal meaning's sweetness is not, however, omitted. "Be active in your functions," says Genius, the emissary of Nature.

> Exert yourselves gaily to leap and dance,
> And rest not, lest your members grow lukewarm.
> All your utensils in the task employ;
> He who works well by work will warm himself.
> Plow, barons, plow—your lineage repair.[38]

The medieval writer, as he takes for his subject the entire range of human activity, whether sacred or profane, is necessarily an erudite man. The titles bestowed on him by a grateful posterity bear witness to his unrivaled erudition. He is *Magnus* or *magister* or *doctissimus . . . magister*, who is equally adept in divine and human readings (*in divinis et humanis scripturis eruditissimus*). "Let us in no manner be cut off from the pursuit of reading," says Cassiodorus in the middle of the sixth century.[39] Late in the twelfth century Marie de France advises the poet, in the prologue to her fables, to devote himself to good writings. It is appropriate that Jean de Meun, as he is supremely faithful to that advice, should be represented, in a portrait executed long after his death, as wearing a Master's biretta.[40] The critical element in this approving of the medieval writer, as the representation attests, is the verity and scope of what he knows. When Chaucer pays honor to predecessors like Alan of

---

[38] Ll. 20064, 20071-77. Lineation follows Robbins trans. Fleming, *Roman*, p. 213, reads this passage as burlesque. The exhortation to "sexual heroics" is "comically undercut by epic agricultural metaphors" lifted from Alan of Lille. One man's meat is another man's poison.

[39] *Institutiones*, p. 71.

[40] Morgan MS 245 (*c*.1415), f. 77v.

Lille and Martianus Capella, it is because their descriptions are "sooth" or true.[41] Alan, as he is myriad minded, is honored as *doctor ille famosus* and *doctorem celeberrimum*. So conversant is Martianus with esoteric lore that a ninth-century commentator who can track him in those snows is venerated as *egregius doctor*.[42] Chaucer himself is esteemed as the "learned Chaucer," even by antiquarians of the new enlightenment like Leland and Speght.

It is, however, the very range of the learning exhibited by these medieval masters that impairs their authority in an age committed to focus and to the enunciating of a single point of view. The earlier age, as it sees no mandatory distinction between poetry and philosophy, tends to confound the two. In its catholicity of interest it tends to cancel priorities, as between the shell and the kernel. In its penchant for scrutinizing "various things" at once, it makes against the establishing of inviolate categories and fixed lines of demarcation. It sees the process of demarcation as entailing a loss in integrity and hence in capacity, like the resolving of the emulsion into its constituent parts. The positive statement of this position is that "consent gives us matured might."[43] The medieval author, inferring the relationship of demarcation and what Alan of Lille calls "dissent," omits to classify separately the splendor of the moon and the light of the sun, or the flow of the stream and the force of the river, or the fruit of the grain and the ear that sustains it. The result is that, in his anatomizing of things, "the pain of an aching head [tends to] pass away into the limbs . . . [and] the blemish of the bitter root [to] be lost in the branches." Abstraction is interdicted, on which the establishing of categories depends. Nothing is anatomized in its ideal or isolated condition—as the ratonalist, who does not grasp the implicit contradiction, might put it: *wie*

[41] *House of Fame*, Bk. II, ll. 985-90.

[42] Remigius of Auxerre, who is also "*in divinis et humanis scripturis eruditissimus*" and "*doctissimus ea aetate magister*," Lutz edn., pp. 1, 6. See the similar titles conferred on Alan of Lille, from the thirteenth through the sixteenth centuries, in Cornog edn., pp. 10-11, 21-22.

[43] II, v; p. 71.

es wirklich war—but always in terms of the total habitation from which its life derives. Music inhabits and derives from the heavenly spheres. The different spacings and speeds of the planets are understood to produce it. And therefore music is defined at least partly in astronomical terms. (In the celestial scale, as elaborated by Remigius of Auxerre, it is the moon that gives forth the deepest note.)[44]

This mingling of kinds is disconcerting to the classifier. He does not know how to take hold of a world presided over by a deity who "conforms his heavenly soul to earth," and so gives example for the conforming of "the cedar to the hyssop, the giant himself to the dwarf, light to murkiness, rich to poor, well to sick, king to slave, purple to sackcloth."[45] His idea is to keep the different genres distinct, and to ascertain what is proper to each. But if he wishes to determine what is proper to a poet and turns for elucidation to the medieval writer, he finds to his perplexity that a poet like Chaucer is also a kind of scientist (as witness the treatise he composes on the astrolabe); that the poet Lucan is a historian as well as a poet (on the authority, among others, of Isidore of Seville), and what is more a philosopher who "invites the curious to determine the hidden causes of the ocean waves" (John of Salisbury); and that poets in general are hardly to be distinguished from "the learned clerks" and "the great philosophers" (Jean de Meun, who cites Virgil and Ennius), or even from the geometricians (the bizarre contribution of Martianus Capella).[46] Of course there are differences, but not generic, only particular differences.

I do not want to overstate here. Servius, in his commentary on the *Aeneid*, as he declines to call Lucan a poet, apparently discriminates between kinds. Lucan, on his view, does not write

[44] Lutz edn., p. 21.

[45] *Anticlaudianus*, v, ix; p. 116.

[46] End of Bk. vi; p. 362 in Dick edn. For John of Salisbury on Lucan as philosopher, see *Metalogicon*, Bk. i, Ch. xxiv, p. 67; iv, 40, p. 269; and as historian, *Policraticus*, Bk. ii, Ch. xix ("*poeta doctissimus si tamen poeta dicendus est, qui vera narratione rerum ad historicos magis accedit,*" Webb edn., i, 441). For Isidore, see *Etymologies*, viii, vii.

poetry but history.[47] Four centuries later, Rabanus Maurus expresses the same opinion and in almost the same language.[48] Lucan, he asserts, cannot be numbered among the poets, "because it is evident that he wrote history and not poetry." You cannot serve cod and salmon. But what shall be said of Rabanus himself, the *primus Germaniae praeceptor*, who combines in one person the roles of theologian, polemicist, mystic, encyclopedist, clerical administrator, and poet? So far as I can tell, the more conventional view is, however, not so jealous of formal distinction. This jealousy, or acuity, begins to be conspicuous only in the early Renaissance. I detect it in Boccaccio, for whom "poets are not like historians, who begin their account at some convenient beginning and describe events in the unbroken order of their occurrence to the end."[49]

Boccaccio, who is writing a defense of poetry, is of course concerned that poets "should be reckoned of the very number of the philosophers." He wants to make the point that they also are workers in the vineyard and hence deserving of attention and regard. That is why he salutes Dante as, not simply "a mere mythographer," but as one who "unties with amazingly skillful demonstration the hard knots of holy theology"—and philosophy and physics. This mingling of kinds does not exemplify the medieval confusion but the new stridency with which the Renaissance seeks to justify the poet. Though Boccaccio is at pains to see that poetry is honored equally with philosophy, he is careful to describe and to consider his poets under a different rubric. "The philosopher," he says,

> by a process of syllogizing, disproves what he considers false, and in like manner proves his theory, and does all this as obviously as he can. The poet conceives his thought by contemplation, and,

[47] P. 129 in Thilo and Hagen edn. respecting *Aeneid*, I, 382: "*historiam composuisse, non poema.*" The idea persists throughout the seventeenth century.

[48] *De Universo*, xv, ii, "De poetis": "*Unde et Lucanus ideo in numero poetarum non ponitur: quia historias composuisse videtur, non poema.*" Migne, *PL*, III, col. 419.

[49] *Genealogy*, xiv, viii.

wholly without the help of syllogism, veils it as subtly and skilfully as he can under the outward semblance of his invention. . . . It is . . . a philosopher's business to dispute in the lecture-room, but a poet's to sing in solitude.[50]

That is the kind of distinction the rationalist has in mind. He does not find it very often in the Middle Ages.[51]

Now the Middle Ages are, on one side, not exactly unfamiliar with distinction or propriety. As medieval society is permeated by notions of class, it is greatly given to the setting up of nicely reticulated hierarchical structures, in which not only the different orders of men but those of the lower animals and also of the plants and minerals occupy their appointed positions. Hierarchy stipulates that the laurel take precedence over the myrtle, and the olive over the oleaster, and that roses be preferred before the wild nard, and hyacinths before the lowly seaweed. But the trouble is that, in the medieval schema, distinction is less of kind than of degree. If the world is divided into many mansions, their separation from one another is not so important as their contiguity. Reticulation is more than demarcation. The firm soil is forever winning of the ocean, and the ocean eating at the flats, and to the end that each effaces what is peculiar to either. Kinds and categories do not so much insist on their differences as confess their affinities: "the swollen torrent requests a wave from the river . . . Narcissus is wont to seek pattern from the parsnip, and the flame of a candle to contribute to the light of day."[52]

This indifference to the weighty matter of mine and thine, than which nothing is more pernicious to the age of Bacon, Burke, and Bentham, has unfortunate consequences for poetry of the open-handed or antediluvian kind. As the prodigal father is succeeded by his more frugal and punctilious son and heir, the older poetry is indicted as making against the order of things. Evidently, it relishes of our old stock in that it takes without

[50] xv, vi; xiv, ix; xv, vi; xiv, xvii.

[51] Clerk and poet and philosopher are generically the same, "Good men who give their lives to learning's quest,/ Becoming doctors of philosophy" (*Roman de la Rose*, ll. 19116-17).

[52] *Anticlaudianus*, ii, i; p. 65.

shame whatever lies in its road; and yet lends without scruple, and to the scandal and confusion of the rationalist, who does not understand why arithmetic, for instance, should be permitted to wear poetry's colors. To Henry Cornelius Agrippa (d. 1535), who epitomizes the irritable wonderment of the Renaissance detractors, poetry is "An Arte that is alwaies hungrie, and eatinge up other mens breade like mise."[53] It gives to Caesar what is owing to Caesar, and also what is owing to God. Or else it reverses that formulation. Partly, this double allegiance is due to the equivocal nature of the poets themselves who, as they seek to be all things to all men, are equally at home in either camp.

The deviousness or promiscuity that is characteristic of them is writ large in the poet Dante, of whom his enemies might complain that he is neither fish nor flesh. The kind of poetry he writes follows predictably. In a more rational time, the poet surveys the choices available to him and compounds unequivocally for a single kind: "either for tragedy, comedy, history, pastoral, pastoral-comical, historical-pastoral, scene individible, or poem unlimited." Dante, as a type of the medieval poet who is not easily parted from his character of Proteus, the multiform god, is more subtle and rapacious. The form or method of treatment he employs in the *Divine Comedy* embraces a whole decalogue of *modi* or kinds. It is "poetic, figurative, descriptive, digressive, metaphorical and, in addition, explanatory, divisible, probative, condemnatory, and explicit in examples."[54] The Bible instructs by stories and parables and metaphors; but so does Dante: it is his *modus transumptivus* or metaphorical mode. Science offers to define and to analyze problems, and logic to prove and controvert. Dante assimilates the methods of science and logic. He is a scientist in that he deals with the explanatory and divisible kinds; he is a logician in that his form of treatment is probative and condemnatory. In his work, all that is congenial to the human spirit finds a place, and philosophy and poetry

[53] *Of the Vanitie and Uncertaintie of Artes and Sciences*, trans. 1569, Elv.

[54] Letter to Can Grande della Scala, *c.*1319; adapted from Lathem and Carpenter edn., Letter xi, p. 196.

walk amicably together. It is, to the dichotomizing temper, an inappropriate pairing.

The charge which Virgil, in the *Inferno*, lays on the poet may be taken as figuring the rationale of the poem:

> That to the full thy knowledge may extend
> Of all this round contains, go now and mark. . . .[55]

It is true, what Dante asserts in the letter to Can Grande, that "The subject, then, of the whole work, taken according to the letter alone, is simply a consideration of the state of souls after death." It is equally true that the subject is the state of souls in their mundane condition, and vested in particular forms:

> The ladies and the knights, the toils and ease,
> That witch'd us into love and courtesy.[56]

Like Aglauros in Purgatory, Dante is prone to remember whence he came. Though Heaven calls and courts his gaze, yet his eye "Turns with fond doting still upon the earth." Dante the eschatologist is also Dante the patriot and Dante the politician, who is deeply engrossed by the corruption of the Papacy, and the discords that assail his native city, as epitomized in the contention of Bianchi and Neri, and Guelph and Ghibelline. The way to salvation is of absorbing interest to him; so is the painting of Giotto and Cimabue, and the poetry of Cavalcanti and Guido Guinicelli. He has an eye for the felicities of San Miniato al Monte, and for the winding course of the Arno. He is attentive also, and more prosaically, to the construction of dikes in the Netherlands, and the origin of Mantua, and the dividing along its length of the Pont San Angelo in the reign of Boniface VIII. The heavens kindle his imagination, but not entirely for theological reasons. It is possible to see him as anticipating Newton, in speculating on the system of gravitational attraction. He is decidedly curious, from his station in Purgatory, about the position of the sun overhead and the course it travels along the ecliptic. This hunger for *res varias* is the clue to his titanic achievement. He might have taken for his motto the moving line from the *Georgics* which Cardinal Newman takes for his,

[55] Xvii.   [56] Purgatory, xiv.

and which seems to me to illuminate equally the triumphant
exploiting of the here and now that characterizes the art of the
Middle Ages, and the reviving in the nineteenth century of first-
rate discursive prose:

Felix qui potuit rerum cognoscere causas.

But if Dante is the greatest of the medieval philosopher-poets,
his uniqueness lies only in the delimiting adjective and not in
the mingling of kinds. The medieval Virgil evinces the same
inexhaustible curiosity and the same willingness to mix together
what is, by later convention, immiscible. Virgil, as Dante describes him, is above all the catholic poet "who every art and science values!" Nothing is too arcane or prosaic to be exempted
from the probings of his inquisitorial eye. Dante's praise of him
is verified: "what silence hides, that know'st thou."[57] His bucolic
and didactic poetry is taken by the Middle Ages as uniting with
his epic to form a biographical relation which corresponds in
little to the diversified nature of all life and all activity. This
Virgil is not a poet but an encyclopedist. But an encyclopedist is
a poet. The fusing of the two is signalized in the medieval creation of Virgil's Wheel (*rota Virgilii*), in which the manifold
correspondences of the poetic achievement are depicted graphi-
cally in concentric circles.[58] It is not the supreme function of this
poet, simply to justify God's ways to man! but more comprehensively and with less portentousness to delineate—what the
Wheel depicts—the hierarchy of poetical kinds, and social kinds,
and also the complementary classes of implements and animals
and places and trees. What Cassiodorus says of the Psalter—
mixing metaphors (as he acknowledges)—may be said of the
medieval achievement as a whole. It "is a heavenly sphere thick
with twinkling stars and a very beautiful peacock adorned by
eyes of many decorous colors; it is indeed the paradise of souls,
containing countless fruits to fatten the human spirit in charming ways."[59]

[57] Inferno, iv, xix.
[58] Following Curtius, *European Literature*, pp. 231-32.
[59] *Institutiones*, p. 83.

216

 VII   The Seeds of Psyche

CATHOLICITY and not exclusiveness is the watchword of the medieval poet. It is also his defense against that medieval critic who, as he bases his attack on the old Platonic position, anticipates the criticism of the Renaissance. He has been met already in the twelfth century, attacking literature in the name of the new dialectics and later of Scholasticism. To the equable view of Jean de Meun that poetry, philosophy, and scholarship are the same, he opposes the more discriminating assertion of St. Thomas Aquinas that poetry is "the least of all the sciences." St. Thomas, although he is a poet himself, will not allow that poetry, like philosophy, has a cognitive function. He seeks, accordingly, to dissolve the ancient nexus of poetry and philosophy. The business of poetry is in his view inferior to that of reason. It is to be distinguished absolutely from the business of theology. Poetry employs figures of speech only to make pictures or as an appurtenance to fabling: in the words of the *Summa*, "to produce a representation." Holy Writ employs them for instruction and hence for profit: in this latter case they are "both necessary and useful."[1]

To a poet like Dante, the distinction is inadmissible. He is able to oppose it, from his house of many mansions, by adducing the philosophical *modi* which define his form of treatment just as fairly and exactly as the purely poetical kinds. The tieing together of the *modi* of metaphor and definition to those of poetry and science (as in the letter to Can Grande) denotes the commingling of pleasure and profit, whose fusion is not arbitrary (as often in the Renaissance) but organic. To paraphrase the definition of Love which Dante offers in the *Vita Nuova*: in the

[1] *Summa*, Pt. 1, Q. 1, Art. 9, Objection 1 and Reply.

circle (which is the poem), the parts of the circumference stand in equal relation to the center. Or—to adapt St. Bonaventura, who is describing the Deity—the poem is a circle whose center is everywhere and whose circumference is nowhere.

But Dante is the last important poet who is able to retort easily and with the old assurance on the critic whose appeal is to use. In the more narrow and eupeptic world which succeeds to the waning Middle Ages, the catholicity and the willingness to accommodate, to which the medieval poet might appeal in his defense, do not constitute a defense but an indictment of poetry. Catholicity has become inimical to use. The Renaissance, as one part of its program to rationalize all mundane business and to express from it the maximum yield, is concerned to fix the circumference of things once and for all. As its commitment is to order, it cannot afford to be endlessly egregious. In the world it inhabits, the center is not everywhere but just here. Its effort is to locate the center and build upon it. In pursuit of that effort it is necessarily exclusive. The hospitality of poetry is therefore anathema to it. What is wanted is not the multiple vision but a singleness of vision, and this in the interest of clarity that the truth of things (or better: Truth) may be discovered and implemented.

> Hands, do what you're bid:
> Bring the balloon of the mind
> That bellies and drags in the wind
> Into its narrow shed.

This is the new injunction. It is enjoined on the artist, not less than on other men, to the degree that he pretends to be useful.

Certainly the art of the Middle Ages is useful in that its purpose is to teach and delight. But it lays no claim to that tremendous and ultimate use which the Renaissance announces: the making over of man. Its commitment is to the achieving of knowledge: *rerum cognoscere causas*. But chiefly it conceives of knowledge as an end in itself. In rationalizing the story of Leah, the fecund woman whom Jacob prefers initially to the barren Rachel, it presents the former as a type of the active or affective life. Rachel, as she is barren, stands for contemplation. That is Dante's construction.[2] But Jacob is understood to make the wiser choice as he comes at last to prefer the contemplative woman, who is satisfied merely to see.[3] According to Hugh of St. Victor, "The things by which every man advances in knowledge are principally two—namely, reading and meditation."[4] That is a voice from the ends of the earth. It is the voice of a world that has been swallowed up forever in the dark backward and abysm of time. This vanished world of the Middle Ages, by virtue of what a more purposive generation will stigmatize as irresponsibility or sloth, can afford (to put it so) to divagate and meander and to be ribald and sober or comic and tragic by turns or even simultaneously.

To be precise about terms here: it is not the employing of different kinds in one work that distinguishes the medieval performance from that of the Renaissance. If the Middle Ages in its dramaturgy manipulate a comic subplot as undersong to the deeply serious burden of the play (as in the *Secunda Pastorum*, the greatest of the medieval mysteries, in which the vulgar story of Mak the sheep-biter recapitulates the birth of Christ), so in the drama of the Renaissance nonsense and high seriousness exist cheek by jowl (as in Marlowe's *Dr. Faustus*, in which the comedy of Wagner the servant recapitulates the tragedy of his master). But what the Renaissance will not tolerate in treating either story is a multiple point of view. It allows of complementarity (the plays of Robert Greene, Marlowe, Dekker, John Ford). The august protagonist is reincarnate on a lower level in the clown. Ambiguity is, however, forbidden. Neither Faustus nor Wagner is good and bad together, "one apple tasted," like Stephen Dedalus (as the medieval psychology returns in our time) or Mark Antony or Chaucer's Criseyde. Milton in his *Areopagitica* speaks to this psychology. "Good and evil we know in the field of this world grow up together almost insepara-

[2] Purgatory, xxvii, 108.

[3] See discussion in Charles S. Singleton, *Journey to Beatrice*, p. 112; Hollander, *Allegory*, p. 151.

[4] Preface to *Didascalion*.

bly"—let us add: comedy and tragedy, foolishness and wisdom, ugliness and comeliness—"and the knowledge of good is so involved with the knowledge of evil, and in so many cunning resemblances hardly to be discerned, that those confused seeds which were imposed upon Psyche as an incessant labor to cull out, and sort asunder, were not more intermixed."

The Renaissance undertakes the labor of culling out. The Middle Ages see it as gratuitous. Intermixing or ambiguity describes the fabric of things. The medieval poet, in telling a serious or epical story, is prone to comic interpolations.[5] Roland and Oliver joke on the field at Roncesvalles. There are no such interpolations in Virgil, nor in the later age in Tasso or Spenser or Milton. In the Second Shepherd's Play, a thievish and mendacious wife insists that the sheep her husband has stolen is a newly born babe. But it is not only the sheep of which the wife is speaking:

> I pray to God so mild,
> If ever I you beguiled,
> That I eat this child
> That lies in this cradle.

It is also the Eucharist: it is the Lamb of God! Nor is there anything blasphemous in the conjunction of these two, or in the vulgarity and homeliness with which the shepherds in the final scene acknowledge their Redeemer. Neither is Mak the villain any less of a villain for his comic Southern speech. There is whimsy, and there is also diabolism, in his drawing of a magic circle about his sleeping companions. He is in the event a bumbling deceiver, and hence comic and even endearing; he is at the same time a type of that more sinister and redoubtable figure who would win us to our harm by the practice of "arts inhibited and out of warrant."

The habit of the mysteries is to blend the two together, like the yolk and white of a single shell. Pontius Pilate, the first vil-

---

[5] Documented in detail (and with appended bibliography) by Caroline Eckhardt, U. of Michigan dissertation, 1971.

lain of the medieval drama, is coincidentally a figure of fun. Chaucer implies this dual aspect:

> Ne abyde no man for his curteisie,
> But in Pilates voys he gan to crie,
> And swoor, "By armes, and by blood and bones,
> I kan a noble tale for the nones."[6]

Herod, like Pilate, is no better than one of the wicked. He is also a blustering comedian who, as he reads a prophecy of the birth of Christ, "kindles with rage, and hurls the book to the floor." His anger, on learning that the Wise Men have prudently omitted to bid him goodbye, is only more risible than terrible. In the famous stage direction, the mingling of fear and laughter is implicit: "Here Herod rages in the pageant [wagon], and in the street also." Or perhaps an equivalence is intended as between the wrathful man and the comedian:

> Another way? Out! Out! Out!
> Hath those false traitors done me this deed?
> I stamp! I stare! I look all about!
> Might I them take I should them burn at a glede.
> I rant! I rave! and now run I wode!

In this same play from the Coventry cycle, Herod, adumbrating a grimly comic scene in *Hamlet*, forces the soldiers who will slaughter the Innocents to swear to their purpose on his sword. I suppose Shakespeare's convenient station as a boy in nearby Stratford-on-Avon to account for his reminiscence of the Coventry play. It is at least an innocent suggestion. But the provenance of Shakespeare's farcical-tragical scene, in which Horatio and his fellows are sworn to silence on Hamlet's sword, is not of particular importance. What is important is the parallel, in "such ambiguous giving out," to the medieval penchant for confounding jest and earnest. "Come on," says the antic Hamlet, as the ghost of his murdered father cries under the stage:

> you hear this fellow in the cellarage:
> Consent to swear.

[6] Prologue to the "Miller's Tale."

The blending of what ought to be immiscible—in character, in plot—is suggested to the Middles Ages (more simply, is exemplified in that period) by the hypostatizing of the great Scriptural stories. The Passion of Our Lord exists forever and outside time. Essential history is always contemporaneous. Or it is the point where all times are present (*"il punto a cui tutti li tempi son presenti"*). Christ is there already when Abraham prepares the sacrifice of Isaac. In the Wakefield play, which concerns the Nativity, the Third Shepherd swears by Christ's cross. We would say he is guilty of an anachronism. From the medieval point of view, his anticipation or collapsing of time is logical, entails no embarrassment. If one reads history "typologically" (the priest Melchisdec in Genesis 14, offering bread and wine, prefigures Christ), chronological barriers go down. Historical decorum is no longer to the purpose. Dress or idiom or architecture are felt as adventitious. Shakespeare's historical plays gloss these observations. "Cut my lace," says Cleopatra to Charmian.

And now the psychological leap: the artist who employs a figural approach to his materials is asserting, whether consciously or not, the oneness of all things and even vice and virtue, which "grow up together almost inseparably." That is why, like Shakespeare or like the Wakefield Master, he can mingle without a sense of indecorum hornpipes and funerals: high and low, risible and tragic. The corollary is parallel structure which truly interpenetrates and which I do not find by and large in Renaissance drama. As the typological method—more precisely the psychology that begets it—sees history not as linear progress but as the recurrence of patterns or figures, it is able to fuse sacred and profane: in the drama, in religious architecture and painting, in church music, and whatever the objurgations of Pope John XXII who anticipates the purist or time-bound man of the Renaissance and later.

> *Dies Irae, dies illa*
> *Solvet saeclum in favilla*
> *Teste David cum Sybilla.*

The Apparition of the Virgin to her constituents, in a painting by the Spanish artist Berruguete (Prado Museum), is not marred but completed by the presence, in a corner of the canvas, of a monstrously comic devil mimicking the sacred scene. At St. Nazaire in Carcassonne a gargoyle adorning the basilica represents two monks evidently engrossed in fellatio. The representation is understood to be comic, reprehensible, disgusting, and altogether appropriate to a house of worship. Carcassonne is in heretic (Albigensian) country, and hence a stopping place for pious Protestant "Tours of the Reformation Lands." What the modern tourist sees is (what he knows already) that the Middle Ages were disgusting.

In the Age of Reason, as the consciousness of "history" intervenes, the fusing of immiscibles or temporal states is no longer possible. New philosophy insists on a single point of view, sponsors a universe that is rigid and constrained. Newton is its prophet in asserting the existence of absolute space and time. It is true that in the art of the later period, discrete-seeming materials continue to be associated. But the association is violent. It makes a felt oxymoron. The interpenetrating of comic and tragic in the medieval drama is not the same thing as the disingenuous yoking together of the two in Renaissance tragicomedy. To Guarini, who is the first to essay this latter form, poetry's "scope is to delight, not to instruct."[7] The clear inference is that classical strictures against the bastard nature of the form do not obtain. Such a play as Guarini's *Pastor Fido*, abjuring instruction, is explicitly frivolous and therefore not amenable to serious consideration. The drama of the Middle Ages is, of course, tragicomedy almost altogether. That is not because its scope is simply to delight, but because it is imitating the equivocal nature of life itself. What the Renaissance invents is, except in Shakespeare, a meditated and a decadent thing. The idea is to have one's cake and eat it. In *Pericles* and the *Winter's Tale*, Shakespeare is only holding up the mirror. The ambiguity of what he sees associates him more intimately to the dark age than to the luminous and

[7] Frank H. Ristine, *English Tragicomedy*, p. 37.

unequivocal psychology of the Renaissance. He is like the medieval artist, for example Van der Weyden who, in representing the Deposition (Uffizi Gallery, Florence), is able to assimilate even the total grief in the faces of those who prepare Christ for burial, by directing the attention above and beyond the open tomb where the Savior is laid, and the crosses which stand on the hill of Golgotha, to the battlemented town where men walk and ride horseback and attend to their daily but not less engrossing concerns.

The more exclusive character of the modern age is suggested, conversely, by the Elizabethan printer who is introducing Marlowe's *Tamburlaine*. His boast is to "have (purposely) omitted and left out some fond and frivolous jestures, digressing and . . . far unmeet for the matter." In the opinion of Renaissance man, to permit these "graced deformities . . . to be mixtured in print with such matter of worth . . . wuld prove a great disgrace to so honorable & stately a historie." Medieval man is not so finicking. His character is given by the commonsensical Theseus, in *A Midsummer Night's Dream*. The point is to the "very tragical mirth" of Pyramus and Thisbe (which strikes off, precisely, the nature of Shakespeare's art).

> Merry and tragical! Tedious and brief!
> That is, hot ice and wondrous strange snow.

Theseus, in whom the rational man is epitomized, is tickled and bemused at the conjunction of these opposites. Essentially, he gives it up: "How shall we find the concord of this discord?" The Middle Ages resolve the question. The Renaissance does not really entertain it.

But Rabelais, Cervantes, John Donne? These more comprehensive figures are also of the Renaissance: and like the rock that stands above the water. The new tide that begins to set, in Italy after Dante, in the France of Marot, in England half a century later does not hurry them with it but isolates them like giant promontories which signal to one another, aloof from the environing age. In the seventeenth century, the sense of the *dis-*

cordia concors is still vivid;[8] only it is recognized more and more as consciously aberrant: what Johnson means in his commentary on the Metaphysicals.

"Discorde makes weake, what concorde left stronge," says the poetaster Thomas Howell,[9] who would have been appalled at what passed for consent or concord in the age before his own. Compare the implication in the complementary saying I have quoted from Alan of Lille. The Renaissance playwright keeps the action of a piece. But if he is merry and tragical, as in the first version of *Tamburlaine* or in the later version of *Dr. Faustus*, that is largely in fulfillment of a vulgar theatrical design, to titillate his patrons with the best of both worlds. Like Polonius, and even as the topless towers are falling, he's for a jig or a tale of bawdy or he sleeps. At his worst he is Thomas Preston, who offers in *Cambises* (1569) "A Lamentable Tragedy Mixed Full of Pleasant Mirth." At his best he is Christopher Marlowe.

I detect him and his slipshod esthetic in the prologue to the Elizabethan interlude, *Like Will to Like* (1568). The title is appropriate for a play which is founded on the proposition that "To please all men is . . . [an] author's chief desire." The medieval author, for example Chaucer in the *Canterbury Tales*, is not inattentive to the different tastes of his readers. No doubt he also writes to please. Least of all is he remiss in pleasing himself. But if in his work, as in medieval literature in general, serious and frivolous jostle for place, that is because life is like that: the bundle of *fasces* in the Dumb Show with which the tragedy of *Gorboduc* commences. In this bad little play, "matters of mirth and pastime" are made to alternate with "matters of gravity" only because the audience might otherwise grow restive. It is to narcotize the "divers men of divers minds" and not to hold up the mirror to nature that "mirth with measure to sadness is annexed." I take the difference to be absolute, as between this

[8] See L. Spitzer, *Classical and Christian Ideas of World Harmony* (esp. pp. 102-7, 125-38), in which the dilating on the word *Stimmung* implies and documents the persistence of the harmonizing habit.

[9] *Devises*, 1581.

essentially mindless view of things whose only fixed principle is to purvey what pleases, and that suggested by Chaucer in a poignant line from the *Knight's Tale*: "Joye after wo, and wo after gladnesse."

It is not to please all men that the medieval maker annexes mirth to sadness. In his work, there is no suspicion of annexing. He knows and inhabits only the one world. He does not turn from jest to earnest (the sense of "comic relief"). He runs the two together. In dramatizing the story of the Deluge, which is the greatest of all tragedies but one, he dramatizes concurrently the comic wrangling of Noah and his wife. Mary Magdalene, as he conceives her, is partly that pathetic figure, the fallen woman. She is also a comic figure who dotes on cosmetics and haggles over their cost with an archetypal funny man called the Unguentarius, who sells preparations for anointing the dead. What, says Duke Theseus, does the price of cosmetics have to do with the crucifixion and resurrection of Christ? The medieval Balaam is tragic, or potentially so, in his willful disputing of the angel's command. "God's hest I set at naught," he announces in his pride; and presumably the audience attending the little play, as presented by the Cappers of Chester, looks pale with fear and pity. In a moment, the audience is laughing. For the ass on which the prophet has entered—"plying his spurs," as an early MS reads—is made to halt suddenly and throw Balaam on his head. (It is Hjalmar Ekdal, in Ibsen, dramatically renouncing his wife and daughter, and then returning for a bite to eat; or Dr. Stockmann, pledging himself to give battle, just as soon as his trousers have been mended.) "What the devil!" cries the tragi-comic hero,

> My ass will not go!
> Served me she never so.
> What sorrow so her does annoy?

At this point—I quote from the stage direction—"he shall beat the ass, and someone in the ass shall speak."

In the medieval drama there is always "A boy underneath

the ass" who, as he is made to bray, gives unity of tone its quietus. To the medieval playwright, it is a unity founded on willful exclusion. Mostly, he dispenses with it. In a fifteenth-century enacting of the Conversion of St. Paul, he associates that august business to the ludicrous squabbling of Paul's servant and an ostler, and a comic episode between the devils Belial and Mercury. In the *Harrowing of Hell*, a play from the Chester Cycle, he depicts the damning of an ale wife who, as she is seized by Satan and his fellow demons, receives from one of them a proposal of marriage. In the Coventry play of the Slaughter of the Innocents, as Herod's men are commencing to murder the little children, he permits an irate woman to rush on stage, armed with a pot ladle. (It is not Niobe but such a one as Noah's Gyb.) The Wakefield Master, in his version of the Murder of Abel, enlivens the somber story with a grotesquely obscene Cain, who evokes fear and trembling and also amusement, as he berates his team of oxen and his truculent helper. The better (on the whimsical and more inclusive view of this playwright) to dramatize the significance of the Day of Judgment, he presents in his play of Doomsday a group of serio-comic devils (it is the nature and the way of devils), discoursing on the evidence they have accumulated against womankind, and suggesting that if Doomsday is deferred for much longer, Hell will have to be vastly enlarged.

The Devil is terrific; and the Devil is an ass. As Cain has his comic fellow in Pikeharness or Garcio, so the Devil, and especially in the later Moralities, has as his companion a comic Vice. "It was a pretty part in the old church plays," writes Samuel Harsnett at the beginning of the more fastidious age, "when the nimble Vice would skip up nimbly like a Jack-an-apes into the Devil's neck, and ride the Devil a course, and belabor him with his wooden dagger"—an accouterment which survives in Shakespeare's dagger of lath—"till he made him roar, whereat the people would laugh."[10] This Vice, metamorphosed, appears again as Miles the student in Greene's Elizabethan comedy,

[10] *Declaration of Popish Impostures*, 1603.

227

Friar Bacon and Friar Bungay. When, however, in the last act of that play he rides to Hell on the Devil's back, it is only laughter that he inspires, unalloyed with fear. "Now surely," says Miles, "here's a courteous devil, that, for to pleasure his friend, will not stick to make a jade of himself." The Devil may be, now an ass and now a prodigy of terror. He can hardly be both at once.

But the more ambiguous face he presents to the old and benighted age is not obliterated in the light of the new. It remains in stone to haunt and affront the imagination. I think, for example, of what was there for Baïf to see not less than for Jacques de Molay: the hideous and ludicrous gargoyle that looked out on the medieval city of Paris from the north tower of Notre Dame.[11] The kind of mind that could conjure up this most equivocal apparition is not given to minimizing the aspect of dread. The medieval "Devil in his feathers, all ragger and rent" (in the language of the Banns which advertized the Chester plays), whose hand grasps a cudgel, whose redbeard is reminiscent of the archtraitor Judas, is sufficiently dreadful. Deformity describes him. His feet are cloven, he wears horns, he is notable and awful for his gaping mouth and great nose and staring eyes. But that is the Devil only on one side. Like Shakespeare's Richard II, who is able to "play in one person many people," he is at once the Prince of Darkness and an unsophisticated clown, pitifully ambitious of out-heroding Herod. In the N. Towne *Fall of Lucifer*, he contrives, by a species of legerdemain which in the last analysis is only human, to amalgamate these two roles in one. The occasion is the casting out from Heaven. It is a momentous occasion and the Devil in his colossal impenitence is equal to it. "Now," he exclaims with Miltonic sonority, as he brandishes a fist at the Victor:

> Now to hell the way I take,
> In endless pain there to be fixed.

[11] Actually it is Viollet-le-Duc who, confronted with fragments of the originals, created the figures on the balustrades of the towers. But the inspiration derives from comparable figures at Rheims.

He adds, with the right mixture of irreverence, vulgarity, and phlegm:

> For fear of fire a fart I crack.

It is a very unmiltonic interjection.

One might cite, by way of comparison and contrast, a detail from Tiepolo's "Rape of Europa" (Accademia, Venice), in which the grave mythological business of the painting is set off (or relieved) by the presence of a urinating cherub. That is studied and deliberate whimsicality. It is precious, it is artistic, and just the sort of thing the Age of Reason is able to assimilate. There is nothing studied in the blending of savagery and scurrile humor which characterizes the Devil of the mysteries. He is, wholecloth, what he is. In the N. Towne *Trial of Christ*, joining buffoonery to terror, he gambols "into the place in the most horrible wise," precisely as Jesus is handed over to Pilate. It is "while that he playeth" that Jesus is dressed to be taken away. This is not what the pedagogue is thinking of when he speaks of comic relief.

The terminology of the pedagogue derives from his intenser view of things. It is a legacy to him from the new men of the Renaissance. Medieval man—unlike Luther, who is on one side of the new generation—is not so confident or narrow as to assert that "Each passage has one clear, definite, and true sense of its own." His practice is to hunt after and to exploit concurrent truths. His reading of the Bible typifies his approach to life and art in general. He posits, not one single and exclusively important meaning, but four different levels of meaning. Luther, in his brave simplicity, rejects the fourfold method. Allegories are "the scum of Holy Scripture." To Luther it is a scandalous rule "that Scripture is to be understood in four ways, literal, allegorical, moral, anagogic." His prescription, "if we wish to handle Scripture aright," is "to obtain *unum, simplicum, germanum, et certum sensum literalem.*"[12] This idea of a single sense commends itself to William Ames, "because otherwise the sence of the Scripture should be not onely [not] cleere and certaine, but

---

[12] Quotations from Farrar, pp. 327, 328.

none at all: for that wich doth not signifie one thing, signifieth certainly nothing."[13]

The medieval exegete, as he is denied a vision of the naked truth, attends—perhaps necessarily—now to the literal level (*sensus literalis*), concerned with historical fact or with the obvious meaning of the words; and now to the allegorical (*sensus allegoricus* or *mysticus*), which has to do with our belief, as embodied in the New Testament and symbolized or prefigured in the Old; and the moral or tropological (*sensus moralis* or *tropologicus*), with right action; and the anagogical (*sensus anagogicus*), with man's last end.[14] This multilevel method of interpreting Scripture is illustrated by Dante. The Biblical phrase he sets for exposition, "When Israel went out of Egypt," is not a simple phrase, as he construes it, "but rather can be said to be of many significations . . . for there is one meaning that is derived from the letter, and another that is derived from the things indicated by the letter." The first meaning he calls literal or historic. The second, which is the allegorical or mystic, as it embraces different levels, designated by different names, is more efficient. On Dante's reading, to consider the letter is to perceive that "the departure of the children of Israel from Egypt in the time of Moses is signified." But that is only to make a beginning. The allegory remains, whose function is to speak to "our redemption accomplished in Christ." But the allegory encapsulates moral and anagogical meanings, which have to do, respectively, with "the conversion of the soul from the sorrow and misery of sin to a state of grace," and with "the departure of the sanctified soul from the slavery of this corruption to the liberty of everlasting glory."[15]

[13] *Marrow of Sacred Divinity*, pp. 170-71.

[14] "Littera *gesta docet, quid credas* allegoria,/ Moralis *quid agas, quo tendas* anagogia": verses given customarily to Nicholas of Lyra, d.1340; D. W. Robertson, Jr. attributes to Augustine of Dacia, *c*.1260. For discussion and definition of the four senses of Scripture, see Hollander, *Allegory*, p. 15 and n. 1, pp. 24-28.

[15] Letter to Can Grande in Lathem and Carpenter edn., p. 193. Aquinas reserves the fourfold allegorical method to Scripture. But Dante, as a number of modern critics have demonstrated, I think convincingly, writes the

Against this complex and extraordinarily ambitious mode of treatment, which had prevailed at least since the time of John Cassian ten centuries before, and which had if nothing else the virtue of stretching the mind, the conventional Renaissance writer, whether secular or sacred, Catholic or Protestant, stipulates one level only, that we may really take hold of what we are asked to accomplish. Wyclif anticipates the new day in affirming that "all things necessary in Scripture are contained in its proper literal and historic sense."[16] This narrowing down is congenial to Tyndale, though characteristically he shifts the emphasis away from the word: "God is a Spirit, and all His words are spiritual, and His literal sense is spiritual."[17] Compare Erigena, writing in the ninth century, for the difference: "the sense of divine utterance is manifold, and like a peacock's feather"—one remembers Cassiodorus—it "glows with many colors."[18] The point is to exclusiveness. Thus Bacon: allegorical poetry is not a complex structure but only "history with its type."[19] As the Renaissance endorses this reductive view, it throws back to the simplistic allegoresis of the early millenarians, like Origen of Alexandria. Its reading is correspondingly more clear and the issue of its reading more compendious. But it has lost the amplitude and richness that belonged to the characteristic medieval method. The result of that method was, in art, a happy melding of antitheses and opposites which an age like the Renaissance, whose commitment is to clarity and thence to accomplishment, cannot possibly countenance.

Commedia in imitation of "God's way of writing." See Hollander in "Dante's Use of 'Aeneid' I," *CL*, xx, 142-56; and *Allegory*, esp. pp. 4ff, 134; and the work of Charles Singleton (cited Hollander, pp. 49-50, 60). For the difference between "modern" (compendious) and medieval, see Donne's treatment, in *Essays in Divinity* (Simpson edn.), p. 75, of the same Scriptural text on which Dante meditates. Donne looks to be doing the same thing, but all that remains in his exegesis is scaffolding.

[16] Farrar, p. 279n. [17] *Obedyence*, O7v-P6v.

[18] *De Divisione Naturae*; Farrar, p. 254.

[19] *Advancement of Learning*, ii, xiii. For the collapsing in the Renaissance and later of the four levels into two, and the separable nature of the two, see E. Bloom, "Allegorical Principle," *ELH*, xviii, 163-90.

Comparison is illuminating between the medieval understanding of allegory and that of the Renaissance. Medieval allegory is not defined by a one-to-one correspondence (the popular misapprehension): this character betokening, absolutely, this quality or characteristic. The analogy is unfortunate because misleading that emblematizes in the husk and kernel of the nut the surface and signification of the work of art. "In the nut," says Fulgentius, whose temper is reductive like that of the Neo-Platonists who are his contemporaries, "there are two parts, the shell and the kernel; so in the songs of the poets there are two, the literal sense and the mystic." Renaissance man, in the teeth of the more expansive medieval construction, accepts the analogy. He sees the shell or letter as extrinsic and hence superfluous, and the underlying or mystic sense not in its triform aspect (*allegoria, moralis, anagogia*) but as indivisible and essentially simple. In consequence of this misunderstanding, he endeavors, as his temperament is secular or mundane, to treat the shell as a façade for the elaborating of curious fretwork (he is a realist, he is a naturalist); or, as he is bitten by eschatology, to discard the shell altogether, the better to come to the nugget of meat it encloses.

This of course is what the Middle Ages are generally supposed to do. I quote from a very eminent modern historian, who seems to me to express nicely the conventional error:

> In the eyes of all [medieval persons] who were capable of reflection the material world was scarcely more than a sort of mask, beyond which took place all the really important things; it seemed to them also a language, intended to express by signs a more profound reality. Since a tissue of appearances can offer but little interest in itself, the result of this view was that observation was generally neglected in favor of interpretation. (Marc Bloch)[20]

But that is to get it backwards. It is because the medieval world does not think it can strike through the mask to find out all the answers and so build the kingdom in which all shall be well that it does attend, more prosaically and more humbly, to appearance. It is only provisionally Platonic. Hence the paradox that

[20] *Feudal Society*, Bk. I, Pt. II, Ch. v, sec. 3.

that age builds best in the here and now that fixes its eyes on the hereafter.

Conceded that the medieval intelligence demands ulteriority even of what looks to be plain. Confronted with the parable of the Wise and Foolish Virgins, it engages in a rumination on number. The Wise Virgins are five to denote the five forms of contemplative life, and hence the five senses of the soul. But the life of the body is comprised in as many senses. These, as they are maleficent in their issue, are expressed in the number of the Foolish Virgins. In this way, the material world is resolved to a language of symbolic signs. And still much remains: for example, the minute and loving observation of the surface, which is the material world, in medieval representations of the Wise and Foolish Virgins, as on the west doorway of Notre Dame. The tale in which they figure is a parable or symbol. It is also a narrative or fact. As such, it is rendered, and unforgettably. Against the French historian, I invoke the art of thirteenth-century France.

Another example: the medieval monastery, as ordered by the famous Rule of St. Benedict of Nursia (d.543), does not look to the world and not even to learning. Its dedication is otherworldly. It pursues a dream of the City of God. But as monasticism engages in that pursuit, it becomes involuntarily an indispensable social institution. At first its importance is religious, and this though no connection with the Church outside the walls had been envisaged. And then it impinges on education and politics and economics. The zeal which inspires the Benedictine monk is very circumscribed in nature. It is to assist in bringing men to eternal life. That is why the Benedictine cultivates the patristic tradition, which is implemented, as Cassiodorus suggests, by the study of classical texts. But it is this monk who copies out in his *scriptorium* all that we possess of the literature of the past. The result of the medieval indifference to the world is civilization, precisely.

In medieval allegory, the tissue of appearance is not extrinsic or unimportant and occasions much interest in itself. It is not to be shucked or neatly disentangled from that more profound real-

233

ity abiding within and beyond it. Henry James, describing himself and the perplexing nature of his art, comes close to describing the allegorical writer of the Middle Ages: and in fact it is only in our time that this complicated and hence more nearly truthful mode of expression has become current once more. The whole work of Joyce is a gloss on the assertion. But here is the passage: "Addicted to seeing 'through'—one thing through another, accordingly, and still other things through *that*—he takes, too greedily, perhaps, on any errand, as many things as possible by the way."[21] That is the counsel of Epictetus and the practice of Dante and Shakespeare. "It is after this fashion that he incurs the stigma of laboring uncannily for a certain fullness of truth— truth diffused, distributed and, as it were, atmospheric." Truth is not isolable but fills the interstices of things. The dancer and the dance are not dissevered without menacing the vitality and even the identity of either.

The poem of Dante attests to the interacting of the two; Chaucer's poetry does also. Chaucer is a kind of allegorist, though not in the sense obtaining today. He works concurrently on a number of levels. (The adverb counts as much as the adverbial phrase.) In the *Canterbury Tales* the literal level, time-bound and involved in the workings of plot, is that of the pilgrimage as a real journey, and the narratives and social intercourse of the pilgrims themselves. The allegorical level is implicit perhaps in the line from Jeremiah (6:16) which introduces the Parson's Tale: "Go out upon the highways." Each tale partakes of the nature of an exemplum, and so establishes the author's concern with morality. But the poem is written also on a timeless or anagogical plane, which is the "parfit glorious pilgrymage to the heavenly Jerusalem."[22] In a later time, this sort of multifarious activity is interdicted. That is because, in Chaucer, the levels are not discrete but in accord with one another. The wart is on the Miller's nose because the Miller as a moral being is gross. He has not risen above his physical nature.

[21] Preface to "The Pupil," 1908.

[22] Norman Hinton, "Anagogue and Archetype," *Annuale Mediaevale,* VII, 66n.

The wart is iconographic: it points or denotes. But it is also very palpable, repulsively so: a real detail depicted realistically. This means it is more than denotative. Its physical integrity is not obliterated by its meaning. But neither does it overawe the meaning. Chaucer's world is, and is thoroughly moralized; and so the literal truth tallies with its rationalizing in allegorical terms. In the words of Alan of Lille: "just as the meaning is wrapped around the material, so the signification of the allegory shines through the material."[23] The levels exist, but they are also one.

Most critics from the Renaissance forward have taken allegory to be an enforcing of ideas already held, by means of a picture writing in which as little color or thickening as possible is lavished on the picture. "Fruyt" and "chaf" no longer intermingle: as in Chaucer, whose predilection for counting pots and pans (Talbot Donaldson's phrase) is rejected as to no "purpose." The surface or picture has no genuine integrity, it is only a vehicle. Its beauty is admitted only as a means of persuading. Symbolism is made to differ from allegory in that the symbol, as Coleridge describes it, "is characterized by a translucence of the special in the individual, or of the general in the special, or of the universal in the general; above all by the translucence of the eternal through and in the temporal. It always partakes of the reality which it renders intelligible; and while it enunciates the whole, abides itself as a living part of that unity of which it is the representative."[24] This, as I see it, is Chaucer's allegory, exactly.

The allegory of the Renaissance, on the other hand, attempts to enforce a separation of the symbol or surface from the reality it is supposed to express. The separation is dictated by a fear that

---

[23] Argument, *Anticlaudianus*, p. 51.

[24] *The Statesman's Manual*, 1816; Angus Fletcher, *Allegory*, p. 16n. R. Delasanta, "Chaucer and the Exegetes," p. 8, distinguishes precisely between "The allegorist [who] codifies and simplifies truth. . . . [and] The typologist . . . [who] measures existential reality not by some rarefied ideal or abstract formula but by another existential reality which does not clarify mystery (as allegory would purport to do) but in fact deepens it."

235

the reality will otherwise be infected and so obscured. It is not an unreasonable fear and it is very poignant in the late sixteenth century, which is concerned with a perfect betokening in the interest of advancing the uncontaminated truth. Obscurity in itself, which is the métier of the medieval poet, is of course inimical to truth. Dante, as he is alive to the danger, admonishes his readers to "mark well the lore conceal'd/ Under close texture of the mystic strain."[25] It is necessary that they make their eyes keen for the truth, for the veil which hangs before it is so subtle of texture that even the most perceptive are apt to "pass it through unmark'd."[26]

It is just this difficulty that the Renaissance complains of. "Must all be veiled," asks George Herbert, of the old-fashioned kind of poetry, "while he that reads, divines,/ Catching the sense at two removes?"[27] The intent of Renaissance man is to approach to the sense as nearly as may be. In prosecuting that intent, he thins the surface of the poem that truth may be conspicuous in the foreground. In other words, he discovers perspective.[28] The Middle Ages know nothing of perspective. Medieval art is marked by simultaneity. It does not heighten or depress. That would be, like the plebs in *Coriolanus*, to "bury all which yet distinctly ranges." In medieval painting everything is foreground, and often in medieval music. The melody in polyphonic or many-voiced music is not reserved to a single voice (as in the part-song of the later age), to which the other voices are subordinated as accompaniment. Rather are all the voices or parts conceded equal interest and importance. The Flemish composer Okeghem does not emphasize this part at the expense of that other. Accordingly, the effect is to direct attention away

[25] Inferno, ix. Robert Hollander (conversation) describes these lines as atypical: one of only two passages in the *Commedia* in which Dante calls attention to one-for-one allegory.

[26] Purgatory, viii.

[27] "Jordan," 1, *The Temple*, 1633.

[28] W. J. Ong relates sixteenth- and seventeenth-century addiction to the allegorical tableau—for example, emblem literature—to the tables and outlines of Ramus. The impulse in each case is to achieve "the reduction of the verbal to the spatial": "From Allegory to Diagram," *JAAC*, xvii, 437.

from questions of primacy. Great peaks and troughs are absent; or say: background and foreground are merged. Shakespeare's aphorism is not applicable here: "When two men ride a horse, one must ride behind." Form in the modern sense is to seek. I am thinking especially of the Missa Mi-Mi.

The same effect is remarkable in medieval allegory, in which the various levels (or planes or voices), moral and literal, anagogical and mystic, do not contend for place but live together as equals. In Langland's poem, Piers Plowman is a type of the *bon laboureur*. He is also the Good Shepherd. Finally, and not least, he is a particular, an indigenous human being. None of these aspects of his multiform character enjoys hegemony over the others.

In the Renaissance this old-fashioned or egalitarian conception of the genre, in which the various levels are allowed to coexist, is superseded. To Jonson's friend and preceptor John Hoskins, "An Allegory is the continual following of a metaphor and proportionable through the sentence, or through many sentences."[29] But a metaphor is simply "a translation of one word onely." And therefore "an Allegorie," as it picks up a number of these one-to-one correspondences, "is called a continued Metaphore."[30] The metaphors of which the *Divine Comedy* or *Piers Plowman* or the *Canterbury Tales* are compounded translate more than one word. Compare Isidore of Seville, who sees books in their translatable or suggestive quality as like a lyre; but a lyre whose cords are of infinite resonance. To vary the metaphor: in medieval allegory "Hills peep o'er hills, and Alps on Alps arise!" The Renaissance, as it is covetous of discrimination, is impatient of many translations or levels. "Th' increasing prospect tires our wandering eyes." Its art is marked by perspective. It endeavors to indicate and to cast in bold relief that one word only in which the truth inheres. Given its endeavor, it is unwilling to tolerate any longer those "Poeticall Clerkes" who, as Thomas Wilson describes them, weave "blinde Allegories, delighting much in their owne darkenesse." The work of the

[29] *Directions for Speech and Style*, c.1599-1600; H. Hudson edn., p. 9.
[30] Henry Peacham the Elder, *The Garden of Eloquence*, 1593.

old-fashioned clerk is brushed with strangeness "as with the wild wing of some bird of the air who might blindly have swooped for an instant into the shaft of a well, darkening there by his momentary flutter the far-off round of sky" (Henry James). The new poet comes out of darkness into the light: he collapses the old levels into one level; in lieu of many meanings he finds out one. Allegory is reduced to its kernel. It is in its import as single or exclusive as metaphor: "An Allegorie is none other thing but a Metaphore, used throughout a whole sentence, or Oration."[31] The translation of many words or meanings gives way to the translation of one. The total displacement of the poem is thereby reduced. Medieval allegory is a more substantial vessel. The Renaissance acquiesces in the diminution in that clarity is gained by it. What it wants is the very reverse of an art the heart of whose mystery you cannot pluck out and define.

In the ideal allegory of the Age of Reason, this equals this. Mystery is dissipated. The work of art is rotated along a horizontal axis, one half of which is surface and the other below. Bilateral symmetry describes it. The end in view is the asserting of precise equivalences. These are not always manifest in nature. The heart of man, as Hermann Weyl reminds us, is an asymmetric screw. But truth to nature is not at issue. The modern maker, who dreams his dream of order and seeks to impose it on flux, is coercive, compulsive. "Symmetry signifies rest and binding, asymmetry motion and loosening, the one order and law, the other arbitrariness and accident, the one formal rigidity and constraint, the other life, play and freedom."[32]

Imperious form, recrudescent in the art of the modern age, pays homage to order and law and has its analog in the prescriptions of classical science. The laws of nature are invariant. If the numbers are in accord by which the scientist fixes everything that exists, if the algebraic expression denoting this and this is the same expression, then the things denoted must be the same. Idiosyncratic character is a casualty of the proposition; transpicuous

[31] *Arte of Rhetorique*, Bk. III.

[32] *Symmetry*, pp. 26, 16 (Weyl quoting the art historian Dagobert Frey).

allegory is contingent on its acceptance. Leibniz, hypothesizing his absolutely translatable monads, is an allegorist of the new dispensation; Shakespeare (*et hoc genus omne*) is reactionary, as he imagines the man whose like we shall not see again. Now, as the wheel turns, Shakespeare and his medieval antecedents are vindicated. "Molecular science," says Clerk Maxwell, "forbids the physiologist to imagine that structural details of infinitely small dimensions"—the monads of Leibniz, one within another stretching to eternity—"can furnish an explanation of the infinite variety which exists in the properties and functions of the most minute organisms."[33]

The prohibition is implicit, the asserting of infinite variety is patent in medieval allegoresis. The tendency is to aggrandizement and thus to obfuscation. Loosening is mystery. The modern tendency is to diminution and thus to clarification. The balloon of the mind is brought within its narrow shed. Already this tendency is working in Boccaccio, who seems in his language to oppose it. "One must bear in mind"—the point is to the myths he is explicating—"that . . . [they] contain more than one single meaning. They may indeed be called 'polyseme,' that is, of multifold sense."[34] It is an impeccably medieval construction and even to the eccentric vocabulary, which derives by way of Dante from the pioneering annotations of Servius so many centuries before. In the word *cano*, writes Servius, laboring the opening verses of the *Aeneid*, there is more than meets the eye: "*polysemus sermo est.*"[35] He proceeds to lay bare the different significations the word encloses. Superficially, Boccaccio is of this old or inclusivist party. In glossing the myth of Perseus and the Gorgon he distinguishes, precisely as Servius might have done, the literal or historical sense, which is the fable itself; and the moral in which "a wise man's triumph over vice and his attainment of virtue" are manifested; and the allegorical, which "figures the pious man who scorns worldly delight and lifts his

---

[33] Quoted D. W. Thompson, 1, 71.

[34] *Genealogy*, 1, 3.

[35] Dante in the Epistle to Can Grande describes as "polysemous" whatever is "of a number of senses." Servius is quoted 1, i, 20.

mind to heavenly things"; and last, the anagogical, which "symbolizes Christ's victory over the Prince of this World, and his Ascension."

And then, having demonstrated that he can perform in the complicated or multilevel kind as deftly as any, Boccaccio gives it all away. He observes that "these secondary meanings, by whatever name, are essentially allegorical." That is Dante's observation to Can Grande. It does not inhibit his continuing perusal. Boccaccio, as he looks to the future, is more impatient than Dante. "But it is not my intention," he proclaims, "to unfold all these meanings for each myth when I find one quite enough."[36] The proclamation is exciting and generally it is fulfilled in proof. Only rarely does Boccaccio, on the word of his

---

[36] I, 3. Seznec, p. 220, quotes C. C. Coulter on the *Genealogy*: the attempt "to reduce the whole of classical mythology to a system . . . marks Boccaccio as a child of the Middle Ages." On the contrary. Seznec himself, p. 222, says erroneously: "Through his method of interpretation [of myth], he places himself" as "essentially a man of the Middle Ages." For a more perceptive reading of Boccaccio's allegorizations, see Hollander, *Allegory*, p. 34. The Renaissance continues the medieval practice of allegorizing myth. That is obvious. Many critics are led to say, therefore, that Renaissance and medieval, in respect of the "moral or theological truths discovered beneath the mask of Fable and in the figures of the gods" are the same. "Nothing of this had actually been invented by the Renaissance. It was . . . the 'rêverie médiévale' to which the Renaissance had succumbed" (Seznec, p. 104). The sameness is evident; more interesting is the difference in the allegorizing, the boiling down. As hatred of paganism revives in the Renaissance (already Boccaccio is uneasy at trafficking in myth), it is countered by artists in the appeal to use. Read myth symbolically and it teaches virtue. Allegory becomes a simplistic probing beneath the surface. Dolce says: "those who will take the trouble to look with discernment not at the surface . . . but at the motives . . . will see beneath the rind of fiction, all the sap of moral and sacred Philosophy" (1554; Seznec, pp. 269-70). Beneath the shell of fable is the "*sapientia veterum*." Under the fruit of fiction, "the stone is hidden." Mythology is taught in Jesuit colleges as it inculcates or discovers philosophical truths: the way Ripa in his *Iconologia* presents it. Painting is like mythology, a means of "rendering thought visible." Emblem literature, which the Jesuits employ as a homiletic instrument, illustrates the teachings of the Christian religion. See Seznec, pp. 263-69.

modern editor, employ the fourfold method of exegesis. Mostly, his interpretations are resolved to the literal and moral: he would say, to the allegorical, a much tidier word as he construes it. Even as he is insisting that Virgil's method is fourfold, he manages a decisive attenuating of the method.[37] The design of the *Aeneid* is, first, to "follow the practice of earlier poets, particularly Homer," by beginning *in medias res*; second, "to show with what passions human frailty is infested, and the strength with which a steady man subdues them"; third, to honor Octavius; and fourth, "to exalt the glory of . . . Rome." But the third and fourth of these motives imputed to Virgil are essentially a single motive; the first, as it is pretty much a matter of technique, does not signify in terms of the conventional classifications. In Boccaccio's *Aeneid*, the four levels, as elaborated by the Middle Ages, have in fact been diminished by half.

Boccaccio's allegoresis is not so spare or so exclusive as Giordano Bruno's in the sixteenth century,[38] or as Bunyan's in the seventeenth. Neither is it so rich or so nicely reticulated as Dante's, only a little earlier. Allegory, as Boccaccio conceives it, is a portmanteau term, and as such it may incorporate a welter of different meanings or surmises. But he is not ordinarily at pains to distinguish among them. As he is disinclined "to unfold all these meanings," he allows a fusion of the moral or tropological sense with the anagogical. He considers it enough to point—and with a sweeping gesture—to the *sensus allegoricus*, which is made the sole referent.

The exegetical vocabulary of the Middle Ages is obviously remote from modern usage. The supersession of this vocabulary and the complicated practice it describes, most of all the involuted psychology that lies behind it—this, on the other hand, has been greatly consequential for the art and history of the modern period. Characteristically the modern artist, as he cleaves to the new and coarser assurance that truth is truth, eschews the *multiplex intelligentia* in his treatment of human

[37] xiv, xiii.

[38] For Bruno as simplistic allegorist, see his treatment of the fable of Actaeon. Santillana, *Age of Adventure*, p. 271.

beings. He idealizes, like Raphael. The range of possibilities is discounted. His representations, whether they are of good or bad, are insistently straight and single. Until the nineteenth century, there are no credible characters in English prose fiction who are truly catholic or particolored, and in the nineteenth century the repertory of such comprehensive characters can be numbered on the fingers of either hand. (Mostly, one finds them in Jane Austen.) Shakespeare offers, in Falstaff and Prince Hal, Hamlet and Brutus, Emilia in *Othello*, real-seeming protagonists who run the gamut in their behavior. To vary the metaphor: each plays in one person more than a single part. After Shakespeare, inclusiveness in character disappears from the stage, first in tragedy, then—as psychology becomes with each decade a little more gross and simplistic—in comedy.

Waiving the few great dramatists of the Restoration, to whom can one point as displaying any inkling of the truth of the Clown's observation in *Twelfth Night*: "Virtue that transgresses is but patched with sin, and sin that amends is but patched with virtue"? What one gets in the theatre, as also in fiction, is not an amalgam or "botching" of sin and virtue, but the delineating of either by turns: caricature. The best contemporary critic of Samuel Richardson, who asserts that "every level in his novel is fully presented," is, I think, begging the question.[39] Where is this plurality of levels? Not in Richardson, not in Fielding, who is a great cartoonist, very dim when he addresses us in a serious vein (*Amelia*). Smollett is more satisfying as he is less ambitious, a naturalist who succeeds as he does not venture to generalize on the human condition. That is Scott's negative success, as the generalizing is his failure. When he offers to be serious, we do not take him more seriously than the Italian librettist who is hunting in the novels for the stuff of a melodramatic extravaganza.

In the eighteenth century, the major artistic talent in fiction is Laurence Sterne, who impresses most as he is idiosyncratic, hardly a novelist in the conventional sense, but who, attempting

[39] I. Konigsberg, *Samuel Richardson*, p. 124.

242

the human heart, confounds bathos and and pathos. In the nineteenth century the great talent is Dickens, who ranks in point
of sheer endowment only second to Shakespeare. But Dickens,
endeavoring to imagine the whole man, who is and is not passion's slave, in whom the elements or seeds of Psyche are nicely
intermixed, is no more persuasive than George Lillo, a century
before. Vice and virtue to Dickens, as generally to the Age of
Reason, are discrete. Scrooge is bad, and then he is good. There
is no accounting for the transition, no intimation that the new
man is nascent in the old, who continues to live *in posse* in his
regenerate state.

But Dickens, like Thackeray, yearns after the Shakespearean
or medieval perception that, as for vice and virtue, there went
but a pair of shears between them. The result is the hero-villain
Steerforth. This version of encyclopedic man, who presents as
in an emulsion the different "levels" or modes of conduct latent
in us all, bears comparison with George Barnwell, the wretched
hero of the *London Merchant*. He is not to be confused with
the real thing: Fabrizio del Dongo "now," Maggie Verver,
Richard II in the dark age before our own.

In the intervening age, the Enlightenment, "modern" times,
the hero or villain lives mostly on a single level. The terms are
denotative. The former signifies "a man absolutely stainless,
perfect as an Arthur, a man honest in all his dealings, equal to
all trials, true in all his speech, indifferent to his own prosperity,
struggling for the general good, and, above all, faithful in love."
The villain epitomizes villainy. He is a man "carried away by
abnormal appetites, and wickedness, and the devil . . . [inclined
to] commit murder, or forge bills, or become a fraudulent director of a bankrupt company." He is a humorous man, in Shadwell's sense, and driven predictably to "be untrue to his troth,
and leave true love in pursuit of tinsel, and beauty, and false
words, and a large income."

These dispiriting but faithful cardboard cutouts are sponsored
by Anthony Trollope, who has arrived at the middle of his own
artistic journey and who, in the novel called the *Eustace Dia-
monds* (Ch. xxxv), is composing what is clearly a manifesto in

243

which the straitness of the modern age is repudiated and a return to the old inclusiveness and intermixing is augured—in Trollope's later fiction, in that of his contemporary George Eliot (*Middlemarch*), in the fiction of the twentieth century. The picture presented in this fiction—James is describing it, in the *Golden Bowl*—is "veiled" with dimness. Behind the veil the protagonists, who are felt as real partly as they are "indistinguishable," loom for a moment into the definite, fade again into the vague. They have lost, "all so pitifully, their precious confidence." Henceforward the writer or psychologist will tell, as once before, not of the self-assured hero and the perdurable villain, but "of the man who is one hour good and the next bad, who aspires greatly but fails in practice, who sees the higher but too often follows the lower course." Heroes of the new or equivocal fiction will be knights with reproach, heroines will doubt as "between the poor man they think they love and the rich man whose riches they know they covet." Villains will be abolished "whose every aspiration is for evil, and whose every moment is a struggle for some achievement worthy of the devil." Tolstoy, who understands that the indubitable villain must be made to love his mother, is predicted. The rational intelligence, which denies ambiguity of persons and situations, is confuted in the persons of Kate Croy and Merton Densher and the situation which is the donnée of the *Wings of the Dove*.

"Instead of the existence of a difficulty," says Trollope sardonically—he is anticipating the conventional reaction to his own ambiguous hero—"there was a flood of light upon his path, so the reader will think; a flood so clear that not to see his way was impossible." One thinks of the flood of light which envelopes and baffles the mistress of Poynton, or the heroine of *Can You Forgive Her?* (whence James must surely have derived his *Portrait of a Lady*). "Oh, Gilbert," cries Isabel Archer, having come at last to full knowledge of her monstrous husband, "for a man who was so fine—!" It is one of the great moments in fiction and it recalls irresistibly the similar scene in *Othello*, when Lodovico confronts the Moor over the corpse of Desdemona and inquires rhetorically:

244

O thou Othello, that wert once so good,
Fall'n in the practice of a damned slave,
What shall be said to thee?

Othello, like Gilbert Osmond, is good and bad together; and
Isabel, like the emissary from Venice, represents concurrently
the angel of disdain and her first cousin, the angel of pity.

The coexistence of disdain and pity, of antinomies whatever
their nature, is the *bête noir* of the Age of Reason and the rediscovery of our own age. See, for instance, the art of Faulkner:
comedy and tragedy within a single rind (*As I Lay Dying*).
The flood of light hypothesized by the reader of nineteenth-
century fiction is not endlessly irradiating; it also casts in shadow.
Lord Jim is "veiled like an Eastern bride." This means that the
single personality is multiple and even mysterious. Without
feeling his shadows, you can never feel his lights. But the same
observation holds of the context and the tesselation of fact of
which the context is elaborated. More than one conclusion or
explanation is potential of the *Turn of the Screw* or the *French
Lieutenant's Woman* or Joyce's *Portrait*. In the ending of the
Golden Bowl, every link between cause and consequence is shuf-
fled away. The intention that remains is "like some famous poetic line in a dead language, subject to varieties of interpretation." Only in the perspicuous atmosphere of Heaven is there
no shuffling. There only, as King Claudius instructs us, "the
action lies/ In his true nature."

The rational intelligence disallows varieties of interpretation.
It does not call things as it sees them; it thinks it calls things
as they are—in science certainly, but also in psychology (Freud
reclaims the Zuyder Zee), in literature (allegory is fined down
in the seventeenth century and later, Shakespeare is clarified:
he is "improved"), and not least in its dealings with history and
mythology. Modern man, confronting the intransigent fact, has
recourse to euhemerism. Chronos, the ancient of years, is reduced to an abstraction and hence divested of mystery. Chronos
is time. The characteristic formula in Renaissance allegorizations or "conversions" of classical story reads (as in Francis

Bacon): *"Pan sive natura/ Cupido sive atomus/ Atalanta sive lucrum,/ Sphinx sive scientia/ Orpheus sive philosophia."*[40]

Bacon, who differs from his more reductive colleagues as he asserts that the fable antedates the moral (it has its own integrity), is himself as thinker and writer impressively metaphorical. In the *Advancement of Learning*, he sneers at Plato as a fabulist or "poet." Shelley in his defense of poetry sees and praises both Plato and "Lord Bacon" as poets. Shelley is right. One can venture the same praise of that insistently prosaic man, Thomas Hobbes. By and large, the modern euhemerist is not so complicated. Sir Charles Lyell in his *Principles of Geology* supposes that "when difficulties arise in interpreting the monuments of the past," the part of "philosophical caution" is to refer these difficulties "to our present ignorance of all the existing agents."[41] Only grasp the agents and difficulty disappears. Man "in his infancy and non-age" stands abashed and irresolute in the presence of mystery. As he grows more assured, says Robert Chambers, he places what has hitherto been mysterious "within that field of order to which it has been the tendency of all science to transfer the phenomena of the world."[42]

Classical fable in its primitive state exists, however, on another plane. Iris is not simply the rainbow. The reluctance of the fabulist to "transfer": his continuing absorption in the irreducible fact lies behind Dr. Johnson's irritable observation that "Every reader of the classics finds their mythology tedious." Walter Bagehot, who quotes this remark with approval, understands that men in the dark age "were afraid of everything . . . the spectacle of nature filled them with awe and dread. They fancied there were powers behind it." Nineteenth-century rationalism is stupefied at this archaic assumption, "cannot think how it could be credible."[43]

[40] P. Rossi, *Francis Bacon from Magic to Science*, pp. 73-134.

[41] Edn. of 1830-33, Bk. i, Ch. xiv. The quotation is eliminated in the revised edn. of 1877. The motto (from Bacon) on the t.p. is faithful, however, to the sense: *"Verè scire est per causas scire."*

[42] *Vestiges of the Natural History of Creation* (1844), "General Considerations Respecting the Origin of the Animated Tribes."

[43] *Physics and Politics* (1867), Ch. ii, "The Use of Conflict," sec. ii.

I have been seeking in these quotations to characterize the psychology of the modern age, still the official psychology to-day. Compare Francis Crick, scoffing at vitalism. The scoffing is justified. That is not what matters but the tone and the posture. Is it necessary to document the wavering of this dogmatic tone in the present? Huxley, girding at the Christian religion, is at once splendid and old hat: "I do not very much care to speak of anything as 'unknowable.' "[44] We, who are his more provisional successors, are "tories of speculation." Our sympathies, as the long past begins to quicken, go not to the yea-sayer or declarative man but to the pious agnostic, as personated by the "unprogressive" courtier Lafeu in Shakespeare's late comedy, *All's Well That Ends Well*. Lafeu the courtier is considering the facile answers afforded by the "scientist" or new philosopher. "They say miracles are past, and we have our philosophical persons, to make modern [prosaic] and familiar, things supernatural and causeless. Hence it is that we make trifles of terrors, ensconcing ourselves into seeming knowledge when we should submit ourselves to an unknown fear" (II, iii).

Modern man has come up from the vale of unknowing. Boccaccio, as often, announces his advent. To Boccaccio, in the treatise on the gentile gods, the rationalizing of mythology is accomplished as "all the existing agents" are known. In reading the literal level of myth, Boccaccio is mostly euhemeristic. That is as one would think. There is nothing the rationalist covets more than a simple and logical explanation of what appears to be out of this world. Prometheus is not the Titan whom Jupiter chains to the rock: he is, more explicably, a teacher of men.[45] The medieval writer occasionally inverts this explication of the text. As the allegorizers of the early Christian centuries receive from the ancient past the myth of St. George and the Dragon— essentially, I suppose, the story of Perseus and Andromeda— they identify the monster with the old idolatrous faith, and the rescued maiden with a province evangelized by the warrior saint.

---

[44] "Agnosticism and Christianity," *Nineteenth Century*, June 1889 (repub. 1894 in *Collected Essays*, 1894-97, vol. v, sec. ix).
[45] IV, xliv.

In the medieval period, this nice equivalence is forgotten. Medieval man finds it more attractive to hypothesize a real dragon from whom a real princess is saved. Renaissance man, as personated in Boccaccio, rejects the hypothesis as superficial.

There is a suggestive precedent for his rationalizing of classical myth. Prudentius, attacking the pagan past (as in the *Contra Symmachum*), is a kind of euhemerist, whose voice is edged with the appropriate condescension: "Every marvel that earth or ocean produces they held a god." On the more sophisticated view of the Christian, who is the *modernus* of his time, Bacchus is reduced to "A young man of Thebes [who] becomes a god because he has conquered India," and Priapus to "an active owner of well-tilled land, a man who was notable for the wealth of his gardens." But more and less than sophistication is evident here. Priapus is also "an arrant whoremonger . . . [who] with exceeding lust used to plague the poor country drabs and couch obscenely amid the willowgroves and thick-set bushes." Only the ingenuous or the wicked deify the Sun: "a bearded old man bends his face to earth and plants kisses (it is all but incredible!) on the legs of bronze-footed horses, and decks with wreaths of roses, or smokes with incense, wheels that cannot turn and reins that cannot bend"—this, because the Sun never varies in its course. The same scorn for mythologizing is evident in Lactantius, who knows very well "How they who were men obtained the name of gods," and who cites as conclusive the judgment of Cicero "that all those who were worshipped were men."[46]

The herald of the new dispensation seeks to divest the past of its magic as part of his program to usher in a more beneficent present. His concern is to disprove false religions (the burden of the first book of Lactantius, as also of the first three books of the *City of God*), and to supersede them with an efficacious truth: "Let not earth be thy god," says Prudentius. "Neither make gods of human virtues." Look to the abstraction which underlies the drossy fable. Like the new men of the Renaissance, he is a progressive. In this character, he applauds the putting

[46] *Divine Institutes,* I, xv.

down of pagan worship, when "Rome withdrew from her long-standing errors, and shook the murky clouds from her aged face." Nothing is more exasperating to him than the spectacle of those moping contemporaries who "keep their eyes closed and will not open them in the light of day." Augustine evinces this exasperation. "But now awake, and rouse thyself," he cries to his fellow Romans. "It is now day."[47]

The Renaissance also, as it is conscious of a new dawning, is impatient of murkiness and error. For that reason it is consistently euhemeristic: rationalizing, in its treatment of classical myth. Bacon, like Lactantius, commits himself to the explicating of fabulous stories.[48] This impulse to reduction has, however, a grander provenance than the enthusiastic propaganda of the early Christian Church. In its insistence on limpidity of surface through which one can look to see something that pertains and can be used, the sixteenth century is most of all like Plato's century. Plato's deprecating of Homer is complemented, in hope it is palliated, by the attempt in Plato's time to allegorize Homer and to vindicate the surface of his poem by making it point past itself. What is central to the various rationalizations is the sinking of the particular in the general. It is central also to Renaissance constructions. The characteristic figure of the new day is synecdoche, not the partaking of the part in the whole but the representing of the part by the whole, the primacy of the general in the particular and hence the attenuating of the particular.

Classical science is incurious of particulars, interested rather in establishing the proposition "that the acts of all living things are fundamentally one." Its eye traverses quickly "the diversities of vital existence." Huxley lumps them together: the flower a girl wears in her hair, the markings of the tortoise shell, the figure a tree makes, or a jellyfish "pulsating through the waters of a calm sea." The rationalist wants to know "what hidden bond can connect" these discrete-seeming phenomena. His happiness is accomplished as "all the multifarious and complicated activi-

---

[47] *City of God*, II, xxix.
[48] In *De Augmentis*, II, xiii, as also in the *Wisdom of the Ancients*.

ties of men are comprehensible . . . [in] categories."[49] What is lost as the categories are delineated? The question does not arise.

This enduring collision in temperament between the empiric and the schematizer is adumbrated by Plato and Aristotle, even though the latter is himself a "scientist" enamored of schematization. There is on the one hand the Least Common Denominator and then there is the integer that eludes breaking down: particles, in Huxley's skeptical phrase, "which are indestructible and unchangeable in themselves; but, in endless transmigration, unite in innumerable permutations, into the diversified forms of life we know."[50] The Platonizing intelligence denies to these particles final integrity. The party of the Stagyrite is their celebrant. Now this discredited party reenters its claim to attention. Against the figure in the carpet or "unity of substantial composition," it is satisfied to contemplate, *pari passu*, the oak and the tortoise, the flower in the hair and the blood coursing in the veins. The thing itself is more engrossing than the hidden bond connecting one thing to another.

Renaissance man is partial to a more cursory mode of inspection and representation. Boccaccio's purpose in scrutinizing pagan myths is "to tear the hidden significations from their tough sheathing" or, less voraciously, to offer "an explanation of the meaning . . . beneath the surface."[51] In fulfillment of this purpose, he removes "the outer mythological covering" to discover that "By Mercury, Virgil means either remorse, or the reproof of some outspoken friend." But to "have added an explanation to each myth" is to have restricted the total area with which the myth can be concerned.[52] To rationalize is to diminish. The rationalizing of Virgil by the Platonic academy of Florence issues in the attenuating of Virgil, as by Pico della Mirandola, and Cristoforo Landino, who reads the *Aeneid* not in the old en-

---

[49] Huxley, "On the Physical Basis of Life," *Fortnightly Review*, Feb. 1, 1869; repub. vol. 1 of *Collected Essays: Methods and Results.*

[50] "On the Physical Basis of Life."

[51] Preface to King Hugo IV of Cyprus and Jerusalem.

[52] XIV, xiv; and Proem.

cyclopedic way but, more exclusively, as a shadowing of the hero's rise from the fleshly business of Troy to the life of pure contemplation, whose emblem is the conquest of Latium.[53] Pico is concerned also with the discovering of a natural religion in which Christian and ancient lore can be combined. It is a significant conjunction. All stories and even sacred stories are emblematic, and the truth they encapsulate is at once simple and generally diffused.

Here the extraordinary vogue of Lactantius among the humanists of the Renaissance takes on meaning. Lactantius is at best a writer of the second rank. Yet the first printed edition of his work is also the first book to be printed in Italy (Salerno, 1465). At least a dozen editions follow before the fifteenth century is out. Praise for the Christian Cicero is founded only in part on his cultivated style. Erasmus honors him most of all for having unified Christianity and the pagan past. That, I think, is why Lactantius comes into his own, after a thousand years in limbo. This early apologist, who sponsors a kind of Christian deism to the end that Rome may be converted to Jerusalem, is esteemed in the Renaissance as having played a more tepid but a more congenial role. His appointed task is seen to be the composing of differences. Like Pico or like Giordano Bruno, he is a syncretist who supplants nice distinctions with a faith that is simple and clear.

The impulse to syncretism is powerful in the early centuries. Boethius, who intends the translation of Aristotle and all of Plato's Dialogues, sets himself to prove "that the Aristotelian and Platonic conceptions in every way harmonize . . . [and] are in agreement with one another at the philosophically decisive points." That is Pico's idea. In the meantime, the Middle Ages are not concocting a specious agreement but simply employing, and whatever material is to hand. On the walls of the cathedral at Amiens the Sibyls are depicted, though they do not harmonize or agree with the saints. Donne, in praise of Aquinas, suggests

[53] See also the rationalizing of Greek myth by Coluccio Salutati, *De Laboribus Hercules*, c.1406.

251

the point at issue: "nothing was too minerall nor centrick for the search and reach of his wit."[54] In token of this omnivorous instinct, the Florentine painter Gozzoli, in his "Triumph of St. Thomas Aquinas" (Louvre), represents the Seraphic Doctor as invested by Aristotle and Plato. The meaning is that he takes from both impartially, though certainly he does not see them as in agreement "at the philosophically decisive points."[55]

The gulf that separates utilizing, freebooting even, from reconciliation is illustrated in the architecture of the enlightened age. Distinct and multiple parts—the environing chapels of the Gothic cathedral—are borne under. An unbroken spatial unit succeeds. The Pantheon is the ultimate church of the Age of Reason. It is a traditional church in that it incorporates a nave and transepts and choir. But these are effaced by the sense of a single and overmastering whole. The huge open square before the church, like that before St. Peter's in Rome, denies idiosyncrasy or clutter or the intimation of historical provenance. The Pantheon, which is completed appropriately in the year of the French Revolution, is truly catholic: it is dedicated to all the

[54] *Essays in Divinity*, ed. Simpson, p. 16.

[55] Seznec sees the fusing of Pagan and Christian as characteristic of the Renaissance (pp. 132-33). The dream of Ficino is realized in the eclectic pantheons of Florence, which lodge Plato and St. Thomas, Christ and Apollo, together (p. 146). But no: the difference between medieval and Renaissance is that between eclecticism, and ecumenicism or catholicity. In the Renaissance *summa*; everything is given its proper place and habit; the medieval *summa* is indifferent to strict propriety. Among the planetary gods sculptured on Giotto's Belltower in Florence is Jupiter, dressed in a monk's robe and holding a chalice in one hand, a cross in the other. The artist is careless of "decorum," is picking up whatever he can use from the different traditions with which he is familiar. The modern age is recognized as he feels a need in himself to honor decorum. By the fifteenth century he has become aware of the incongruity in vesting a Pagan god in Christian habiliments. He goes back in his representations to Greek and Roman originals. In this sense the Renaissance "is the end of a long divorce" (Seznec, pp. 188, 213). On the wall of the sixth-century baptistery in the little church at Venasque (near Avignon) is a bas-relief fragment of an angel and what looks to be an old man plucking fruit from a tree. Maybe this man is Abraham or Adam, and the angel the Roman goddess of victory. No one knows, and in the Dark Ages it does not matter.

gods, radically unlike the provincial abbey church of St. Gene-
vieve, which it replaces. Nearby on the Rue Valette lived John
Calvin, and that is also a congruent fact. Calvin is the great
clarifier who opposes the naked Truth, in which other and lesser
truths are swallowed, to the *multiplex intelligentia*.

In the sixteenth century the clarifying treatment is applied
once again to Christian doctrine, and to classical poets like
Homer and Virgil. It is not restricted, however, to the past.
Ariosto, the greatest of the moderns, receives the treatment.
Within a decade of the publication of the *Orlando Furioso*
(1530), the meaning-mongers are at it. The first edition of the
poem with rationalizations included appears before the middle
of the century.[56] Thereafter most editions are published "*con le
allegorie.*"[57] Tasso, since he is later in time than Ariosto and
therefore more enlightened, writes his own allegory of the
Gerusalemme Liberata (1581), but after the work is finished—
rather like Spenser, though on a far greater scale than Spenser,
rationalizing the *Faerie Queene* after the fact. Edward Fairfax
in his translation reprints Tasso's allegory, which justifies all
previous epic poetry in that it is "informed" with latent and
serious meaning.[58]

The definition of the new or transpicuous allegory—and it is
here that eccentricity and change are most apparent—is first,
that the truth to be comprehended is resolved to either/or (so
Thomas Wilson: "under the . . . [tale] is comprehended some
thing that perteineth, either to the amendment of maners, to the

[56] Venice, 1542.

[57] Simone Fornari, *La Spositione sopra L'Orlando Furioso*, 1st part
Florence 1549, 2nd 1550. Harington, appending an "Allegory of the
Poem" to his trans. (1591), levies on Fornari. Oratio Toscanella, *Belleze
de Furioso*, Venice, 1574, offers also an "allegory of the proper names."

[58] *The Recovery of Jerusalem*, 1600. The *Odyssey* and *Divine Comedy*
are seen as emblematizing the life of contemplative man, and the *Iliad* the
civil life. The *Aeneid* is an amalgam of both. In Tasso's poem, "The army
compounded of divers princes, and of other Christian soldiers, signifieth
Man, compounded of soul and body, and of a soul not simple, but divided
into many divers powers." Goffredo is Understanding, "lord over the other
virtues of soul and body." Rinaldo is Ireful Virtue, second only to Reason.

knowledge of the trueth, to the setting forth of Natures work, or els the understanding of some notable thing done");[59] and second, that the "excellent knowledge" which the poet is proffering and which he conceals beneath the surface of the poem is yet so close to the surface as to shine through it with utter clarity: "when one thing is told . . . by that another is understood." In this way the Renaissance (whose spokesman is John Harington)[60] cuts through the old complexity, which it takes to be confusion, and arrives at the heart of the matter. From now on allegory, as it is faithful to the type, will manifest a one-to-one correspondence. Thomas Wilson and Thomas Lodge furnish examples of the new and precise equivalence. The story of Danae and the shower of gold means, on Wilson's more clear and narrow perception, "that women have bene, and will be overcome with money." The fall of Icarus is as exclusive in its meaning and hence as appliable: "Nowe what other thing doeth this tale shewe us, but that every man should not meddle with things above his compasse."[61] Lodge points as with a ferrule to "the person of Saturne [in which] our decaying yeares are signified," and to that of "angry Juno" which deciphers "our affections," and to "the person of Minerva" which represents "our understanding." His instinct is to be done with alternatives: he proclaims that "When they faine that Pallas was begotten of the braine of Jupiter, their meaning is none other but" and so forth. He wants his reader to see that in Aeneas is described "the practice of a dilligent captaine," and in Prometheus the creation of man, and in Narcissus "the fall of pryde." It appears to him that in Apollo "all knowledge is denotated."[62] It is the apposite word.

Edmund Spenser, the greatest writer of allegory produced by the Renaissance in England, owes formal allegiance to the principle of exclusiveness in the service of use. His mode of proceeding in the *Faerie Queene*—potting his doctrine in a syrup of cherries or emblematizing his scheme of the virtues in a gal-

---

[59] *Rhetorique*, III.
[60] Quoted Smith, II, 202.　　　[61] *Rhetorique*, III.
[62] *Defense of Poetry* (1579); Smith, I, 65-66.

lery of transparent cutouts—is or appears to be painfully clear and impeccably useful. But despite the incessant reduction and simplification, Spenser is not thoroughly attuned to the demand of his time that he communicate the unoccluded truth. Frequently he delights in the surface of his story and can be detected indulging it. His political satire, *Mother Hubberds Tale* is, like the *Faerie Queene*, at least quasi-allegorical. But whether the surface is denotative is moot. Perhaps Lord Burghley lurks beneath it, or Simier the French ambassador, or Alençon the pretender to the hand of Elizabeth. It is the business of the Spenser Variorum to say. But didacticism is a casualty of this mocking of exegesis. As a didactic poet, Spenser is wanting.

As the lust for the naked truth burns more fiercely in the seventeenth century and later, the entanglement of esthetic surface and moral or political signification is more successfully avoided. Comparison is relevant between the plays of an Augustan like John Gay and an Elizabethan like John Lyly. In the *Beggar's Opera*, it is evident that Peachum the fence is a *nom de guerre* for the Prime Minister Walpole. Of course he is more than that. Still, Gay's primary intention is clear. In Lyly, the man of an earlier generation, that intention is absorbed in the fabric of the play. I am thinking of the tedious speculation which hovers about the characters of Lyly's *Endimion* and attempts, without notable success, to pin them down. In Spenser, there is the same baffling of positive identification. Dryden's *MacFlecknoe* is not so obscure as Spenser's *Mother Hubberd*; it is therefore more efficient a polemic. *Pilgrim's Progress* can be reduced to its homiletic intention; Spenser's intention in the *Faerie Queene*, given his preoccupation with the surface, is often mysterious.

The function of allegory, as the sixteenth century conceives it, is basically tutorial. Harington acknowledges this function in applauding the *Orlando Furioso* as "containing in effect a full instruction against presumption and despair." Spenser merits the applause of his contemporaries in that, far more than Ariosto, he is out to fashion a poem that contains. The *Faerie Queene* illustrates the advanced critical and ethical positions of its time—

255

as enunciated, for example, by Sidney—in that it goes beyond pointing the right course of conduct and endeavors to bring us to the right. It is a poem of action which seeks not merely to imitate the good for the instruction and delectation of its readers, but to metamorphose its readers. Its habit and end are kinetic.

But throughout the poem and warring with the kinetic impulse is another, whose issue is a reveling in the surface without specific intention other than delighting, which may be self-delighting. Between the jars of these two divergent impulses, I would locate the idiosyncrasy and the excellence of the *Faerie Queene*. The excellence is partial in that it is founded on loss. Spenser does not achieve the more nearly perfect union that is Chaucer's achievement, in which the moral and esthetic impulses are wed. After Spenser's time, poetry manifests increasingly one impulse or the other: on the one hand *Gondibert*, on the other *Paradise Regained*.

The comparison with Milton is especially apt. There is no wavering in him between idea and execution. By and large he is faithful to his governing precept, as set forth in the first book of *Paradise Lost*: "Before all temples, the upright heart and pure." Spenser is not so resolute. In the *Faerie Queene* contention is discernible as between the rigor of the gnomic prefatory verses and the letter to Ralegh—in these, Spenser is paying homage to the partisans of the naked truth—and the ample and obfuscatory treatment of this episode and that. In his descriptions of the impregnating of Chrysogone, or the bathing of Diana, or the lotus land in which Acrasia dwells, Spenser, whose end is indubitably moral, jeopardizes the end and gives hostages against it. This Spenser is the poet of Keats's bathetic and engaging verses, who "by Mulla's stream/ Fondled the maidens with the breasts of cream." So lavish is he of detail and so careless of its implication that the Bower of Bliss or the amours of Paridell begin to quicken with an interest independent of the total context and even inimical to it. The esthetic surface trenches on and contaminates the idea. Only rarely does this happen in Milton, who is more dogged than Spenser and more modern. Milton

256

lashes himself to the mast and so he sails by temptation. His thought and scheme permeate his longer poems absolutely. The reader, despite the Romantic misconstruing of Satan in *Paradise Lost*, is never permitted to lose sight of the meaning. Whatever the doubts of Blake or Shelley, there is no doubt but what Satan is the villain of the poem, and not only by intention or proclamation but in proof.

This is not to say that Milton forbears to indulge or to decorate the surface. *Paradise Lost* is a monument of the decorative style. It differs from the *Faerie Queene* in that adornment and meaning are kept discrete. The meaning is not obscured by the surface and not much informed and supported by it either. In Chaucer, the moral and esthetic responses run in tandem. Spenser often confounds the two, and that is unfortunate. Milton dissevers them, and that is disastrous.

To this penchant for dissevering I attribute the growing vogue of naturalism, as also the fantastic torturings of nature which succeed to it in the seventeenth century. The depicting and proliferating of concrete detail in everything that is tangential characterizes the age whose primary impulse is to simplification and abstraction. As abstraction waxes in important matters, the irrelevant surface is increasingly figured. Classical religion attaches its gods to material objects (Ceres is corn, Gaia is earth), exactly as these gods begin to forfeit their identity.[63] The same process is observable in the euhemeristic allegories of the early centuries and the Renaissance. In the fifteenth century mysticism is renascent, and Gothic architecture enters, I think sequentially, on its decadent or ornamented phase: austerity and deprivation in first and last things find their complement in redundance of detail. A century later the mysticism of St. Theresa and St. John of the Cross is complemented by the building of cathedrals, in Spain and also in Spanish America (Tepozotlan), for which Baroque is too pallid a word. In these cathedrals the passion for adornment comes to seem, as it is pointless, a hysterical gesticu-

---

[63] Barfield, *History in English Words*, pp. 92-93; Hinks, *Myth and Allegory*, pp. 27ff.

257

lating in the void.[64] As the surface of things is understood not to count, it is either neglected or else it is taken as offering a fair field for amusement. The conceit is suppressed or else it is manipulated in extravagant and essentially irrelevant ways. In 1671 Milton publishes *Samson Agonistes*: it is polemical and reformist and therefore it is spare. In the following year Dryden publishes the *Conquest of Granada*, a mindless entertainment and hence teeming with figures whose function is solely to bedizen. "Sublime subjects," says the author, "ought to be" not informed, but "adorned with the sublimest, and consequently often with the most figurative expressions."[65]

Absorption in the fact, which may have no reference except to itself, preoccupies the artist and sculptor; and also the musician, who is often concerned in the late Middle Ages to achieve an intimate relation between the music and the words he sets. But the achievement is desirable not for affective but for pictorial reasons. The primary intention is mimetic. This intention describes almost the whole surviving repertory of poems set to music in the early Tudor period.[66] It is *art pour l'art* that the fifteenth century is adumbrating here: in music (the contrapuntalist masters, of whom Joannes Okeghem is the great exemplar), and also in architecture (the Flamboyant style of late Gothic, as elaborated in such churches as St. Maclou in Rouen or the monastery of St. Jeronimo in Lisbon), and in painting (the *diableries* of Hieronymous Bosch, Patinir, Breughel the

[64] See, for example, the fantastic retable at Oviedo in northern Spain or—an earlier illustration—the decorated porches and wrought columns within the church in the monastery of St. Jeronimo, Lisbon. Wellek, paraphrasing Georg Weise (in *Concepts of Criticism*, p. 90), locates this "tendency towards arbitrary inorganic decoration in the history of the arts and literature always at the end of a period."

[65] Essay on *Heroic Poetry and Poetic License*, 1677. More radically the poet, conceiving of all language as superficial, will play with words as if they were mechanical counters: so the revival in the Renaissance of number poetry, as of poems which seek to fulfill a typographical design.

[66] See the music collected in the *Fayrfax MS* (British Museum); and, for the same effect, the conventional counterpoint of the songs in *Ritson's MS* (BM), dating also from the end of the fifteenth century.

Elder, Pieter Huys).[67] The new music of the Elizabethans, though it may employ the techniques of naturalism, will interest itself in brute fact: in communicating the nuances of the matter to be set, not because it desires a more nearly perfect delineation of what is (the masses and motets of Okeghem) but because it sees that delineation as serving an end beyond itself. The ulterior end is not static but dynamic: not simply an awareness but action upon awareness. It is the transformation of man.

The triumph of ulteriority in the later sixteenth century does not require by any means a superseding of naturalistic art. Naturalism flourishes and later exfoliates in its various perversions (Gongorism, Marinism; in architecture the Churrigueresque style), and even as the art of the moral maker grows more imperious and austere. What is required is the acknowledgment that truth to nature is not a primary truth. The parallel is inescapable to the language of men of science like Galileo and Descartes, who insist on precisely this division between what is primary or real and what is secondary or evanescent. But the primary truth is not concrete, it is abstract. Breughel the Elder is sufficiently concrete and perhaps he is more serious and successful than the connoisseurs of ulteriority. It is difficult to see him, in paintings like "Mad Meg" or "Flemish Proverbs," as an affective artist. The pseudo-Rabelaisian *drolatiques*, like the ornamental grotesques or *sogni dei pittori* of sixteenth-century Italy, are convincing (if bizarre) as representation: and emphatically and exclusively ornamental.[68] It is open to an Elizabethan composer like Thomas Weelkes to cultivate the lesser truth (to display his consummate skill in disposition), as in the imitative madrigal on the nightingale. Implicit, however, in the applause

[67] For Bosch, see especially "The Hay Wain," "The Table of the Mortal Sins," "The Temptations of St. Anthony" (two copies), "The Garden of Delights"; for Joaquin Patinir (1480-1524), "Passage of the Stygian Lake," "Landscape with St. Jerome" (aptly titled: the saint is less than the landscape), "The Temptations of St. Anthony" (with Quintin Massys); for Breughel the Elder (1525-69), "The Triumph of Death"; for Pieter Huys (1519-81), "Fantasia Grotesca." All illustrations from the Prado.

[68] Kayser, *Grotesque in Art and Literature*, p. 180.

he receives is the stipulation that only craft or cunning is in-volved. It seems to him as to many of his contemporaries that one kind of composition is appropriate to truth telling, another to secular or self-indulgent art. "A knee walks lonely through the world," says Christian Morgenstern, who is presumably pull-ing our leg.

As truth is easy of access, its presentation is aloof from craft or technique. The truth of Holy Scripture is "open to all, and even those of least penetration" (Augustine).[69] It needs no "such explication whereby light may be brought to it from something else" (William Ames).[70] Samuel Howe, the preaching cobbler, declares for the "sufficiency of the spirits teaching" as against the "profane, vaine bablings" of the seven liberal and gratuitous arts. Since "The Saints are all taught of God . . . they need no outward teaching by men brought up in humane learning."[71] Giordano Bruno supposes, like the Prophet, that "Whosoever walketh in the way, yea, and even fools, shall not err therein." That is why he finds it easy to sneer at his disputatious contem-poraries, "those sticklers for niceties who are nowadays infesting Europe." Luther, who is not inclined to stickling, wonders at the "need for interpretation when Scripture is entirely clear." His adversary Erasmus had better "give up his human wisdom" and "learn to know Christ and be strong."[72] But Erasmus does not need to be admonished.

The strength that works miracles is not a function of intelli-gence, says Tyndale, but faith.[73] The Platonist or enthusiast be-lieves that, as faith quickens within him, he must come to the possession of truth. Given this intensely optimistic belief, the art of the Renaissance will be a fiercely single-minded art, al-ways driving toward the imparting of the one truth which, when achieved, engenders action. Its characteristic concern will be with clarity, that the truth may be discovered and implemented. Thus

[69] Epistle cxxxvii, 18.
[70] *Marrow of Sacred Divinity*, pp. 170-71.
[71] Quoted in Thomas Hall, *Vindiciae Literarum*, 1654, D2.
[72] Isaiah xxxv, 7, 8; Santillana, *Age of Adventure*, pp. 248, 136, 143.
[73] *Obedyence*, H5v.

the quest for the plain style in poetry and music, and in either art the abrading of the surface. But when the poet or the composer is simply fooling about, not intent for the moment on climbing Jacob's ladder, he will do the naturalistic thing without pretension. In this way it happens that a preoccupation with technique for its own sake characterizes an age which is dedicated on its serious (its dominant) side to the exploiting of technique in the service of salvation.

The sixteenth-century composer Luzzaschi is the serious man. He sets to music Dante's *Quivi sospiri*. His contemporary Dascanio is the self-delighted technician. He imitates the noises of El Grillo, the cricket. Each man (each side) is represented in William Byrd who, as he expresses (not fuses) them both, epitomizes the late sixteenth and early seventeenth centuries in England. Byrd's dominant side is serious and finds expression in his Latin and English church music. But Byrd in another vein is indulgent of technique for its own sake: "his *Virginella* and some others of his first Set cannot be mended by the best Italian of them all" (Henry Peacham).[74] He is careful, however, to keep his seriousness and his frivolity distinct.

The ardors of frivolity may sponsor an art that is naturalistic or grotesque. But whether it seeks to delineate nature with absolute fidelity or to offer a highly mannered approximation of nature, it remains an inferior or merely technical thing. As such, and though it will require great pains and expertness, it is not taken as engaging the higher truth. One might suppose this intermediate kind of activity to be reserved to the nominalist, whose eyes are necessarily averted from the heavens. But that does not follow. The Platonic temperament, if it is attracted at all to the representing of sensuous experience, emphasizes technique, and often in perverse or exaggerated ways, exactly as it

[74] *Compleat Gentleman*, p. 100. Perhaps Byrd is the creator of Variation-form, the first musician to play with a popular song by ornamenting the melodic line with as much cunning as art allows. He is in any case not above composing variations for the virginal on secular song tunes like *O mistress mine* or in setting Ariosto (*Orlando*, I, v, 42) in his *Sonets and Pastorals*.

declines to concede it any ultimate importance. Art does not mediate between the unknown and the known. But though it is not requisite in detecting the truth, it is in lesser ways a source of delight. The humanist or idealist may devote a lifetime to the cultivating of art. Only he will understand that what he is doing is, in the last resort, tangential.

Sir Philip Sidney, to the degree that he evinces this understanding, typifies the new or rational man. As a pastoral poet or writer of sonnets, Sidney is first of all an innovator. His preoccupation with technique is manifest in his constant seeking out of fresh tasks, as many as he can muster and as arduous as possible in the proceedings they enjoin on the poet. But when Sidney turns psalmist, his writing, though still inventive prosodically, is no longer so pestered with rhetorical devices. That is not surprising: Sidney is dying out of "poetry" into life. As he wishes to come to the heart of the matter, he does not allow much expansion of imagery or manipulating of tropes. Metaphor, which on his reading is always a gratuity, is here an impropriety: the more lofty subject on which the poet's mind is bent permits of no adornment.

Wan hope is the motive for metaphor. Human fallibility makes a precise equivalence unattainable. One has resort, therefore, to inference and analogy. Cassiodorus understands that "in view of the condition of earthly affairs, the heavenly truth is announced to us, in accordance with our intellectual capacity, by means of parables and dark sayings." In support of this more humble reading of things, the medieval man adduces Psalm LXXVII: "I will open my mouth in parables, I will utter dark sayings from the beginning."[75] Quintilian's observation is also a concession: "many things with us have no recognized names, so that we are driven either to metaphor or periphrasis."[76] Contrasting his native Latin to Greek, Quintilian laments "our poverty of synonyms." The poverty is endemic in all language. What Sidney says is true: "for wordes are but wordes, in what language soever they bee."[77]

---

[75] *Institutiones*, p. 112.   [76] *Institutio Oratoria*, XII, x, 34.
[77] Letter no. XXXVIII (to his brother Robert) in Feuillerat edn., III, 125.

But Sidney believes that after all we can apprehend the naked truth. And so, as he is serious, he discards the analogical way. His translation of Psalm xix (*Caeli enarrant*) summarizes the rationalist position, which rests on the belief that the truth is ascertainable and simple.

> There be no eyne but [can] reade the line
>   From so fair book proceeding,
> Their Words be set in letters great
>   For evry body's reading.

On this affirmation the Renaissance establishes its program to build the kingdom of God on earth. In the inspiriting words of the Spanish humanist Juan Vives, "Truth stands open to all. It is not as yet taken possession of. Much of truth has been left for future generations to discover."[78] But the task of future generations is not so much to discover the truth as to proclaim it.

[78] Preface to *De Disciplinis*, 1531.

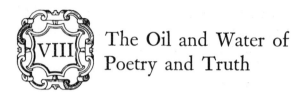

The Oil and Water of
Poetry and Truth

MAN in the dark age supposes, congruently, that truth is couched in dark sayings (Psalm LXXVII). Modern man, the denizen of the age of gold, takes his text from the more hopeful prophet of the Book of Numbers: "With him will I speak mouth to mouth, even apparently, and not in dark speeches" (12:8). Apparent speaking, the perfect accessibility of truth, suggests that art is supererogatory.

But the early seventeenth century is the Age of Shakespeare? It is, however, the immensity of Shakespeare's achievement that sponsors the identification. The eccentricity of the achievement is discounted. Shakespeare as psychologist and maker is not giving a lead to his contemporaries. Already the times have passed him by. The singleminded impulse by which the age is more correctly perceived is made to look disconcertingly thin by the generosity or mindlessness Shakespeare evinces. Henry Adams suggests—he is describing the endless refinements of light and color in the apse at Chartres—that even the utmost power of expression as manifest in the greatest artists of all time has been capable of expressing no more "than the reaction of one energy on another, but not of two on two."[1] It is partly a mysterious phrase but if I take its meaning, I think Shakespeare refutes it, as when in *King Lear* Edgar tells us that "Ripeness is all"—a line that is forever—and old Gloucester rejoins banally: "And that's true, too." Each line has its perfect integrity. In Shakespeare's art, the product of a mind "never violated by an idea," the art of the medieval maker is summed and transcended, and then it disappears. The man whom Gerard Janssen imagines in the chancel at Stratford, who wears the mask of Buddha, is

[1] *Mt.-St.-Michel and Chartres*, p. 159.

unique in his own time as he possesses the ability to hold in suspension antithetical truths without forfeiting his sanity or his power to discriminate.

Antony and Cleopatra illustrates this ability best. The asp that Cleopatra handles is an emblem of Cleopatra as the serpent of old Nile; and also the serpent in the Garden of Eden who brought death into the world and all our woe; and concurrently a pretty worm who is doing his kind. Cleopatra, who invites it, who has the aspic in her lips, is Eve the seductress; and also a lass unparalleled whom everything becomes: who is dressed by the devil, and who makes defect perfection. Antony, a man who is the abstract of all faults, is also a digest of infinite virtue. Antony is dishonored and condemned in that he kisses away the greater cantle of the world. But Antony is also honored and justified in rating a single tear of Cleopatra's above all that is won and lost. And so no definitive judgment may be uttered about him. He cannot be placed. No Truth inheres in him. But that is intolerable to an age whose business is with judging and doing. After Shakespeare the mind refuses to entertain together such divergent possibilities. It is either Dryden and a fatuous commending of The World Well Lost, or Racine in *Bérénice* (a much more considerable business but pretty nearly as exclusive), opposing to self-gratification the greater imperatives of *raison* and *honneur*.

In the seventeenth century the skepticism or tolerance which is the nourishing of art yields to the conviction that we can come to enabling conclusions. The essential displacement is anterior to Shakespeare, whose magnitude conceals but does not repair the infectious optimism mining all within. That optimism is something new under the sun. Certitude denotes it. There is finally no doubt but what Dryden's Antony is right to reject the claims of the world. There is no doubt that Titus, in Racine, should affirm them. But doubt is endemic in Shakespeare. It envelopes his characters and the situations they inhabit. For example *Troilus and Cressida*:

> My mind is troubled like a fountain stirred,
> And I myself see not the bottom of it.

The result is that declarative statement is made merely vulgar.

But not forever. The new philosopher and his satellites, in art, in politics, in religion, proclaim an end to dubiety. "Hypotheses non fingo!" That is Sir Isaac Newton, throwing out his chest. The man who lives equably with the unknown is not affronted by the presence of doubt; neither is he paralyzed by it. Ambiguity is the "natural" condition. "To hold two opposed ideas in mind at the same time, and still be able to function"—this is not so much the test of intelligence as it is the mark of health.[2] Incertitude is existential and as such is acceptable to the healthy man. His perception of things is unmotivated (he has no ax to grind) and hence more nearly true. Modern man in what he sees is motivated intensely, wills an end to doubt. As his understanding swells, the ignorant fumes are banished that disable the reason from choosing in unequivocal ways. In the more rational art of the later seventeenth century, equivocation is relegated to the dark age whence it came. The new clarity that supervenes is, however, not a goal to be achieved at last. It is given from the beginning. The seeds of Psyche have been parted.

But if the Word (the meaning) is perfectly clear, the meticulous couching of the Word, which is the business of art, loses its justification. That is only the logical conclusion. Easy to avoid it! Sidney and other partisans of poetry avoid it by promulgating the metaphor of art as medicine. The choice of metaphor is agreeable in the context of the late sixteenth century. To the utilitarian, it suggests that poetry is homeopathic. It gratifies the instinct of the rationalist to clarify and resolve by analyzing poetry into constituent parts. There is the palliative that wins us with a pleasant taste; and there is, concealed beneath it and distinct in its function, the salutary emetic. Stephen Gosson, the contemner of poetry, resembles Sidney, who endeavors to defend it, in distinguishing two contrary aspects of verse. The first, which is pleasure alone, is emblematized in the mindless and bootless preoccupation of "The fool that comes into a fair gar-

[2] After Scott Fitzgerald in "The Crack-Up"; and Maslow, in *Motivation and Personality*, p. 295.

den [and] likes the beauty of flowers and sticks them in his cap."
There, "they wither without profit." The typically sensuous
reader of poems who "picks out their flowers for his own nose
is like a fool." If, however, he emulates "the physician [who]
considereth their nature and puts them in the pot," he will find
that "they serve to the health of the body." Poems are to be
valued not as they are good or bad, but as "their sweet smell"
is fortified and made acceptable by "their virtue" or power.[3]

Other metaphors announce this same division. Nashe separates the "greene and flourishing leaves" from the "fruite hidden in secrete" beneath their shadow. Meres echoes him, commending the "many things verie profitable to be knowne" which
bide beneath the surface of "poems, figures and fables," even
as "in a Vine clusters of grapes are often hidde under the broade
and spacious leaves." Alternatively, Meres likens the division
to that between the insubstantial flower, which may be a noxious
flower, and the bag of honey it encloses: as the bee is directed
by the one to the other, so the philosopher is made to extract
profit "out of obscene and wanton Poems and fables."[4]

None of these writers looks very hard at the flower. It has no
value in itself but only an intermediate value—rather like "the
haune" or husk which men must penetrate or strip away "before
they can come at the karnell" (Nashe). This ancient and simplistic figure of the husk and kernel is refurbished by Sir John
Harington, and to the end that "the litterall sence (as it were
the utmost barke or ryne)" is seen as protecting "a second rine
and somewhat more fine . . . nearer to the pith and marrow . . .
[which is] the Morall sence."[5] If the meaning or sentence is the
vital spark, art is the integument. Though, says Sidney, "the
inside and strength" of Plato's Dialogues "were Philosophy,
the skinne as it were and beautie depended most of Poetrie."[6]

---

[3] *Schoole of Abuse*, E2v.

[4] Smith, I, 331 (*Anatomie of Absurditie*); II, 309, 312 (*Palladis
Tamia*). For the flower and the honey, see Nashe and Whetstone in Smith,
I, 332, 59.

[5] *Briefe Apologie*, 1591; Smith, II, 201.

[6] *Apologie*; Smith, I, 152.

A demeaning separation is effected, as between the vizard and the thing itself. Art, which is the vizard, is related to what it covers only by contiguity. The function of art, like that of the diabolic harmony in Milton's Hell, is only to ravish or beguile:

For eloquence the soul, song charms the sense.[7]

The defenders of poetry are contending for superficies: mere "gards of Poesie" with which the writer of history and philosophy "trymmeth both theyr garments" (Sidney). The identifying of art with facing or decoration is understood to characterize "the greatest part of Poets [who] have apparelled their poeticall inventions in that numbrous kinde of writing which is called verse: indeed but apparelled, verse being but an ornament."[8] Sidney's point is that a Dichter need not write in verse. My point is to the phrasing: the way verse is construed. Harington, as often, takes his cue from Sidney in describing the "part of Poetrie, which is Verse" as the "clothing or ornament of . . . [the matter]." The verse is dispensable; still, it "hath many good uses": it gives assistance to the memory; it is especially graceful for its "forcible manner of phrase"; chiefly, it affords "pleasure and sweetness to the eare which makes the discourse pleasaunt unto us often time when the matter it selfe is harsh and unacceptable."[9] Enter Lady Macbeth adjuring her husband: "Look like the innocent flower,/ But be the serpent under't."

It is convenient to remember Dante who, in the *Vita Nuova*, discusses personification as a form of tropology. He is aware that there are poets who employ it "without consideration," which means to no organic purpose. These are to be indicted "as having no reason in what they write." Dante's practice, like theirs, is to "rhyme under the semblance of metaphor or rhetorical similitude." But "afterward, being questioned thereof," he can "rid his words of such semblance, unto their right understanding." The point here (despite the separableness which

---

[7] *Paradise Lost*, II, 556.

[8] Smith, I, 192, 159. For the sixteenth-century reading of the rhetorical surface as ornament alone, see M. Prior, *Language of Tragedy*, p. 25.

[9] Smith, II, 206.

Dante allows) is not that sense and similitude are unrelated. The point is that they tally. The similitude is not justified as mnemonic or forcible or cozening. It is justified inferentially in that it ratifies the sense. That is why it is possible to paraphrase the poem: to rid the argument of its metaphorical semblance. The symbolist remains discontented. Metaphor, as he apprehends it, is more than ratification. And hence he is led to speak of the heresy of paraphrase. Dante is not formally a symbolist, though on my reading his poetry is not so amenable to paraphrase as he suggests. But neither is he a decorative poet who fixes a gulf between the understanding and the form.

To the modern writer, Puttenham, for instance, the figure or form evokes praise as it is new or surprising. It does not partake of the life of the meaning; it apparels the meaning. Two kinds of poetical ornament are distinguished, one of which stirs the mind, and the other "th' eare onely by a goodly outward shew set upon the matter." Each kind or garment is produced by figures of speech, "some serving to give glosse onely to a language, some to geve it efficacie by sence."[10] The gloss or outward show is acceptable as it burnishes and includes a different thing than itself. The "out-side of . . . [Poesie], which is words, or . . . Diction" is, to Sidney, a mask or blind under which the Greek philosophers appeared to the world. The task of the reader is to find out the secret places "under the vayle of fables" where Hesiod and Homer elaborated their home truths, or Aesop ("under the formall tales of Beastes") his "pretty Allegories." These are "wrapped within the folde of the proposed subject."[11]

Let me recur for the crucial difference to Alan of Lille, who observes in the *Anticlaudianus* that "just as the meaning is wrapped around the material, so the signification of the allegory shines through the material." In the Renaissance, the interpenetration which characterizes medieval practice disappears. Meaning and material are discrete. "The vanitie of tales is wonderful," says Thomas Lodge (who is rendering the Latin of Campano); "yet if we advisedly looke into them they will seme

---

[10] Bk. iii, Ch. iii. [11] Smith, i, 152, 206, 167, 158.

269

and prove wise"—as witness the fables of Ovid and Virgil in which "under the persons of beastes many abuses were dissiphered." It is the looking into—*introspiciantur*—that is decisive.[12] The wonted formula is to speak, first and with some embarrassment in qualification—this, as touching style or surface; and then to overset the qualification by detecting the "good Morrall lessons . . . therein contained."[13] The participle is important as enforcing a separation between fruit and chaff. The poem is not an integer.

I do not suggest that medieval man apprehended, as an indivisible thing, the text he was perusing. Mostly, he gives primacy to the deeper meaning and wishes to isolate it. That is the implication in this sentence of Peter Lombard: "The historical sense . . . is for beginners, the moral for the advanced, the mystical for the perfect."[14] But the historical sense is not treated perfunctorily. The kind of value imputed to it is illustrated by the twelfth-century master and Chancellor of Paris, Peter Comestor, in the prologue to his great summary of biblical history (*Historia Scholastica*). Peter is called the Comestor or Manducator in that he has eaten and digested the Scriptures in their entirety, not omitting what the later age miscalls the husk or awn. He is conscious of levels; at the same time he is conscious of the whole. To put it another way: "History is the foundation . . . allegory the wall . . . tropology the roof." A preoccupation with the letter is supremely useful, by analogy to a digging of the foundation. Accepting the analogy, Roger Bacon, who is more

---

[12] Though Chaucer "be lavish in the letter, his sence is serious" (Lodge, *Defence of Poetry*; Smith, I, 65, 69). "Though the manner of his stile may seeme blunte and course . . . yet . . . a man shall perceive" much beneath it (Webbe, *Discourse*; Smith, I, 241). Ovid's "worke of greatest profitte [*Metamorphoses*] . . . though it consisted of fayned Fables . . . and poeticall inventions, yet being moralized . . . and the trueth of every tale beeing discovered," shows itself to Webbe "a worke of exceeding wysedome and sounde judgment." So the Eclogues of Theocritus, Virgil, and Spenser: "Although . . . they . . . seemeth commonlie in appearaunce rude and homely . . . yet doo they indeede utter in the same much . . ." and so forth. Smith, I, 238, 262.

[13] Webbe in Smith, I, 264.   [14] Smalley, p. 245.

a scientist in the conventional or empirical sense than his greater
namesake, urges that geometry be employed in glossing Scripture, "in order that Noe's ark, the tabernacle with all its furniture, the temple of Solomon and Ezechiel may be described
physically." If this physical description is scanted, says Bacon,
"it is not possible for the literal sense to be known, nor, in consequence, the spiritual."[15]

The conviction of dependency is central to the medieval reading. Medieval man, who sees the letter as preliminary, nevertheless is intrigued by the letter. In any case, he does not see it
as a vehicle only. Herbert of Bosham, the secretary and biographer of Becket, differs from his more restive successors, the
platonizing churchmen of the Age of Reason, in paying honor
to what is of the surface. "I am not striving," says Bosham very
humbly, "after an understanding of the difficult spiritual senses,
but with the animals that walk the earth, I cleave to earth, attending only to the lowest sense of the letter of the Psalter."[16]
It is a fruitful attending.

In the Middle Ages, the sign, despite the intervention of
Plato, still participates in the referent. Indifference to the letter
is not praised as a stripping away of the veil. It is censured as a
neglecting of the foundation. The word is a pointer and also the
incarnation of reality. The drift is not yet confirmed from the
symbol to the thing it signifies. The figurative is more than figurative; it is also substantive.

Millenarian zealots, as they anticipate the imminent ending of
all things, look without relish on what is literal or of the surface.
Their impulse is to come at once to the spiritual sense that lies
beneath. The impulse is heretical and is accordingly condemned,
as in the Montanists of the second century, men obsessed with
the spirit. Gregory the Great smacks of their heresy. What I
should call his Platonic character is conveyed in medieval representations, for example at Chartres, where the ghostly dove at
his ear dictates the books whose writing, in lesser men, depends
on the patient observing of fact. Gregory is indifferent to obser-

[15] Smalley, pp. 242, 330.　　[16] Smalley, p. 188.

vation, as in his commentary on the vision of Ezechiel. The dimensions of the altar, which so concern and so interest the prophet that he gives them specifically "after the cubits" (43: 13-15), are nothing to him; or rather, they constitute an envelope which he tears in his impatience. The impatience is destructive of the commentary. To Richard of St. Victor, the disciple of Hugh, Gregory's exposition of the vision of Ezechiel is wanting: "what it means literally he does not say."[17]

This same unwillingness to scrutinize the letter describes St. Bernard of Clairvaux. The great and greatly beautiful monastery of Cluny, the light of the world, moves him only so far as to provoke the indignant question: "Will the light only shine if it is in a candelabrum of gold or silver?" As he gazes on the carvings which adorn the cloisters of his order, he wants to know what "these fantastic monsters [are] doing" and "To what purpose are here placed these creatures, half-beast, half-man, or these spotted tigers?" To the ascetic spirit, what is palpable is nugatory. "Surely," says Bernard, "if we do not blush for such absurdities we should at least regret what we have spent on them!" Like the platonizing Pneumatic he really is in his heart, he urges a friend to abandon as gratuitous his studies of the Prophets and to enter the school of piety at Clairvaux. "O," he cries, with the true eschatological fervor, "had you once tasted a little of the fat of corn that filleth Jerusalem, how gladly would you leave their crusts to be gnawed by the lettered Jews." The crust is the text or surface. The Jews are lettered—a term uttered in contempt—as they are literally minded.[18]

I see this scorn for the surface as peculiar and portentous: in it, the millenarian of the early Christian centuries and of the twelfth-century renascence salutes and prefigures the man of the greater Renaissance. Each understands perception in terms of use, is contemptuous accordingly of whatever is "superficial." This suggests that perception in the modern age is purblind: doggedly motivated (the guarantee of myopia), rubricizing, and

---

[17] *Prologus in visionem Ezechielis*; Smalley, pp. 92, 108-9.

[18] Mâle, *Gothic Image*, pp. 48-49; Bernard's *Letters*, cvi; Smalley, p. 173.

always auxiliary to action. "It isolates that part of reality as a whole that interests us; it shows us less the things themselves than the use we can make of them . . . we scarcely look at the object, it is enough for us to know to which category it belongs." Bergson, who associates disinterested perceiving with painters and sculptors, musicians and poets, might be treating more comprehensively of those medieval men whose senses are "less adherent to life," as the compulsive personality misconceives it. "When they look at a thing, they see it for itself, and not for themselves. They do not perceive simply with a view to action; they perceive in order to perceive—for nothing, for the pleasure of doing so. . . . It is therefore a much more direct vision of reality that we find in the different arts; and it is because the artist is less intent on utilizing his perception that he perceives a greater number of things."[19]

Let us substitute for the artist the unmotivated personality: man in the Middle Ages. This man, who builds cathedrals and slaughters Turks and Jews, has no end in view? The question is gratuitous, answers itself. What is meant in the description of him as a man less "impelled" than his successors is that, characteristically, he is satisfied to pause a little. Like Hugh of St. Victor, he censures those who, reading Scripture, "leap straight from the letter to its spiritual meaning." It appears to him that if the surface is only a vector which points past itself, "then the metaphors and similes, which educate us spiritually . . . have been included in the Scriptures by the Holy Spirit in vain." Those men, those eschatologists, are not acute but myopic to whom "The outward form of God's word seems . . . like dirt." As they "trample it underfoot, like dirt, and despise what the letter tells . . . [them] was done physically and visibly," the total meaning which they covet is necessarily diminished. It is this venerating of the letter and the sense that a neglecting of it entails a diminution of the whole that I should describe as distinctively medieval. To Hugh of St. Victor, whom I take in this particular to epitomize the old-fashioned point of view, what is carnal and visible is also of the sacrament. "But hear!" he ex-

---

[19] From *Creative Evolution*, quoted Maslow, pp. 298-99n.

claims, admonishing his more austere and simplistic contemporaries, "that dirt, which you trample, opened the eyes of the blind. Read Scripture then, and first learn carefully what it tells you was done in the flesh."[20]

Recovering the letter is a great preoccupation of the Renaissance, for example in patristics. But the letter the exegete is hunting is not written on the surface. He finds it hidden or contained "in a cloake of simplicitie" or "in some prety and pleasant covert." Nashe, in a vivid and vulgar image, sees him as having "fished out" the moral.[21] That done, he may turn his back on the rest of the afternoon.

The antithetical view, that the style or treatment is not merely a vehicle but of critical significance in itself, is met so infrequently in the Renaissance as to seem, when one encounters it, profoundly eccentric. Mostly the critic directs his attention to the matter. Is it sufficiently serious or "poetic"? It is startling to read, in Francesco Patrizzi's *Della Poetica* (1586), that "the matter comprised in science, in art, in history, can be a convenient subject for poetry and poems provided that it be poetically treated." But if any subject is tractable, primacy will belong to the treatment and not the subject. Latent or residual here, I suspect, is the medieval notion of the *topos* or set theme, which one takes as given and proceeds to dispose as expertly as he can. The pith is in the *dispositio* or handling. But that is flat heresy in the year of Sidney's death. Ramus has supervened, who gives primacy not to disposition but to invention. That is the heart of the Ramistic revolution. Webbe is Ramistic in honoring Chaucer chiefly for his "sharpe and eger inventions," and Gascoigne in stipulating that "The first and most necessarie poynt . . . to be

[20] *De Scripturis*, v, 13-15; Smalley, pp. 93-94.

[21] Smith, I, 322. Antecedent quotations from Webbe, I, 264, 262, 241. O. B. Hardison, *Enduring Monument*, defends Renaissance literary criticism against the charge of "intellectual naïveté" and advances the proposition that sixteenth-century didactic critics have much to say about the nature of poetry that commands our continuing respect. I think the proposition most persuasive as it emphasizes the insistence of the older criticism on the social significance of art (pp. 187-94). This emphasis is perhaps what Shakespeare, who is the most "political" of writers, absorbs.

considered in making of a delectable poeme is . . . to grounde it upon some fine invention." His counsel to the poet is to "stand most upon the excellencie of . . . Invention, and sticke not to studie deepely for some fine devise." Believing that the manner is ancillary, he takes it as self-evident that, the matter "beying founde, pleasant woordes will follow well inough and fast inough."[22]

The Middle Ages are not so sure. That is why they emphasize *dispositio*. But in this emphasis, the *topoi* are not neglected. Paradoxically the Renaissance, as it honors invention and deprecates technique, is left at last with *dispositio* alone. For the *topoi* are a casualty of what is essentially an exalting of the individual inspiration. The reliance on the inner light, typified in Descartes' rejection of all outer authority, begets a contempt for history and a belief in the capacity of the individual man to stand as an individual against the present moment, always seen as existing *in vacuo* and not to be explained in terms of antecedent time. "I am myself alone." The rationalist, who despises history and tradition, must settle in the end for the promptings of his lonely and isolated ego. At last he has no alternative but to rack his own brains.

Canonical opinion, in positing a division between fruit and chaff, does not insist, or not yet, on rejecting the latter altogether. Nashe justifies a cursory attention to the manner in suggesting that "true things are rather admirde if they be included in some wittie fiction, like to Pearles that delight more if they be deeper sette in golde." The metaphor derives from Ascham: "And even as a faire stone requireth to be sette in the finest gold with the best workmanshyp . . . so excellencye in learning . . . [should be] joyned with a cumlie personage." But Ascham is shrewder than Nashe and not so modern in defending comeliness and workmanship as something more than superficies. He perceives and stigmatizes the unwisdom in saying, " 'What care I for a

---

[22] Webbe in Smith, I, 241; *Certayne Notes*, 1575; Smith, I, 47-48. To Jonson, translating and approving Horace, the chief desideratum is "thy matter first to know." "Where the matter is provided still,/ There words will follow, not against their will."

mans wordes and utterance, if his matter and reasons be good.' "
He is aware that those who "care not for wordes but for matter . . . make a devorse betwixt the tong and the hart" and so
do grievous harm to learning. History is Ascham's warrant here.
"Marke all aiges," he asserts, "and ye shall surelie finde that,
whan apt and good wordes began to be neglected, and properties
of . . . [Greek and Latin] to be confounded, than also began ill
deedes to spring, strange maners to oppresse good orders, newe
and fond opinions to strive with olde and trewe doctrine."[23]

Even so late as the middle of the seventeenth century, isolated
voices continue to be heard in protest against the facile opinion
that a preoccupation with language is "needlesse, and uselesse."
Scripture itself, says Webster's clerical opponent Thomas Hall,
"as it is a Text consisting of words" must remain a closed book,
failing "the help of Arts." This text is "ful of Rhetorick, many
Tropes and Figures . . . abundance of Metonymies, Ironies,
Hyperboles, Hypallages." The truth inhering in it, "like Treasure, lies deep and hidden, and cannot be found without search,
and study."[24] Hall's reactionary proposal is "to dig into those
Sacred Minerals, for the better finding out of . . . [the figures
of speech] which lye hid there."

> For the bare reading of the Scriptures, without searching into its
> heavenly mysteries and meaning, is like the comming into a Treas-
> ury, wherein we see many costly things folded up, and some ends
> appearing out, but when they bee all uncovered, then doth their
> glory more affect us.[25]

It is a noble passage and emphatically out of date.

If palaces are more comely as they are adorned "with unnecessary painting"—already Boccaccio is drawing the inference—
"artistic embellishment" is defensible, "though it is of no prac-

[23] Smith, I, 329, 2, 6.

[24] *Vindiciae Literarum*, Preface, Blv-2, A3-v. "Hypallage": when the
order of the words is changed. Hall (*Rhetorica Sacra*, Ml-v) illustrates
from Job XVII, 4: "Thou hast hid their heart from understanding. Thou
hast hid understanding from their heart."

[25] *Rhetorica Sacra*, 1654, L3-v.

tical use whatever." Boccaccio's analogies are not especially lucky. "Of what use," he inquires, "is the hair on the head?" and answers: "None, as all agree." The reason a stag has horns or a bird "gay plumage" is, as he supplies it, a pretty reason: it is "For embellishment and nothing else." So with his own practice, in which "an occasional story [is] mingled with the substance" only "for ornament's sake."

Boccaccio proceeds to claim for his writing a very potent "usefulness, public and private, in which its greater value resides."[26] The usefulness may be conceded for it is, in this context, neither here nor there. What is important is the separation of matter and manner and the defense of the latter as "valuable . . . merely on the score of ornament." Subsequent writers will do a little better than this. They will say gay plumage as sexually attractive, and hence as serving to further the propagation of the species (the justification of gay plumage and sexuality alike); or they will observe, with Richard Morison, the translator of Juan Vives, that "moral precepts pleasantly set out in feat colors of witty phantasys, both creep faster into our bosoms and also tarry there with much more delectation and profit, than they would, being plainly spoken."[27] But the creeping and tarrying are not really to the purpose. The otiose principle has been established. Art is excrescent. It is the husk which envelopes the kernel. Between the two there is no affinity. There is only proximity. Art does not inhabit the inner core of things. It merits approbation not as it is truthful but as it is cunning. The function of art is to adorn.

The critique of art which the Renaissance sponsors is unfortunate. But the art itself? Some readers—those who are charitable—will suppose that the view of two ages, one exalted at the other's expense, suffers from bad luck in that the Renaissance provides our greatest era in poetry. I acknowledge that I am not logically so rigorous as, say, Yvor Winters in asserting an immediate connection between bad art and bad critical thinking. Yeats is wooly minded, and as a poet incomparably superior to T. Sturge Moore. Ben Jonson in his criticism is undistinguished,

[26] *Genealogy,* xv, i.
[27] *Introduction to Wisdom* [1540?], A3.

277

he thinks too little and not very acutely; and he is tenably the supreme lyric poet in English. Marlowe, who as psychologist is elementary when put against the Wakefield Master, has no peer in the drama save one. And so on. Still I would argue that there lives within that flame of love which is the colossal achievement of the Renaissance "a kind of wick or snuff that will abate it." Murky thought and a dubious psychology, given time, bring in their revenges: the death of tragedy, the decay of the discursive style in the poetry and prose of the late seventeenth century and after. Discursiveness, truth to life are a casualty of the proposition that truth is open and shut.[28]

Longinus in the third century, as he is not persuaded of the easy accessibility of truth, sees the vehicle and its burden as more intimately connected. Grandeur "is never dissociated from use and profit." I take this to mean that style is not extrinsic but partakes of the life of the whole. Hence Quintilian's observation two centuries earlier that "True beauty is never divorced from utility."[29] If, however, the conviction grows that truth is simple, and discernible without particular effort ("Their Words be set in letters great For evry body's reading"), the grandeur or beauty which environs the truth will come to seem an inorganic accouterment. It will follow from this position that the most excellent style is the absence of style. (That is the genesis of the "plain style" of Jonson.) To render the Word artfully is not to render it more precisely. Art does not enable nor does truth require the trappings of romance. Tasso, as he indulges romantic business, labors to no purpose: he was "a Christian Poet, whose Religion little needs the aids of Invention." The writer is Davenant who, as he is something less than a Christian or serious poet, may give a loose rein to invention. Already he conceives

---

[28] Hardison, whose drift is not mine, nonetheless ends up asserting "the indubitable truth that the effect of a poem is often quite independent of the intentions and literary theories of the author" (*Endless Monument*, p. 188). So Sidney and Jonson, in their dual role as poets and as theorists and readers of literary theory. Enter the intentional fallacy, and Lawrence's dictum: "Never trust the author, trust the tale."

[29] *On the Sublime*, 36, i; *Institutio*, VIII, iii.

it as a self-engendering thing, approximating to high nonsense or fancy.[30]

It is still possible to defend the accouterment which is art as seductive or protective or dignifying, by analogy to the sugar-coated bolus or the flower or the husk or the setting of a stone. But these ancillary functions imputed to it do not make good the decisive loss entailed in the view of art elaborated by the Renaissance as against that of the Middle Ages. Compare, with Sir Philip Sidney, the Victorines on the letter of the Scripture. The difference is absolute, like that between the organic beauty of pillars which function as support of an edifice for living: beauty allied to use (as in Peter Comestor's metaphor of the foundation), and the ostensible beauty, which in the last analysis is a meretricious thing, of those pillars or fake pilasters stuffed with rubble whose function is only to adorn. As one conceives of art under this latter aspect, he will associate it increasingly with technique: he will understand that art is a *tour de force*, the intention of which is not to divine the truth but to enhance the prestige of the artist. If, conversely, one believes that art should concern itself at least partly with eliciting or divining, he will logically attack conspicuous art as making against that concern. Longinus is logical in commending the appearance of simplicity (which is not the same thing as simplicity itself): "A Figure looks best when it escapes one's notice that it *is* a Figure"; and Quintilian in observing that "The chief business is to dissemble art, so that numbers may seem to flow of their own accord, not to be fetched and forced into service.[31]

Renaissance critics and artists, as they wish to communicate the truth of things, appear to embrace this self-effacing doctrine. Jonson insists that "The true Artificer . . . not run away from nature, as hee were afraid of her; or depart from life, and the likenesse of Truth." The "onely Art" is "so to carry it, as none but Artificers perceive it."[32] That is the position Sidney affirms

---

[30] Preface to *Gondibert*, 1650.

[31] *On the Sublime*, 17, i; *Institutio*, IX, iv, 147.

[32] *Discoveries*: a commonplace book, precisely, the bulk of which is taken from others.

in deriding the misguided pedant who, "using Art to shew Art, and not to hide Art (as . . . he should doe), flyeth from nature, and indeede abuseth Art."[33] But Sidney himself uses art to show art and more consistently and audaciously than any other important English poet. The famous double sestina, "Yee Gote-heard Gods," is a triumphant illustration. The numerological sonnet in correlative verse, also from *Arcadia*, as it is less than triumphant, offers a more suitable gloss:

[1]Vertue, [2]beawtie, and [3]speach, did [1]strike, [2]wound, [3]charme,

[1]My harte, [2]eyes, [3]eares, with [1]wonder, [2]love, [3]delight:

[1]First, [2]second, [3]last, did [1]binde, [2]enforce, and [3]arme,

[1]His workes, [2]showes, [3]suites, with [1]wit, [2]grace, and [3]vow's might.

I explain the very striking disparity between precept and practice by suggesting that Sidney is mostly not intent on rendering nature but on flying from nature to another and an unrelated sphere where questions of verity are displaced by questions of art, which means in his lexicon of technique.

That is not always so. Sidney is sometimes a notable poet in the plain style. But even when verity is at issue, as in the Metaphrase of the Psalms, the precept is not enacted: art is not used to hide art: essentially, art is disused. This further paradox or contradiction is traceable to Sidney's more fundamental belief that truth requires no courting. The medieval opinion may be gathered from an exposition on the Octateuch by the twelfth-century abbot, Andrew of St. Victor, who is famous in his own time and later as one who expounds the Bible *ad litteram*. "How hidden is truth," observes this protagonist of what is called rather too easily the Age of Faith—

how deep she dwells, how far she screens herself from mortal sight, how few she receives, how laboriously they seek her, how few (they are almost none) may reach her, how partially and piecemeal they drag her forth. She hides, yet so as never wholly to be hidden. Careful seekers find her, that carefully sought, she may again be found.

[33] Smith, I, 203.

The Age of Reason felicitates itself in having attained to a perfect apprehending of the truth. Medieval man is more skeptical
and not so forthputting, and hence his belief that "None may
draw ... [the truth] forth in her completeness, but by degrees.
The fathers and forefathers have found her; something is left
for the sons and descendants to find. So always: she is sought;
something is still to seek; found, and there is something still to
find."[34]

The medieval artist eschews (until the medieval period approaches its term) a superfluity of decoration as entailing a blurring of the goal. Very obviously, there is no eschewing of art.
Sidney's explosive insight is to see these two as one. At the heart
of his esthetic is the austere or fanatic proposition, unstated in
the *Apologie* but writ large in the verse, that when truth is in
the lists art is best hid by the virtual exclusion of art; but when
the pursuit or, better, the presentation of truth is intermitted,
when the serious man is content in an idle hour to indulge or
amuse or glorify himself, rhetoric (in its pejorative sense) is
to be heightened. The heightening is lucky. Opportunism—the
commitment to rhetoric—turns out to be the right way to make
poetry, as also to discover the "truth." Sidney is a great poet.

The preoccupation with technical expertise—tropology, lavish ornamentation—is conceived as a preoccupation with the husk
or awn. But technique is of poetry. And now the crucial identification: poetry is the husk. First the husk and kernel are divided.
Now poetry is defined in terms of the former. Its appeal is not
to the intellect but to the ear or the viscera. It is the song that
charms the sense. Poetry is fancy.

When Carlyle announces, some centuries later, that "all right
Poems are [Songs]," he means to distinguish them from rational utterance. The "mystic unfathomable song" of Dante is
known to be poetry in that it eludes comprehension. In prose,
on the other hand, "What we want to get at is the *thought* the
man had, if he had any: why should he twist it into jingle, if
he *could* speak it out plainly?"[35] Thought is alien to poetry

---

[34] Smalley, p. 124.   [35] *The Hero As Poet.*

whose "proper and immediate object," says Coleridge, "is the communication of immediate pleasure." In this it differs from a more substantial activity like science, whose "proper and immediate object . . . is the acquirement, or communication, of truth."[36] While the poet dreams a "summer dream beneath the tamarind tree"—it is Poe who is describing him, sympathetically he thinks —the scientist, "whose wings are dull realities," is engaged in tearing the Naiad from the water and rooting out the Hamadryad from the wood. Of course the poet scorns and fears him:

> How should he love thee? or how deem thee wise,
> Who wouldst not leave him in his wandering
> To seek for treasure in the jewelled skies.[37]

But really to look at the skies is to denude them. The distinctive support of poetry, says Matthew Arnold, is imagination. Intelligence, conversely, is "the ruling divinity of prose."[38] An instructor of Oscar Wilde's at Trinity College, Dublin, would have been a poet, "If he had known less." Ruskin, who taught Wilde at Oxford, was in fact "a great poet . . . and therefore of course a most preposterous professor; he bored you to death when he taught, but was an inspiration when he sang."[39] Poetry is the antithesis of teaching. Poetry consists in "an elevating excitement of the Soul" and not at all in "the satisfaction of the Reason": Poe on the *Poetic Principle.* "Its sole arbiter is Taste." It does not pretend to hold a mirror to Nature. There are "chasmal differences between the truthful and the poetical modes of inculcation. He must be theory-mad beyond redemption who, in spite of these differences, shall still persist in attempting to reconcile the obstinate oils and waters of Poetry and Truth." The poet creates with the careless rapture of Ralph Waldo Emerson, who folds his arms beside the brook and lets the passing cloud indite his letters for him.[40] Composition is most successful when "the intellect [is] released from all service," or else when it is "inebriated." The result is that the poet is able to fashion, like

[36] *Biographia Literaria*, Ch. xiv.   [37] "To Science."
[38] *The Literary Influence of Academies.*
[39] Harris, *Wilde*, p. 33.   [40] "The Apology."

Emerson himself, only a vignette or still life. The metaphor of the ignorant traveler describes him: he "throws his reins on his horse's neck, and trusts to the instinct of the animal to find his road."[41] This bemused and intoxicated person agrees with Wordsworth in holding "the critical power very low, infinitely lower than the inventive." He himself cannot be tasked with the fribbling intervention of mind. But neither will he allow it to the critic who, as he exercises his intellectual function, is supposed to be impervious to "the finer influences of a thing so pure as genuine poetry."[42]

These are the voices of Romanticism. They are heard first, however, in the Renaissance and for that reason I summon them here. I do not mean to come on in the hectoring vein like Irving Babbitt. In our reading of poetry we are all "romantic" (except for the isolated moralists among us, like Yvor Winters), and mostly that is to the good. I think we agree with Poe that "with the Intellect or with the Conscience . . . [poetry] has only collateral relations." This agreement makes us as critics potentially far more penetrating than the vulgar homilists of the Italian Renaissance with whom modern criticism begins. It is only that, like Poe, we are not sufficiently catholic. The poet never teaches, is exclusively a fantasist who inhabits a plane tangential to reason. But that is what Davenant supposes.

The equation between poetry and fancy, which is fathered customarily on the nineteenth century, is suggested already early in the sixteenth.[43] Tyndale assumes its validity in girding at Thomas More and "his poetrie where with he bylte utopia." The question Tyndale puts is rhetorical: "What maye not Master More saye by auctoritie of his poetrie?" The answer, I suppose, is that nothing is forbidden him, and not simply because

---

[41] *The Poet.*

[42] Quoted by Arnold in *The Function of Criticism at the Present Time.*

[43] Monk says, in his treatise on *The Sublime*, p. 5: "It has become a truism that in the art and theory of the eighteenth century are to be found all or about all of the ideas and methods that we usually associate with that unhappy term *romantic*." I would revise to read: about all of these ideas and methods are nascent in the Renaissance.

the poet is mendacious as the more febrile critics allege, but because considerations of truth or falsity are not at issue in the medium in which he works.[44] Though poetic figures "be occupied of purpose to deceive the eare and also the minde, drawing it from plainnesse and simplicitie to a certaine doublenesse," this abuse of the real or departure from it does no harm. Since the poet is not judicious but only suasive and then only in trifling matters, and since "all his abuses tende but to dispose the hearers to mirth and sollace by pleasant conveyance and efficacy of speach," it follows to Puttenham that these abuses "are not in truth to be accompted vices but for vertues."[45]

But more than this will follow. Reasonable men, as they are forced to believe their ears, will begin to "deride and scorne . . . [poetry] as superfluous knowledges and vayne sciences." It will seem to them with some propriety that "who so is studious in th' Arte . . . [is to be called] in disdayne a phantasticall; and a light headed or phantasticall man (by conversion) . . . a Poet." Agreeing with Puttenham that "the common people, who rejoyse much to be at playes and enterludes," do so by virtue of "their naturall ignorance,"[46] they will conclude, as he does not, that this same ignorance defines a rejoicing in any of the arts. Even if they remain sympathetic, like the printer Richard Field who first publishes the narrative poems of Shakespeare, they will be conscious of the fanciful nature of the stuff in which they trade. Field expresses this consciousness in addressing Puttenham's *Arte of English Poesie* to the Lord Treasurer Burghley. Necessarily he boggles a little at the task, "Perceyving . . . the title to purport so slender a subject, as nothing almost could be

[44] *Answer to More* [1530], N8, O1, A7.

[45] "Our maker or Poet is appointed not for a judge, but rather for a pleader, and that of pleasant and lovely causes and nothing perillous, such as be those for the triall of life, limme, or livelyhood, and before judges neither sower nor severe, but in the care of princely dames, yong ladies, gentlewomen, and courtiers" (III, vii). The next step is taken by the academic philosopher Jacopo Mazzoni who, in a *Defense of Dante* (1572, 1587), classifies poetry under Sophistic instead of Dialectic.

[46] I, viii; II, ix.

more discrepant from the gravitie of your yeeres and Honorable function, whose contemplations are every houre more seriously employed upon the publicke administration and services."[47] The discrepancy is between poetry and reality. The province of poetry is not the business of life but romance.

This new and invidious definition takes strength from Sidney's redacting of the doctrine of idealism. What Sidney is doing, or rather prescribing, is generally misconceived by modern readers of the *Apologie*. On the one hand, he is confounded with Shakespeare, refining the truth to body it forth more precisely. What does it mean, a modern critic inquires, that Sidney's poet "nothing affirmes"? It means that in his verse this poet "embodies, dramatizes, makes real the truth, preserves and intensifies experience."[48] But that is simply wrong. The poet of the *Apologie* does not embody experience. He does not love it very much. The second and more plausible misconception: Sidney gets high marks, especially in our own time, as he is supposed to prescribe for the "pure" poetry of the twentieth century. The poet "nothing affirmes, and therefore never lyeth."[49] His responsibilities begin in dreams. He has read somewhere that in the Emperor's palace at Byzantium there is a tree of gold and silver and artificial birds that sing. And in fact there are poems of Sidney's, particularly in the *Arcadia*, that are like this golden bird ("formes such as never were in Nature"). I think there are yearnings in the *Apologie*, not wholly grasped by the writer who conveys them, toward a Symbolist poetry, the song alone without reference to signification.

But always Sidney pulls back. The "good invention" at a remove from banality to which the poet is committed turns out to be not *art pour l'art* but falsification, not an adumbrating of Wallace Stevens and Paul Valéry but a tedious enjoining of the Platonic lie: poetic justice. The poet does not labor "to tell

[47] Smith, II, 2.
[48] P. Spacks, "In Search of Sincerity," *College English*, XXIX, 598.
[49] Smith, I, 184.

285

you what is, or is not, but what should or should not be."[50] Sidney in the event is disappointing and familiar.

Like the moral maker today, Sidney carries a great burden. It is to annul the Platonic indictment that poetry impoverishes by representing an inferior reality in lieu of the higher or plenary truth. "And it was written of Socrates," according to one of the *mysomousoi* or poet-haters, "that he was but ill or slenderly brought up in Poesie, because he loved the truth."[51] Sidney himself, as he finds the inference unacceptable, seeks to whiten his fellows with the Socratic candor by affirming that "of all Writers under the sunne the Poet is the least lier." Now, to represent an inferior reality (the secondary truth of Plato and Descartes) is to lie. But the "Poet can scarcely be a lyer" for he does not depict the truth in its conventional habiliments, which means as one meets it in the highway. Other critics, Webbe for instance, insist that the matter "which the Poet handleth" be stamped with "an Image of trueth."[52] Hobbes takes this position in his polite exchange with Davenant. Dissenting "from those that think the Beauty of a Poem consisteth in the exorbitancy of the fiction," Hobbes asserts that "the Resemblance of truth is the utmost limit of Poeticall Liberty." Sidney, in contending for a wider freedom, is more acute. Perceiving the force of the Platonic objection to what is conceived as a similacrum of the thing itself, he absolves the poet of the arduous and possibly trivial labor of depicting this resemblance.

But he does not exact of him a more nearly veracious depicting. For Sidney is not concerned with the plenary truth. He is sufficiently a Platonist to believe (in Hoby's words) "that the skirt of our garments shoulde not carrie a stinche of life."[53] He

---

[50] Smith, I, 185. Creation belongs to God, is not yet the province of a poet. "Whatever early sixteenth-century critics may appear to us to say, it is always best to assume that they are thinking of a poet's work as fiction-making, not as creation: their verb is *effingere*, not *creare*" (G. Shepherd, ed. Sidney's *Apology*, pp. 62, 155-56).

[51] I. G., *A Refutation of the Apology for Actors*, 1615, E3.

[52] Smith, I, 184, 342, 251.   [53] Smith, I, 344.

endeavors to remove the poet from his lowly habitation on the bestial floor and to translate him to a golden and more fastidious world, abounding "with pleasant rivers, fruitful trees [and] sweet smelling flowers" where, I think, the rivers never run to the sea and the ripe fruit never falls. In the brazen world of Nature there are no lovers so true as Theagines, no friends so constant as Pylades, no heroes so valiant as Orlando. In the intense inane to which the poet is going, these wants and disappointments are all to be made good.

> Who quarrels over halfpennies
> That plucks the trees for bread?

The new poet parts company with the painful realist who is "captived to the trueth of a foolish world." Preferring to brute fact "the vigor of his owne invention," declining to be "inclosed within the narrow warrant of . . . [Nature's] guifts, but freely ranging onely within the Zodiacke of his owne wit," he will "growe in effect another nature, in making things either better then Nature bringeth forth, or, quite a newe, formes such as never were in Nature." In this prodigious work of amelioration, he will far surpass the servile realist who counterfeits what is set before him. The poet Sidney envisages is more excellent as he is more benevolent and less scrupulous: "having no law but wit," he will represent what is "fittest for the eye to see."[54]

But this wit which inspires him and also constitutes the sole authority he is willing to acknowledge is not to be equated with intellect. As Sidney construes it in the *Apologie*, wit is synonymous with fancy. From that construction, much mischief ensues. Only a few years earlier, Ascham had defined *Euphues* as "he that is apt by goodness of wit, and appliable by readiness of will, to learning." Here the old-fashioned or conventional sense is implicit. Wit to Ascham is wisdom or intellect or reason. This is the sense it bears to Shakespeare:

> Then all too late comes counsel to be heard
> Where will doth mutiny with wit's regard.[55]

[54] Smith, I, 156-59, 170, 185.   [55] *Richard II*, II, i, 27-28.

287

Sidney endorses this older definition:

> Vertue alas, now let me take some rest,
> Thou setst a bate betweene my will and wit.

But already he perceives in the word a double meaning or second sense, as in the engagingly humorous and self-critical injunction: "Peace, foolish wit, with wit my wit is mard."[56] Wit is concurrently reason and fancy. In the *Apologie*, the primary meaning is suppressed.

There is precedent for this. Lyly in *Euphues* is remembering Ascham. *Euphues* is "The Anatomy of Wit." But to Lyly, the wit that denotes his protagonist makes him inept and unready. It is a form of self-indulgence and hence subversive of right reason. In Lyly, wit is posed against reason. Dr. Johnson describes what has happened, though he errs by more than a century in locating the event: "it was about the time of Cowley that *wit* which had been till then used for *intellection*, in contradistinction to will, took the meaning, whatever it be, which it now bears."[57] This new meaning which associates wit to fancy is taken by Sidney as defining the poet's milieu. The prodigious forms which he discovers, not in Nature but in the firmament of his own imagination, as they have no correspondence in Nature are not open to criticism as unveracious but only as unconvincing. The poet has no law but wit or fancy, and therefore it is not germane to indict him as holding up a distorted mirror to Nature. He does not pretend to delineate Nature. His boast is to "borrow nothing of what is, hath been, or shall be" but rather to envisage and depict "what may be, and should be." His function is to dash the cup from Socrates and to devise in hell new punishments for the tyrant who condemned him to death. On earth, the valiant man rots in his fetters and the evil man expires peacefully in bed. In the fanciful zodiac where the poet ranges "All friends shall taste the wages of their virtue,/And all foes

[56] *Astrophil and Stella*, nos. 4, 34.
[57] *Life of Cowley.* "Wit" meaning "fancy" goes back *c.*40 years before Lyly. See W. G. Crane, *Wit and Rhetoric in the Renaissance*, Ch. ii; W. G. McCollom, "The Role of Wit in 'MAdo,'" *SQ*, xix, 169.

the cup of their deservings." The poet will show you in the latter "nothing that is not to be shunned" and in the former "each thing to be followed."[58] His task is to repair the human condition or else to transmute it.

This sophisticated apology which seeks to annul the Platonic indictment of poetry by affirming, not in guilty but in triumphant ways, the equivalence of poetry and fiction, is not wholly original with Sidney. Bernardo Daniello a half century earlier is willing to allow on ancient authority a "mingling [of] true things with false and feigned, because the Poet is not bound, like the Historian, to describe things as they actually are and have happened, but such as they ought to have been."[59] But this poet is conducting an experiment and, like the scientist, in a controlled or ideal state. He is approximating more nearly to the truth by casting the truth in relief.[60] To come to the truth he heightens or interpolates or divests his representations of irrelevant detail. In the making of these interpolations and excisions, the imagination governs. To the ancients, however, imagination, as it performs this governing function, is not to be identified with fancy but with craft. Neither is it opposed absolutely to the fact. Imagination retrieves and redintegrates the fact. It is not a more congenial but "a wiser craftsmistress than Imitation." (I am quoting from the Greek rhetor Philostratus, on whom Keats drew by way of Burton for the story of *Lamia*.) "Imitation will fashion what she sees, but Imagination what she has not seen, for she will suppose it according to the analogy of the real."[61] The coordinate clauses tally with Sidney's reading. Sidney's innovation is in contemning the analogy. The older writer is more faithful to it exactly as he reorders what appears to be true.[62] If he suppresses the particular exemplification, it is not from

[58] Smith, i, 159, 170, 168.

[59] *Poetica*, Venice, 1536.

[60] Jonson in *Discoveries*: The poet is one "that fayneth and formeth a fable, and writes things like the Truth."

[61] *Life of Apollonius*; quoted Saintsbury, *History of Criticism*, i, 120.

[62] So Jonson, translating Horace: "For, being a Poet, thou maist feigne, create,/ Not care, as thou wouldst faithfully translate,/ To render word for word."

289

parti pris but because he sees it as idiosyncratic. His purpose is a penetrating to the truth of things, and so he declines to make a fetish of unlicked experience. Years follow on Macbeth's usurpation of the throne, and still sin does not pluck on sin. Shakespeare, collapsing time, does not violate but only clarifies the ultimate truth. In this sense he idealizes or speaks, in Sidney's phrase, to "the universall consideration." But that is not what Sidney's poet is about in elaborating "a perfect patterne." His pattern does not find corroboration in fact, and even given the poet's license to tug history into shape. But though his utterance may be cryptic or at odds with the truth, he is not to be censured as lying. He cannot be censured for "the Poet . . . nothing affirmes, and therefore never lyeth."[63]

It is an interesting assertion and its consequences for the future of poetry are immense. The poet has become a contriver of fictions. Wilde's dictum that "a picture is a purely decorative thing" is already potential in the formulations of Sidney and his disciples. Poets, says Puttenham, emulating Oscar, "devise and make all these things of them selves, without any subject of veritie."[64] To idealize has come to mean, as in our vulgar modern sense, to bark up the wrong tree.

It is unctuous talk to the new authoritarians, who are quick to grasp and applaud its implications. James I, as he is eager to buttress in practical ways the doctrine of divine right, is pleased to take at face value the stipulation that poetry never affirms. He construes it as a pledge of allegiance. Agreeing with Sidney (and with Ramus before him) that "Invention is ane of the chief vertewis in a Poete," James concludes that "it is best . . . [to] invent your awin subject your self" and not be "bound, as to a staik, to follow that buikis phrasis quhilk ye translate."[65] That is Sidney's conclusion. He sees it as ennobling the poet in that it permits him to overgo the brazen world in his imaginative representations, and as acquitting the poet of the charge of

---

[63] Smith, I, 167-68, 184.

[64] Wilde, "The English Renaissance of Art" (New York lecture, 1882), quoted Harris, p. 54; Puttenham, I, i.

[65] Smith, I, 221.

mendacity in that it secures for those representations freedom from conventional assessment. Sidney, enfranchising the poet from the trammels of fact, does not propose to lessen but to magnify his role. Sidney's poet is not a jester who truckles to the court but a seer who stands above it.

But the King is more relentless a logician. He sees how to wrest the conclusion, which derives from a lofty estimate of poetry's business, and to the end that poetry and vacuity are made the same.[66] Adhering to the proposition as Sidney expounds it, that "though . . . [the poet] recount things not true, yet because he telleth them not for true, he lyeth not,"[67] James observes demurely that as the poet is pinnacled in the zodiac of his own wit, creating forms which have no provenance in Nature and which are neither true nor false, he can scarcely have occasion or justification to meddle in princes' matters. The poet Mayakovski, as an ironical contemporary reminds us, "died because he had trespassed on territory to which he was a stranger."[68] Across this interdicted territory the old-fashioned poet, who has never heard of freedom of speech, travels freely. See the *Roman de la Rose*. The new poet in his movements is more constricted, is "wary of wryting any thing of materis of commoun weill" except as he writes nonsensically ("Metaphorically"), or as he is satisfied to flog a dead horse by treating what is "opinly knawin." He has abdicated his mundane station. Now he is instructed that mundane matters "are too grave materis for a Poet to mell in." It is not an unreasonable conclusion. Henceforward the poet's station is in the nursery or the boudoir. That is what the empyrean comes down to. As he is wise, asserts the King in an amusing piece of casuistry, he will omit entirely to trench on public business lest he fail to "essay . . . [his] awin Inventioun."

There is an element of dessert in this disingenuous contracting

---

[66] Quintilian on his own time is instructive: "It was the Interest, therefore, of Tyrants, to debilitate and cripple every Species of Eloquence. They scarcely had any other Safety." Trans. William Guthrie, 1756; quoted W. Irving, *Providence of Wit*, p. 52.

[67] Smith, I, 185.   [68] *Hope Against Hope*, p. 27.

of the poet's domain. The poet himself is first to reject as too narrow the warrant of Nature's gifts. He can hardly expostulate or not as he takes thought when the courtier Puttenham, reaffirming the royal prescription, depicts him as "never medling with any Princes matters nor such high personages."[69] But he does not expostulate. He comes wittily to terms. The poet Edmund Waller is his spokesman. As befitting a humble (and sagacious) entertainer who dances attendance at Court, Waller writes first in celebration of Cromwell, and then as the wheel turns of Charles II. But the King is displeased. His panegyric, he complains, is not so successful as that handed up to the Protector. Waller answers: "Sir, we poets never succeed so well in writing truth as in fiction." It is Sidney's defense in a nutshell.

The esthetic which informs the defense or capitulation takes a while to sink in: Donne, Herbert, Marvell, other poets of price who are not only suasive but cogent are to come. Later in the seventeenth century, the equation between poetry and fancy is confirmed. Poetry, as Thomas Shadwell understands it, is very much a matter of artificial birds that sing. Though Shadwell as a playwright is possibly more rational than Shakespeare, he is not so poetical, which means so adept in fantastical business. "For the Magical part," he acknowledges readily, "I had no hopes of equalling Shakespear in fancy."[70] The distinction, in which Shadwell is satisfied to acquiesce, is between Prospero the conjuror and Theseus the rational man. Poetry is conjuring.

On this principle Bishop Sprat undertakes to clear the memory of his friend Abraham Cowley. Because of an equivocal passage Cowley had written in introducing a collection of his poems, he is criticized as an opportunist whose loyalty is given only to the time. But the attack has no basis, or so Sprat alleges in his life of the poet, for "what he there said was published before a Book of Poetry, and so ought rather to be esteemed as a Problem of his Fancy and Invention"—the coupling is laconic now—"than as the real Image of his Judgment."[71]

[69] I, xiv.
[70] Preface to the *Lancashire Witches*, 1681.
[71] *Life of Cowley*, 1668, a⁷.

Not surprisingly, the mage or poet, given the terms of this defense, is sometimes at pains to conceal his affiliation to the puerile trade at which he labors. Sprat, who does not perceive the irony, makes it a point of praise in Cowley that "None but his intimate friends ever discovered he was a great Poet, by his discourse." Cowley beguiles expectation. He is intelligible. He is, however, phenomenal in this: "He had a firmness and strength of mind, that was proof against the Art of Poetry it self."[72] As the poet matures, he is apt to repudiate this rhapsodic or prestidigitory art as an adolescent diversion. Donne, as he grows older and hypothetically wiser, is taken as repudiating his songs and sonnets and preferring to them a more solid ecclesiastical career. "The recreations of his youth were poetry," says his biographer Walton in a fine compendious phrase. Cowley, who supposes that "the Marriages of Infants do but rarely prosper," is mature and rueful in reflecting on "the diminution or decay of my affection to Poesie; to which I had contracted my self so much under Age, and so much to my own prejudice in regard of those more profitable matches, which I might have made among the richer Sciences."[73]

Dryden, who reads poetry under the same rubric and yet continues to cultivate it, is not so faithful to his gray hairs. In his criticism and often in his practice, the gulf widens between poetry and truth. Since poets "have only their fancy for their guide," they "may let . . . [themselves] loose to visionary objects, and to the representation of such things as depending not on sense, and therefore not to be comprehended by knowledge, may give . . . [them] a freer scope for imagination." The poet, "speaking things in verse which are beyond the severity of prose," inhabits a world of gossamer stuffs. His task is fulfilled as the high nonsense he fabricates succeeds in diverting the reader. Enough if he is "pleased with the image, without being cozened by the fiction."[74] (Aureng-zebe unsheathes his dagger of lath.) As the

---

[72] d2ᵛ. [73] Preface to *Works*, 1656, B4.

[74] "Of Heroic Poetry," preface to the *Conquest of Granada*, 1672; *Heroic Poetry and Heroic License*, 1677. The pioneering treatment of Dryden as thinker, and the bases of his thought, is Bredvold's *Intellectual*

image mirrors such things as depend not on sense, so delight becomes "the chief, if not the only end of poesy."[75] Dryden is not eccentric in announcing this dubious proposition. To Cowley also, "the main end of Poesie" is "to communicate delight to others."[76] But as the poet has no commerce with the brazen world of fact or sense, he cannot address himself to the understanding. He is an entertainer.

Because they endorse this conception of poetry's business, the Augustans, who detest enthusiasm in religion or in rational discourse, are able to applaud enthusiasm in the arts. Quaking and shaking, the indulging of sentimental or fantastic or irrational behavior, is forbidden to the churchman. His task is to inculcate the truth. But Shaftesbury does not forbid irrationality to the poet.[77] Neither does Hume, in allowing unbridled license to the poetic imagination. A "poetical enthusiasm" differs necessarily from "a serious conviction," since poems "are connected with nothing that is real." To Hume it is obvious how "the least reflection dissipates the illusions of poetry, and places the objects in their proper light." Among these illusory objects are "winged horses, fiery dragons, and monstrous giants." In poetry, nature is ostracized or "totally confounded." But poets are to be pardoned this confounding, "because they profess to follow implicitly the suggestions of their fancy."[78] John Dennis confers the same equivocal pardon, in separating those passions which are rooted in objective reality from the merely subjective kind like woe or wonder. The latter, as their nature and provenance are not amenable to reason, are made appropriate to the disheveled

---

Milieu of JD. As the introduction makes clear, the book is written (ostensibly) to controvert the view of Dryden as "an expert craftsman with an uninteresting mind." To me, that is just right as description. To say so is not to disparage the great scholar I am quoting or the great poet he is defending.

[75] *Defence of an Essay of Dramatic Poesy,* 1668.

[76] Preface, 1656, B4v.

[77] *Characteristics of Men,* 1711, 1st and 5th treatises.

[78] *Treatise of Human Nature,* 1738, Bk. I, Pt. III, sec. x; Pt. I, sec. iii; Pt. IV, sec. iii.

art of the poet, who writes above his lintel the fateful words, *Je ne sais quoi.*[79] The young Edmund Burke, perusing this motto, discovers in sublimity the hallmark of the greatest art. But the sublime and the incoherent are essentially the same.[80] To the author of *Cato*, ruminating on the Pleasures of the Imagination, the hallmark of art is illusion, which is the bane of the practical man and, at the same time, the indispensable resort of the poet.[81] The quality of *Cato* follows predictably. *Cato* is an imposition. Like tragedy in general, as Goldsmith defines it in a very casual and hence illuminating phrase, it is marked by "The pompous train, the swelling phrase, and the unnatural rant."[82]

Hypothetically, this canting and mock-serious art is entertaining. It is not especially instructive. Dryden, as he is the most eclectic of critics, which means partly the least consistent, is not willing to forego instruction altogether and despite his professed allegiance to pleasure. And so he makes room for instruction but only "in the second place," and on the principle that "poesy only instructs as it delights." It is, superficially, a principle to which one is tempted to give his assent. Implicit in it, however, is a denigrating of consequential business. The ante-

---

[79] *Advancement and Reformation of Modern Poetry,* 1701.

[80] *A Philosophical Enquiry into the Origin of Our Ideas of the Sublime and Beautiful,* 1757. The growing identification of the sublime and incoherent is hinted at or corroborated in hundreds of details by Ogden and Ogden, *English Taste in Landscaping in the Seventeenth Century,* esp. pp. 134-51. Among the subjects of late seventeenth-century painting and engraving most popular in England were the forest scene, the moonlight landscape, the waterfall, mountain scenery (often marked by "horror"), the "prospect" (not so much depicted as "suggested"), the ruin piece. In the Restoration, the old distinction between ideal and topographical landscape begins to disappear. This breaking down is one way of looking at or glossing Sidney's assertion that the poet's commerce is not with the brazen world and that, at best, he "nothing affirms." It is exciting and perhaps not surprising to read (p. 163): "The whole history of landscape painting from Patinir to Turner might be written in terms of the process by which this distinction [between real and ideal] disappeared."

[81] Addison, *Spectator,* nos. 411-21.

[82] *Essay . . . on Sentimental and Laughing Comedy,* 1773.

diluvian poet—Chaucer, Dante—would have written that poetry delights only as it instructs. He is, however, a casualty of the Ramistic revolution which, in the way of such sanguinary enterprises, concludes with an inverting of the premise on which it was fought. This premise is that invention is more than disposition. Consequential business takes precedence over art. But greatly to invent is to repudiate the brazen world. In course, invention becomes inspiration. The poet is left with chimeras. But these, as they are not comprehended in knowledge, can hardly proffer instruction. They will signify, therefore, only as they are elaborated (or disposed) with sufficient cunning to entertain. In this manner, as art abjures life, disposition obliterates invention.

It is an old story. Quintilian on the Silver or decadent Age, when "The Care of *Words* succeeded to that of *Things*; real Beauty was stifled under false Ornament; and pretty Thoughts filled the Room of noble Sentiments" is not less cogent in the Age of the Augustans.[83] To the giant race before the flood, poetry is valuable as it speaks to the way of the world. Now the waters recede and Dryden is discovered, proclaiming the equivalence of poetry and rodomontade. Donne, who misses this equivalence, is blamed for "perplexing the minds of the fair sex with nice speculations of philosophy, when he should engage their hearts, and entertain them with the softnesses of love."[84] The critical error of the Metaphysical poets, says William Drummond, is that in reforming poetry they have "endeavoured to abstract her to Metaphysical ideas, and Scholastical Quiddities, denuding her of her own Habits, and those Ornaments with which she hath amused the whole World some Thousand Years."[85] Poetry is naked without the ornamentation that denotes her, but not as the truth is naked. "When all is done," observes Sir William Temple, "Human life is, at the greatest and

---

[83] Trans. Guthrie; Irving, p. 52.

[84] Drummond in Alvarez, *School of Donne*, p. 184.

[85] *Familiar Epistles*, letter to Arthur Johnson, c.1625-30; Alvarez, p. 153.

the best, but like a froward Child, that must be Play'd with and Humor'd a little to keep it quiet till it falls asleep, and then the Care is over."[86] Poetry's function is to participate in this humoring. Poetry is a bauble or else a soporific.

This of course is what the Puritan believes, and it is why he will fight to the death against poetry with pretensions but will indulge the sort of nonsense which approves his conception of poetry as a kind. His attitude toward music is illuminating. Without question, much secular music is published and therefore sanctioned in the Commonwealth period. The appearance of John Playford's *English Dancing Master* (1651) and the publication by Playford of works by Matthew Locke and Orlando Gibbons are notable examples. They suggest that the connection of Reform to dour business is mostly a fetish of Sir Toby's. Under the rule of the Saints, music remains popular at Oxford and Cambridge. Private instruction continues to flourish. The itinerant performers called waits play, as before, in the taverns. Masques, as by Davenant and Shirley, are presented, and to the accompaniment of music and dancing. Bach on the Continent is able to find employment at the Calvinist court of Coethen, at which he composes his French Suites and the Brandenburg Concerti. Milton, Wither, and Marvell, among poets of the new persuasion, certainly persist in their devotion to music. So does John Bunyan. Even Cromwell who, like Milton, kept an organ in his home, is supposed by Anthony à Wood to have "loved a good voice and instrumental music well."[87] Cromwell, in Marvell's phrase, is like "David, for the sword and harpe renown'd."[88]

But the essential point to grasp in this condoning of music and even delighting in it by the party of Reform is that music does not signify in first and last things. A laconic remark of John Evelyn's is suggestive. The Puritans, he says, "have trans-

---

[86] Conclusion to essay *Of Poetry*, 1704.
[87] Scholes, *Music and Puritanism*, p. 41.
[88] "A Poem Upon the Death of O. C."

lated the organs out of the Churches to set them up in taverns."[89]
That is to say: there is nothing wrong with music so long as
it is understood to be a peripheral activity. Even in church the
playing of an organ is permitted—after the service is done.

On this analogy, the bitter animus against the playhouse, concurrently the sanctioning of certain kinds of theatrical entertainment, become explicable. The poetic drama, as it offers to criticize
life, pretends to a significant role. Bodin, in his *Commonwealth*,
tells how Solon the magistrate, "having seene the Tragedie
of *Thespia* plaied, did much mislike it." The dramatist who
says easily, "It was but a play," is answered and reproved: "No,
but this play turnes to earnest."[90] The Puritan closes the theatres.
But he is not concerned to break a butterfly. With his tacit approval, rope dances and mummings and acrobatic acts persist in
the Commonwealth period. Not every theatre is dismantled. At
the Red Bull, which evades the general proscription, public per-
formances of that debased dramatic entertainment called the
droll are tolerated. What engenders such unexpected toleration
is, I suppose, the emasculated nature of this fragment or snippet
of a play, which abstracts from the whole a single scene of farce,
like Falstaff's account of the robbery at Gadshill or the clowning
of Nick Bottom or the colloquy of the gravediggers in *Hamlet*.
The patron of the droll humor is precisely that froward child
who must be played with a little until he falls asleep.

He is titillated in this same mindless way at the opera, which
is also allowed by the Puritan party while the legitimate drama
remains forbidden. There is no inconsequence in this. Dryden
makes that plain, in defining opera as "a poetical tale, or fiction"
—the correspondence between the two being patent—"represented by vocal and instrumental music, adorned with scenes,
machines, and dancing." Verisimilitude is reserved to the adornment. "The supposed persons of this musical drama are generally supernatural, as gods, and goddesses, and heroes, which at

[89] *A Character of England*, 1659; Scholes, p. 27. Puritan ordinances
against music in divine service met with a good deal of opposition.
[90] P. 645.

least are descended from them, and are in due time to be adopted into their number." But these supernal heroes, unlike Orpheus and Alceste, do not speak to human nature in the conduct that describes them:

> The subject . . . [of an opera], being extended beyond the limits of human nature, admits of that sort of marvellous and surprising conduct which is rejected in other plays. Human impossibilities are to be received as they are in faith; because, where gods are introduced, a supreme power is to be understood, and second causes are out of doors.[91]

When Davenant in the first of these emancipated productions turns rational causation out of doors, he fills up the hiatus by dwelling on "the art of perspective in scenes" and causing "the story [to be] sung in recitative music."[92] In the hurly that ensues, as music vies for attention with the shuttling of backdrops in and out of grooves, the telling of a consequential tale is omitted and the censor stays his hand. His political complexion does not matter. In this respect, republican and royalist are the same. *Macbeth* is agreeable to either as it is metamorphosed, and to the end that it is "excellent . . . especially in divertisement"— as Pepys describes an improved production (1672) "with alterations, amendments, additions, and new songs." If to go to the play is, in Pepys' phrase, to go "to the opera"—he is remembering an evening at the Duke's Theatre in Lincoln's Inn Fields —then it is permitted to go to the play. Shakespeare's *Macbeth* is, however, interdicted: it makes mad the guilty and appalls the free. Davenant's *Macbeth* (1666), "being in the nature of an opera," occasions no protest: "drest in all its finery, as new clothes, new scenes, machines, as flyings for the witches, with all the singing and dancing," it is only a mammet to bemuse the froward child. The poet Mandelstam, in exile, is fearful of

---

[91] Preface to his own opera, *Albion and Albanius*, 1685. The description is appropriate of Italian and French opera, mostly dominant in the period. See Dent, *Foundations of English Opera*.

[92] *The Siege of Rhodes*, 1656.

his life. "Tell him to calm down!" says a condescending warder. "We don't shoot people for making up poetry."[93] One knows what he means.

Plato, in his more general anathematizing of art, had spoken from just this same contemptuous point of view two thousand years before. Now the artist, in his work and in pronouncing on the work, appears to validate the Platonic characterization. This unlikely event I attribute to the eupeptic crusade which is Humanism. "Blessed are those who take the sword in their hands," says the Essene in Koestler's novel, "those who build towers of stone to gain the clouds, who climb the ladder to fight with the angel." But the poet, as he joins with the sons of man, is not blessed. What he conceives as a warrior's habit is only a coster-monger's coat, "Covered with embroideries/Out of old mythologies." The sword he flourishes lay yesterday in Wardour Street. It does not inflict much damage unless on himself. To the quarrel between poetry and philosophy, which had sponsored through many centuries so many embittered and sanguinary exchanges, there is after all a comic denouement.

[93] *Hope Against Hope*, p. 51.

IX Procrustes' Bed

THE POET is committed to fabricating a golden world and the result is a world of *papier-mâché*. But the mendacious poet, the father of lies, does not hold the field alone. A rival tradition, whose chief intention is heuristic, enlists the poet in the regiment of virtue. The medieval wholeness is broken. Art is an insubstantial pageant or else it is a tractate.

The chief imperative enjoined on this instrumental art of the rival tradition is clarity. That is why didactic poetry, which obliterates nice distinctions in the service of truth, often verges on bathos. The imperative is pragmatic. As art is dedicated to action and to the communicating of truth that action may be realized, its intermediate goal is transparency. If it is to be affective or expressive, it must first be made absolutely clear. The mortifying of allegory follows.

But all kinds and genres are clarified now. The Italianate resort to *sposizione* or explication is made native to England. Readers are edified by the margin. Dark conceits are illuminated, as by Spenser's friend E. K. who annotates in the *Shepherd's Calendar* whatever Spenser had left cloudy. The "trade of gloss or translations" becomes a thriving trade, that men may see more surely where they are going.[1] This trade of interlineating does not differ so much from that plied by the iron-age exegete like Fulgentius (*id est . . . id est*) or the makers of the Glossa Ordinaria. It differs absolutely from that of the typologist, who is supplanting one reality with another, more complex. In the Renaissance, only the One remains. The burden of the new criticism, which enters on its first great period in English, is accordingly a laying down of rules and cautels, this on the sanguine

---

[1] Quoting Nashe, preface to *Menaphon*.

principle that "art be but a certaine order of rules prescribed by reason."[2] As the rules are enabling, to heed them is to garner a preciseness of communication such as had not flourished before. The expectation is of a miraculous harvest, "if English Poetrie were truely reformed, and some perfect platforme or Prosodia of versifying were by . . . [the poets] ratified and sette downe."[3]

The first plank in this platform is an insistence on rigorous form. Ariosto, by the middle of the century, is denigrated as indifferent to form. His habit is to begin at the beginning and go straight on to the end. His instinct is the medieval instinct to tell the whole story. In his progress he is so inclusive or hospitable as to incur a charge of promiscuity. The instinct of the new critics is for exclusiveness and meticulous pattern. They detest equality in art. Their habit is to begin *in medias res*, to arrive more quickly at the heart of the matter. Sidney in the *Apologie* is their spokesman: "if they will represent an Historie, they must not . . . beginne *ab ovo*, but they must come to the principall poynte of that one action which they will represent." The more artful poet "thrusteth into the middest, even where it must concerneth him, and there recoursing to the things forepast, and divining of things to come, maketh a pleasing analysis of all."[4]

Ariosto is not conducive to analysis or rationalization. The Ariostoan reticule—and the art of helter-skelter in general, like the panoramic drama of the Middle Ages and its successor the chronicle play—is therefore abjured as chaotic and formless. It aspires, says Ben Jonson,

> To make a child now swaddled, to proceed
> Man, and then shoot up, in one beard and weed,
> Past threescore years.

Sidney, in an amusing passage, illuminates the merely linear progress it goes: "two young Princes fall in love. After many traverses, she is got with child, delivered of a fair boy; he is lost, groweth a man, falls in love, and is ready to get another child;

[2] Puttenham, I, ii.
[3] Webbe in Smith, I, 229.
[4] Sidney in Feuillerat edn., p. 39; Spenser's letter to Ralegh.

and all this in two hours space; which how absurd it is in sense
even sense may imagine, and art hath taught."[5] Antonio Minturno, legislating for the romance, understands that Ariosto is
myriad-minded. That is his vice: "for Truth is one," says Minturno.[6]

In obedience to this requirement of the single truth a new kind
of heroic poem is attempted, as by Giovanni Trissino, a self-conscious reformer who sees himself as impressing form on the literature of Italy where indiscipline and misrule had been before.
The *Orlando Furioso* abounds in romantic and fantastical matter; Trissino, in his *Italia Liberata dai Goti* (1548)—the title itself is a manifesto—eschews it for the real or historical thing. His
supernatural apparatus is not fabulous but Christian. Most of all
he is committed to unity of action: his plot is constructed "of one
single great action, which has a beginning, a middle, and an
end."[7] The English playwright and poet Nicholas Grimald, who
plumes himself on having "united in one and the same action a
story covering several days, and different periods of time," anticipates the future in perceiving that the various incidents of
which his Latin resurrection play is compounded "could easily,
and without trouble, be reduced to one stage setting."[8] Tasso is
not so servile in deferring to classical rules; still, it is his constant
opinion that "unity, in spite of critical disputes, in spite of Ariosto's success without it and of Trissino's failure with it, is vital."[9]
Truth is rendered in close conformance to the tables of the law.
The panoramic dramatist, a kind of heathen, misreads or ignores
them. In his plays romantic matter triumphs over reality and
correctness of composition is to seek. He is a fabulist and anarch

---

[5] Feuillerat edn., p. 197.

[6] *L'Arte poetica*, 1563; C. S. Baldwin, *Renaissance*, p. 168.

[7] Dedication to the Emperor Charles V.

[8] Dedication to *Christus Redivivus*, 1543.

[9] *Discorsi dell'arte poetica*, 1587; Baldwin, *Renaissance*, p. 177. In support of this opinion, Tasso writes a theoretical preface to his first heroic
poem (*Rinaldo*, 1562), defending unity of interest and action. In prepara-
tion for the *Gerusalemme Liberata*, he composes two sets of critical discourses, the first of which follows Trissino in stipulating for the epic poem
an historical and Christian theme.

who "first grounds his work on impossibilities; then in three hours . . . runs through the world, marries, gets children, makes children men, men to conquer kingdoms, murder monsters, and bringeth gods from Heaven, and fetcheth devils from Hell."[10]

Prescriptive action is indicated and is not long in arriving. When Castelvetro comes down from the mountain, having witnessed a prospect of the bright time preparing, he brings with him another commandment. This is the celebrated Doctrine of the Unities. It is enunciated for the first time in the sixteenth century and that is appropriate: perhaps by J. C. Scaliger in the sixties, more probably, in any case more insistently by Castelvetro a decade later. In formulating the doctrine (in his commentary on Aristotle), Castelvetro appeals to the truth that everybody knows, and that is characteristic: "it is evident that, in tragedy and in comedy, the plot contains one action only . . . because the space of time, of twelve hours at most, in which the action is represented, and the strait limits of the place in which it is represented likewise, do not permit a multitude of actions." Already the architect and painter Sebastiano Serlio had undertaken to explain, in his treatise on perspective, how an artificial sun might be made to rise at the beginning of this circumscribed action and seen to move on its course, "and at the end of the play . . . made to set with such skill that many spectators [should] remain lost in wonder."[11]

Not only the skill of the designer is wonderful but the propriety with which he signalizes the unity of time. Aristotle had spoken only for unity of action. The Renaissance adds and canonizes two unities more, and so extends the empery of rule that much further. This aggrandizing is congenial to Sidney, the first writer in English to profess allegiance to the new formulation. Sidney, as befitting his intelligence and tact, is not so hard and fast as the educers of truth by rule who come after him. Neither is he so catholic a critic as Cinthio, who stands against his time in asserting that Aristotle's precepts "do not extend save to the

---

[10] Whetstone, dedication to *History of Promos and Cassandra*, 1578.
[11] *Architettura*, trans. Robert Peake, 1611, Bk. II (1545).

poems which *are* concerned with a single action."[12] Sidney is with the time, or rather before it, as in his criticism of the tragedy of *Gorboduc*. That the play is a static thing is not his objection. He reprehends it because "it is faulty both in place and time, the two necessary companions of all corporal actions." In Sidney's intenser view, "the stage should always represent but one place, and the uttermost time presupposed in it should be, both by Aristotle's precept and"—here the rationalist speaks—by "common reason, but one day."[13] Milton, a century later, is not more rigorous than this: "The circumscription of time . . . is, according to antient rule and best example, within the space of 24 hours."[14]

Given these strictures, it will be obvious that Spenser is no more suitable a model than Ariosto. The *Faerie Queene* is not faithful to the unities and hence it violates precept and affronts common reason. "There is," complains Dryden, "no uniformity of design in Spenser."[15] The *Faerie Queene* does not answer to the need of the new dispensation for an epic poem constructed on rationalist lines. The fulfilling of that need awaits the coming of Milton. In the interim, it is Sidney who supplies it more nearly than Spenser—or, more accurately, tries to supply it, for when put against the *Arcadia*, Spenser is clarity itself. Sidney, nonetheless, is the more considerable figure, and the *Arcadia* and not the *Faerie Queene* the true representative of the spirit of its time. As his passionate endeavor is to bring order from chaos, Sidney fulfills the definition of the artist, and in fact it is in the *Apologie* that the word *artist* with all it connotes appears for the first time in English. Forsaking the old-fashioned and loosely articulated romance, the artist or régisseur creates what is essentially a five-act play. In the first part or prótasis, he introduces his moral tale of self-indulgence. The plot thickens: abdication has its issue; that is the business of the second part or epistasis. Catastrophe succeeds, and conducts to the peripeteia or reversal; and at length to the moment of anagnórisis, which is the discov-

[12] *Discorso dei Romanzi*, 1554.   [13] Smith, I, 197.
[14] Preface to *Samson Agonistes*, 1671.
[15] *Essay on Satire*, 1693.

ery of ultimate truth. Each of the first four acts is followed by a series of eclogues. Decisively unlike the *intermezzi* or mere diversions they resemble, these pastoral interpolations serve to advance and confirm the themes that have been bruited before. The whole is thereby made formal, but in the sense of organic and not mechanical form. If what happens does not always happen *propter hoc*, that is because Sidney is too militant to be unreservedly honest.

Poetry, as it is founded on number, is not organic but arbitrary in form. So, the rationalist rejects it. But if he is a friend to poetry, like Sidney or Thomas Campion, he will seek to come to terms with his perception by calling for a new prosody. Sidney says: "Let us some grammar learne of more congruities."[16] The impulse to congruity is the source of the aversion to rhyme in the sixteenth and seventeenth centuries, and the campaign to supplant it with quantitative measure. Jonson, who is very nearly supreme among rhymers, nonetheless engages in a "Fit of Rime against Rime"—whimsically, of course, but also, as his *English Grammar* attests, because he is alive to its Procrustean nature. Rhyme cozens "Judgement with a measure, But false weight."[17]

Partly the aversion is inspired by what is taken to be the dark provenance of rhyme, which the Age of Reason associates with the Latin verses of the medieval church. Rhyming poetry is too inclinable "to dance after the . . . pipe of inveterate antiquitie."[18] That is Puttenham's objection, as when with superb sweep he envisages "the Clergy of that fabulous age wholly occupied . . . in writing of rymes and registring of lyes."[19] The mendacious habit of "rude beggarly riming" was "brought first into Italy by

---

[16] *Arcadia*, Second Eclogues, #30.

[17] Jonson commends English "natural" rhythm as "both sweet and delightfull, and much taking the eare"; but is distressed at its lack of "regard to the Quantite of Syllabes." That "our Tongue may be made equall to those of . . . Italy, and Greece," he extols the virtues of "Artificiall" or quantitative verse (in the *English Grammar*, Bk. I, Ch. vi).

[18] Nashe in a polemic against Gabriel Harvey: *Foure Letters Confuted*; Smith, I, 317; Rubel, p. 106.

[19] II, 15.

Goths and Huns, when all good verses and all good learning too
were destroyed by them, and after carried into France and Germany, and at last received into England."[20]

Not parochial bigotry or pride but the opposition of lying to
learning, of expressive form to the jigging vein of the pretenders
to form, most inspires the revisionists and accounts for their rude
vociferation. Spenser's Eckermann, E. K., as he abhors "what in
most English writers useth to be loose, and . . . ungirt," is
prompted "to scorn and spew out the rakehelly rout of our
ragged rimers."[21] In this intemperate language there is a kind of
fitness. Truth is at issue: "the curiositie of rime" makes against
it.[22] As one hunts the letter or the right or chiming sound, the
bigger game he should be seeking eludes him.[23] The critic who
grasps the magnitude and nature of the issue condemns the fry
of "wooden rimers" as so many "blind bayards." The adjective
tells most heavily against them: "this tynkerly verse which we
call ryme" is responsive to the ear alone.[24] That is the gravamen
of Thomas Campion's indictment. With more exactness and implication than any of his contemporaries, Campion distinguishes
the intolerable fault of rhyme, as the reformers conceive it,
"which is, that it inforceth a man oftentimes to abjure his matter
and extend a short conceit beyond all bounds of arte."[25]

[20] Ascham in *Scholemaster*; Smith, I, 29. This is the explanation of
Thomas Blenerhasset's disdain for the "Gotish kind of riming" (induction
to the *Complaint of Sigebert* in *A Mirror for Magistrates*, edn. of 1578),
as of Milton's rejection of rhyme as "the Invention of a barbarous Age"
(note on the versification of *PL*).

[21] Dedication to *Shepherd's Calendar*; Smith, I, 131. So Webbe on the
"rabble of bald rimes" or "brutish Poetrie" (Smith, I, 229, 301, 240,
246).

[22] Francis Meres in *Palladis Tamia*, 1598; Smith, II, 314.

[23] So the poetaster William Warner: as we "run on the letter we often
run from the matter; and being over-prodigal in similes we become less
profitable in sentences and more prolixious to sense" (*Albion's England*,
1589; Hunter, p. 280).

[24] Richard Stanyhurst in his trans. of Virgil, 1582; Webbe, quoted
Smith, I, 240.

[25] *Observations in the Art of English Poesy*, 1602; Smith, II, 331.

To the charge of abjuring the matter, most poets are able to rejoin only with difficulty. Their business is the disposing of formal propositions. "Why is my verse so barren of new pride": that is an approximation, in Renaissance terms, of the *topoi* or *meletae* of the medieval poet. To the question, the sonneteer addresses himself. But in the hammering out of an answer, opportunism supervenes: certain responses and kinds of responses are dictated or precluded by the exigencies of rhyme and meter: Shakespeare's sonnets move often to unexpected conclusions. I suppose Shakespeare, contemplating this fact, to have been relatively free of perturbation.

The rationalist is not so complacent. He makes it a capital offense that the rhyming poet should handle his subject "as tyranically as Procrustes the thiefe his prisoners, who, when he had taken, he used to cast upon a bed, which if they were too short to fill, he would stretch them longer, if too long, he would cut them shorter" (Campion).[26] What gives offense in this behavior is not its summariness but its indifference to endemic form. Stretched on the tyrant's bed, Truth is disfigured. The result of this lopping and chopping is an arbitrary pattern created by the artist in his role as the willful Procrustes. There is, however, another pattern which antedates the artist and is implicit in the stone. This other he will educe and enfranchise, as he is enamored of Truth. Once more, he holds his warrant from Plato.

To enfranchise what has hitherto been fettered or defaced he experiments with quantitative measure. His preoccupation with quantity matches his insistence on what is literal and one. Each is an aspect of the grand endeavor to elaborate a more nearly expressive form. To prosecute this endeavor, the Protestant reformer seeks to adjust the Psalms to classical metres.[27] Earlier in the century, Trissino the Hellenizer, whose zeal for Truth

---

[26] Smith, II, 331.

[27] Scipio Gentili, whose so-called epic paraphrases are dedicated—congruently—to Sidney, as also his trans. into Latin hexameters of the 4th book of the *Gerusalemme Liberata: In XXV Davidis Psalmos Epicae Paraphrases*, 1584; *Plutonis Concilium*, 1584.

had led him to devote twenty years to the writing of a classicistic epic, essays the creation of an unrhymed Italian verse.[28] As the Platonic impulse waxes in England, so does the emulating of classical metre. The new critic commends as "the true kind of versifying . . . [the] imitation of Greeks and Latins" and looks "towards the framing of some apt English Prosodia," that order may be born out of chaos.[29] That is the aspiration of the humanists assembled at Cambridge, the forcing house of rationalist ideas. Cambridge is Ramist and Puritan in its sympathies, Oxford Aristotelian and leaning towards the Crown.[30] Already at Cambridge in the 1540s, the humanists Cheke and Ascham and Bishop Thomas Watson had canvased the possibility of assimilating quantity to English. The Rev. Thomas Drant, at Cambridge a little later, codifies their proposals and passes them on to the next generation: Sidney's rules for the writing of quantitative verses are "the very same which M. Drant devised . . . [though] enlarged with M. Sidneys own judgement."[31]

The new prosody is not only commended but attempted by the poets. Sometimes the issue of their attempt is surprising. One example will be enough. Abraham Fraunce, who is seeking

[28] Trissino's *Sophonisbe* (1515), a tragedy modeled on the Greeks, and his *Italia Liberata* (1548) are each "freed from rhyme": the meaning and the goal of his *versi sciolti*. Other writers carry forward the work of reclamation: in Italy, Claudio Tolomei, who stipulates the rules on which the new poetry will be patterned (*Versi e Regole della Poesia Nuova*, 1539); in France, Jean Mousset, who renders Homer in hexameters (1530), and Jean-Antoine de Baïf, who seeks to restore Hebrew "quantities"; in Spain, Consalvo Periz, the friend of Ascham, who translates the *Odyssey* into unrhymed Spanish verse (1553), and is honored by Meres as one who had "by good judgement avoided the faulte of ryming" (Smith, II, 315).

[29] Webbe in Smith, I, 278, 302. Puttenham undertakes to "shew how one may easily and commodiously lead all those feete of the auncients into our vulgar language" (II, xiii).

[30] Joseph Glanvill, entered in Exeter College, Oxford, laments "that his friends did not first send him to Cambridge, because . . . new philosophy and the art of philosophizing were there more than here in Oxon" (Anthony à Wood in Cope, *Glanvill*, p. 2).

[31] Spenser to Harvey, October 1579.

to attach the purse of Sidney's earnest and ingenuous sister, that archetypal bluestocking the Countess of Pembroke, purports to show her how easily the ancient feet may be led into English.

> There shal Phillis againe in curtesie strive with Amyntas,
> There with Phillis againe in curtesie strive shal Amyntas,
> There shal Phillis againe make garlands gay for Amyntas,
> There for Phillis againe gay garlands make shal Amyntas,
> There shal Phillis againe be repeating songs with Amyntas,
> Which songs Phillis afore had made and song with Amyntas.[32]

When Thomas Nashe inquires "whether riming be poetry" and refers an answer "to the judgment of the learned,"[33] he is answered by the learned in their own practice. The school in which that practice is hopefully perfected is the so-called Areopagus, whose master is Sidney and whose pupils include Spenser and the poet Edward Dyer and Gabriel Harvey as a tolerated sizar. The self-conscious intention of this little group of dedicated reformers is to achieve an unalloyed purity by effecting "a general surceasing and silence of bald rimers." Spenser is momentarily exalted by the prospect of driving out the counterfeit coin of rhyme: "in stead whereof they"—his fellows of the Areopagus—"have, by authority of their whole Senate, prescribed certain laws and rules of quantity of English syllables for English verse, having had thereof already great practice, and drawn me to their faction."[34] Significantly, Spenser is only temporarily of the faction. He writes, conscientiously and without much success, two poems in the new manner and then returns,

[32] Quotation (at random) from the *Countesse of Pembrokes Yvychurch*, 1591. Fraunce is imitating the experiments with quantity of Marlowe's friend Thomas Watson (appended to his Latin version of *Antigone*, 1581), whose Latin *Aminta* (1585) he translates into hexameter verse (1587). Other examples: Stanyhurst's preposterous "observation of quantities" in his trans. of Virgil, 1582; Richard Barnfield's *Hellen's Rape* (in *Poems*, 1598); Fraunce's *Countesse of Pembrokes Emmanuel*, 1591. Campion's experiments are in a class apart: Campion is a poet.

[33] *Anatomie of Absurditie*; Smith, I, 329.

[34] Spenser to Harvey (1579), who develops the figure of rhyme as counterfeit; Smith, I, 89, 101.

mole-like, to the darkness of rhyme. Sidney is more perse-
vering.[35] His experiments are not simply an attesting to virtu-
osity but are deliberately decorous. Mostly, it is the noble
strangers in his romance who speak in measured verse. Accentual
iambics are reserved, as more native, to the native Arcadians.

This concern with decorum, with what Puttenham calls
"everything in his kinde,"[36] comes partly from an indecorous
attending on Horace, the great prescriber of characterization
according to type. Old men are to be always, like Shakespeare's
Nestor (but not like Shakespeare's Timon), "praisers of the
times when they were young," and this not for economy's but
propriety's sake. Here, from the beginning of the sixteenth century, is a codifying of the more narrow understanding of
propriety:

> It were not fitting a heard or man rurall
> To speake in termes gay and rhetoricall.
> So teacheth Horace in arte of poetry,
> That writers namely their reason should apply
> Mete speeche appropring to every personage,
> After his estate, behavour, wit and age.[37]

The prescription is widely accepted in the Renaissance. "To
work a comedy kindly"—which is naturally—"grave old men
should instruct, young men should show the imperfections of
youth, strumpets should be lascivious, boys unhappy, and clowns
should speak disorderly."[38] Two centuries later, Dr. Johnson is
still concerned with these tidy correspondences. On his view,
Shakespeare's desire (as expressed in the Chorus to *Henry V*)
that "princes [might] . . . act And monarchs . . . behold the

---

[35] He attempts classical hexameters and, in his sonnets, aristophanic,
elegiac, and sapphic verse. In the *Arcadia*, he writes anacreontics and, in
imitation of Catullus and Horace, the phaleuciac and asclepiadic.

[36] III, xxiii; and also Ch. xxiv.

[37] Alexander Barclay, the first poet to compose formal eclogues in the
vernacular, in his *First Eclogue, c.*1514.

[38] Whetstone, dedication to *Promos and Cassandra,* 1578. The same
correspondences are insisted on by the playwright and musician Richard
Edwards, in the prologue to *Damon and Pythias,* S. R., 1567.

swelling scene," sins against what is proper or kind. In requiring such activity of princes and monarchs, Shakespeare "does not seem to set distance enough between the performers and spectators."[39] Truth is simple. "One thing becometh pleasant persons, an other sadde." Royalty and the vulgar crowd are disjunctive. "Every one must observe . . . fitnesse" or "be fitted accordingly" in terms of his "dignity, age, sex, fortune, condition, place [and] Country."[40] In the right or congruent kind of play, as opposed to the Shakespearean reticule, "each thing . . . [is] duly assigned to its proper place."[41] Not the poet but the rationalist is the type of Procrustean man.

Procrustes is old, and he is new: a classical apparition and of the Renaissance. Medieval man does not pay much heed to his morbid insistence on propriety, which is security. I think that is because there is no conviction of ultimate security (there is no hysterical compulsion to it) in the Christian Middle Ages. "The foxes have holes, and the birds of the air have nests, but the Son of Man hath not where to lay his head." This root sense of insecurity in first and last things is central to the old-fashioned psychology, before the new learning came up. "We have no way of saving ourselves."[42] That is the medieval understanding, in the teeth of Pelagius, and it explains the indifference of man in the dark age to rubricizing: decorum, on which salvation in the modern age is understood to depend.

Modern man believes that the truth is not only simple, it is efficacious: "ye shall know the truth, and the truth shall make you free." And therefore confusion is not to be tolerated in discriminating among kinds. The objection is fierce and understandable to writers "who use one order of speech for all persons,"[43] as does Shakespeare, who is sometimes the prisoner of his blank

---

[39] Quoted Walter Whiter, *Specimen of a commentary on Shakespeare*, 1794, p. 204.

[40] Webbe, translating Horace; Smith, I, 292.

[41] Nicholas Grimald, dedicating his Latin drama on the Resurrection of Christ (1543).

[42] Following Alan W. Watts, *The Wisdom of Insecurity*, pp. 9, 26.

[43] Whetstone in Smith, I, 59-60.

verse or else so magnanimous as to allow the same grandiloquence to the villain and the hero, to Achilles and Ulysses, to Hotspur and Hal, and even to a hired bravo as in *Macbeth*. A coward is to certify in each syllable to his cowardice, like Clinias in Sidney's *Arcadia*; and a boor to his boorishness, like Sidney's Dametas. (But the illustration is wanting in rigor. Sidney, says Ben Jonson to Drummond, "did not keep a decorum in making every one speak as well as himself." Even "Dametas sometymes speaks Grave sentences." That is a fault in Guarini as well—in the *Pastor Fido*, the shepherds in their eloquence are so many versions of the poet. It is, parenthetically, the characteristic fault or perhaps only the condition of the novels of William Faulkner.) In the more lucid art to which the Age of Reason aspires, a fool is not to speak like a sapient sir nor a courtier like a clown nor a shepherd like a courtier.[44]

To defer to Horace and his enjoining of consistency is agreeable: the Renaissance cites precedent wherever it can. But what is more to the point: this perfect consistency has got to obtain if art is to fulfill its function of teaching and enforcing. In the medieval drama, as a corner of this function is scanted, there is no great objection to robing the Pharisees as Catholic ecclesiastics or to providing Caiphas and Annas with a pair of mitres. "Essentially," a high priest is a bishop. The medieval maker is not always so cursory. St. Stephen, who is stoned to death, is sometimes made to honor decorum: a statue in the abbey church of St. Ouen in Rouen represents him with stones in his hand. Mostly, however, the medieval idea of decorum is more random and less compendious. A very general feeling for essentiality determines the allotting (as in the Newcastle cycle) of the Noah play to the shipwrights or watermen and the play of the Magi to the goldsmiths and that of the Flight into Egypt to the stable keepers. The Disputation in the Temple has to do in part with lawyers, and hence it is to the lawyers that the presentation of this

---

[44] Propriety in speech is illustrated by George Turberville (translating the pastorals of Mantuan, 1567, into rustical 14ers), who uses "the common country phrase according to the person of the speakers in every egloge as though indeed the man himself should tell his tale."

313

play is assigned. The play of the Last Supper, by a species of synecdoche in which only one part does duty for the whole, goes "appropriately" to the bakers. The election by the guild of its patron saint bears traces of this haphazard analogizing, in lieu of transparent denotation. Mary Magdalene, who is a woman of many sides, is the choice of the perfume-makers because she had anointed the feet of Christ. Christopher, who carries the infant Christ on his shoulders, is the patron of the porters. There is in that coupling an approach to the Renaissance conception of decorum. Precise or denotative fitness is, however, not so readily apparent in the connection of the tanners to St. Bartholomew who was flayed alive, or of the chandlers to St. John because he was immersed in boiling oil.

To the Renaissance critic, incongruous associations of this kind give scandal as they are taken to be obfuscatory. That is why he demands a more punctilious adherence to type. For the same reason, he reprehends the intermingling of light and shadow. If a play—like Grimald's *Resurrection*—is serious, it is to incorporate "no frivolous epigrams, no jokes about love, no silly talk, no mimes, no dialogue of the lowest types of men." That is Sidney's position and Ben Jonson's. Sidney is the dominant poet in his time; Jonson is the dominant playwright, if not in his own time, certainly to the age succeeding. Each is actuated by imperatives which are characteristically of the Renaissance. This is to say: the exciting cause of the insistence on decorum is that same impulse to clarity as informs the campaign against rhyme. Horace is useful in that he affords the needful or venerable text, as when he interdicts the mixing of kinds. If Truth is to be realized, these also will have to be exclusive or single. But that is self-evident: "If a painter chose to combine a human head and a horse's neck, and to clothe limbs brought together from all sorts of bodies with varied plumage—to make what is a lovely woman above end hideously in a black fish-tail below—you would laugh when he exhibited his work." (It may be objected, as by Spenser in the *Faerie Queene*, imagining his Duessa, or Shakespeare in the *Tempest*, his Caliban, that there are more things in Heaven and earth than are dreamt of in the Horatian

314

philosophy. The objection, however, will fail of endorsement. These creatures of the poet and playwright, as they are prodigious are objects of laughter, like the strange calf with five legs or the six-year old boy with the great thing in Ben Jonson.)

But what occasions the laughter, even more than the eccentric character who is not properly a character at all, is the equivocal nature of the total performance, whether painting or poem or play. The Calvinist is true to type in desiring to burn the Van Eycks' "Adoration of the Mystical Lamb," which affronts him with its mingling of Sibyls and Prophets. The new or post-Tridentine Catholic resembles the Calvinist. In the eighteenth century at Vézelay, the monks plaster over the great figures of the facade, which are like no thing in nature. Macaulay is wrong, in his famous panegyric on the enduring vitality of Rome. The Church of the Middle Ages expires at Trent. Reformation and Counter-Reformation are, in their proclivities, the same. Each puts period to the medieval delight in the blending of immiscible things. Each opposes itself to obscurity, as to the representing of a multiple truth. To equivocate is to lie: the artist who covets truth will engage that his work be of a piece.

Equivocation means the acknowledging of myriad possibilities. Where many things are potential, no one thing is certain. Contingency rules. The modern maker, in art, in science, owes allegiance to predictability. His God does not throw dice. *Hoc non licet modernis*. The medieval maker, who reads history not in terms of the adamantine net but "providentially," must lay all that happens to caprice. His God is unconstrained, like the world he inhabits. No doubt divine Providence is informed by design: but no one can parse it, or not before the fact. That is a more sympathetic way of glossing the medieval instinct for inclusiveness and indifference to coercive form. The beginning of wisdom is the fear of the Lord. Compare with the Scriptural saying the text from Francis Bacon: Knowledge is power.

The less sanguine understanding of the past is manifest in its contempt for decorum. The base-blooded art it sponsors is epitomized for the Renaissance in those hybrid entertainments, familiar to the Middle Ages and congenial to the promiscuous temper of dramatists like Shakespeare, entertainments which, as Sidney describes them, "be neither right tragedies nor right comedies."[45] (Sidney's right hand runs on without reference to his left. His greater poetry, associating owls and nightingales, doleful and pleasant business, enacts triumphantly just that blending of immiscibles which the criticism proscribes.) It is hard to exculpate Shakespeare, whose practice is to "make a clown companion with a king" and permit him to outjest the heart-struck injuries of his master; or who in "grave councils . . . allows the advice of fools," as Feste and Touchstone are allowed, and Thersites.[46] But Shakespeare is old-fashioned and soon to be superseded. His kinship is not with progressives like Jonson but with the makers of the medieval mysteries. It is a disabling kinship. Plays like the Wakefield *Killing of Abel* (in which Cain the assassin is allowed to be amusing), and the *Secunda Pastorum* (in which the coming of the Lamb of God is parodied in the theft of a sheep), and the York *Birth of Jesus* (in which a January-like Joseph, grumbling about the weather, is almost a figure of fun); or *Pericles* and *Much Ado About Nothing* and the *Winter's Tale* are taken by the legitimatists as verifying Horace's prediction that "such a picture" as he had drawn in his *Epistle* "will find its match in a book where, as in a sick man's dreams, the forms are idly fictioned, so that neither head nor foot belongs to a single kind."

This play of mingled kinds is called by Sidney "mongrel tragicomedy." Under that title he reprehends not only the confounding of forms but also the want of decorum in the bringing together of disparate emotions and attitudes within a single form, whether comic or tragic.[47] Decorum is violated by the figure known as oxymoron or seeming contradiction and the ecumenicism associated with it. The rationalist, unless he is concocting an entertainment to please the squeaking boys: revising *Hieronimo* like Ben Jonson, or fabricating like Thomas Preston "A lamentable tragedy mixed full of pleasant mirth," abhors oxy-

---

[45] Smith, I, 199.   [46] Whetstone in Smith, I, 59.

[47] Gascoigne (*Certain Notes*, 1575) anticipates Sidney: "to intermingle merry jests in a serious matter is an indecorum."

moron as the ultimate befuddling. This abhorrence impels Sidney to forbid the playwright to "match Horn-pypes and Funeralls."[48] By and large, the prohibition is honored in the Renaissance. Either music is excluded from tragedy altogether or else it is admitted, on analogy to the Italian *intermedii*, as a frankly inorganic diversion "to the intent the people might be refreshed and kept occupied" and to offer "relief . . . if the discourses have been long" (Puttenham).

The aversion to mirth in funeral—for example, to the singing of the grave digger in *Hamlet*—dictates the conventional hostility to the organic participation in tragic business of the clown, who is also the chief musician of the adult acting companies. The comic interludes and musical cues in such a play as *Dr. Faustus* are admissible in that they are partly irrelevant. Marlowe mixes Plautus and Seneca only as he desires to please. That is generally true of the Elizabethan or Jacobean playwright. Tourneur in the *Revenger's Tragedy* and Marston in *Antonio and Mellida* and Chapman in the *Revenge of Bussy D'Ambois* are only enlivening their plots but not really enforcing them, as they intersperse music and dance. Shakespeare as often is peculiar, in evincing a less rigorous conception of decorum. Music in his tragedies, and even comic music, is admitted as an integral part of the total artistic design. He does not relieve the pathos depending on Juliet's supposed death by the incongruous presence of the jesting musicians: he intensifies it. After all it seems to him deeply congruous that Peter the clown should call in his grief for "some merry dump" to ease him: Shakespeare's reading of things is less in debt to the decorous consistency of theory than to the unexpected coupling which is fact. Shakespeare indulges oxymoron, not as Marlowe does, to titillate, but to signalize the paradoxical nature of life itself.

His allotting of song to female protagonists, like Desdemona, sets him apart even further. Mostly, as they conform to the prescriptions of decorum, tragic heroines before Shakespeare do not venture to sing. Desdemona's Willow Song is, of course, rendered by a boy. But Shakespeare's use of adult song is also

---

[48] Smith, I, 199.

marked by an unwillingness to accept just what theory prescribes. Decorum interdicts public singing as improper to aristocratic persons.[49] Shakespeare, very typically, flouts this prohibition. Pandarus sings in company; so does the gentleman Balthasar in *Much Ado About Nothing*, and the noble Amiens in *As You Like It*. In each case, the social prejudice is acknowledged: the singer is made to protest his insufficiency, in accordance with Castiglione's precept that a courtier should "come to show his music as a thing to pass the time withal, and as he were enforced to do it."[50] But the protest is unavailing. Even Hamlet, though he does not sing, delivers snatches from ballads and songs, like Ophelia.

This characteristic refracting of the norm is dramatized most notably in the two songs assigned to Iago. It is said of Othello that he "to hear music . . . does not greatly care."[51] Othello is known thereby as a man "fit for treasons, stratagems, and spoils." Lorenzo in the *Merchant of Venice* inveighs against him: "Let no such man be trusted." Iago, on the other hand, has music in himself: he is known as honest Iago. (Cassius also "hears no music." In this he differs from the gentle Brutus. But Brutus, whom melody pleases, is not less an assassin.) In Shakespeare, as the decorous stereotype is distorted, the expectation of the auditor is beguiled. He is compelled to repudiate convention and the surface of things, to which decorum is necessarily confined. And so he learns to perceive the visage in the mind. Procrustes, in his insistence on decorum, never gets so far as this.

That the villain should sing lends support to the hypothesis that Robert Armin, as the chief singer of Shakespeare's company, played the part. But Armin is a famous clown, and Iago is a demi-devil, and decorum disallows any mingling of the two. Casting is type-casting, except apparently on Shakespeare's eccentric and more audacious understanding. To the common-garden

[49] So Ascham in *Toxophilus*, 1545: "much music marreth men's manners."

[50] *Courtier*, Bk. II.

[51] The "general" whom the Clown is describing in this quibbling speech is the vulgar, the common people; but also, I think, the Moor.

critic, this audacity is like a red flag. What does it mean to speak of Romeo as a dove-feathered raven or ravening lamb? and how is one to take Mercutio, who lightens in dying; or Desdemona, who sings a smutty song; or John of Gaunt, who puns on his deathbed? "Can sick men play so nicely with their names?" Decorum denies the possibility. The medieval theoretician resembles his successor in associating a lofty style to the discussion of "universal things or persons" and a middle style to middling things. Vulgar matter requires a corresponding declension.[52] The categories tend, however, to merge, as in the medieval approach to epic poetry, which condones the "mixing [of] filthy matters with jests, wanton toys with unhonest, or noisome with merry things."[53] Dante on the stairs of Purgatory is able to poke delicate fun at himself, earning a smile from Virgil, when he touches his fingers to his forehead and compares himself to a man who can tell "from the becks of others" that he is marked, I suppose like the cuckold (xii). As unseemly comparisons like these are permitted, comedy and tragedy are no longer felt as being distinct. But on their formal separation depends their identification.

But decorum governs not only in the suiting of the speech to the speaker who, if he is tragical, will utter only "the big and boisterous words," and if comical only the little. Decorum governs also in the poet's choosing of prosodic form. Ideas and emotions, as they are simple and analyzable, are amenable to perfect denotation. Uncommon or tragic business argues rime royal; common business, "commoun verse."[54] Between the two a line of demarcation is drawn. You cannot serve cod and salmon. In the conventional critic—Puttenham, King James—there is no thought of blurring the line, to bemuse the reader and to quicken his perception. In nature all things are clear. Art imitates nature. When Chaucer seeks a metre for the *Canterbury Tales*, he hits on pentameter couplets. These, says the critic with a kind of affable condescension, "be but riding ryme." Because

[52] Geoffrey de Vinsauf in Faral, *Les Arts poétiques*, p. 312.

[53] Webbe in Smith, i, 294.

[54] See the equivalences posited by James VI under "Kyndis of Versis" (Ch. viii in his *Treatise*, 1584), and by Puttenham, i, xxxi.

he sees them as proper for jocular business, he excuses them in Chaucer (who is wholecloth a jocular poet) as "neverthelesse very well becomming the matter of that pleasaunt pilgrimage." What is more than pleasant in the *Canterbury Tales*—the Knight's Tale, the Reve's Prologue—is outside his ken and so escapes his censure as being cast in an unsuitable metre. That he is purblind is, however, partly by the way. As one accepts the twofold proposition that truth is patent unless obscured by bad art, and that art is an instrument in the building of the New Jerusalem, he will agree that censure ought to be visited on those who violate decorum and defer the new day that is coming.

Characteristically, the poet and playwright—waiving the inevitable laggards and misbelievers—are concerned to hasten the day. And now, in the later years of the sixteenth century, the common player is recruited to their side and made to assist in the endeavor. On the medieval stage his facility in doubling had enabled him to carry as many as four parts in a play. This facility persists into the reign of Elizabeth. In the tragedy of *Horestes*, only six players are required (on the evidence of the casting charts) to manage twenty-seven different roles. Significantly, the roles these players assume are likely to be antithetical in nature. In the fifteenth-century morality, *Mankind*, Mercy, who succors the hero, and Titivillus the comic vice, who seeks the hero's damnation, are the business of one man. An anonymous morality from the earlier years of Elizabeth's reign assigns to one player the title role of New Custom ("a Minister"), and Assurance ("a Virtue"), and also and impartially that of Avarice ("a Ruffler"). No sense of incongruity hovers about these transitions from evil to good. In the homiletic drama of the 1560s, Honest Recreation converts easily to Irksomeness (as in the *Marriage of Wit and Wisdom*, in which the actors must carry, on the average, better than three parts to a man).[55]

[55] In Preston's *Cambises* (in which 8 players suffice for 38 parts), the whore Meretrix, a comic figure, becomes the tragic Otian, who sees his father skinned alive. In Bale's *Three Laws*, each of the supporting actors represents one of the saving laws and two of the vices. The actor who portrays the Law of Christ is also Sodomy and Ambition. In this way 5 play-

Partly, the tradition of the doubling of opposites is dictated by dramatic convenience. The typical morality displays an alternating pattern; the troupe that presents it is restricted in size. In one scene Humanum Genus is solicited by the Vices, in another by the Virtues. It is simply expedient that he who plays Carnality should also play Continence: the two are unlikely to be on stage together. But if the doubling of opposites is convenient, it is also a comment on the inclusiveness of the medieval temper. Life is a *discordia concors*. The ill-assorted pairing yokes together like and like. This sense of the rightness of complementarity persists until relatively late. In a play by George Peele, twenty-six actors encompass more than twice as many roles. That is an illustration of the old versatility, still notable in the closing years of the sixteenth century though not so spectacular as before. The troupe has grown larger; nonetheless, it has not yet acquired a fatal feeling for the proprieties.[56] Shakespeare also remains a laggard in his willingness to allow incongruous pairings. "The tragedy of the first emperor, Julius Caesar," as a German traveller remembers, was "excellently performed by some fifteen persons," although there are forty speaking parts in that play.[57]

But as the medieval taste for oxymoron commences to pall, these transitions from like to unlike begin to occasion uneasiness. It is by the 1590s no longer a praise that the player, like Proteus, should enact diverse roles in one person. The Christian functionary and the Moslem—one man, in Peele's drama—are properly antinomies. The sleight-of-hand that enables the same

---

ers manage 14 parts. Piety turns to Ignorance in William Wager's *The Longer Thou Livest the More Fool Thou Art*, and Lust to Sapience in the *Trial of Treasure*. Discussion follows Bevington, *From "Mankind" to Marlowe*, Ch. VII, "Doubling Patterns"; and Bentley, *Shakespeare and His Theatre*, pp. 32-33.

[56] *The Battle of Alcazar, c.*1594.

[57] The traveller is Thomas Platter. Bentley, pp. 124-25. Even at the end of his career, as in *HVIII* in which 41 speaking parts are required, Shakespeare needs no larger a cast than that which had presented the 13 speaking parts of *Othello*.

player to represent them involves a kind of lying. Proteus is the equivocal god. To heed decorum is to take care "that he which represented some noble personage in the Tragedie bee not some busy foole in the Satyr."[58] The medieval practice of doubling opposite roles is abandoned for the more decorous (the more truthful) practice of doubling roles that are like. The result is a monstrous burden on the actor who—to give but one example, this, from a play of the 1580s—is made to present a Catholic Cardinal and also a Scotch Papist, even though the two characters appear just once and almost together, with a mere seven lines separating their presence on stage. Certainly it would be simpler and technically more efficient for the player to enact, not a pair of villains whose entrance is nearly simultaneous, but in one scene a villain and in the next a virtuous man. But truth is more than convenience, and the modern playwright a truth teller who is "alwaies ware, DECORUM, to exceede."[59]

Coeval with the decline of the doubling of opposites is the ascendancy of type-casting, indebted also to simplistic notions of truth and a sterner allegiance to it. The actor, as he is decorous, is no longer a jack-of-all-kinds. He begins to approximate to the character actor. In a company like the Admiral's Men, big and boisterous roles, if they are generically related—as the swaggerers Barabas and Tamburlaine and the Guise are related—are not given indifferently to Gabriel Spencer or Robert Shaw or Martin Slater but, as by right of specialization, to Edward Alleyn. First the doubling of opposites is interdicted, and then, as literalism grows more insistent, even the doubling of characters who are like.[60]

The next step is to make inviolate integrity of sex. No longer

[58] Webbe in Smith, I, 294.

[59] The playwright is Nathaniel Woodes, who is describing himself in the Prologue to his morality, *Conflict of Conscience* (printed 1581).

[60] John Marston in his induction to *Antonio and Mellida* (1602) laments the necessity of even a single pairing of roles. Thomas Heywood's *Silver Age* requires for 32 parts the merging of two companies, that integrity may be preserved. Bentley (p. 125) records exceptions to the trend (11 actors handle 21 parts in Heywood's *Fair Maid of the Exchange*); which, however, remain exceptions.

is it suitable for men or boys to play women, as in the theatre of the Renaissance and (by and large) on the medieval stage. "Nay, faith," says Flute, the literal-minded man, "let me not play a woman; I have a beard coming." With the Restoration, literalism triumphs absolutely. No squeaking Cleopatra boys the greatness of the real Cleopatra: "she here," in the posture of a whore. From the late seventeenth century, a whore is a whore in the grain. That is what realism means.

It is the same in the physical makeup of the theatre, and that is possibly surprising. For the drama of automatism is by its nature not much concerned with the presenting of indigenous men and women. The corollary ought to be a withering of mimesis, and in fact this is just what occurs. But realistic representation does not wither. The same principle governs as in the Flamboyant cathedral: as it is understood that truth is generic and does not inhere in the surface, every inch of the surface is adorned. In the theatre of expressionism, which is ascendant from the fifteenth century forward, the wart on the Miller's nose is attended to more narrowly just as his idiosyncrasy as a total human being is denied. The comic villain Parolles in *All's Well That Ends Well* is sufficiently peculiar to be permitted on stage under his own recognizance: "Simply the thing I am shall make me live." If real peculiarity is, however, not conceivable (unless to Shakespeare who, as often, is *sui generis*), a special code will have to be formulated in order that the protagonist may be known.

This elaborating of a code: a series of denotative hallmarks, is exactly what has been happening in the allegorical poem as the peculiar persons in that poem are absorbed more and more in the type. Here decorum confesses its real meaning. Decorum means codification or the concerting of signs. It is involved, by definition, with superficial dissimilarities or tokens, for with the coming into being of the new or heteronomous man, essential dissimilarities are abraded. The genus is overmastering.

The drama of automatism, like the allegorical narrative in its latest development, or like the morality play, endeavors to sink the particular in the general. The kind of character which re-

323

sults is, in Jonson's sense, the humorous character. He is a cartoon: a type, and not least when he is most aberrant; and he holds the stage, first in tragedy and then later in comedy, for the next three hundred years. I think it is tenable to assert that the tragic protagonist disappears from the drama almost on the retirement of Shakespeare. After the death of Farquhar (1707), there are no palpable characters in comedy either. This long interregnum endures until the advent of John Synge, at the beginning of the twentieth century. One remembers Kate Hardcastle: but not so tangibly as Beatrice in *Much Ado* or Cherry in the *Beaux Stratagem* or Millamant in the *Way of the World*. In the declining years of the drama, Charles Surface is the representative hero, and whether he is making love or conniving at murder or addressing himself to the gallows. (In this latter role he is apt to speak of the far, far better thing he is doing.) The representative heroine is Paula Tanqueray, who only pretends to flesh and blood.

One touch of nature makes the whole world kin. Nice or lower-case discrimination is disused with the acknowledgment that truth is simple and law is pervasive. There are no important differences between x and y. The result in the theatre is necessarily the triumph of realism, which gives a factitious solidity to the shadows which flit across the stage. But realism is not to be confounded with mimesis. I suppose the two to be in constant opposition, and the true or mimetic thing to diminish in proportion as the vulgar simulacrum is enlarged.

In the drama of automatism, realistic representation comes into its own. Otway, who manipulates stick figures, is more realistic than Shakespeare or Webster; Pinero, who cannot manage a protagonist even so elusive as the hero of *Venice Preserv'd*, is more realistic than Otway. The acme of realistic representation is the art of the Grand Guignol, in which substantial character has evaporated altogether.

The morality is of course to be distinguished from these later essays in puppeteering. In each case, character is reduced to a notation: to Good Deeds and Confession in the *Summoning of Everyman*, to Thorowgood and Trueman in the *London Mer-*

chant, to Belcour the noble savage in Cumberland's *West Indian*, to Courtly and Meddle and Dazzle and Pert in Boucicault's *London Assurance*. But the morality agitates serious business: at its heart is the *psychomachia*. The secular morality or animated cartoon is given over increasingly to *son et lumière*. That is a necessary consequence of the initial commitment to expressionism. As the fifteenth-century playwright declines to sift or scrutinize concrete exemplifications, his way with ideas grows more coarse and less convincing. After all, the morality, despite its lofty purpose, represents a dead end. The purpose that informs it is passed on to Shakespeare, whose entire *oeuvre* is a dramatizing of the *psychomachia* but always in particular terms. (The addiction to particulars is a legacy to him of the other great medieval tradition, which is the mystery play.)

The expressionist technique is inherited by Marlowe and Jonson, great dramatists in practice, unfortunate as preceptors to the following age. In this latter age, as the intelligence of the playwright is forbidden its proper nutriment, the analytic habit atrophies and real content disappears from the play. The designer is called into the playhouse, first of all to define the new cipher hero: to set him in an apprehensible context. As the protagonist shrinks to an abstract factotum, visibility depends on real habiliments, like the jewel-encrusted costumes in the paintings of Carlo Crivelli. The function of the designer is to answer in pictorial ways the impatient question, whose point grows sharper with the passing of each decade: who is man, that we should be mindful of him? Character is evicted, and then consequential business. As the eighteenth century goes down to the nineteenth, what remains to the theatre is expertise: Tom Robertson rattling door knobs and shifting cups and saucers. By the time of de Loutherbourg (1740-1812), the designer is indispensable to the play. It rests with him to proclaim the Emperor's new clothes.

"Hamlet without words": that is the goal as it is the necessary resort of the theatre of rationalism. In the achieving of this goal, decorum—cosmetology—is of critical importance. But decorum is hardly served by the unworthy scaffold of the Globe or the street pageant of the medieval innyard. The art of a Serlio or an Inigo Jones, which is the meticulous elaborating of simulacra, is baffled by the old convention of unlocalized place. In the medieval drama, place is where one says it is. But this implausible convention is not coercive of belief. The verisimilar constructions which compose the set of the new Italian play—"so many streets, so many palaces, and so many bizarre temples, loggie, and various kinds of cornices"—are more imposing, says Vasari, as they are "all so well executed that it seemed that they were not counterfeited, but absolutely real."[61]

In the crude theatre of the mysteries and the panoramic play, the auditor is required to suspend his disbelief. The requirement is not especially onerous so long as he inhabits an historical context whose reality he is able to endorse. "Three rusty swords, And help of some few foot and half-foot words" are felt to suffice in the locating and representing of "York and Lancaster's long jars." The Age of Reason, as it inhabits a more shadowy world, demands a more decorous representation. This demand is enacted by the rude mechanicals in Shakespeare's comedy. If Pyramus and Thisbe are supposed to meet by moonlight, it is important to discover whether "the moon [doth] shine that night we play our play." Bottom, who is exercised by this question, is the type of the decorous man. "A calendar, a calendar! Look in the almanac!" Serlio anticipates him in the agitation he reserves to whatever is peripheral. "Oh immortal God!" he cries ecstatically, "what wonder it was to see [on stage] so many trees and fruits, so many herbs and diverse flowers."[62]

Comparison is odious to that *soi-disant* stage on which the mysteries are performed: a stage so indifferent to demarcation and to clarity of line as to allow the manger in which Christ is born to stand cheek by jowl to the throne where Herod gives judgment, and to indicate the nature of either only by the rapid sketching of a few metonymic deails. Between the fixed stations which are the *domus* and *sedes*, each of which is utilizable for an infinite variety of scenes, action flows without let and hence without discrimination across a playing area (*platea*) which may

[61] Quoted Campbell, *Scenes and Machines*, pp. 51-52.
[62] *Architettura*, Bk. II, 1545.

represent, as the dramatist supposes, the ascent to Golgotha or the road to Damascus or the passage through the Red Sea. His easy supposition is possible in that he is intent most of all on the consequential transactions of real human beings. That they move in the world is *ipso facto*. That is why, like the outraged father in *Othello*, the dramatist, in establishing his setting, has only to affirm. "This is Venice," says Brabantio.

But the rationalist is not so easily persuaded. He is the observer of phylogenetic resemblances. He cannot tell the players without a playbill. He does not know, any more than Iago, how one woman should differ from another. He is unwilling to assume that color is only skin deep, for on that assumption propriety, which means security, is menaced. To achieve the certain identification on which security depends, he insists that setting be denotative or prescriptive. Typically, it does not suffice to Sidney that the playwright should work on our imaginary forces, as does the medieval maker who, careless of decorum, presents "a common castle in which to crown, scourge, perform the Last Supper and other things."[63] What pretends to be everything is nothing. That is the first objection. The second is to the barefaced nature of the pretence. "What childe is there that, comming to a Play, and seeing Thebes written in great Letters upon an olde doore, doth beleeve that it is Thebes?" The medieval stage, as it is dynamic and polyscenic and relatively plain, affronts and exasperates the rational man, who thinks it simply nonsense to have or pretend to "have Asia of the one side, and Affrick of the other, and so many other under-kingdoms, that the Player, when he commeth in, must ever begin with telling where he is."[64]

That is what Shakespeare compels him to do, as when he brings in—to the scandal of Ben Jonson—"a number of men saying they had suffred Shipwrack in Bohemia, wher ther is no Sea neer by some 100 Miles." In his comparative unconcern with a superficial verity, Shakespeare is like the medieval playwright. He is also superior to the medieval playwright, most of whose

[63] Donaueschingen Passion Play, *c.*1485.
[64] Sidney in Smith, I, 185, 197.

productions remain a donnish pleasure, remote in quality not only from Shakespeare's achievement but from that of his principal contemporaries. But the mysteries and moralities are the soil whence Shakespeare springs. What associates Shakespeare to the past and accounts in part for his transcendence is the non-representational character of his art. In the First Folio, as in editions of the plays throughout the seventeenth century, place headings are conspicuous by their absence. Mostly, location, if it is specified at all, is merely theatrical.[65] Scene divisions are scanted and often ignored. Of the original quartos of Shakespeare's plays, only *Othello*, the very latest (1622), is divided into acts.[66] In *Antony and Cleopatra*, in *Romeo and Juliet*, the play is a continuous whole. Old Capulet's ball is concluded: Romeo, alone on stage, utters two lines: at once his scurrile companions appear and speak at length, presumably in "another part of the forest." Now Romeo, as they leave him, answers to their taunting: and now, without intermission, the balcony scene begins. It is all of a piece, unbroken in its combustible progress by front curtains and intervals and shifting of sets, and as such it is unbearably confusing to reasonable men like Nicholas Rowe (1709) and Lewis Theobald (1733) and Thomas Hanmer (1744), who would like to know where we are and who make it their business to tell us.[67]

But showing is still better than telling. Shakespeare's Verona is only a cursory notation. Castiglione, who plays a part in the staging of the new Italian theatre, indicates the right way of ekeing it out. His scene is more authentic and therefore more assuring than Shakespeare's merely verbal evocation in that it is "laid in a very fine city, with streets, palaces, churches, and

[65] What one gets is something like this, from *Julius Caesar*: "Enter Brutus in his Orchard" (ii, i, 1); or this, from *Titus Andronicus*: "They goe up into the Senate house" (i, i, 63). Change of place is denoted, as in *Romeo and Juliet*, by the direction: "They march about the Stage" (i, v, 1).

[66] W. W. Greg, *Shakespeare First Folio*, p. 168.

[67] Rowe first resolves and shatters the play to a fixed number of segments. In *A&C* he distinguishes 27 different settings, Hanmer 42.

towers, all in relief, and looking as if they were real, the effect being completed by admirable paintings in scientific perspective."[68] Shakespeare, although he is sometimes lavish of description, is not able to engineer so convincing a triumph as this. That is no part of his intention. His art, if judged from the point of view of the designer, is only a tissue of language: evanescent in nature, as he himself confesses; or else it depends on the kind of crude imposture which Ben Jonson anathematizes in the prologue to *Every Man in His Humour*. What is wanted in the theatre is not assertion or clumsy pretence, as in *Henry V* or *Cymbeline* or *King Lear*, but a realistic representation,

> Where neither chorus wafts you o'er the seas,
> Nor creaking throne comes down the boys to please:
> Nor nimble squib is seen to make afeard
> The gentlewoman; nor roll'd bullet heard
> To say, it thunders; nor tempestuous drum
> Rumbles, to tell you when the storm doth come.

It is a reproach that Shakespeare's Rosalind should be required to say, "This is the Forest of Arden," or that Edgar in *Lear* should have the countenance to ask us if we do not hear the sea. The new men undertake to make the question and the bald announcement gratuitous. They create a theatre that is illusionistic (no more paltering about the Cliffs of Dover), and also monoscenic and static (no more pretended hurrying from Alexandria to Athens to Sicily to Rome). If in this theatre the scene is supposed to change, it does really change in physical fact, that the tailor's dummy who is the hero may take color from a real-appearing place. The primacy of place, as opposed to integrity of persons, is suggested by the architect and scene painter Nicola Sabbattini (1574-1654). "First of all," he asserts, "when you are planning to give a performance, it is necessary to . . . [have] space sufficient both for the various machines employed to present heavenly, terrestrial, marine, and infernal apparitions and for . . . distant prospects and perspective views."

[68] Production of Cardinal Bibbiena's *La Calandria*, 1513. Campbell, *Scenes and Machines*, p. 50.

Enforcing of belief devolves on the carpenter. It is subverted as the player—like King Lear—is made to apostrophize and so to conjure up the storm: an approximation of real lightning is necessary: Sabbattini, so long as he is granted sufficient space for his machines, engages to provide it. There is about his proceedings a certain inconsequence. Take a board one foot in width, says Sabbattini to the playwright who, like Archibald MacLeish in the presence of Elia Kazan, had supposed that he had written a play. Cut this board in zig-zag patterns, cover with gold leaf and place a candle just behind. To simulate the lightning in the collied night (but the phrase is dispensable), open and close the rifts quickly.[69]

This simulating is not casual: the physical counterfeit has got to pass current. Serlio, who understands very well how "To make a planet or other heavenly body pass through the air," grounds his art on the proposition that "all must be so far back that neither the thread nor the wire can be seen."[70] In this way it happens that sleight-of-hand becomes more engrossing than the words (or "business") assigned to the player. The governing fact in the production of the play is the expertness of the designer in the fabricating of scenes and machines. His office is "the arousing of wonder among the spectators . . . [and] the imitating, so far as possible, of the natural and the real."[71] The order of precedence that obtains in the modern theatre is given by the architect and engineer Joseph Furtenbach (1591-1667): "first of all, the eye loves to look on something beautiful; second, the ear is charmed by the accompanying music; and third, the mind takes vivid delight when the soul-stirring players, coming forward, make graceful discourse."[72]

In the attenuating of this third element, the aggressive genius of Inigo Jones, the first of the English régisseurs, is decisive. That is perhaps unjust: the preeminence of the régisseur is a contingent phenomenon. In the beginning is the impoverishing of

[69] Campbell, p. 157.   [70] *Architettura*, Bk. II.

[71] Sabbattini, *Pratica* [Manual] *di Fabricar Scene e Machine ne' Teatri*, Bk. I, 1638.

[72] *Architectura Civilis*, 1628.

credible discourse, concurrently the decline of mimesis. Jonson, who lampoons his more successful collaborator as "tireman, mountebank and Justice Jones," is partly faithful to his own abundance of black bile. "Poets, though divine, are men." On the other hand, Jonson has cause. "Painting and carpentry are the soul of masque." I do not suppose that Viscount Haddington and his consort attended so closely to the words supplied by the poet for the marriage masque of the *Hue and Cry after Cupid* (1608) as to the ingenious labors of the tireman who contrives that "on the sudden, with a solemn music," a bright sky come from clouds to discover "first two doves, then two swans, with silver geers, drawing forth a triumphant chariot." Graceful discourse after this is surely gratuitous. In the masque, says Samuel Daniel, "The art and invention of the architect gives the greatest grace and is of the most importance; ours, the least part and of least note." That is because nature abhors a vacuum.

In the first half of the seventeenth century, the architect or designer, having found his way into the tent, rapidly preempts it. Marvell's verses are apposite:

> Nature that hateth emptiness,
> Allows of penetration less—

where penetration means the occupying of the same restricted space by two bodies. Jonson expostulates from more than personal pique. In the swamping of the drama by ancillary business, the writer is menaced where he lives:

> Shows! Shows! Mighty shows!
> The eloquence of masques! What need of prose,
> Or verse, or sense, t'express immortal you?

This writer, who cannot enlist the aid of the *scena ductilis*, is scarcely able to part a cliff in the midst and reveal within "an illustrious concave, filled with an ample and glistering light, in which an artificial sphere . . . made of silver, eighteen foot in the diameter," turns perpetually.[73] But what the age demands is just such a compelling representation, not the " 'sculpture' of

---

[73] Campbell, pp. 170-71.

331

rhyme." The poet or playwright, as he fails to comply, is expendable. By the reign of Charles I, the play is no longer the thing but the glistering sphere. The masque, says Aurelian Townshend, the new favorite at Court, is "nothing else but pictures with light and motion."

This cunning delineation of pictures is required to persuade a skeptical audience of the truth of what it sees, or perhaps to make it forgetful of the vacuum at the heart. It is open to Hamlet, the product of a more ingenuous age, to impose on the gullible Polonius:

> Do you see yonder cloud that's almost in shape of a camel?

> By the mass and 'tis like a camel indeed.

Sabbattini, whose audience makes a fetish of what is clearly discernible, cannot rely on such ready assent; and therefore he engages by means of pulleys and levers to fashion palpable clouds that move across stage, and do really change in shape and size, and even dissolve into parts as they descend.[74] It is not his business to inspirit the auditor (who is the spectator now) by verbal evocations, but to fabricate superficies. For that reason he does not inquire how to catch the conscience of the king (what conscience? what king?) but "How to Transform a Man into a Rock or a Similar Object." To hold up the mirror is, on his more literal understanding, to "Make the Sea Rise, Swell, Get Tempestuous and Change Color," or to contrive that, in that sea, "Dolphins and Other Marine Monsters [will] Appear to Spout Water While They Swim."[75]

As contact with the springs of reality grows more remote, the attempt to establish conviction grows more desperate. This attempt engenders the theatre of cruelty which dominates in the waning years of the Renaissance drama: "Enter Giovanni with a heart upon his dagger" (John Ford, imitating Artaud). This revolting apparition is not peculiar to the seventeenth century. Cruelty abounds in the theatre from the 1560s forward, as in the mock-Senecan plays of Preston and Kyd: Hieronimo biting off

---

[74] *Pratica*, Bk. II, secs. 37-49.   [75] Bk. II, secs. 25, 26, 30, 34.

his tongue, the bladder of blood that drenches the stage of *Cambises*. Shakespeare in his apprentice work is not sparing of sanguinary business which has no point but itself: "Enter Lavinia, ravished, her hands cut off, and her tongue cut out." But the early Elizabethans are as boys tormenting flies (or as ruffians baiting bears or bulls in Paris Garden) when compared to their hysterical successors in the Jacobean and Caroline period. It is only to titillate that George Peele brings on stage the heroic Moor, Muly Mahomet, with a quivering lump of lion's flesh on the point of his sword, or that Preston causes the bleeding heart of a little boy to be cut from his body. But it is to impinge, to corroborate the fact of a real presence, that Webster contrives the hideous murders of Brachiano and the Duchess of Malfi.

For existence itself is moot. To live and die is to

> Fall in a frost, and leave . . . [one's] print in snow;
> As soon as the sun shines, it ever melts,
> Both form and matter.[76]

Webster flays his characters that he may know them. "The appearing are fantastic things, mere shadows."[77] In this more tenuous world of the Jacobeans, apprehension necessitates physical violence. It is Addie Bundren in Faulkner's novel: "only through the blows of the switch could my blood and their blood flow as one stream." In Kyd, violence is gratuitous and it is savored. In the mature Shakespeare, it is the dreadful consequence of abdication. Webster (or Ford or Tourneur) resembles Kyd in his innocence of cause. But he does not trade in sensation for its own sake. It is simply that, in his plays (in the world as he conceives it), there are no results but only events.

> We are merely the stars' tennis-balls, struck and bandied
> Which way please them.[78]

That is like Gloucester in *Lear*, on the gods who kill us for their sport. But Gloucester does not speak for the playwright. In the

---

[76] *Duchess of Malfi*, v, v.
[77] Fletcher in the *Wild Goose Chase*, I, iii.
[78] *Duchess of Malfi*, v, iv.

drama of automatism, this mordant view of things is possibly as tenable as any other. Knowledge dissolves in painful surmise: "I am in a mist"—Bosola, dying—"I know not how." To establish identity, to elicit the words by which his protagonist flares momentarily into life: "I am Duchess of Malfi still"—Webster condemns his fated heroes to an ignominious death. The question torments him: "Or is it true thou art but a bare name, And no essential thing?" The question is as bizarre as any in the Renaissance drama. In the inflicting of pain, an answer is potential. "If it hurts me enough," says a character in D. H. Lawrence, "I shall know I was alive." And hence the material in which the playwright deals: "Gives her a dead man's hand. . . . Here a dance of Eight Madmen. . . . Enter Executioners, with a coffin, cords, and a bell. . . . the executioners . . . strangle the Children." Identity is realized by a bearing witness to horror. In Webster, horror is a means of grace.

As the playwright is able to pierce to the quick, he achieves the brief emergence of his protagonist from the fantastic shadows in which being is dissolved: "Cover her face; mine eyes dazzle: she died young." The objectification of life is the Dumb Show in the *Duchess of Malfi*. It is a pompous charade, somnambulistic in character, essentially enigmatic. From this charade the protagonists, moving by rote, as if under water, seek for a luminous instant to break free. The way to freedom is through suffering, whether one endures it or inflicts it. To ravish or be ravished is to escape from the flux.

In the mimetic drama, for example in *Romeo and Juliet*, the playwright is able to refer, without looking over his shoulder, to the social and political context within which his protagonists play out their more meaningful play. In the drama of automatism, this context tends more and more to be fabricated of brummagem stuff. In this connection, compare John Ford, and notably as he revises Shakespeare's early tragedy in the egocentric melodrama, *'Tis Pity She's a Whore*. With the reopening of the theatres after the Restoration, the context has vanished altogether. *Venice Preserv'd* takes place in a wax works. The protagonist is a puppet dancing spasmodically in air. Tragedy descends perforce to the squalid nether regions where mere realism is regnant. It is indistinguishable from the cockpit. This means that its appeal is necessarily visceral, and exclusively so. In an old-fashioned drama like *Henry V*, the appeal is largely, though not entirely, to the ear and thence to the intelligence. In the drama that supersedes it, the appeal is to the eye alone. (I except, as irrelevant, the crashing of cymbals and the making of mellifluous sounds.)[79]

The medieval dramatist is not impervious to the attractions of literalism and does what he can to make his imposture go down. An earthquake apparatus (in a barrel) is available to him, and a Hell Mouth with two large eyes and sometimes "a nether chap."[80] His concern with clear or decorous enacting is attested in a play performed by the Grocers of Norwich, in which God, creating Eve, lifts "a rybbe colleryd red" from Adam's side. If he wishes to represent the Fall of Man, he endeavors first of all to purchase a spade for Adam and a distaff for Eve, and "a pece of tymber for an apeltrie," and "a clamp and other yron work" to keep the tree from coming down. When he dramatizes the Day of Doom, he hires a carpenter to make three worlds for burning, at a cost of three shillings and eight pence.[81] But the guild accounts for the N. Towne cycle suggest how remote and ingenuous is his approach to the literal truth. Entries that call for half a yard of Red Sea, and two worms of conscience, and a link or torch to set the world on fire do not argue a vastly credible representation.

In the waning Middle Ages, this dramatist of meager technical resources begins to cope with much greater enthusiasm with the demands of a more decorous theatre. It is an index of the renascent age. But it is only an index or "obscure prologue."

[79] If Davenant could get hold of more ample resources,
    Then his contracted Scenes should wider be,
    And move by greater Engines, till you see
    (Whilst you Securely sit) fierce Armies meet,
    And raging Seas disperse a fighting Fleet.
                            (Prologue to *Siege of Rhodes*, Pt. ii)
[80] Drapers' Pageant, Ludus Coventriae cycle.
[81] Craig, *English Religious Drama*, pp. 279, 296.

More conclusive advances must wait on other times and more imperial persons—like Stanislavsky, who will insist that if cherry trees are heard falling off stage, real cherry wood must take the blows of real axes; or like Sir Henry Irving, who introduces the scene curtain (1881) to hide the marchings and counter-marchings of 135 stagehands, property men, and gas men, whose job is to handle the elaborate set pieces which are the only *raison d'être* of the *Corsican Brothers*. "But, sir," says Ellen Terry, "why don't we rehearse together?" And Irving answers, "O, we're all right! What I've got to fear are those limelight men. They're the people we've got to rehearse."[82]

But what the nineteenth century will perpetrate in the theatre is signalized and predicted already, in the triumph of Procrustes three hundred years before. The praise bestowed on the poet of the *Shepherd's Calendar* "for his due observing of decorum everywhere, in personages, in seasons, in matter, in speech,"[83] is owing not so much to Spenser as to the Age of Reason, actuated as it is by the impulse to nail the truth once and for all.

[82] M. Menpes, *Henry Irving*, p. 35.
[83] E. K., quoted by Webbe in Smith, 1, 263.

X The Watch That Ends the Night

THE IMPULSE to congruity is hopeful, and like so much else in the ambiguous history of Renaissance thought, like the fevered insistence on the value of time, it is a despairing impulse as it communicates revulsion from the world of phenomena in which antinomies jostle endlessly for place. The amorphous world is denied as the régisseur elaborates his decorous *ensemble*. Obsessive form, which is founded on purgation or willful exclusion, opposes the more catholic language of earth. The opposition governs along the entire spectrum. Not only poetry and the drama but music is put to its purgation. In each case the idea, which is primary, is categorized and assigned its proper domicile. Possibly the domicile is more restrictive than before. The gain envisaged is, however, a greater preciseness of communication. No confusion is to wait on the transmission of the idea.

The mathematician Mersenne, as he is concerned most of all to enforce the idea, attends as closely in his musical theorizings to the choice and pronunciation of the words as to the music that supports them. He wants to be sure that each word is appropriate and distinctly audible, and hence that no shade of the meaning escapes. On this latter consideration depends the whole strength of the piece.[1] If, as in the music of the later sixteenth century, the commentary, which makes for action, is exalted, it will follow that whatever tends to obscure the commentary is bad. All that is not the word enfetters the word—for example, the swirling vocalizes of an earlier songbook like the Fayrfax

---

[1] *Quaestiones*, 1623, cols. 1565-72. Mace, "A Reply," p. 300, quotes from a letter (1698) of the mathematician John Wallis (who appears to echo the strictures of Vossius, *De poematum cantu et viribus rhythmi*, 1673): monody is more suitable than "Compounded Musick" as it follows the "just measures" and "true Accents" of words.

MS, associated with the longueurs of the court of Henry VIII before the new learning came up. The saying of the Book of Common Prayer is also an admonition: "Christ's Gospel is not a ceremonial Law . . . but it is a Religion to serve God, not in the bondage of the Figure or Shadow, but in the freedom of the Spirit." Erasmus, reproving English musicians as indifferent to clarity, their allegiance being given to the Shadow, enunciates the new point of view:

> Modern church-music is so constructed that the congregation cannot hear one distinct word. The choristers themselves do not understand what they are singing, yet according to priests and monks it constitutes the whole of religion. . . . In college or monastery it is still the same: music, nothing but music. There was no music in St. Paul's time. Words were then pronounced plainly. Words nowadays mean nothing. . . . If they want music, let them sing psalms like rational beings, and not too many of these.[2]

Obfuscation of the message is death to the spirit. But life, in the form of innovation and experiment, peers through the hollow eyes of death. Quantitative settings are seen as making for clarity. The parallel to poetry is close. In either art, quantity is cried up by the new men "in imitation of the Greeks and Latins of that better age."[3] But if clarity as the instrument of a moral purpose is everything, counterpoint must go since it makes against the sense of the words. And so the new quantitative settings are monodic. Still better is the solo song with instrumental

---

[2] Stevens, *Music and Poetry*, pp. 78-79.

[3] Baïf to Charles IX on the *Académie de Musique et de Poésie* (1571), of which he is co-founder. See F. Yates, *Giordano Bruno*, pp. 323-24. The purpose of the *Académie*, to establish, advance, and join together quantitative music and poetry, is anticipated by the Austrian scholar Petrus Tritonius, who sets the odes of Horace *secundum naturas et tempora syllabarum et pedum* (1507). Baïf, the epitome of the new man (he is translator, psalmist, reviser of orthography, metrical reformer, compiler of sententiae, and the real initiator of quantitative verse in France), writes 3 books of chansons in *vers mesurés* (quantitative notation), which are set by contemporary composers. "Jodelle before him had written some that were better" (Théodore-Agrippa d'Aubigné).

accompaniment, which gains on and replaces the older music "bated with fugue" because it is more audible and therefore more efficient. It is another instance in which the Protestant and the new or counter-reforming Catholic are essentially one. Each tends to look with the same dubiety on polyphonic music and for the same reason. Each fears that the Word will be lost in the interweaving of the voices. A consequence of this fear is the disusing of the contrapuntal choral style, which dies everywhere in Europe at about the same time and is succeeded by a homophonic or more lucid conception of choral texture and, later, by the explicit phrases of recitative.

The decline of the madrigal is coeval with the exacerbating of the impulse to clarity.[4] One has only to listen to the lively essays of Thomas Morley (d.1603), in whose compositions liveliness and obscurity are inseparably wed, to understand why the form will not do. I think of the madrigal for four voices, beginning, "In every place, fierce Love," in which the voices, overlapping to the delectation of the ear, effectively prevent the auditor from taking the sense of the words. For the air or solo song, which already is displacing the madrigal in popular esteem, this complaint does not hold.[5] Unlike the madrigal, the air is a homophonic or more nearly translucent composition in which the voices or parts move in step with one another and do not muddy the message by pursuing independent directions. If it is printed to be performed as a part song and not as a solo with lute or viol da gamba, it assigns the melody as by right to the highest voice or cantus and relegates the other voices to accompanying roles.

Not to be too solemn: the singing of madrigals requires (and gives pleasure to) a group of singers; the lute song, the air

---

[4] The Flemish school of madrigal composers is extinct with the death of Orlando Lasso (1595). In Italy the vogue wanes with the appearance of Monteverdi, in Germany with that of Schuetz, who honors the Lutheran principle that the people must be able to follow the words. England, as often, is a little behind the times.

[5] The popularity of the air dates from the closing years of the century, with the publication of the first of John Dowland's three books (1597).

allow one to please himself; monody, treated here as "subversive" of the older music, makes possible the greatest of musical forms, which is opera. All these afford pleasure—to us, who possess them all and do not care to winnow and choose. I see our predecessors, on the other hand, as committed to winnowing. The new primacy of the air or solo song means that the claim of this or that recalcitrant part to equal interest goes unhonored, is reduced to rule.

The rule is compendious. Like epigrams in poetry, says Thomas Campion, are airs in music: "then in their chief perfection when they are short and well seasoned." Campion, the partisan of quantitative verse, is also and appropriately a maker of the new music. What the new men chiefly relish in either art is the heart of the matter, in this case "A naked air without guide, or prop, or color but his own."[6] What they cannot stomach is confusion, and hence their hostility to singing in parts. That hostility, occasioned by a fear of losing the Word, occasions in turn a going back to simple melody, the naked line of sound unembellished by Figure or Shadow; and so begets the great Protestant hymns of Germany and England, indubitably great, but also restricted in range and characterized by a notable economy of rhythmic means. It begets also the rise of declamation, as in the Passion music of Heinrich Schuetz.[7] To insure that the saving words of the text will come through, only a very subdued instrumental background is permitted. The utterance is clearer than polyphony allows but, to my ear, too clear, and hence on the way to being coarse. Schuetz is not coarse; his music is greatly austere: but I think it tenable to suggest that the vogue of *falso bordone*—as Carlyle would put it: speaking the narrative out plainly, not twisting it into jingles—implies for the future the disusing of art. "What we want to get at is the *thought* the man had, if he had any." As words come to dominate number,

[6] Campion, preface to *A Book of Airs*, 1601.

[7] Since the Evangelist, who plays the role of Expositor in Schuetz's Easter oratorio ("History of the Resurrection of Jesus Christ," 1623) is intent most of all on the Word, his narration is partly declaimed.

340

music becomes not merely more simple but simplistic. "O promise me," etc.

In the Middle Ages and even so late as the time of John
Dunstable (d.1453), words are subservient to music. Medieval
music is dominated by number. But that relationship is abhorrent to the Renaissance which, as it exalts the message, must
make the words supreme. Thomas Morley, in the century after
Dunstable, despises his great predecessor as given to dittying:
the fitting of words to music. Dunstable, suggests Morley, essaying a horrid pun, treated words like a dunce. Morley's notion
and that of his contemporaries is that the music should be fitted
to the words, the better to implement the meaning or message.
Music after the Reformation is dominated by word. What happens in the drama is superficially different, essentially the same.
The nature of the medium makes the difference. In music, it is
number that contends against meaning; in the drama, paradoxically, it is language. As the desire is to realize clarity that meaning may be implemented, the word is depressed as against the
speaking picture. The result is that same clarity which trenches
on coarseness. At last, the result is imagism without signification.[8]

The greatest of English composers, William Byrd, in asserting that vocal music is excellent as it is "framed to the life of
the words" is not proclaiming a manifesto but only a truism. By
and large it has gone unchallenged since. The highest praise

---

[8] Though poetry per se is bitterly attacked, only the draconians wage
a concerted warfare against music in the Renaissance. Lasso, Monteverdi
are only conspicuous among the secular masters who are honored throughout Europe. The performer, like the famous singer Ludovico Zacconi
"lives surrounded by great admiration and esteem and is everywhere received with open arms" (*Practical Music*, 1592). The favoring of music
by the privileged classes in the sixteenth and seventeenth centuries is like
that of poetry, and is not surprising. (The connection between these arts
and noble patronage is documented in my *War Against Poetry*.) But
poetry is widely rejected, and absolutely, as its "meaning" is clamant.
Music is accepted in provisional ways: as the didactic meaning takes precedence over number, or as the musical composition is conceived as an ancillary (inconsiderable) diversion.

Byrd's editor and biographer allows to his subject is owing to his "power for devising the exact musical phrase to suit the words."[9] The Spanish composer Victoria, setting the text of the Mass, is concerned to reproduce in musical notation the actual rhythm of the spoken word—for example, the phrase *et it-er-um ven-tur-us est* of the Credo.[10] Campion aims chiefly, in his English airs, "to couple my words and notes lovingly together."[11] How far the primacy of number has been attenuated by the beginning of the seventeenth century and the old relationship reversed is attested by Byrd himself, who affirms that "as one meditates upon the sacred words and seriously considers them, the right notes, in some inexplicable manner, suggest themselves quite spontaneously."[12] The wind-swept lyre of the Romantics is not so very far behind.

As the "return of the brutal Middle Ages" is augured, the reactionary practice of the medieval composer is dusted off and resumed. Virgil Thomson suggests this practice in describing his treatment of a text by Gertrude Stein: "My theory was that if a text is set correctly for the sound of it, the meaning will take care of itself." Allegiance is to number or sound, and so the question of tonal illustration does not arise: "birdie babbling by the brook or heavy hangs my heart."[13] What happens to "meaning" as the primacy of sound is established? Perhaps the question is gratuitous.

The Renaissance composer does not think so. As he is conscious of its purport in narrow ways, he undertakes a syllabic treatment of the words that are set, the end being once more to heighten those words so completely that the Truth they embody cannot fail of communication.[14] Classical precedent is available

[9] First quotation from t.p. of Byrd's *Psalmes, Songs, and Sonnets*, 1611; second from E. H. Fellowes, *William Byrd*, pp. 27, 57.

[10] In the motet *O Magnum Mysterium*.

[11] *Two Books of Airs*, c.1613.

[12] Latin address to his patron Lord Northampton in *Gradualia*, Lib. 1, 1605; Fellowes, pp. 27-28.

[13] *Virgil Thomson*, p. 90.

[14] Schuetz pursues this end in employing for the "Resurrection" syllabic recitation without measures.

here; Campion invokes it. "The lyric poets among the Greeks and Latins were first inventors of airs, tying themselves strictly to the number and value of their syllables."[15] The gain in clarity potential in that more strict connection is not lost on the Elizabethans and their successors. One syllable is given one note; "high" or critical words are given high notes or greater time value. In a little while, the method is commonplace.[16] For example, Isaac Watts:

> A thou-sand a-ges in Thy sight Are like an ev'-ning gone;
> Short as the watch that ends the night Be-fore the ris-ing sun.

The Protestant, as also the new Catholic who is sponsored by the Council of Trent, has recovered the truth. He does not require polyphonic (or rhetorical) investigation. Like the blind seer Tiresias as Milton describes him, he is "wiser for his loss of sight."[17] He has got to the kernel. Or else like Peter Ramus, who divorces rhetoric and logic, he conceives the former as involved only with delivery or style. But as truth is patent, style is gratuitous. Cicero, the supreme stylist, is a casualty of this formulation. "What do I care," asks Erasmus rhetorically, "for an empty dish of words . . . mumped from Cicero"; and adds inconsequently, "I want all Cicero's spirit."[18] The dish of words,

[15] *A Book of Airs,* 1601.

[16] When John Merbecke, attempting to produce a vernacular liturgy, modifies the traditional plain chant, his settings are wholly syllabic (*Boke of Common praier noted,* 1550). Syllabic treatment characterizes the printed music accompanying the text in John Hall's *Court of Virtue,* 1565. Donahue, "Sarum Liturgy," *American Benedictine Review,* p. 458, finds this treatment suggested already by Cranmer in the reign of Henry VIII.

[17] Elegy VI to Charles Diodati, trans. William Cowper.

[18] *Ciceronianus,* 1528; Huizinga, *Erasmus,* p. 171. For the rising hostility to Ciceronianism in the sixteenth century, see N. Rudenstine, *Sidney's Poetic Development,* Ch. IX: "Sidney and Ciceronianism," pp. 131-48. Thomas Wilson, rejecting Cicero's "large vein and vehement manner of eloquence," prefers to it the "plain familiar manner of writing and speaking" he associates with Demosthenes (*The Orations of Demosthenes,* 1570). The opposition of the two great orators recapitulates in miniature the opposition of medieval and modern. Gabriel Harvey is "modern" in describing his own writing as "stripped of all rhetorical copiousness and

343

like Sidney's medicine of cherries, is instrumental. Its office is to
work its own extinction (the natural end of all didactic or provisional art). When Bishop Sprat, condoning the poetic strategy
of alluring men to the truth, suggests that "This was a course
which was useful at first, when men were to be delightfully
deceiv'd to their own good," he is anticipating a more enlightened time in which deception will no longer be required.[19]

Already in the sixteenth century, the reformer sees this hap-
pier time as in prospect. That is why he opposes himself even to
settings of the Psalms and rejoices when Coverdale's metrical
version is suppressed and burned by Henry VIII.[20] The singing
of Psalms means voices raised in unison, "conjoint voices," and
that means necessarily a deliberate or "set form" of praise. But
deliberation is spiritual death. To the really draconian reformer,
the only admissible singing of the Word is extempore solo singing, the lifting of one's voice in obedience to the moving of the
Spirit within. Humphrey Clinker is obedient to the Spirit.

But the end is not yet. Even better than extemporized singing—this is the conclusion to which the argument inexorably
conducts—is no singing at all. Sing Psalms if you must sing (but
not too many!), says the humanist a little scornfully to his weak-
er brethren. He is willing to concede them a staff on which to
lean as they hobble toward the Truth. He himself is enamored

---

gloring more in its furniture of subject matter than in its parade of
words" (*Ciceronianus*, 1577).

[19] *History*, quoted Willey, p. 208. Even Plato "still preserved the fable,
but refuseth the verse" (Harington in Smith, II, 203). The preserving
is an expedient: the Greek poet-physicians availed themselves of sugar
candy "seeing the world in those days was unperfect" (Lodge, *Defense
of Poetry*, p. 5). When the stomach is not so finicking, the fable and all
that is associated with it can be refused. But the fable is poetry's reason
for being.

[20] At the end of the Injunctions issued by Henry VIII in 1539 is a
catalog of forbidden books, which includes (among those attributed to
Coverdale) "Psalmes and Spiritual Songes drawn out of the holy Scripture." Henry's fear is of Lutheran heresy: Coverdale is translating from
German. The fear that agitates the extremist wing of the Puritan party
strikes deeper.

344

of silence. He would be colder and dumber and deafer than a fish. "Yea, let them hear," adjures the preacher Thomas Becon, "whose office is to sing in the church, that they must sing to God, not in the voice but in the heart."[21] The rest is silence.

Surely it is wrong to associate Erasmus, the prince of intellectuals, with a bigoted reformer like Thomas Becon? But each, in the matter of superficies, stands on the same ground. Erasmus is closer to his great antagonist Luther, the decrier of reason, than to his fellow Catholic Abbot Suger, four centuries before.

In the fourteenth century music and poetry had begun to move apart, each being cultivated more and more exclusively in technical and generic terms, as of polyphony or rhetoric. The reformers of the sixteenth century, as they are indebted to classical theory and desirous of producing an ethical effect, demand and consummate an intimate union of the two, but a union in which expertise is belittled and in which the content or kernel is esteemed above the form: the husk or awn. The reunion of music and poetry in the later sixteenth century is an arbitrary reunion. Nevertheless, and given the imperatives which produce it, this forced conjunction is deeply influential on the practice of Elizabethan madrigal and lutenist composers, and also and not least on the understanding and basic assumptions of the cultivated nonprofessional who knows what he likes or should like. Hooker, who reverences music as "A thing which delighteth all ages and beseemeth all states," interdicts in church music as "unsuitable harmony" such harmony "as only pleaseth the ear." What only pleases, displeases. So far from adding "either beauty or furtherance," delight that has no end beyond itself "doth rather blemish and disgrace" the matter, which is the heart of the business.[22]

In time even the matter or kernel, just because it is formal and codified, goes the way of its ostentatious cover. No music, not even church music, is sanctioned. The reforming Bishop of

---

[21] Stevens, p. 79.

[22] *Ecclesiastical Polity*, 1597, v, xxxviii, 1, 3. For the increasing dissociation of music and poetry in the sixteenth century, see J. Mazzaro, *Transformations in the Renaissance English Lyric*.

Ossory, John Bale, casts "away the nutte for mislike of the shell." Music, he thinks, any music, is "the very synagogue of Satan."[23] What is left are sensations and feelings, not formalized but inchoate: felt in the blood and felt along the heart.

It is the same in theology. First the elaborate ceremonies of the Church are discarded as husk:

> No hallowed oils, no grains I need,
> No rags of saints, no purging fire.[24]

To a preoccupation with the husk—grains or rosary beads—succeeds a scrupulous concern with the pith or sense those ceremonies had figured. Erasmus, who enjoins this concern, epitomizes the age of scriptural and patristic erudition.[25] But as the claims of disputation and ceremony are disvalued as against the claims of scholarship, so in the next age scholarship is made less than insight. This is the age of Martin Marprelate, who cares nothing for the learning of the bishops but only for the naked Word as he divines it. His saying is that of the Waldegrave Prayer Book (c.1585): "whatsoever is added to this word by man's device, seem it never so good, holy or beautiful, yet before our God . . . it is evil, wicked, and abominable."[26]

The sequence holds for poetry also. Not merely the crucial business but the whole business of poetry is made increasingly the communicating of home truths. The form of poetry, the fictions and pleasing patterns in which the essential stuff is enclosed, is tolerated at first only as a lure or bolus. As we grow stronger and less dyspeptic we can dispense with the form: we can put away poetry altogether. So Francis Bacon withers into the truth.

Bacon, in his avidity to grasp the naked truth, is very modern.

---

[23] The first phrase is from Nashe, quoted Smith, 1, 330. Bale says: "Neither shall the sweet organs, containing the melodious noise of all manner of instruments and birds, be played upon, nor the great bells be rung after that, nor yet the fresh descant, pricksong, counterpoint, and fa-burden be called for in thee" (Stevens, p. 79).

[24] Sir Henry Wotten, "A hymn to my God."

[25] For the enjoining, see his preface to the New Testament.

[26] Stevens, p. 76.

Like his successors in the age of classical science, he is disinclined to "wonder at a puppet-show, if . . . [he] can look behind the curtain."[27] As he wishes to take hold of the hidden abstraction, he does not attend much to the curtain itself, or vizard or painted sheath. "It is the Body, not the Shadow, that dispatcheth the businesse."[28] Style is shadow (one remembers Erasmus) or, what agrees more precisely with its superficial attractiveness, style is "The flower [that] delighteth to-day, and fadeth tomorrow," of little moment against "the fruite [that] edifieth and endureth."[29] The new Platonist—like Galileo on one side—spurns "the lovely flowers of rhetoric" as they "are followed by no fruit at all."[30]

The world is no longer in its nonage, and so the spurning is appropriate. The root and branch reformer, as he sees the provisional nature of the defense of poetry, concludes and announces that the time is ripe to jettison poetry altogether. "The season of Fiction is now over."[31] That is Jeremy Bentham, writing in the apogee of the Age of Reason. The kingdom on earth is in process of accomplishment. All the vexing problems—even death, with which the master of utility takes order in his will—have been vanquished, or else their resolution is in train. Of what further use are the sentimental illusions which, in the view of modern man, are poetry's stock in trade?

We have come down to the present. Poetry, as it continues to endure in the present, is mostly faithful to the dichotomized reading of its function elaborated in the late sixteenth century. Poetry is banal jingling: the music of Rod McKuen, hypotheti-

[27] *Advancement of Learning*, Bk. I.

[28] Gabriel Harvey in his invective against Robert Greene; Smith, II, 237.

[29] Harvey in *Foure Letters*, 1592.

[30] Cf. Nashe in *Anatomie*: "leaving theyr words we would cleave to their meaning, pretermitting their painted shewe we woulde pry into their propounded sence" (Smith, I, 322); Stanyhurst in his trans. of Virgil: "slising thee husk and cracking thee shel," he bestows "thee kernel upon" the reader (Dedication, 1582); Chaucer, "casting away the chaff of superfluity, and shewing the picked grain of sentence" (Caxton's preface to *Canterbury Tales*, 1484).

[31] *Westminster Review*, Jan. 1824; quoted Halévy, p. 134.

cally delightful; or it is kinetic, a blow to the head, and so fulfills the vulgar purpose stipulated by Ron Karenga, an apt pupil of the Platonizing theorists of the English Renaissance: "All art must reflect and support the Black Revolution and any art that does not discuss and contribute to the revolution is invalid."

In the narrow passage between these dispiriting alternatives, the genuine poetry of the twentieth century, not militant and not open and shut, beats up against the wind. It does not often confess the sovereign power of reason, for reason and poetry are at a remove. The poet Donald Hall, quoting with approval a stanza of Marianne Moore's, declines to offer a rational paraphrase but not as he is deferential, rather as the meaning of the lines "is not available to the rational mind." If poetic utterance is independent of reason, where does it come from? The poet answers: from "sea-serpented regions/ 'unlit by the half-lights of more conscious art.' "[32] The prepositional phrase is derisory, a contradiction in terms. "That is why I like to live in Italy," says D. H. Lawrence. "The people are so unconscious." The poet, conceiving of the intellect as a bit and a bridle, answers only to his blood "as being wiser than the intellect." (The exclusivism of Lawrence is perhaps a little less deplorable than the deifying of rationality by the cock-sure intellectuals of the Age of Reason.) Rejecting the fribbling intervention of mind, the poet "makes himself a seer through a long, prodigious, and rational disordering of all the senses" (Rimbaud).[33] The public to which he was used to appeal responds by drawing a sanitary cordon around poetry and poets:

> You either drive them mad, or
>   else blink at their suicides,
> Or else you condone their drugs,
>   and talk of insanity and genius. (Ezra Pound)[34]

The poet from the beginning has been identified with madness. But Plato, who proposes the identification, means to confer honor on poetry. (In his judgment of this art, he is notably

[32] Quoting "Novices"; *Marianne Moore*, p. 14.
[33] Quoted Kayser, p. 168.   [34] "Salutation the Third."

equivocal.) The poet or *vates*, as deific frenzy takes him, speaks with an oracular voice. The modern auditor of poetry perceives and acknowledges the frenzy, is skeptical as to its provenance. What is the source of his contemptuous or negligent reading? I think it is the baffling of great expectations. He has been taught by Boccaccio and the tiresome panegyrists of the English Renaissance, whose names are no longer current but whose doctrine is current, to expect all things of poetry. In promise, by insistent proclamation, poetry is the *vade mecum*. That is how Professor X continues to present it. His students in their uneasiness are wiser. "And it is because of this, because imaginative realization can enhance the statement of a meaning and augment its practical effect, that poetry has become identified with meaning, and with truth, and wisdom, and morality, and all those things that look greatly into the future" (Max Eastman). But the association of poetry with these abstract desiderata is spurious. "Poetry but lends itself to them. It is of its own nature foreign to them all."[35]

In our own time the Renaissance pretension is threadbare. The poet is the butt of contempt. Still the notion persists that, like the *aruspex*, he has something uncanny up his sleeve. He is, accordingly, the object of superstitious regard. Put these two dichotomies together. The poet is showered with uncritical adulation—this, for his riddling pronouncements on the Poetry Circuit (one understands a fury in his words but not the words)—and then is buried upside down in a hollow tree where one discovers Allen Ginsberg, the poet as magus: priest and charlatan together.

The priesthood of art is "not to bestow upon the universe a new aspect, but upon the beholder a new enthusiasm": not to discover but to dispose, for all the "discoveries" have been entered from the beginning. There is nothing new in first and last things. Already Sophocles knows them all. What is truth in art? It "is not discovery of facts or addition to knowledge, it is the exercise of propriety" (Kenneth Burke). The lameness or little-

---

[35] Eastman, "The Practical Value of Poetry," in Bader and Wells, *Essays of Three Decades,* p. 442.

ness of the definition is just right. Compare Sir Philip Sidney for the hyperbolic point of view. Thoreau, though he seems a little to denigrate poetry, has got the idea. "Great prose, of equal elevation, commands our respect more than great verse, since it implies a more permanent and level height, a life more pervaded with the grandeur of the thought. The poet only makes an irruption, like a Parthian, and is off again, shooting while he retreats; but the prose writer has conquered like a Roman, and settled colonies."[36] The discrimination is precise. Poetry settles nothing and does not conquer, except prosodically.

Here is a felicitous conjunction, of Max Eastman distinguishing that function which is aloof from the business of poetry (he calls it the bestowing of a "new aspect"), and Wallace Stevens, describing inferentially (in "Le Monocle de Mon Oncle") the character of poetic utterance as "An ancient aspect touching a new mind." This touching or communion is of the essence of poetry's achievement and to say that it has utility is only to confess the poverty of critical discourse.

Let us take hands, then, with the Renaissance militants and perverse apologists for poetry and their avatars in the present time, and agree that poetry is useful; but let us redefine our terms in the interest of greater exactness and implication. The misconceiving reader equates the usefulness of poetry with its issuance in action, purposive behavior—as when, in the 1590s, Harington reading the bucolic poetry of Virgil is impelled to drive the plough. But this issue is illegitimate. Richard Wilbur, in the poem called "Objects," memorializes the "devout intransitive eye / Of Pieter de Hooch." The adjectives suggest the difference between the kinetic instinct which treats objects as contingent phenomena and wants to do something with them; and the powerful activity of art, which is certainly engaged but not finally transitive, which is satisfied to celebrate or render. The artist is diffident, repudiates the illative voice. Wilbur's poem, "The Giaour and the Pacha," furnishes a nice or precise setoff to the purposive estheticians of the Renaissance, takes us

[36] From section entitled "Friday" in *A Week on the Concord and Merrimac Rivers.*

350

back to Quintilian (and the medieval reader) who supposes that art becomes wholly pure only as "it withdraws from action and can rejoice in the contemplation of itself." In the Delacroix painting—the *topos* Wilbur is disposing—the Giaour on horseback prepares to destroy the hated adversary he has finally brought low. And abruptly, like Prospero in the climactic action of the *Tempest*—which is the negation of action—he stays his hand. As the purposive instinct is dissipated, the horseman is changed: he becomes in that moment a work of art:

> the cloak becomes aware
> Of floating, mane and tail turn tracery;
> Imbedded in the air, the Giaour stares
> And feels the pistol fall beside his knee.[37]

This is not to assert that poetry is static, only that it has no circumscribed objective. It is not programmatic: political, or not in the conventional acceptance of the word. "My songs are kandym"—tenacious plants—"in the waste land," says the Communist poet Hugh MacDiarmid. The function of these songs is not "to combat the leper pearl of Capitalist culture"—that is what the poet thinks—but, more comprehensively, to put "a withy round sand": to fend against erosion, not least in the heart, to make a permanent domicile, transcending place and time, where capitalism and socialism are nonce words.

"Politics is about grievances that something can be done about. And poetry is about grief that nothing can be done about" (Robert Frost). The Marxist poet who thinks that "it is no time to pity the roses when the houses are burning" is like those eschatologists, St. Augustine and St. Jerome, who will us to avert our eyes from little business and look to the millennium or City of God. (The advent of the heavenly City is conditional on the deferring of little business and is accordingly forever unrealized.) Enobarbus in the play, as he is not so exclusive, is paradoxically more efficient: "Every time Serves for the matter that is then born in't." Poetry, which may pity the roses or the poor or dilate on grief or its obverse, is restricted in its domain of possibilities

---

[37] Following Donald Hill, *Richard Wilbur*, pp. 38-39.

only as it "does not translate anything/ does not explain anything/ does not reject anything/ does not grasp the whole/ does not fulfill any hopes."[38]

Roger Ascham in the sixteenth century describes the diligent search to which he and his fellow partisans of the new poetry are committed: "we seeke soch one in our schole to folow, who is able alwayes, in all matters, to teach plainlie, to delite pleasantlie, and to cary away by force of wise talke" (*Scholemaster*, 1570). Almost four hundred years later, William Carlos Williams is reflecting on the new poetry of the twentieth century. "What were we seeking?" he inquires; and answers simply: "the poetic line" (*Autobiography*, 1951). What is in question is not the kingdom on earth, as heretofore; and is not necessarily of less moment.

The "inverted humanist" of the twentieth century, who is conspicuous in the Soviet Union but not resident exclusively in that country, is dissatisfied with this succinct response. (He does not estimate its audacity.) Affecting the role of critic, he rounds on his supposititious "comrades," Shostakovich, Myaskovsky, Prokofiev: "your atonal disharmonic music is organically alien to the people . . . we absolutely do not accept . . . [contemporary] music. There is no harmony in it, no order."[39] The criterion of value is that of the ethical theorists in the beginning of the modern age. Art is validated only as it speaks out or conduces. Wilde in the *Soul of Man Under Socialism* sees, on the contrary, how in art "speaking out" is atonal, disharmonic. (He is discussing in Shelley's poetry the jarring note of rebellion.) "The note of the perfect personality is not rebellion, but peace." This is not to discommend Shelley's radical politics but all angry adhering, which presupposes exclusion, rejection. Imagine Joseph de Maistre as a poet.

The poet at peace with himself courts or "disposes" the Lord's truth wherever he finds it. One does not need to comment on

[38] Tadeuz Rózewicz in 1966, reversing his earlier opposition to the "poetry of roses"; T. Z. Gasinski, *MQR*, x, 29-30.

[39] Quoted by the cellist Mbtislav Rostropovich in a letter to the Soviet press, 31 October 1970 (*NYT*, Nov. 16, 1970, p. 35M).

the matter of his poetry, unless to note that his eye is circum-ambient. In the Renaissance a breach is opened between the content of poetry, gauged and selected now with regard to use and purport, and the form, conceived as excrescent. The modern ideologue who accepts this division and puts his money on the poet's "thought," warns us off as he is patently wrongheaded. The death of poetry is accomplished, however, not in the depressing of form against content—Sidney's Metaphrase of the Psalms, Shelley's verses on Castlereagh—but in the laconic assumption that form and content are discrete. To suggest that poetry is "metre-making argument" is implicitly to credit this assumption. Take the next step, and one is saying with Margaret Fuller (or with Tolstoy on Shakespeare) that a great work of art demands a great thought. The saying is plausible—it goes far to explain the inflated reputation of a "serious" or "moral" poet like Edmund Spenser—and I think most of us as readers of poetry, schooled in the humanist tradition, make no question but what it is valid. In fact it is lifted from the gospel of the Philistines and ought to stick in our craw. T. S. Eliot is more considering, in observing of the work of a contemporary poet that, "For a mind of such agility, and for a sensibility so reticent, the minor subject . . . may be the best release for the major emotions."[40]

Milton chooses to sing, not of King Arthur but of "One greater Man," in the conviction that a greater poem must follow. But the greatness of *Paradise Lost* does not reside in the idea or major subject, rather in the nice cohering of idea and idiosyncratic technique and perception (the singular personality of the poet).

In the *New Criticism*, J. C. Ransom, who is discussing the subordination in the writing of Yvor Winters of the poetic to the moral interest, turns to examine the old Horatian formula. Poetry is to teach but also to delight. In our time, he suggests, concern has grown increasingly with Horace's rider, "a concern as to how a moral discourse which goes to all the trouble of being technical poetry distinguishes itself from a moral discourse

---

[40] Introduction to the *Selected Poems* of Marianne Moore, 1935.

in prose. That is the critical problem." The answer to the problem lies in the "gratuities" of poetry—in Donne the hermetic syntax, the zeugma; the electing by Emily Dickinson of a naïve prosody abstracted from the hymnal; the constant resort in Shakespeare to circumstantiation, tautologous substantives, the adverbial phrase: "the whiff and wind of his fell sword," "unregarded age in corners thrown": matter which, from the standpoint of paraphrase, is off the "point," and is therefore disallowed by Procrustean or literal-minded man.

Milton's idea in *Lycidas* appears inconsiderable when isolated or reduced to its intellectual "kernel." Wherein lies the greatness of *Lycidas*? I suppose in the diapason or form, as in the interstitial business on which the poet attends as he goes his meditated progress, rationalizing the fortuitous event or the ways of God to man.

> Bring the rathe primrose that forsaken dies,
> The tufted crow-toe, and pale jessamine,
> The white pink, and the pansy freaked with jet,
> The glowing violet.

The conferring of importance on things which do not count is the peculiar accomplishment of poetry and explains why the old-fashioned or poetic psychology is mostly discredited in the modern age. Prospero, abjuring his art in the conclusion of the *Tempest*, remembers inconsequently the dark meadow grass the fairies make by moonlight: "green sour ringlets . . . Whereof the ewe not bites." The remembering is generous, the qualifying phrase absolutely concessive—and therefore indispensable. When in *Richard III* the ghost of Warwick indicts the perjured Clarence "That stabbed me in the field by Tewksbury," the localizing word weighs with the indictment. It matters to Escalus, the connoisseur of superficies, that the hapless Claudio in *Measure for Measure* "had a most noble father!" To Angelo, the abstracting intelligence, it does not matter.

The penchant for boiling down is alien to Shakespeare, characteristic of his greatest contemporaries and successors: Descartes in the *Discourse on Method* distinguishing essential content from the evanescent form, Galileo the philosopher of mechanism reducing form to iconology.[41] The image is not primary—the visible world—but the disembodied idea in the image. See for a literary gloss the collections of florilegia like the *Polyanthea* (1507) of Nannius Mirabellius, or the emblems of Alciati, or the mythological treatises—"compendia," precisely—of Cartari and Cesare Ripa. The extrinsic detail is denotative: like the eagle, the thunderbolt, and sceptre by which Jupiter is figured; and it is always—if Jupiter is intended—the same. What is truly indigenous—not merely cosmetological—is denied. On the denial rest the triumphs of new philosophy. Mathematics, says an eminent practitioner of this science, is fond of giving the same name to different things (Henri Poincaré).[42]

Aldous Huxley in the *Doors of Perception* sees how recognition is contingent on myopia: how, exactly as in Renaissance allegory, our potential consciousness of the visible world is "funneled through the reducing valve of the brain and nervous system" and with the result that only a "measly trickle" emerges. "To formulate and express the contents of this reduced awareness, man has invented and endlessly elaborated those symbol-systems and implicit philosophies which we call languages." But the characteristic vocabulary or symbology of the Age of Reason victimizes the man who employs it "as it confirms him in the belief that reduced awareness is the only awareness and as it bedevils his sense of reality, so that he is all too apt to take his concepts for data, his words for actual things."[43] The insistence in this vocabulary on symmetry and sequence destroys the actual thing. It sins against the Holy Ghost.

What is this mysterious and unforgivable sin? It is to treat people as ciphers, to deny integrity to the man in his habit as he lived. "What happens to a Russian, to a Czech, does not interest me in the slightest," says Heinrich Himmler. "How horrible,

---

[41] Galileo is a great empiric, but only by turns. "It has often been maintained that Galileo became the father of modern science by replacing the speculative, deductive method with the empirical, experimental method. I believe, however, that this interpretation would not stand close scrutiny": Einstein, introducing a new trans. of the *Dialogue Concerning the Two Chief World Systems*, p. xvii.

[42] In D. W. Thompson, I, 139.   [43] P. 23.

fantastic, incredible it is that we should be digging trenches . . . because of a quarrel in a faraway country between people of whom we know nothing": Neville Chamberlain on the eve of the Second World War.[44] The source of the incredulity or indifference is myopia, the incapacity to perceive the world as substantially there. Leibniz is myopic in his willful replicating of monads which are assumed to be forever the same. Against the insipid world of perfect replication is the discontinuous world of the twentieth century, made up of particles which in some sense are *sui generis*. This world is harder to negotiate and also more nutritive because more nearly true.

Classical science proclaims that nature can follow only one road, "the road which was mapped out from the beginning of time to its end by the continuous chain of cause and effect." The new science of Planck, and Einstein his unwilling adherent, is probabilistic. "It cannot predict with certainty which state will follow which; this is a matter which lies on the knees of the gods—whatever gods there be."[45]

Man in the Age of Reason assures himself that he knows everything or will know everything soon. The hatred of agnosticism evinced by the classical Marxist is necessary hatred. Agnosticism gets at him where he lives. It is therefore understood to be "undermined and refuted by experience and practice. Science every day extends and deepens our knowledge of the content of existence. Nothing which exists can be regarded in principle as unknowable; the only valid distinction is that between what is already known and what is not yet known."[46] This assurance is, however, conditional. It is required, first of all, that one affirm the mathematical lie.

> They will get it straight one day at the Sorbonne.
> We shall return at twilight from the lecture
> Pleased that the irrational is rational.
> (Wallace Stevens, "Notes Toward a
> Supreme Fiction")

[44] Quotations from Shirer, *Third Reich*, pp. 937, 403.
[45] Sir James Jeans, *The Mysterious Universe*, p. 22.
[46] Rosenthal and Yudin, p. 14, "Agnosticism."

Descartes is able to get it straight as he shuts his eyes and ears to the perplexing variety of the physical world. "In the uniform lucidity of his closed senses . . . he is certain of seeing that which he sees."[47] The older age is more catholic, acceptive as it is satisfied to contemplate the indestructible integer, the associating of disparate persons and things, the possibility of madness in reason, "divinest sense" in madness: King Cophetua and the Beggar Maid, the Bedlam in *Lear,* the mad king himself "crowned with rank fumiter and furrow weeds."

Yeats in a letter to the poet Sturge Moore signals the return of a more circumstantial mode of perceiving, a less cursory mode of being: "I try always to keep my philosophy within such classifications of thought as . . . to include in my definition of water a little duckweed or a few fish. I have never met that poor naked creature H_2O."[48] The idiom is of the twentieth century, the psychology is reminiscent. The receptivity of the Middle Ages to phenomenal things is epitomized by that tenth-century abbot of Cluny who says on his deathbed, *Domini, dilexi decorum domus tuae*: "Lord, I have loved the beauty of thy house."[49] The contemporary poet reaffirms this mundane love, repudiates concurrently the mythology of the proximate past in his saying: "No ideas but in things" (W. C. Williams). The poet is bidding us dwell in the carnal and mysterious surface, in the consciousness of "style." We are to attend not solely to the point or kernel but to the entire canvas, not least to its irrelevancies: "Whereof the ewe not bites." His reactionary and inspiriting proposal is that modern form is abnegation. What it offers is ready comprehending, the simple man or fact who is sign and referent. What it precludes is the Shakespearean range of possibilities: the ambiguous man who is good and bad together, in an unexpected sense "himself alone."

On the conceding of integrity, the *discordia concors*, tolerance depends: the approbation of life as it really consists. We are back to Oscar Wilde, anathematizing in the work of art the jarring

[47] Foucault, *Madness and Civilization*, p. 94.
[48] R. Ellmann, *Yeats the Man and the Masks*, p. 261.
[49] Majolus, 4th abbot, in Duckett, *Death and Life*, p. 210.

note of rebellion. "When a painting is silent"—I am quoting
the abstract painter Serge Poliakoff—"it means it is successful."[50]

Artistic silence is not, however, the silence of the grave and
what the artist makes is not inert like a headstone. Emerson's
belief that "the most private is the most public energy" is borne
out in the "dynamic" activity of a poet like Dante, who undertakes "to remove those living in this life from a state of misery
and to guide them to a state of happiness." The poet or trans-
mogrifier, working on the imagination, calls up the Pisgah-sight
and assigns it a habitation in the present. As he enforces unexpected connections, he is necessarily subversive. To turn the
coin, and resume and modify the association of poetry and politics: in a more catholic sense, the poet is always political. "There
is no such thing as genuinely non-political literature" (George
Orwell).[51] Arnold, in his last words as Professor of Poetry at
Oxford, explains what this means. He has been asserting that
literature has nothing to do "with ready-made judgments and
watchwords"—let us say, with the homilies of the preacher or
the shibboleths of the political hack—but not because it is des-
sicated, rather as it is vital, committed. "It seeks to do away
with classes; to make the best that has been thought and known
in the world current everywhere."

The first clause is the exciting clause, the second begins to
trench on the proselyting esthetic of the fathers of humanism
from whom Arnold derives. Egalitarian, "activist," social: these
words, if one applies them exactly, are definitive of poetry, and
even though it is never translated concretely as by plebiscites
and political battles. "We have not stopped our adversaries' advance"—Arnold is speaking for Oxford but his words have a
ramifying force, suggest the quickening activity of poets like
himself—"we have not marched victoriously with the modern
world; but we have told silently upon the mind of the country,
we have prepared currents of feeling which sap our adversaries'
position when it seemed gained." In the matter of poetry, that
is the true kinetic power and makes clear why the poet, whatever

[50] In *NYT*, Nov. 16, 1970.
[51] P. 112 in "The Prevention of Literature" (*Shooting an Elephant*).

his political prepossessions, is the natural enemy of the despot. "In this country," says the widow of Mandelstam, "all real poetry is outrageous."[52] One can omit the adverbial phrase.

In the lexicon of humanism, kinesis is more narrowly defined. Activism is parochial, serves a delimited end. The artist collaborates in the endeavor "to make reason and the will of God prevail." This duty is enjoined on him by Renaissance critics, beginning with the Italians in the generation after Dante. The intention of Terence, says one of the benevolent company, "was to show the ugliness of foul things so that men would abstain from them . . . and to propose to them the praiseworthy and virtuous and honest ones so that they might embrace them and adorn themselves with them. Just as tragedy . . . induces men to abstain from acting wickedly, so comedy, by means of laughter and jokes, calls men to an honest private life" (Giraldi, 1566).[53]

Activity addressed to a putative good takes precedence of showing forth and perceiving. The question of delight, in life, in art, does not arise except as delight is instrumental. The Renaissance humanist and his successors to the present consign it surprisingly to the merely theoretical labors of science. The seeker after truth, who derives his contentment in estimating the nature of things, is not so practical as the poet—just that. And so the scientist is left to his abstruse incantations. Copernicus is only a theoretician; that is why he gets the papal imprimatur. "Science has this which is different from art . . . [it] takes as its subjects things which although they may be known do not necessarily lead to action; but Art does not take for its subjects things which, when they are known, cannot much more easily lead to action" (Castelvetro, 1565-71). The artist is beneficent, committed to a job of work; the scientist pleases himself. The definition or assignment is certainly preposterous—like the characteristic formulae of the Age of Reason it allows of no middle ground—and explains why the poet who denies the inordinate commitment to use must abandon altogether the heuristic role

[52] *Hope Against Hope*, p. 92.
[53] In B. Weinberg, *Literary Criticism in the Italian Renaissance*, I, 289.

359

in which his function is exhausted and proclaim himself a sciolist or trifler.

But the difference between science and poetry has also to do with generosity and candor. "Science tolerates every material, whether it be decent, or useful, or dishonest, or harmful to the world; but art does not tolerate any subject which is not decent and useful to the world."[54] With some such wretched formulation as this, the modern age begins. Here is how it ends, or rather how our more hopeful and magnanimous present is suggested. To the man of letters, says Chekhov, not less than to the chemist, "there is nothing unclean in this world. . . . The artist should not be a judge of his characters or of what they say, but only an objective observer." The humanist confounds two different ideas: "the solution of the problem and a correct presentation of the problem. Only the latter is obligatory for the artist."[55] The artist deceives others and possibly himself as he plays the role to which humanism commits him. The definition of humanism is the purposeful interpenetrating of life and art.

The contemporary poet in his obliqueness or whimsicality seems to abort the connection. Mandelstam says, in his *Journey to Armenia*: "A plant is an event, an occurrence, an arrow." It is a good cryptic retort on the message-mongers of the twentieth century, as on their predecessors four centuries ago. The description is tenable of poetry: except that the arrow which is the poem does not fly like a vector straight to its preordained mark—which is not yet disclosed and not least to the poet—but is like that "childhood proof" Bassanio adduces in the *Merchant of Venice*, in proposing to shoot an arrow in the air. "What follows is pure innocence."

Bassanio's line is enigmatic and perhaps it is disingenuous: Shakespeare at any rate knows what he is doing. But if the play is not innocent or artless, the hero of the play is recognized, in the event he is vindicated, as he declines to prosecute a meditated scheme. The proper involuntariness which describes him

[54] Castelvetro in Weinberg, I, 292.
[55] Quotations from J. L. Styan, *Chekhov in Performance*, p. 340.

gets its comment in a line from *Cymbeline*: "Fortune brings in some boats that are not steered." Against this line, which is reverberant in Shakespeare's work from the earliest comedies to the late romances, one wants to set the deifying of praxis by the modern maker: the reanimating of an ancient illusion, man the master of his fate who is most himself as he is forthputting, grapples with the angel. In this grappling or contending, the artist pays homage to the Prince of Darkness: for us or against us, "on to the bound of the waste." Shakespeare in his sentence takes leave of the Manicheans. The polemical voice is stilled. There is no adversary, no goal whose contours we are able to perceive, and hence in the ideal case no purposive behavior. What there is, in terms of art, is delineating—which, as it is utterly faithful, works a metamorphosis, does really conspire to bring in that golden world for which Sidney in ambiguous ways is yearning.

Sidney and his contemporaries move naturally, with no sense of disjunction, beyond the confines of poetry to require of us the intentional life. That is as they are faithful to the ethical bias of humanism. We want to follow in their track—I think we must follow if we are really to come to terms with the humanists of the Renaissance and so dispel the confusion in which they have involved us—to put the "humanist" question but with a different bias: to what degree is a commitment to the intentional life subversive of the ends and purposes of our being?

The humanist does not of course put the question in so many words; he begs it. The indifferent man, he asserts, should be thrown in the mire "by those who travel on both Sides of the Way, for pretending the Benefit of the Road, without contributing to the making it either Safe or Good." Sir Richard Steele, who prescribes this hardy usage, is humanist: activist in supposing that life is continual struggle and figured metaphorically in the choosing up of sides.[56] How reactionary is the voice of Andrew Marvell, who declines to participate in the Civil War because "the Cause was too good to have been fought for."[57] Mar-

[56] Steele in the final number of the *Englishman.*
[57] *Rehearsal Transpros'd*, 1672-73.

vell's small body of great poetry is like his equable politics before the Restoration, and antipathetic to the modern spirit which makes contention an article of faith. As the motive of art is not to pay homage to the visible world but to recast it, so the motive of life is not simply to live but to query and reconstitute the basis of living. "The philosophers have only interpreted the world in various ways; the point however is to change it" (Marx).[58] Really we are all like the artist, marching as to war; or say that his militant function is assimilated to ours.

Already Petrarch proclaims this function: "It is better to will the good than to know the truth."[59] The galvanic dictatorships of the twentieth century are predicable of this astonishing affirmation. What is fascism but willing without knowing, action without thought? Hitler, who tells his people that "the Age of Nerves of the nineteenth century has found its close with us," is looking to the day when, "from the shifting waves of a free thought-world there will arise a brazen cliff of solid unity in faith and will." As that day is realized, *homo sapiens* abdicates his ancient responsibility. "It does not matter what you think," says Heinrich von Treitschke, "so long as you obey."[60]

Petrarch, ruminating *On His Own Ignorance*, is reacting to the mock-learned man who is tumid with the fever of many books ingested. He is telling us how little we know. Who has not felt in himself the same welling of anger at the pretension to learning, as also the benevolent impulse to leave off theorizing and to make a better world, and who is disinclined to share Petrarch's satisfaction in the rustic title, a good man, as opposed to the inflated title, a man of letters? Petrarch has got hold of a cantle of the truth, and I think we join him in wishing goodbye to mere eloquence—as, two centuries later, Sidney bids goodbye to him. But eloquence is amenable to a range of definition, and not certainly to be posed against that "inborn reason"

---

[58] 11th of the *Theses on Feuerbach*, 1845.

[59] P. 105 in *On His Own Ignorance*, ed. Cassirer *et al.* "*Satius est autem bonum velle quam verum nosse*" (Capelli edn., p. 70).

[60] Quotations from Shirer, *Third Reich*, pp. 230, 110, 99.

for which Petrarch is contending. It is true—what Nietzsche suggests in his comments on *Hamlet*—that knowledge kills action which needs the veil of illusion; and also true that knowledge which has no vent in action makes the sterile or inhuman man—not Hamlet but Gilbert Osmond. This is to say that every pregnant observation demands restatement or qualifying in terms of its opposite. Thoreau's "Simplify!" meets Lear's "Reason not the need!"

The civilization of the High Middle Ages I take to mark in important ways the apogee of human achievement. In chronicling this achievement, one had better find room for the Roman Catholic patriarch of Jerusalem in the time of the First Crusade who compels the Orthodox priests of that city to reveal, under torture, the whereabouts of the true Cross. The saying of Petrarch and his successors in the Age of Reason is insufficiently comprehensive: radical, elliptical. Petrarch, the first "modern" man, is pernicious not as he is wrong but for the bias and weight he accords his particular truth.

The bias of humanism: modernism is in favor of provisionality. The good is always on the horizon and therefore living now is anticipatory, the watch that ends the night.

> Everything is dead
> Except the future. Always everything
> That is is dead except what ought to be.

History, the long night, is repudiated as it is not convicted of "sin." It constitutes no more than "the closing chapter of the prehistoric stage of human society."[61] Contemplation is the hebetude of the Dark Ages. Knowledge (never mind how one achieves it) is for action. "The great questions of the day will not be settled by resolutions and majority votes"—rather, says Bismarck, "by blood and iron." Shaw is "modern" in asserting that "Activity is the only road to knowledge." Herzen is "medi-

---

[61] Marx, *Introduction to the Critique of Political Economy*. Stevens, whose lines (from "The Statue at the World's End") are assigned to a vulgar Marxist, might be quoting Marx himself.

eval" in suggesting another point of view: "To understand is already to act."[62]

All one's experience suggests that Shaw is right. But consider John of Salisbury, a mighty worker in the world, who dismisses the valorous activity of many years as "time trifled away." The characterization is certainly unjust: Chartres is standing, partly because John labored there as its bishop. But I think what is latent in the disvaluing of activity is the sense that the end it serves is a tentative end and the good it achieves very fragile. "All things fall and are built again," conceivably Chartres itself. Medieval man is not indolent or quiescent, only he is skeptical. Modern man commits himself to action in the belief that the knowledge he is harnessing is going to make the critical difference. The living center of history he discerns as residing "in the will and ideality of man himself" (Benedetto Croce, who might be quoting Protagoras or the eupeptic philosophers of the Renaissance and later). He is an exorcist, who thinks he can lay all the ghosts. Or he is like a new Pygmalion. His art remakes the old Adam. "Grace" is unnecessary. Modern man is Pelagian.

New philosophy, which tends to think that knowledge confers absolute power, is corrected in the light of events: "The broken wall, the burning roof and tower/ And Agamemnon dead." What follows is a salutary awareness of human fallibility. "We are all frail": Angelo's discovery, in *Measure for Measure*. This awareness, of everything the modern age denies, is the condition of health. Life is forever going down to darkness—the wisdom of the Reve's Prologue—"bleeds away, even as a form of wax" against the fire: the famous metaphor of Descartes, as anticipated by Shakespeare, and understood here in a sense not intended by the philosopher of unchanging form.

> Man is in love and loves what vanishes,
> What more is there to say?

[62] Bismarck on becoming Prime Minister of Prussia (Shirer, p. 94). Shaw is quoted in the "Revolutionist's Handbook," appended to *Man and Superman*; Herzen in *From the Other Shore*, end Ch. IV.

The question is rhetorical. As one opens himself to contingency, is satisfied to dwell on "the razor's edge of Now," he is fulfilled. As he would save his life he must lose it. The forfeit is an act of enfranchisement. One relinquishes the "principle of self" (Nietzsche in the *Birth of Tragedy*) and is free to inherit the earth.[63]

But this abdication or letting go—the realization that one's hands are not on all the ropes—is not to be equated with supineness. One grapples, like Suger, with those existential problems which beset every man in his time, while understanding that for those problems there is no solution. Tragedy is the full life meeting the unshunnable death. Health, which is founded on the tragic sense of life, is not learning to adjust, to rationalize; it is a confronting in first and last things of our endemic incapacity to adjust. One reaches at the kingdoms of the earth with outstretched arms: and discovers in the end that he has parted but the shadow with his hand.[64]

Pelagianism, which I take to be the modern heresy par excellence, derives from a belief in the efficacy of contractual change. All problems are located in the culture and hence are rationalizable. "Away with erotic problems." Nikolai Chernyshevsky, the nineteenth-century Socialist who puts them to flight, typifies the optimistic intellectual in the high tide of the Age of Reason. As for erotic problems, "The modern reader has no interest in them." That is as he declines to credit the ills our flesh is heir to. "He is concerned with the question of perfecting the administration and the judicial system, with financial questions, with the problem of liberating the peasant."[65] "Jeremiah," diagnosing

---

[63] Following Bugental, pp. 298, 323; Shostrom, pp. 63-65; Karen Horney (after Ruth Benedict) on the opposition of Apollonian and Dionysian, *Neurotic Personality of Our Time*, pp. 270-74; Maslow on work and play, pp. 291-93. The comparison of life to the wax which "Resolveth from his figure" is from *King John*, v, iv, 23-25. Yeats is quoted, "Nineteen Hundred and Nineteen."

[64] Paraphrasing Shakespeare in *3HVI*, I, iv, 68-69.

[65] Review of Turgenev's story, "Asia" in *The Contemporary*, 1860. The tepid a-sexual ending of Chernyshevsky's famous novel, *What Is To Be Done?* dramatizes the proposition.

problems that are organic as opposed to contractual, is banished by the promoters of sweetness and light as Hebraic. The prescriber of release or encounter techniques, perceiving that a young subject "is beginning to feel frightened and guilty," suggests easily that the "culture is already getting to him." Change the culture (will the good) and the happiness of this subject is assured.[66] There is in the prescribing no intimation of what Shakespeare calls "the imposition hereditary ours." The behaviorist discounts heredity or history. "A neurosis is an internal, nonorganic barrier to need fulfillment."[67] This means, a neurosis is external.

Man is good as he is natural, uncorrupted by externals: the psychology asserted some centuries before J.-J. Rousseau in the pastoral poetry of the Renaissance. Shakespeare's pastoral hero is Caliban, his "natural" man is a fool. The contemporaries of Guarini and Sannazaro are more sanguine. Not the warrant of Scripture but the natural goodness of the shepherds, denizens of the Golden Age, earns them the honor of attending on the birth of Christ. As the debacle which is history supervenes, the pastoral world is disoriented by the erecting of nonorganic barriers to need fulfillment. The Golden Age goes down. Man since the Renaissance spends himself in the endeavor to repossess this primal time. That is why he is always looking over his shoulder or rejecting or ravishing the present in favor of a kingdom still to come.

> But yet the state of things require
> These motions of unrest,
> And these great Spirits of high desire,
> Seeme borne to turne them best.

The incessant agitation Samuel Daniel is describing in his verses on Ulysses, the characteristic modern hero, takes its rise from self-disgust. Why else is it required always to be up and doing? Medieval man, who knows himself concupiscent and does not proclaim an equivalence between goodness and the natural condition, is able—as his art attests—to accept without boggling the

---

[66] W. C. Schutz, *Joy: Expanding Human Awareness,* pp. 251-52.
[67] S. and G. Putney, *The Adjusted American,* p. 130.

good and imperfect together. Modern man is more fastidious. It is a trouble to him. The Elizabethan poet Sir John Davies is is his spokesman. Davies is reflecting, in the poem called paradoxically *Nosce Teipsum*, on the equivocal condition of the soul:

> we could gladly think from God she came;
> Fain would we make Him author of the wine,
> If for the dregs we could some other blame.

In the ability to discriminate as between dregs and wine, medieval man is sadly lacking. Pope Innocent, who discriminates successfully, contemns the world and the flesh in favor of a better world hereafter, is a harbinger of morbid times to come.

Morbidity in this context means an obscure need to reject and reconstitute. It is directed insistently against all ambiguous or particolored things, looks on man with the unloving eye of a Cubist. The preoccupation in Renaissance criticism with decorous representation is morbid. The type or genus has, however, this advantage. It is resistant to good pity and therefore congenial to the "rational" societies of the modern age, in which man becomes something to be built from, not for. "What is life? Life is the Nation. The individual must die anyway" (Hitler).[68] Morbidity turned outside in the effort to ameliorate our present discontents is expressed as humanitarian zeal. This is not the same thing as saying that every humane man is a crank. The zealot who like Brutus is exorcising some sick offense within his mind requires the making over of man. Total revolution is total rejection. The zealot has no patience with the old-fashioned or ecumenical poet. Brutus to Cassius: "What should the wars do with these jigging fools?" He is indifferent to the modest labors of a tentative empiricist like Freud as he "cannot show the way," as he offers "not a therapy . . . [but] only a diagnosis. The analyst vainly exposes the regressive nature of the neurotic's solution, if he cannot himself provide a better solution. And Freud cannot." He has "no new truth to offer." That is just right, and of poetry not less than psychology.

It does not occur to the devotee of new truth—as represented here by Christopher Caudwell—to suppose that there is no "so-

[68] Quoted Shirer, p. 933.

367

lution," that man is not to pursue regeneration, whether in the Lord or in a temporal-political church, but more simply to accept himself, perhaps to forgive himself the lot.

> Lord, let the Angels praise thy name.
> Man is a foolish thing, a foolish thing,
> Folly and Sinne play all his game.
> His house still burns, and yet he still doth sing,
> *Man is but grasse,*
> *He knows it, fill the glasse.* (George Herbert)

Perceiving that liberty has always proved an illusion—in the Roman and the feudal era, in the era of the bourgeois: modern times—he goes on in his externalizing way to assign a cause. Men in history have failed as they have sought to maintain the hegemony of the few: "they failed and man is still everywhere in chains, because they did not share the pursuit of liberty with their slaves, their serfs, or the exploited proletariat."[69] But that is not why they failed or why man is still everywhere in chains.

The crier-up of new truth, infected with the provisionality or perfectibilitarianism that comes in with the Renaissance, bitten to frenzy with what is miscalled divine discontent, is too busy at his labors of reconstituting to court acceptance: merely to live. Like Thomas Buddenbrooks, enacting the role of the hysterical bourgeois whom Marx anatomizes in the *Communist Manifesto*, he is forever redoing his environment, in hope redoing or annihilating himself. The present horror is a consequence. If one is gloomy by temperament or perhaps merely theatrical, he will see it as a conclusion. For example, Spengler: "Before us there stands a last spiritual crisis that will involve all Europe and America. In this very century, I prophesy . . . a change of feeling will overcome the will-to-victory of science. The great masters are dead. The curtain falls. The Culture is irremediably in ruin. The final battle is at hand."[70] And so on.

Here, one might put period to the dismal history of the Age of Reason. But a different ending is detectable, at any rate it is

[69] Quotations from Caudwell, *Studies in a Dying Culture*, pp. 182, 10.
[70] Conflated from *Decline of the West*, Chs. x, xix, xxi.

potential, in the same materials. This more hopeful ending is hypothesized by a victim and critic of the morbid humanitarianism that distinguishes the modern age, and I think we should read it in emblematic ways. "Russia once saved the Christian culture of Europe from the Tatars, and in the past fifty years, by taking the brunt on herself, she has saved Europe again—this time from rationalism and all the will to evil that goes with it."[71] I suppose salvation, the waning of the darkness, to follow as the record of the past is taken to heart. In this limited sense, Marx is right. On the remembrance of things past the interring of the past depends, as also the absolving of the future.

The Platonizing critics of the fourteenth century and later reject the quotidien world, and erect over against it a more settled habitation. The fierce desire they manifest to better the lot of their fellowmen, to annul the unlooked-for accident, to make the course of history conform to a rational plan, begets the acceptance of *raison d'état*, at length the a-rational leader who announces that the cause is in his will. Stalin is the last legatee of the Age of Reason. To the architects of the New Jerusalem, the earth and its usufructs (they are sure to partake of them someday!) are worth the destruction of the present. Having sacrificed the present, they fail to inherit the earth.

"What is to be done?" This question, which informs the hopeful polemics of western socialism to the present, functions as the title of Chernyshevsky's bland utopian novel of the 1860s. Dostoevsky, who sees that the question is implicitly rhetorical as it appeals to material progress, answers rudely: "There is absolutely nothing to be done." Against the optimistic faith in social engineering, he poses the sick—and overmastering—fancies of the Underground Man: and accommodates them. His negative resolution is aloof from willing, contractual change, and appears in its simplicity almost simplistic: "for a brotherly loving principle to exist, one has to love."[72] The resolution is negative because

---

[71] N. Mandelstam, *Hope Against Hope*, p. 329 (also p. 162).

[72] Durgy edn., p. xv. "But what do I care if . . . [my sick fancy] is not supposed to exist? What does it matter, since it exists in my desires, exists as long as my desires exist? . . . I will accept all the derision, and will still not say that I am full when I want to eat" (p. 35).

—in our terms, which hark back uncannily to the discredited psychology of the Middle Ages—it is founded on skepticism and nonstriving. Let us unclench the fist: that is what Dostoevsky is saying.

The contemporary psychologist, commending to us "the law of reversed effort," is pouring old wine in new bottles. The pursuit of wisdom, humility, courage, which the humanist makes the whole business of life and art, is a bootless pursuit as these are goals which "forever evade any effort to achieve them."[73] One may seek knowledge, like Bacon; one may not seek to be wise. The rationalizing philosophers grasp this truth only piecemeal. Schopenhauer says: "Man can do what he wills but he cannot will what he wills." The second clause is certainly true and corroborated by Dostoevsky's anti-hero; the first is true only of externals. The rustic title, a good man, which Petrarch covets in the beginning of the modern age, is independent of willing. "Virtues are not accomplishments and cannot be learned. They must be deserved, but their possession is a matter of grace."[74] That is very like St. Odo, the man of the Dark Ages, proclaiming his ill character—and "the mercy which was always looking down on me."

The mercy on which salvation depends, if it is earned, is nonetheless a gratuity. What this means, for the Cluniac monk, in hope for ourselves, is not indifference but reticence, a withering of the impulse to self-assertion.

> From strength to strength go on,
> Wrestle and fight and pray,
> Tread all the powers of darkness down,
> And win the well-fought day.[75]

The autonomous man is definable as the man who does not put himself forward. He turns a deaf ear to all importunate voices,

[73] Watts, *The Wisdom of Insecurity*, p. 9; L. H. Farber, "Faces of Envy," *Review of Existential Psychology*, I, 134.

[74] Farber, pp. 134-35.

[75] Charles Wesley, "Soldiers of Christ, Arise."

to Ulysses and also to Circe. He is like the work of art, as I conceive it. Shelley is more penetrating than the Manicheans in supposing, not the "Protestant" contention "of truth with false-hood . . . the good or evil side," but more subtly of modesty and stridor. "Poetry and the principle of Self, of which money is the visible incarnation, are the God and Mammon of the world."[76] As this contention is lucky in its issue, purposive be-havior—the principle of self—gives way to agnosticism and a becoming reserve. "Fortune brings in some boats that are not steered."[77]

The humanist, who is always girding up his loins, finds the proposition effeminate. He "would fain do something . . . con-tribute something to the sustenation of the whole," believing that "we are not sent into this world to suffer but to do": John Donne on his "modern" or decanal side.[78] To drift is to suffer. What, then, is man's appointed business? Shaw answers vividly, in the conclusion to *Heartbreak House*: "Navigation. Learn it and live; or leave it and be damned." Already the ship is head-ing for the rocks, which wait their chance to destroy it. So much is predictable of ships and rocks and our melodramatic turn of mind, now for a long time.

But the opposite of the navigating or purposive man is not the quietist. Each is an elliptical personality. The way of Leah completes the way of Rachel. In the plenary personality, each is included. Consider the rebuke Christ visits on the Gentiles be-cause they stand idle in the marketplace of the world, forbearing to labor in the vineyard; consider also the preferring to Martha of her sister Mary who, as she does nothing, is said to have

[76] *Defence of Poetry*. The "strife of truth with falsehood" is imagined by James Russell Lowell and is familiar from the Hymnal ("Once to Every Man and Nation").

[77] "It is because Humanity has never known where it was going that it has been able to find its way": Wilde on *The Critic As Artist*, p. 359 in *Intentions* (1891). So the subtitle of Wilde's essay: "With some remarks upon the importance of doing nothing."

[78] In a letter to Sir Henry Goodyer, Sept. 1608; and in *Pseudo-Martyr* (quoted Gosse's *Donne*, I, 253).

"chosen that good part, which shall not be taken away from her" (Luke x:42). These ambiguous sayings suggest the poverty of the old alternatives commended to us by our study of the past: the role of the activist, whose commitment is entire; that of the contemplative, who folds his hands. A more ample role is assigned to the angel who descends from the beatific center, the eye of the storm where agitation is hushed, to trouble the waters of the pool at Bethesda that the sick who bathe there may be healed. The plenary personality, the garment of the best and brightest and adumbrated as yet only faintly in them, is that of the active-contemplative who forsakes the conventual life and enters in the world, who stands ready, in the phrase of Meister Eckhart, "to come down from the seventh heaven in order to bring a cup of water to his sick brother."[79] Let us be clear, however, whose thirst the cup of water is intended to assuage. The active-contemplative—in the Middle Ages John of Salisbury, in the Renaissance Thomas More or Herbert the parson of Bemerton, in our time such a man as Klaus von Stauffenberg or Dietrich Bonhoeffer—enters into the world for disinterested reasons, is not laboring "merely" to save his own soul.

By the same token: to be skeptical of steering (the quotation from *Cymbeline*) is not to see the intellect as a bit and bridle. The poet James Dickey believes profoundly in instinct—like the rest of us, as we are wise. In his art, in his life, he is "consciously working toward an unconscious act."[80] Consciousness is not negated. In the accomplishing of the act, the intellect collaborates. Ralph Waldo Emerson elects, however, to go it alone. He would say he is self-reliant. Emerson from the beginning throws the reins on the horse's neck.

The crime of rationalism is to couch possibilities in terms of either/or, as when we are summoned "up the ladder from intuitive concepts to abstract ideas."[81] But the summons to blood prescience by the spastic totalitarians of the twentieth century or

[79] Quoted by Huxley in the *Doors of Perception*, p. 42.
[80] *Self-Interviews*, p. 59.   [81] Weyl, *Symmetry*, p. 145.

the new solipsists of the drug culture who make their own "real-ity" is not emancipation. It is the mutilated man, reacting. So with the resurgence in the present of astrology, witchcraft, mil-lenarian religions like the Process Church of the Final Judg-ment.[82] Aldous Huxley under mescalin sees naked existence, "what Adam had seen on the morning of his creation." This comprehensive vision, which the modern age denies, is not con-tingent, however, on the forfeiting of intellect. It is from old times the possession of the artist, I suppose of any man "whose perception is not limited to what is biologically or socially use-ful."[83]

The ending end—Sidney's phrase, urged against him—is to slough off the limitation: the canonizing of use and praxis, the reading of life as instrumental merely and so the postponing of life in the present in favor of the heavenly city. "The sabbath was made for man, and not man for the sabbath" (Mark 11:27). Still the "Pharisees" remain unpersuaded. Hence the need of returning to the scene of the crime: uncovering in the past the etiology of the present. It is greatly to the good to assert—with Karl Popper, with Norman O. Brown—that now at length we are to live instead of making history; it is idle to suppose that we can be done with history, escape from it once and for all. That is what Marx supposes. Communism, the supreme expres-sion of rationalism, though it is greatly hagiographical, is not really historical. And so the past is discounted. But the past is

[82] "People all over the world are turning, often desperately, to the over-looked corners and freaks that were never completely systematized. Hence our fascination for the junk and rejects of the industrial process . . . [as for] the slippery stuff that never found a place in it." For example, astrol-ogy: "Do you know what people are saying when they ask your sign? They are saying I want to relate to you, to be intimate with you in this kooky, interesting, groovy way—a way that is going to blow the minds of those god-damned rationalists" (Harvey Cox in *Psychology Today*, April 1970, pp. 62, 45). The latter Foucault presents as feeling shame in the presence of unreason, thrusting into secrecy whatever is aberrant. Endlessly, "the age of reason confined" (p. 62).

[83] *Doors of Perception*, pp. 17, 33.

the matrix from which our life derives. Only the suicidal instinct rejects it. "Ceremony's a name for the rich horn/ And custom for the spreading laurel tree." The point, in spite of Marx, is not to change or abolish the past. The point is to understand it. That is what it means, to awaken from the nightmare which is history.

The "final movement of society" hypothesized by the modern millenarian commits us eternally to a nomadic and savorless round.[84] Life is not being but becoming: the tenor of our rhetoric from the beginning of the modern age.

> All the past we leave behind,
> We debouch upon a newer mightier world, varied world,
> Fresh and strong the world we seize, world of
> > labor and the march,
> Pioneers! O pioneers!

Matthew Arnold, as he is a great rhetorician, is in this vein a notable culprit, and it is right that in bidding farewell to Oxford and seeking to descry the future—always, a better future—he should levy on St. Augustine: "the night is spent, the day is come forth." How familiar and depressing it is, the old eschatological rag: Porphyry and Plotinus, St. Jerome in the fourth century, Joachim of Flora, Cromwell anticipating the Perpetual Synod of Saints, Edward Bellamy in the final chapter of his Utopian romance looking to the kingdom on earth—but not yet!

It is almost a hundred years since Bellamy saw his powerful vision of the iceberg floating southward, undermined by warmer waters and churning the sea to yeast in token of its imminent destruction. And still the vexatious system, which the iceberg presents, is with us—not of course in its particulars but generically: for the system is not a tissue of industrial and social relations. It is endemic in ourselves.

The corollary is hardly despair. Expiation is to no purpose. That much the Protestants, "toiling up new Calvaries ever,"

---

[84] Quoting Caudwell, *Illusion and Reality*, p. 296.

374

have taught us. Good works avail nothing, or not as they are dictated by an ulterior end. What follows? I suppose that one estimates the flaw in the grain and accepts it.

> *Man is but grasse,*
> *He knows it, fill the glasse.*

Concluding his autobiography, Eldridge Cleaver, a militant salvationist of the immediate present, mingles good hope and despair: "we will build a New City on these ruins." But there are no ruins: no Carthaginian peace in which the past is exterminated; neither is there a new city in prospect. The Golden Age, if it exists at all, does not lie in the elusive future nor yet in the irretrievable past. So far, just so far, the ebullient spirits of the Renaissance are vindicated. History is not beginning tomorrow. The Golden Age is now.

Works Consulted

I have not listed well-known authors who are quoted in the text— like Aristotle, Descartes, Thomas Carlyle—unless reference is to page or signature number in a particular edition. Neither have I listed many Elizabethan authors—like Painter, Fenton, Chapman—who are cited in footnotes but from whom I am quoting at second hand. When quotation is from an original source which I have consulted, as opposed to an anthology, I give the source and author here. STC numbers (for books printed between 1475 and 1640) and Wing numbers (between 1641 and 1700) are appended, where available.

Abelard, *Petri Abaelardi Opera*, ed. Victor Cousin, Paris, 1859.

Adams, Henry, *Mont-Saint-Michel and Chartres*, Boston and New York, 1905.

Adams, Joseph Quincy, ed., *Chief Pre-Shakespearean Dramas*, Boston, 1924.

Agrippa, Henry Cornelius, *Of the Vanitie and Uncertaintie of Artes and Sciences*, trans. Ja.[mes] San[ford], London, 1569. STC 204.

Alain de Lille, *The Anticlaudian*, trans. and with an introduction by William Hafner Cornog, Philadelphia, 1935.

Alciati, *Andreae Alciati Emblematum Libellus*, Paris 1536.

Allen, Don Cameron, *The Legend of Noah: Renaissance Rationalism in Art, Science, and Letters*, Urbana, 1963.

Alley, William, *The Poore Mans Librarie*, London, 1571. STC 375.

Alvarez, A., *The School of Donne*, London, 1961.

Ames, William, *Conscience with the Power and Cases Thereof*, trans. from Latin, London, 1639. ? 1643 (not listed STC).

———, *The Marrow of Sacred Divinity*, London, 1642. (STC 558: [1638?] edn.)

Arber, Edward, *see Stationers' Register.*

Arendt, Hannah, *The Human Condition*, Chicago, 1958.

Armstrong, Elizabeth, *Ronsard and the Age of Gold*, New York and London, 1968.

Arp, Halton, "The Need for a New Kind of Academic Responsibility," *AAUP Bulletin*, LV (Sept. 1969), 366-68.

Artaud, Antonin, *The Theater and Its Double*, trans. M. C. Richards, New York, 1958.

Atkins, J.W.H., *English Literary Criticism*, New York, 1943.

Augustine, St., *Epistles*, vols. 34, 44, 57, 58 in *Corpus Scriptorum Ecclesiasticorum Latinorum*, ed. Al. Goldbacher, Pragae, F. Tempsky; Lipsiae, G. Freytag, 1895-1923.

———, *On Christian Doctrine*, trans. D. W. Robertson, Jr., New York, 1958.

Babington, Gervase, *A very fruitfull Exposition of the Commaundements by way of Questions and Answeres*, London, 1583. STC 1095.

Bader, Arno L., and Carlton F. Wells, *Essays of Three Decades*, New York and London, 1939.

Bagehot, Walter, *Physics and Politics* (1867), Boston, 1956.

Baker, Herschel, *The Race of Time*, Toronto, 1967.

Baldwin, C. S., *Renaissance Literary Theory and Practice*, New York, 1939.

Baldwin, William, *Canticles or Ballades of Solomon*, London, 1549. STC 2768.

Bale, John, *Index Britanniae scriptorum*, ed. Reginald Lane Poole, Oxford, 1902.

Bamborough, J. B., *Ben Jonson*, London, 1970.

Bannatyne, George, *The Bannatyne Manuscript Writtin in Tyme of Pest 1568*, ed. W. Tod Ritchie, 4 vols., Edinburgh and London, 1934.

Barfield, Owen, *History in English Words* (1953), Grand Rapids, 1967.

Baxter, Nicholas, trans., *The Lectures of J. Calvine . . . uppon the Prophet Jonas*, London, 1578. STC 4432.

Bellamy, Edward, *Looking Backward 2000-1887*, Boston, 1887.

Bentley, Gerald Eades, *Shakespeare and His Theatre*, Lincoln, Nebr., 1964.

Bevington, David M., *From "Mankind" to Marlowe*, Cambridge, Mass., 1962.

Bloch, Marc, *Feudal Society*, trans. L. A. Manyon, Foreword by M. M. Poston, Chicago and London, 1961.

Bloom, Edward A., "The Allegorical Principle," *English Literary History*, XVIII (1951), 163-90.

Boas, George, *Rationalism in Greek Philosophy*, Baltimore, 1961.

Boccaccio on Poetry, trans. Charles G. Osgood (1930), Indianapolis and New York, 1956.

Bodin, Jean, *The Republic*, 1576; trans. Richard Knolles, *The Six Bookes of a Common-weale*, London, 1606. STC 3193.

Bolgar, R. R., *The Classical Heritage and Its Beneficiaries*, Cambridge, 1954.

Bolton, Robert, *Some Generall Directions for a Comfortable Walking with God*, London, 1625. STC 3250.

——, *Works*, London, 1641. STC 3224.

Bonhoeffer, Dietrich, *Act and Being*, trans. Bernard Noble, New York, 1961.

Bowen, Catherine Drinker, *Francis Bacon: The Temper of a Man*, Boston, 1963.

——, *The Lion and the Throne: The Life and Times of Sir Edward Coke (1552-1634)*, Boston, 1956.

Brathwait, Richard, *The English Gentleman and the English Gentlewoman*, London, 1641. Wing 4262.

Bredvold, Louis I., *The Intellectual Milieu of John Dryden*, Ann Arbor, 1934, reprinted 1956.

Brinsley, John, *A Consolation for Our Grammar Schooles*, London, 1622. STC 3767.

Brown, Donald L., "Black Power: An Analysis," *Illinois Quarterly*, XXXIII (Sept. 1970), 30-46.

Brown, Norman O., *Life Against Death*, New York, 1959.

Bugental, J.F.T., *The Search for Authenticity*, New York, 1965.

Burke, Peter, *The Renaissance Sense of the Past*, New York, 1970.

Bush, Douglas, *Mythology and the Renaissance Tradition in English Poetry*, Minneapolis, 1932.

Butler, Samuel, *Life and Habit*, London, 1878.

Calendar of State Papers, Domestic Series. Edward VI to James I. 1547-1625, 12 vols., ed. Robert Lemon and M.A.E. Green, London, 1856-72; *Charles I. 1627-9*, 2 vols., ed. John Bruce, London, 1858-59.

Campbell, Lily B., *Divine Poetry and Drama in Sixteenth-Century England*, Berkeley and Los Angeles, 1959.

Campbell, Lily B., *Scenes and Machines on the English Stage during the Renaissance*, Cambridge, 1923.

Campenhausen, Hans von, *The Fathers of the Greek Church*, London, 1963.

———, *The Fathers of the Latin Church*, London, 1964.

Cardano, Girolamo, *The Book of My Life (De Vita Propria Liber) by Jerome Cardan*, trans. Jean Stoner, New York, 1930, London, 1931.

———, *Cardanus Comforte*, trans. Thomas Bedingfield, London, 1573. STC 4607.

Carew, Thomas, *The Poems*, ed. Rhodes Dunlap, Oxford, 1949.

Case, John, *The Praise of Musicke*, Oxford, 1586. STC 20184.

———, *Speculum Moralium quaestionum in universam ethicen Aristotelis*, London, 1585. STC 4759.

Cassiodorus Senator, *An Introduction to Divine and Human Readings*, trans. and ed., Leslie Webber Jones, New York, 1946.

Castiglione, Baldassare, *The Courtier*, trans. Thomas Hoby, London, 1561. STC 4778.

Caudwell, Christopher, *Illusion and Reality*, London (1937), 1950.

———, *Studies and Further Studies in a Dying Culture*, New York (1938, 1949), 1958.

Chamberlain, John, *The Letters of*, ed. Norman E. McClure, 2 vols., Philadelphia, 1939.

Chambers, Edmund K., *The Elizabethan Stage* (1923), 4 vols., Oxford, 1961.

———, and F. Sidgwick, *Early English Lyrics*, London (1907), 1966.

Chambers, Robert, *Vestiges of the Natural History of Creation* (1844), New York, 1857.

Chernyshevsky, N. G., *What Is To Be Done?* trans. Benjamin R. Tucker, New York, 1961.

Chettle, Henry, *Kind-Harts Dreame*, London [1592]. STC 5123.

Cleaver, Eldridge, *Soul on Ice* (1968), New York, 1970.

Collier, Jeremy, *A Defence of the Short View of the Profaneness and Immorality of the English Stage*, London, 1699. Wing 5248.

———, *A Short View of the Immorality, and Profaneness of the English Stage*, London, 1698. Wing 5263.

Comparetti, Domenico, *Vergil in the Middle Ages* (1895), trans. E.F.M. Benecke, London, 1966.

Cope, Jackson I., *Joseph Glanvill Anglican Apologist*, St. Louis, Mo., 1956.

Courcelle, Pierre, *Late Latin Writers and Their Greek Sources*, trans. Harry E. Wedeck, Cambridge, Mass., 1969.

Cousin, Jean, *Études sur Quintilien*, 2 vols., Paris, 1935-36 (reprinted Amsterdam, 1967).

Cowley, Abraham, *The Works*, London, 1668. Wing 6649.

Cox, Harvey, *The Feast of Fools*, Cambridge, Mass., 1969.

————, and T. George Harris, "Religion in the Age of Aquarius," *Psychology Today* (April 1970), pp. 45-47, 62-67.

Craig, Hardin, *English Religious Drama of the Middle Ages*, Oxford, 1955.

Crane, William G., *Wit and Rhetoric in the Renaissance*, New York, 1937.

Crashaw, William, *The Parable of Poyson. In Five Sermons*, London, 1618. STC 6024.

Crews, Frederick, "Do Literary Studies Have an Ideology?" *PMLA*, LXXXV (May 1970), 423-28.

Crick, Francis, *Of Molecules and Men*, Seattle and London, 1966.

Crosse, Henry, *Vertues Common-wealth: or The High-way to Honour*, London, 1603. STC 6070.

Cullen, Patrick, *Spenser, Marvell, and Renaissance Pastoral*, Cambridge, Mass., 1970.

Curtius, Ernst Robert, *European Literature and the Latin Middle Ages* (1948), trans. Willard R. Trask, New York, 1953.

Dalgarno, George, *Ars Signorum, vulgo Character Universalis et Lingua Philosophica*, London, 1661. Wing 128.

Dante, *A Translation of Dante's Eleven Letters*, by Charles S. Latham, ed. George R. Carpenter, Boston and New York, 1891.

Darwin, Charles, *The Autobiography*, ed. Nora Barlow, New York, 1958.

————, *The Origin of Species* (1859), New York, 1871.

Delasanta, Rodney, "Chaucer and the Exegetes," *Studies in the Literary Imagination*, IV (Oct. 1971), 1-10.

Dent, Edward J., *Foundations of English Opera: A Study of Musical Drama in England during the Seventeenth Century*, Cambridge, 1928.

Dent, R. W., "Marlowe, Spenser, Donne, Shakespeare—and Joseph Wybarne," *Renaissance Quarterly*, XXII (Winter 1969), 360-62.

Dering, Edward, *A bryefe and necessarie Catechisme or Instruction*, London, 1572. STC 6679.

Dickey, James, *Self-Interviews*, ed. Barbara and James Reiss, Garden City, New York, 1970.

Dimitroff, Georgi, *United Front Against Fascism*, New York, 1935.

Donahue, Sister Benedict J., "Sarum Liturgy and Plainsong: From Latin to English in Tudor England," *American Benedictine Review*, XXI (Dec. 1970), 443-69.

Donne, John, *The Anniversaries*, ed. Frank Manley, Baltimore, 1963.

———, *Essays in Divinity*, ed. Evelyn M. Simpson, Oxford, 1952.

———, *The Life and Letters*, ed. Edmund Gosse, 1899; reprinted Gloucester, Mass., 1959, 2 vols.

———, *The Sermons*, ed. George R. Potter and Evelyn M. Simpson, 10 vols., Berkeley and Los Angeles, 1962.

Dostoevsky, Fyodor, *Notes from Underground*, ed. Robert G. Durgy, trans. Serge Shishkoff, New York, 1969.

Du Bellay, Joachim, *La Défense et Illustration de la Langue Française* (1549), Paris, n.d.

Duckett, Eleanor, *Death and Life in the Tenth Century*, Ann Arbor, 1967.

Eckhardt, Caroline, "Arthurian Comedy: Perspectives on the Hero," University of Michigan dissertation, 1971.

Edwards, Jonathan, *The Nature of True Virtue* (1755), Ann Arbor, 1960.

Eiseley, Loren, *Francis Bacon and the Modern Dilemma*, Lincoln, Nebr., 1962.

———, *The Unexpected Universe*, New York, 1969.

Ellmann, Richard, *Yeats the Man and the Masks*, New York, 1958.

———, *see* Wilde.

Else, Gerald F., *Aristotle's "Poetics": the Argument*, Cambridge, Mass., 1963.

Faral, Edmond, *Les Arts Poetiques du XIIe et du XIIIe Siecle*, Paris, 1924.

Farber, Leslie H., "Faces of Envy," *Review of Existential Psychology and Psychiatry*, 1 (Spring 1961), 131-39.

Farrar, Frederic W., *History of Interpretation* (1886), Grand Rapids, 1961.

Fast, Howard, *Literature and Reality*, New York, 1950.

Felheim, Marvin, "Comic Realism in 'Much Ado About Nothing,'" *Philologica Pragensia*, VII (1964), 213-25.

Fellowes, Edmund H., *William Byrd*, Oxford, 1923.

Feltham, Owen, *Resolves*, London, 1628. STC 10756.

Fernandez, Dominique, "Three Types of Resistance to Freud," *Diacritics* (Fall 1971), Ithaca, New York, pp. 8-15.

Fleming, John V., *The Roman de la Rose: A Study in Allegory and Iconography*, Princeton, 1969.

Fletcher, Angus, *Allegory: The Theory of a Symbolic Mode*, Ithaca, New York, 1964.

Foucault, Michel, *Madness and Civilization: A History of Insanity in the Age of Reason*, trans. Richard Howard, New York, 1967.

Fraser, Russell, *The War Against Poetry*, Princeton, 1970.

Fredegar, *The Fourth Book of the Chronicle of Fredegar*, ed. and trans. J. M. Wallace-Hadrill, London, 1960.

Freud, Sigmund, *Civilization and Its Discontents*, trans. Joan Riviere (1930), New York, 1958.

———, *Collected Papers*, trans. Joan Riviere, 5 vols., New York, 1959.

———, *The Interpretation of Dreams* (1900), trans. A. A. Brill, New York, 1950.

Fulgentius, *Allegoria Librorum Virgilii* [*Virgiliana Continentia*], in *Auctores Mythographi Latini*, Lugduni Batavorum Amstelodami, 1741.

G., I., *A Refutation of the Apology for Actors* (1615); with Heywood's *Apology* (1612), ed. Richard H. Perkinson, New York, 1941.

Galileo, Galilei, *Dialogue Concerning the Two Chief World Systems*, trans. Stillman Drake, Foreword by Albert Einstein, Berkeley and Los Angeles, 1967.

Gascoigne, *see* Prouty.

Gasinski, Tadeusz Z., "Signs of Dissent in Recent Polish Poetry," *Michigan Quarterly Review*, x (Winter 1971), 29-37.

Giamatti, A. Bartlett, *The Earthly Paradise and the Renaissance Epic*, Princeton, 1966.

Glanvill, Joseph, *The Vanity of Dogmatizing*, London, 1661. Wing 834.

Goodwin, James, ed., "Six Ballads, with Burdens, from MS. No. CLXVIII in C.C.C.C.," xiii, London, 1844.

Gosson, Stephen, *The Ephemerides of Phialo. . . . And a short Apologie of the Schoole of Abuse*, London, 1579. STC 12093.

———, *Playes Confuted in five Actions . . . by the waye both the Cavils of Thomas Lodge, and the Play of Playes*, London [?1590]. STC 12095.

———, *The Schoole of Abuse*, London, 1579. STC 12097.

Gramont, Sanche de, "Our Other Man in Algiers," *New York Times Magazine*, Nov. 1, 1970, pp. 30-31, 112, 114, 116, 118-19, 126, 128.

Gramsci, Antonio, *The Open Marxism of*, trans. Carl Marzani, New York, 1957.

Greg, Walter W., *Pastoral Poetry & Pastoral Drama* (1905), New York, 1959.

———, *The Shakespeare First Folio: Its Bibliographical and Textual History*, Oxford, 1955.

Gregory of Tours, *History of the Franks*, trans. Ernest Brehaut, New York, 1965.

Greville, *Sir Fulke Greville's Life of Sir Philip Sidney etc. First Published 1652*, Oxford, 1907.

Grimald, Nicholas, *Archipropheta*, Cologne, 1548.

H., J., *This Worlds Folly*, London, 1615. STC 12570.

Halévy, Elie, *The Growth of Philosophic Radicalism* (1901-4), Boston, 1955.

Hall, Donald, *Marianne Moore: The Cage and the Animal*, New York, 1970.

Hall, John, *The Court of Virtue*, London, 1565 (ed. R. A. Fraser, London, 1961). STC 12632.

Hall, Thomas, *Rhetorica Sacra: Or, A Synopsis of the most materiall Tropes and Figures contained in the Sacred Scriptures*, London, 1654.

————, *Vindiciae Literarum, The Schools Guarded*, London, 1654. Wing 441.

Hardison, O. B., Jr., *The Enduring Monument: A Study of the Idea of Praise in Renaissance Literary Theory and Practice*, Chapel Hill, North Carolina, 1962.

Harris, Frank, *Oscar Wilde: His Life & Confessions*, New York, 1941.

Hartnoll, Phyllis, *Shakespeare in Music*, London and New York, 1964.

Henderson, Archibald, *George Bernard Shaw: Man of the Century*, New York, 1956.

Herzen, Alexander, *From the Other Shore* and *The Russian People and Socialism*, trans. M. Budberg and R. Wollheim, London, 1956.

Heywood, Thomas, *An Apology for Actors* (1612); with I. G.'s *Refutation* (1615), ed. Richard H. Perkinson, New York, 1941.

Hieroglyphics of Horapollo, The, trans. George Boas, New York, 1950.

Hill, Donald L., *Richard Wilbur*, New York, 1967.

Hill, Robert, *The Pathway to Prayer, and Pietie*, London, 1613. STC 13473.

Hilliard, Nicholas, *A Treatise Concerning the Arte of Limning* (1624), Oxford, 1912.

Hillyer, Robert, "Poetry's New Priesthood," *The Saturday Review of Literature*, XXXII (June 18, 1949), 7-9, 38.

Hinks, Roger, *Myth and Allegory in Ancient Art*, London, 1939.

Hinton, Norman, "Anagogue and Archetype: The Phenomenology of Medieval Literature," *Annuale Mediaevale*, Pittsburgh, 1966, pp. 57-73.

Hitler, Adolf, *Mein Kampf*, Boston, 1943.

Hobbes, Thomas, *The English Works of*, ed. Sir William Molesworth, London, 1839, I (reprinted 1966).

Holland, John, *The Psalmists of Britain*, London, 1843.

Hollander, John, *The Untuning of the Sky: Ideas of Music in English Poetry 1500-1700*, Princeton, 1961.

Hollander, Robert, *Allegory in Dante's "Commedia,"* Princeton, 1969.

————, "Dante's Use of 'Aeneid' I in 'Inferno' I and II," *Comparative Literature*, xx (Spring 1968), 142-56.

Horney, Karen, *The Neurotic Personality of Our Time*, New York, 1937.

Hoskins, John, *Directions for Speech and Style*, ed. Hoyt H. Hudson, Princeton, 1935.

Howell, Thomas, *Devises*, London, 1581. STC 13875.

Howes, Alan B., *Yorick and the Critics: Sterne's Reputation in England, 1760-1868*, Hamden, Conn., 1971.

Hudson, Hoyt H., *The Epigram in the English Renaissance*, Princeton, 1947.

Hugh of St. Victor, *The Didascalicon*, trans. Jerome Taylor, New York, 1961.

Huizinga, Johann, *Erasmus and the Age of Reformation*, trans. F. Hopman (1924), New York, 1957.

————, *The Waning of the Middle Ages* (1924), New York, 1954.

Hume, David, *A Treatise of Human Nature*, London, 1738.

Hunter, G. K., *John Lyly: The Humanist as Courtier*, London, 1962.

Huntley, Frank L., *Jeremy Taylor and the Great Rebellion*, Ann Arbor, 1970.

Huttar, Charles, "Poems by Surrey and Others in a Printed Miscellany Circa 1550," *English Miscellany*, ed. Mario Praz, Rome, 1965, pp. 9-18.

Huxley, Aldous, *The Doors of Perception* and *Heaven and Hell*, New York, 1963.

Huxley, Thomas Henry, *Collected Essays*, 9 vols., New York, 1894-97.

Irving, William Henry, *The Providence of Wit in the English Letter Writers*, Durham, North Carolina, 1955.

Isidore of Seville, *An Encyclopedist of the Dark Ages*, ed. and trans. Ernest Brehaut, New York, 1912 (includes part of *Etymologies*).

Iversen, Erik, *The Myth of Egypt and Its Hieroglyphs*, Copenhagen, 1961.

Jean de Meun, and Guillaume de Lorris, *The Romance of the Rose*, trans. Harry W. Robbins, ed. Charles W. Dunn, New York, 1962.

Jeans, Sir James, *The Mysterious Universe*, New York and Cambridge, 1930.

Jerome, St., *The Letters of*, trans. C. C. Mierow, notes by T. C. Lawler, London and Westminster, Maryland, 1963.

John of Salisbury, *The Early Letters (1153-1161)*, eds. W. J. Millor and H. E. Butler, revised C.N.L. Brooke, London, 1955.

————, *Historia Pontificalis (Memoirs of the Papal Court)*, trans. and ed. Marjorie Chibnall, London, 1956.

————, *The Metalogicon*, trans. Daniel D. McGarry, Berkeley and Los Angeles, 1955.

————, *The Policraticus*, 1st, 2nd, and 3rd books and selections from the 7th and 8th, trans. Joseph B. Pike, Minneapolis, 1938.

————, *Policraticus*, ed. with introduction by C.C.J. Webb, 2 vols., Oxford, 1909.

Junius, R. [?Richard Younge], *Compleat Armour Against Evill Society*, London, 1638. STC 26111.

Kayser, Wolfgang, *The Grotesque in Art and Literature* (1957), trans. Ulrich Weisstein, Bloomington, 1963.

Kermode, Frank, *The Sense of an Ending*, New York, 1967.

Konigsberg, Ira, *Samuel Richardson & the Dramatic Novel*, Lexington, Kentucky, 1968.

Kristeller, Paul Oskar, *Renaissance Thought*, I, New York, 1961; II, 1965.

Lactantius, *The Works of*, trans. William Fletcher, 2 vols., Edinburgh, 1871 (vols. 21 and 22 in *Ante-Nicene Christian Library*, ed. Alexander Roberts and James Donaldson; I: *Divine Institutes*; II: *The Epitome of the* "Divine Institutes").

Laneham, Robert, *A Letter* [1575], ed. R. C. Alston, Menston, England, 1968.

Levin, Harry, *The Myth of the Golden Age in the Renaissance*, Bloomington and London, 1969.

Litz, A. Walton, *Introspective Voyager: The Poetic Development of Wallace Stevens*, New York, 1972.

Lodge, Thomas, *A Reply to Stephen Gosson's Schoole of Abuse, in Defense of Poetry, Musick, and Stage Plays*, London, 1579-80 (no t.p., no imprint). STC 16663; reprinted London, 1853 (with Lodge's *Alarum against Usurers*, 1584).

Longinus, *On the Sublime*, ed. D. A. Russell, Oxford, 1964.

Lukács, Georg, "The Importance and Influence of Ady," *New Hungarian Quarterly*, x (Autumn 1969), 56-63.

———, *Realism in Our Time*, trans. J. and N. Mander, Preface by George Steiner, New York and Evanston, 1962.

Lyell, Sir Charles, *Principles of Geology*, 2 vols., New York, 1877.

McCollom, William G., "The Role of Wit in 'Much Ado About Nothing,'" *Shakespeare Quarterly*, xix (Spring 1968), 165-74.

Mace, D. T., "A Reply to Mr. H. Neville Davies's 'Dryden and Vossius: A Reconsideration,'" *Journal of the Warburg and Courtauld Institute*, xxix (1966), 296-310.

Macrobius, *Conviviorum Saturnaliorum Libri Septem*, ed. Franciscus Eyssenhardt, Leipzig, 1868.

———, *Les Saturnales*, ii (Livres iv-vii), ed. François Richard, Paris, n.d.

Magnus, Philip, *Sir Walter Raleigh*, New York, 1956.

Mâle, Emile, *Religious Art in France of the Thirteenth Century*, 1913; republished as *The Gothic Image*, New York, 1958.

Mandelstam, Nadezhda, *Hope Against Hope: A Memoir*, trans. Max Hayward, introduction by Clarence Brown, New York, 1970.

Mao Tse-tung, *Problems of Art and Literature*, New York, 1950.

Marcuse, Herbert, *Eros and Civilization: A Philosophical Inquiry into Freud* (1955), New York, 1962.

Marie de France, *Die Fabeln*, ed. Karl Warnke, Halle, 1898.

———, *Fables*, ed. A. Ewert and R. C. Johnston, Oxford, 1942.

Martianus Capella, Dunchad: *Glossae in Martianum*, ed. Cora E. Lutz, Lancaster, Pa., and Oxford, 1944.

388

WORKS CONSULTED

————, Iohannis Scotti (Joannus Scotus, Erigena): *Annotationes in Marcianum*, ed. Cora E. Lutz, Cambridge, Mass., 1939.

————, *The Marriage of Mercury and Philology*, ed. Adolfus Dick, Leipzig, 1925.

————, Remigii Autissiodorensis (Remigius of Auxerre): *Commentum in Martianum Capellam*, ed. and with an introduction by Cora E. Lutz, Leiden, 1962.

Maslow, Abraham H., *Motivation and Personality*, New York, 1954.

Mason, H. A., "Wyatt and the Psalms," *Times Literary Supplement*, Feb. 27, 1953, p. 144; Mar. 6, 1953, p. 160.

Matthew of Vêndome, *see* Faral.

Mazzaro, Jerome, *Transformations in the Renaissance English Lyric*, London and Ithaca, New York, 1970.

Menpes, M., *Henry Irving*, London, 1906.

Mersenne, Marin, *Quaestiones Celeberrimae in Genesim*, Paris, 1623.

Miner, Earl, *The Metaphysical Mode from Donne to Cowley*, Princeton, 1969.

Monk, Samuel H., *The Sublime* (1935), Ann Arbor, Mich., 1960.

Mulcaster, Richard, *The First Part of the Elementarie*, London, 1582. STC 18250.

Myers, Walter E., *A Figure Given: Typology in the Wakefield Plays*, Pittsburgh, Pa., 1970.

Nashe, Thomas, *Pierce Penilesse*, London, 1592. STC 18371.

————, *The Works*, ed. Ronald B. McKerrow (1904-10), revised F. P. Wilson, 5 vols., New York, 1966.

New Program of the Communist Party U.S.A., New York, 1966.

Northbrooke, John, *A Treatise wherein Dicing, Dauncing, Vaine plaies or Enterludes with other idle pastimes . . . are reprooved*, London, 1579. STC 18671.

Odo of Cluny, St., *The Life by John of Salerno and the Life of St. Gerald of Aurillac by St. Odo*, trans. and ed. Dom Gerard Sitwell, London and New York, 1958.

Ogden, Henry V. S., and Margaret Ogden, *English Taste in Landscape in the Seventeenth Century*, Ann Arbor, Mich., 1955.

389

Ong, Walter J., "From Allegory to Diagram in the Renaissance Mind," *Journal of Aesthetics and Art Criticism*, XVII (1959), 423-40.

Ordericus Vitalis, *The Ecclesiastical History of England and Normandy*, trans. Thomas Forester, 4 vols., London, 1853 (New York, 1968).

Origen, The Writings of, trans. Frederick Crombie, Edinburgh, 1869.

Orwell, George, *"Shooting an Elephant" and Other Essays*, New York, 1945.

Overseth, Oliver E., "Experiments in Time Reversal," *Scientific American*, CCXXI (Oct. 1969), 88-101.

Ovide Moralisé en Prose (Texte du Quinzième Siècle), ed. C. de Boer, Amsterdam, 1964.

Owen, W.J.B., "The Structure of 'The Faerie Queene,'" *PMLA*, LXVIII (Dec. 1953), 1079-1100.

Panofsky, *see* Suger.

Peacham, Henry the Elder, *The Garden of Eloquence*, London, 1593. STC 19498.

Peacham, Henry the Younger, *The Compleat Gentleman* (1622), ed. G. S. Gordon, Oxford, 1906.

Perkins, William, *A Case of Conscience*, n.p., 1595. STC 19667.

———, *A Direction for the Government of the Tongue*, London, 1615. STC 19692.

Petrarch, Francesco, *De sui ipsius et multorum ignorantia*, ed. L. M. Capelli, Paris, 1906.

———, *On His Own Ignorance*, in *The Renaissance Philosophy of Man*, ed. Ernst Cassirer, Paul O. Kristeller, J. H. Randall, Jr., Chicago, 1948, pp. 47-133.

Philo Judaeus, The Works of, trans. C. D. Yonge, 4 vols., London, 1854-55.

Planck, Max, *Where Is Science Going?* trans. James Murphy, New York, 1932.

Plato, *The Dialogues*, trans. B. Jowett, 4 vols., Oxford, 1953.

Plutarch, *De Audiendis . . . Poetis*, trans. Simon Ford as "How a Young Man Ought to Hear Poems," II, 42-94 in *Essays and Miscellanies (Moralia)*, 5 vols., Boston, 1906.

Popper, Karl R., *The Open Society and Its Enemies* (1945), 2 vols., New York and Evanston, Ill., 1963.

Praz, Mario, *The Flaming Heart*, Garden City, New York, 1958.

———, *Studies in Seventeenth-Century Imagery*, 2 vols. (Vol. II a bibliography of emblem books), London, 1939.

Primaudaye, Peter de la, *The French Academy*, trans. T. B., London, 1586, 1594.

Prior, Moody E., *The Language of Tragedy*, New York, 1947.

Prouty, C. T., *George Gascoigne, Elizabethan Courtier, Soldier, and Poet*, New York, 1942.

Prudentius, *Works*, trans. H. J. Thomson, 2 vols., London and Cambridge, Mass. (Loeb Classics), 1949.

Prunières, Henry, *A New History of Music: The Middle Ages to Mozart*, trans. Edward Lockspeiser, New York, 1943.

Putney, Snell, and Gail J. Putney, *The Adjusted American: Normal Neuroses in the Individual and Society*, New York, 1966.

Putt, S. Gorley, *Henry James: A Reader's Guide*, New York, 1966.

Puttenham, George, *The Arte of English Poesie*, London, 1589. STC 20519.

Rabanus Maurus, *De Universo*, c.844, J.-P. Migne, *Patrologiae Latinae*, III, To. 5, Paris, 1864.

Raby, F.J.E., *A History of Christian-Latin Poetry from the Beginnings to the Close of the Middle Ages*, Oxford, 1953.

———, *A History of Secular Latin Poetry in the Middle Ages*, 2 vols., Oxford, 1957.

Rainolds, John, *Th'Overthrow of Stage-Playes*, Middleburg, 1599. STC 20616.

———, *The Summe of the Conference betwene John Rainoldes and John Hart. . . . Whereto is annexed a Treatise intitled, Six Conclusions Touching the Holie Scripture and the Church*, London, 1584. STC 20626.

Rand, Edward Kennard, *Founders of the Middle Ages* (1928), New York, 1957.

———, *Ovid and His Influence*, New York, 1928.

Randall, John Herman, Jr., *The Career of Philosophy from the Middle Ages to the Enlightenment*, 2 vols., New York and London, 1962.

Ransom, John Crowe, *The New Criticism*, Norfolk, Conn., 1941.

Rauh, Sister Miriam Joseph, *Rhetoric in Shakespeare's Time*, New York, 1947, revised 1962.

Recorde, Robert, *The Whetstone of Witte*, London, 1557. STC 20820.

Remigius, *see* Martianus Capella.

Richard de Bury, *The Philobiblon*, ed. and trans. Andrew Fleming West, New York, 1889.

Ripa, Cesare, *Iconologia*, Padua, 1611.

Ristine, Frank H., *English Tragicomedy: Its Origin and History*, New York, 1910.

Robertson, D. W., Jr., *A Preface to Chaucer*, Princeton, 1962.

Robinson, Marie N., *The Power of Sexual Surrender*, Garden City, New York, 1959.

R. R. [Richard Rogers], *The Practice of Christianitie*, London, 1618, 1623. STC 21221.

Rollenhagio, Gabriele, *Nucleus Emblematum Selectissimorum*, Cologne, 1611.

Rollins, Hyder E., *Old English Ballads*, Cambridge, 1920.

Rosenthal, M. M., and P. Yudin, *Short Philosophic Dictionary*, trans. as *Handbook of Philosophy*, ed. and adapted Howard Selsam, New York, 1949.

Rossi, Paolo, *Francis Bacon from Magic to Science*, trans. Sacha Rabinovitch, London, 1968.

Rubel, Veré L., *Poetic Diction in the English Renaissance*, New York, 1941.

Rudenstine, Neil L., *Sidney's Poetic Development*, Cambridge, Mass., 1962.

Saintsbury, George, *A History of Criticism and Literary Taste in Europe from the Earliest Texts to the Present Day* (1900), 3 vols., Edinburgh and London, 1961.

———, *Loci Critici*, Boston and London, 1903.

Sambucus, *Emblemata, cum aliquot nummis antiqui operis, Ioannis Sambuci*, Antwerp, 1564.

Sannazaro, Jacopo, *Arcadia and Piscatorial Eclogues*, trans. Ralph Nash, Detroit, 1966.

Santillana, Giorgio de, *The Age of Adventure*, New York, 1956.

392

————, *The Crime of Galileo*, Chicago, 1955.

————, *The Origins of Scientific Thought*, New York, 1961.

Schaff, Philip, *History of the Christian Church* (1910), 8 vols., Grand Rapids, Mich., 1964.

Scholes, Percy A., *Music and Puritanism*, Lausanne doctoral thesis, 1934.

Schumpeter, Joseph, *Economic Doctrine and Method*, trans. R. Aris (1912), London, 1954.

Schutz, William C., *Joy: Expanding Human Awareness*, New York, 1967.

Servius, Marius, *Servii Grammaticii qui feruntur in Vergilii carmina commentarii; recensuerunt Georgius Thilo et Hermannus Hagen*, 3 vols., Leipzig, 1881-1902.

Seznec, Jean, *The Survival of the Pagan Gods* (1940), trans. Barbara F. Sessions, New York, 1953.

Shirer, William L., *The Rise and Fall of the Third Reich*, New York, 1960.

Shostrom, Everett L., *Man, the Manipulator*, New York, 1968.

Sidney, Sir Philip, *An Apology for Poetry*, ed. Geoffrey Shepherd, Edinburgh, 1965.

————, *The Prose Works*, ed. Albert Feuillerat (1912), 4 vols., Cambridge, 1962.

Simpson, Percy, *Studies in Elizabethan Drama*, Oxford, 1955.

Singleton, Charles S., *Journey to Beatrice*, Cambridge, Mass., 1958.

Skinner, B. F., *Beyond Freedom and Dignity*, New York, 1971.

Smalley, Beryl, *The Study of the Bible in the Middle Ages*, Oxford, 1952.

Smith, G. Gregory, ed. *Elizabethan Critical Essays*, 2 vols. (1904), Oxford, 1950.

Smith, Henry Nash, "Something Is Happening But You Don't Know What It Is, Do You, Mr. Jones?" *PMLA*, LXXXV (May 1970), 417-22.

Spacks, Patricia Meyer, "In Search of Sincerity," *College English*, XXIX (May 1968), 591-602.

Spargo, John Webster, *Virgil the Necromancer: Studies in Virgilian Legends*, Cambridge, Mass., 1934.

393

Whythorne, Thomas, *The Autobiography of*, ed. James M. Osborn, Oxford, 1961.

Wickham, Glynne, *Shakespeare's Dramatic Heritage*, London, 1969.

Wilde, Oscar, *The Artist As Critic*, ed. Richard Ellmann, New York, 1968.

Wilkins, John, *A Discovery of a World . . . in the Moone*, London, 1638. STC 25640.

Willey, Basil, *The Seventeenth Century Background* (1934), New York, n.d.

Williamson, George, *The Senecan Amble: A Study in Prose Form from Bacon to Collier*, Chicago, 1951.

Wilson, Thomas, *The Arte of Rhetorique*, London, 1553. STC 15799.

Wolfe, Bertram D., *Three Who Made a Revolution*, Boston, 1955.

Wolin, Sheldon S., *Hobbes and the Epic Tradition of Political Theory*, Los Angeles, 1970.

Wybarne, Joseph, *The New Age of Old Names*, London, 1609. STC 26055.

Yates, Frances A., *The French Academies of the Sixteenth Century*, London, 1947.

————, *Giordano Bruno and the Hermetic Tradition*, Chicago, 1964.

Zamyatin, Yevgeny, *A Soviet Heretic: Essays by*, ed. and trans. by Mirra Ginsburg, Chicago and London, 1970.

Index

Books and authors to whom passing reference in the text is frequent are cited in this index only when referred to in conjunction with a particular point.

397

278; and Shakespeare, 317; and
T. Watson, 310n.

Marot, Clement, and artistic form,
224; and religious music, 131n.

Marprelate, Martin, 346

Marriage of Mercury and Philology,
and artistic form, 172, 201-202

Marriage of Wit and Wisdom, 320

Marston, John, on decay of nature,
36; and decorum, 317; and
doubling, 322n.; and printing,
104-105; and utility, 99

Martial, and epigrams, 32; and
John of Salisbury, 206

Martianus Capella, and allegory,
172; and artistic form, 201-202,
204-205, 207-208, 211; and
learning, 210-11; and Remigius,
166

Marvell, Andrew, and didactic
poetry, 133; and music, 297;
on poetry and fancy, 292; and
politics, 91, 361-62; and realism,
331

Marx, Karl, on history, 363 and n.,
368-69, 374; and progress,
15; and purposiveness, 362;
and rationalism, 356

Maslow, Abraham, 138n., 266n.,
273n., 365n.

Mason, H. A., 126n.

Mason, Sir Josiah, 80

Massinger, Philip, 98 and n.

Massys, Quintin, 259n.

Matisse, Henri, 84

Matthew of Vendôme, 28

Maxwell, James Clerk, 239

Mayakovski, Vladimir, 291

Mazzaro, J., 345n.

Mazzoni, Jacopo, 284n.

"medieval," defined, 43

Menpes, M., 336n.

Merbecke, John, 343n.

Meres, Francis, on art as ornament,
267; and progress, 24; and
quantity, 309n.; and rhyme,
307n.

Merie Tales, 138

Mersenne, Marin, and music, 65
and n., 337 and n.

Metalogicon, and artistic form,
205; and poetry, 167; and
progress, 26

Metamorphoses, moralizations of,
72

Metamorphosis (Kafka), 86

Michelangelo, Buonarroti, as
modern artist, 50; and Shaw,
113

Middle Ages, and allegoresis,
161-84; and approval of poetry,
167, 173-84; and architectural
form, 197-98; and contemplative
life, 54-55; and decorum, 316;
and drama, 52, 190-95, 221,
226-29, 302-303, 313, 316,
335 and n.; and Golden Age,
6; and mingling of comic and
serious, 220-29; and music, 64-
65, 197, 258-59, 341; and
occultism, 47; and organic
form, 185-219; and present,
53-55; and progress, 19-22;
and Renaissance art, 49; and
Renaissance contempt for, 4;
and teaching and delighting,
50-53; and troubadours, 133-34;
and typology, 222; and unity of
surface and meaning, 270-73,
275, 278-79